International Journal on Advances in Systems and Measurements

2017 vol. 10 nr. 3&4

Printed from e-media with permission by:

Curran Associates, Inc.
57 Morehouse Lane
Red Hook, NY 12571

Some format issues inherent in the e-media version may also appear in this print version.

Printed by Curran Associates, Inc. (2018)

International Academy, Research, and Industry Association (IARIA)
412 Derby Way
Wilmington, DE 19810

Phone: (408) 893-6407
Fax: (408) 527-6351

petre@iaria.org

Additional copies of this publication are available from:

Curran Associates, Inc.
57 Morehouse Lane
Red Hook, NY 12571 USA
Phone: 845-758-0400
Fax: 845-758-2633
Email: curran@proceedings.com
Web: www.proceedings.com

The *International Journal on Advances in Systems and Measurements* is published by IARIA.
ISSN: 1942-261x
journals site: http://www.iariajournals.org
contact: petre@iaria.org

Sponsored by IARIA
www.iaria.org

International Journal on Advances in Systems and Measurements
Volume 10, Number 3 & 4, 2017

Javier Calpe, Analog Devices and University of Valencia, Spain
Jaime Calvo-Gallego, University of Salamanca, Spain
Maria-Dolores Cano Baños, Universidad Politécnica de Cartagena,Spain
Juan-Vicente Capella-Hernández, Universitat Politècnica de València, Spain
Vítor Carvalho, Minho University & IPCA, Portugal
Irinela Chilibon, National Institute of Research and Development for Optoelectronics, Romania
Soolyeon Cho, North Carolina State University, USA
Hugo Coll Ferri, Polytechnic University of Valencia, Spain
Denis Collange, Orange Labs, France
Noelia Correia, Universidade do Algarve, Portugal
Pierre-Jean Cottinet, INSA de Lyon - LGEF, France
Paulo Estevao Cruvinel, Embrapa Instrumentation Centre - São Carlos, Brazil
Marc Daumas, University of Perpignan, France
Jianguo Ding, University of Luxembourg, Luxembourg
António Dourado, University of Coimbra, Portugal
Daniela Dragomirescu, LAAS-CNRS / University of Toulouse, France
Matthew Dunlop, Virginia Tech, USA
Mohamed Eltoweissy, Pacific Northwest National Laboratory / Virginia Tech, USA
Paulo Felisberto, LARSyS, University of Algarve, Portugal
Javad Foroughi, University of Wollongong, Australia
Miguel Franklin de Castro, Federal University of Ceará, Brazil
Mounir Gaidi, Centre de Recherches et des Technologies de l'Energie (CRTEn), Tunisie
Eva Gescheidtova, Brno University of Technology, Czech Republic
Tejas R. Gandhi, Virtua Health-Marlton, USA
Teodor Ghetiu, University of York, UK
Franca Giannini, IMATI - Consiglio Nazionale delle Ricerche - Genova, Italy
Gonçalo Gomes, Nokia Siemens Networks, Portugal
Luis Gomes, Universidade Nova Lisboa, Portugal
Antonio Luis Gomes Valente, University of Trás-os-Montes and Alto Douro, Portugal
Diego Gonzalez Aguilera, University of Salamanca - Avila, Spain
Genady Grabarnik,CUNY - New York, USA
Craig Grimes, Nanjing University of Technology, PR China
Stefanos Gritzalis, University of the Aegean, Greece
Richard Gunstone, Bournemouth University, UK
Jianlin Guo, Mitsubishi Electric Research Laboratories, USA
Mohammad Hammoudeh, Manchester Metropolitan University, UK
Petr Hanáček, Brno University of Technology, Czech Republic
Go Hasegawa, Osaka University, Japan
Henning Heuer, Fraunhofer Institut Zerstörungsfreie Prüfverfahren (FhG-IZFP-D), Germany
Paloma R. Horche, Universidad Politécnica de Madrid, Spain
Vincent Huang, Ericsson Research, Sweden
Friedrich Hülsmann, Gottfried Wilhelm Leibniz Bibliothek - Hannover, Germany
Travis Humble, Oak Ridge National Laboratory, USA
Florentin Ipate, University of Pitesti, Romania
Imad Jawhar, United Arab Emirates University, UAE
Terje Jensen, Telenor Group Industrial Development, Norway
Liudi Jiang, University of Southampton, UK
Kenneth B. Kent, University of New Brunswick, Canada
Fotis Kerasiotis, University of Patras, Greece
Andrei Khrennikov, Linnaeus University, Sweden
Alexander Klaus, Fraunhofer Institute for Experimental Software Engineering (IESE), Germany
Andrew Kusiak, The University of Iowa, USA

International Journal on Advances in Systems and Measurements
Volume 10, Numbers 3 & 4, 2017

CONTENTS

Safe Transitions Between a Driver and an Automated Driving System

Rolf Johansson
Zenuity, RISE
Göteborg, Sweden
e-mail: rolf.johansson@zenuity.com

Jonas Nilsson
Zenuity
Göteborg, Sweden
e-mail: jonas.nilsson@zenuity.com

Annika Larsson
Autoliv Development
Vårgårda, Sweden
e-mail: annika.larsson@autoliv.com

Abstract—**This paper presents a methodology for achieving functional safety for an automated driving system (SAE Level 4) with respect to safe transitions between the driver and the system. Safety analysis and assessment of an implementation example show how to allocate safety requirements on Human-Machine Interface (HMI) components to handle the risks of unfair transition, mode confusion and stuck in transition, respectively. The methodology is appropriate for different assumptions on driver failures. The paper shows how to identify safety requirements on the HMI components, given that there is an assumption of a set of single, double or multiple failures by the driver. Results from this example show that it is sufficient to allocate safety requirements on the sensor and the lock of a control to ensure safe transitions. No safety requirements are needed on visual feedback to the driver, e.g., displays.**

Keywords-functional safety; automated driving system; HMI; safety assessment.

I. Introduction

Presently, the most critical factor for road vehicle safety is the behaviour of the driver. There are different estimates, but a common understanding is that driver mistakes in the last seconds before a critical situation is a contributing factor of more than 90% of serious accidents. However, drivers are competent in general to drive safely and handle most risky situations well.

The potential safety benefit of increased vehicle automation is undoubtedly large but it is important that the extra risks coming from potential failures of automation are limited to a minimum. More advanced functionality and intelligence implemented in the vehicle means that more of the responsibility to drive safely shifts from the driver to functionality implemented in the vehicle. In the discipline of functional safety, there are methods to assess risks of malfunctioning electrical/electronic (E/E) implemented functionality, and to reduce these sufficiently. For road vehicles, ISO26262 is the functional safety standard.

This paper is an extension of [1] and focuses on higher levels of driving automation in on-road vehicles, where the Automated Driving System (ADS) may be given full responsibility for a safe behaviour in traffic. According to the taxonomy and definitions in J3016 [2], we can say that on level 4 (L4) automation, the ADS inside its operating driving domain (ODD) takes full responsibility, including fallback, for the Dynamic Driving Task (DDT).

Regarding the responsibility of the driver, the precise L4 definition says that when in charge, the ADS is responsible for the DDT "...without any expectation that a *user* will respond to a *request to intervene*".

The introduction of an ADS with full responsibility for the DDT, implies that the problem of traffic safety for an L4-equipped vehicle can be decomposed into three subproblems:

1. Safe driving when the ADS is in charge
2. Safe driving when the driver is in charge
3. Safe transitions between the driver and the ADS.

The first point is obvious when stating that the ADS is responsible for driving, and may be the major functional safety challenge for L4-equipped vehicles. The second point includes specific topics coming from the introduction of L4-equipped vehicles. This is because the introduction of an ADS may lead to, e.g., that the driver by mistake relies on an inactive ADS. A special case under the second point, is when the driver makes a mistake of what vehicle he/she is inside now. Such a mistake may hence cause a traditional non-ADS-equipped vehicle to become unsafe because the driver thinks there is an ADS in it. That case is not elaborated in this paper having focus on L4-equipped vehicles. The third point is the focus of this paper.

Having functionally safe transitions, implies showing absence of malfunctions in the ADS transition functionality that may lead to unacceptable risks. This includes risks related to the interaction between the driver and the ADS. One key question is what are reasonable human mistakes and misuse? Consequently, human factors expertise is a vital part to achieve functional safety.

Note that this paper focuses on the functional safety of an ADS and as a part of this analysis use human factors expertise, not the other way around. The goal of functional safety is to show that the remaining risk for the system (e.g., the ADS) in its context is *reasonable*. Human factors (HF) in safety, on the other hand, focus on *optimizing* the safety of the driver-vehicle system, but do not have the ambition to show that all risks (due to, e.g., system malfunctions) have been sufficiently mitigated.

The contribution of this paper is a method for achieving functional safety for an L4-equipped vehicle with respect to safe transitions between the driver and the ADS. Note that according to the definition of L4, we need to achieve this under no assumptions that the driver will take back control within a bounded time.

This paper is organized as follows. Section II refers to related work. Section III describes the new hazards related to the driving mode transitions introduced by SAE L4. In Section IV, we discuss how to define a safe transition and the acceptable level of tolerance to driver mistakes. Section V elaborates on possible implementations using a system example and corresponding functional safety analysis and assessment. Finally, Section VI presents concluding remarks.

II. Related Work

As the existing autonomous systems within the automotive industry are still in their infant stages and the majority of them still are semi-autonomous (i.e., SAE L1-L2) at time of writing, these systems are excluded from the state-of-the-art comparison. The interested reader may study results from several research efforts on this topic; PReVENT, HAVE IT, ADAPTIVE and INTERACTIVE to mention a few.

A. Related Work in Automotive

There are two general strategies how to consider the interaction between the driver and the ADS. SAE L4, which is the focus of this paper, uses by definition the more conservative strategy where there are no assumptions that the driver can take back control within a bounded time. We can call this an autopilot with full responsibility for safety, as it does not need to rely on any responsiveness from the manual driver to stay safe.

Automotive research within human factors and transitions of control have focused on the less conservative strategy and consequently SAE L2 and L3 vehicles. This is a research question that is currently very much investigated [3] [4] [5]. A rather recent overview of what controllability assumptions that are reasonable for different levels of vehicle automation is also found in [6]. Research on L3 vehicles has focused on how transitions may take shorter or longer time to complete, as drivers who are not in control will sometimes prioritize other tasks over driving. Results indicate that the time needed for a safe and completed transition of control following an ADS request for transition, ranges from about 7 seconds to over 30 seconds [3] [7]. Thus, it may be difficult to allow drivers to be out of the driving loop and still expect them to accept and succeed in resuming control within a short time period.

It has also been shown that it may take drivers several seconds to control the vehicle manually without reduced performance, following a forced resumption of manual control [8]. This reduction in controllability are however at a very detailed level, and other research has indicated that about 7-10 seconds after being forced to resume manual control, drivers are able to avoid critical situations as well as before activating automation [3].

Much research effort has also been spent on optimizing the design of the HMI to alert drivers to the need to resume control from L2 and L3 vehicles. Results have indicated that it is preferable to show the driver what the vehicle is "aware" of so drivers can handle the situation if needed [9] [10] [11]. The known accidents that have been attributed to vehicle automation so far, have been caused by automation limitations in handling the DDT and the driver feeling so safe as to cease monitoring its limitations.

There are also simulator studies suggesting that human drivers may change their driving behaviour when taking back control from an autopilot [12]. This is not considered in this paper as we focus on functional safety rather than design of the HMI or autopilot driving behaviour.

B. State-of-the-art comparison with other industries

This section describes technology, systems and concepts from other industries where similar problems arise caused by mode confusion and unsafe transitions. The focus has been on nuclear, avionics and rail since these industries deal with complex systems, exist in a regulated environment and all demand active users for proper operations. Experiences from other industries give valuable insight into how to design interfaces and processes that ensure safe transitions in the context of autonomous driving.

The two major players in the civilian avionics industry, Boeing and Airbus, apply different philosophies regarding automation. Boeing implements a strict assisting role for technology and automation, where the pilot always acts as the final authority. Airbus rather sees automation as a way of enhancing flight performance by assisting the responsible pilot. This subtle difference in philosophy causes different problems, where the Boeing strategy allows the pilot to perform errors that may cause accidents and the Airbus strategy may interfere and prevent the pilot from performing necessary manoeuvres needed for safety in extreme situations [13] [14]. One approach cannot, however, necessarily be said to be safer than the other as aviation accidents are very rare.

In military avionics, there is a system called Auto Ground Collision Avoidance System (Auto GCAS) that monitors the pilot's response in certain situations and if the pilot does not respond to an alarm, the system takes over and performs the necessary manoeuvre. After avoiding the threat, control is returned to the pilot. Inagaki describes this as situation-adaptive autonomy where authority over a system is transferred between human and machine agents [15]. A similar system in the automotive industry is that of forward collision warning with automated emergency braking, where the warning comes first, and if the driver does not respond to the warning, automated emergency braking intervenes.

However, the main point of reference within both civilian and military avionics is that an educated pilot is always responsible for operation of the airplane with the help of coordination and information from air traffic control, differing from the automotive situation envisioned in SAE L4-5. In aviation, there are also several protocols for transitioning control, be it between pilot and co-pilot (pilot flying and pilot not flying) or between pilot and autopilot. In emergencies, civilian pilots generally have several minutes to diagnose a problem and try different countermeasures, being able to consult each other while doing so.

Within the nuclear industry there are numerous processes for operators to monitor. This is handled with different interfaces displaying process information. One main control board represents the state of the system and operators are specially trained on how to read it. The main control board is assured to high safety integrity and acts as the primary source of information should different sources provide inconsistent information. Nuclear operators are well educated with the processes and the system and are regularly trained in handling risky scenarios. They also use binders which contain detailed information on what procedure to follow given different error messages and states of the main control board. Some tasks that could be automated have not been, in order not to make the operators passive and complacent to changes in the system state [16].

In modern nuclear power plants, there are specific procedures ensuring correct decisions are made even in emergencies regarding the operation of the nuclear plant. Regulations state that the plants are to be designed in such a way that operators always have a 30-minute window to search for, deliberate and perform a procedure. In other words, the plant is fully autonomous for 30 minutes at a time [16]. There are also mechanisms for actions at high safety levels that require several users to acknowledge the actions independently in order to perform it. The time allowed for deliberation is, thus, much longer than in automotive or any other vehicle industry.

Studies from the rail industry have analysed operator workload and the possibilities of it causing human errors. Two main ways of managing human performance have been formulated, through either technology or human resource management. Assessment of individual possibilities to manage the required workload has been performed through psychometric testing, as well as limiting workdays and issuing regular breaks [17].

When reviewing earlier experiences from the nuclear, avionics and rail industries we make three important observations. One: In nuclear, rail, avionics and space the time available to operators are on the minute scale, sometimes tens of minutes. This means incidents in those contexts allow for perception, deliberation, and action. Automotive often operates in much shorter time scales in the realms of seconds and milliseconds, leading to much shorter response times mainly allowing for perception and action. Two: Within these industries, the technical solutions are operated by educated users, certified to use the specific equipment, and trained on a regular basis. This is not the case in automotive, where most countries only require one driving test during the entire lifetime of the driver. Three: These industries rely heavily on safety procedures, regulating what is to be done and in what order. These procedures are often written on paper and can be physically viewed in case of emergencies. These industries also often operate in controlled environments and operators handle incidents in cooperation with colleagues supporting them.

Translating information displays such as those in the nuclear industry into the automotive setting is problematic, as most of the information sources' primary purpose in cars is to enhance and ease the experience rather than to provide safety-assured information on the system state. Also, the displays in nuclear demand training for the operators and are not self-explanatory. Adaptive interface features linked to specific task requirements with consistency in interface design across different modes of system operation is recommended for the users to effectively apply mental models [18]. As the automotive setting makes it difficult to limit usage periods, the technology and interfaces must be designed to ensure safe usage under these different circumstances.

III WHAT CAN CAUSE THE ADS-EQUIPPED ROAD VEHICLE TO BECOME UNSAFE

One interpretation of a hazard analysis & risk assessment (HA&RA) today according to ISO26262 is that the vehicle itself is considered safe, if it only puts the driver in situations that are possible to manage safely. The driver is ultimately responsible for safe driving, and the malfunctions of the vehicle should be restricted in such a way that the driver can keep the vehicle in a safe state. The explicit method for determining the requested Automotive Safety Integrity Level (ASIL), restricting a certain hypothetical vehicle failure, is to measure three factors: exposure (E), severity (S) and controllability (C). The two first factors are the traditional ones that are part of the definition of risk, i.e., a combination of probability and severity. The third factor is the one that considers that the driver may sometimes have a possibility to keep the vehicle safe, even though the ordinary (safety-related) functionality is failing.

When we shift from a situation where a manual driver has the ultimate responsibility, to highly automated driving where the manual driver and the ADS are alternating, this will have an impact on the HA&RA. So, what will become different when going to SAE L4? This new challenge has partly been addressed in [19].

As a starting point, we require the same from an ADS as from a driver. This means focusing on a safe style of driving, making the driver or ADS capable to handle also unexpected events. When programming an ADS, this is what we cover on the tactical level [2] [20] [21] [22]. The ADS should always choose to perform the manoeuvres in such a way that reasonable, but still unexpected, situations could be handled safely. For example, the decision whether to initiate an overtaking manoeuvre is on the tactical level. An optimistic decision to overtake may place the vehicle in a situation where avoiding one accident may cause another. The solution to this dilemma is of course to initiate an overtaking manoeuvre only when the entire operation is foreseen to be possible to fulfil in a safe manner.

Note the contrast to Advanced Driver Assistance Systems (ADAS), where the vehicle takes over mainly on the operational time scale, maintaining as steady-state as possible, and then assumes the manual driver to continue according to the (maybe revised) tactical plan. The ADAS functionality today does not take the ultimate responsibility to drive the vehicle safely. Firstly, it operates on the operational time scale, and does not revise tactical plans. Secondly, it only assists the driver. In SAE L4 when responsibility is transferred from the driver to the ADS, there is no longer an assistance relation. The transfer means that from then on, the ADS is fully responsible for driving the vehicle safely.

Given that the ADS can drive safely once in command, the HA&RA must also cover the transitions between the driver and the ADS. In SAE L4, these transitions introduce three new types of hazards, namely *unfair transition, mode confusion* and *stuck in transition*. These are described in detail in the following sections.

A. *Unfair transitions*

It may be complicated for the driver to make a proper override of what is perceived as a failing or unsafe tactical decision of the ADS. This is because drivers may find different tactical solutions to a certain driving situation, and each of these may be correct. It may be hard for a driver to distinguish an unsafe tactical decision from a one that is just different from his or her own favourite pattern. Even more, it may be hard to continue to fulfil a tactical plan of another driver if the responsibility is transferred in the middle of the intended sequence. This difficulty is both for a driver to continue a plan of the ADS, and for the ADS to continue what has been initiated by the manual driver. Problems can arise in terms of non-driving task engagement, safe headways, and the knowledge of other road vehicles' positions.

If the manual driver realizes that the ADS has handed over responsibility, without the manual driver agreeing to this, this is a new risk to consider when entering SAE L4. We can say that the manual driver is put in a situation of *unfair transition*. For a driver with the same understanding of the traffic situation and the control of the vehicle, the situation may be possible and easy to handle, but an unfair transition may put the driver in a situation where continuing to drive can be difficult. For example, the driver may be engrossed in a non-driving related task and therefore take a long time to resume manual control [7].

The problem of unfair transitions may appear in both directions. It is reasonable to assume that the automated driver can drive safely as long as it can choose its own tactics. This is a far easier task than being able to understand and solve arbitrary situations.

To summarize, if the responsibility is transferred from one driver to the other, this must include a confirmation from the receiving driver. Otherwise, the transition may be regarded as unfair, and it is a non-negligible risk that the second driver is incapable of handling the situation, on both operational and tactical time scales.

B. *Mode confusion*

In order to make the entire trip from start to stop safe, it is critical that the two drivers always agree which of them currently is in charge. If they misunderstand each other, there is a risk that either there are two drivers trying to control the vehicle, or there is no one taking care of the ride. Both these potential *mode confusions* need to be addressed.

If we allow both the manual driver and the automated driver to override each other, there is an obvious risk that the resulting non-harmonized commanding of the vehicle may result in dangerous situations. This is especially probable because the two drivers most likely make different tactical decisions now and then, and as consequence regard the operative command of the other as faulty. For safe driving in SAE L4, it is important to reduce the risk of this reciprocal *override*. Note that this does not necessarily exclude the opportunity to adjust operational tasks such as lane position, within bounds that the responsible (driver or ADS) agrees with.

It is perhaps even more obvious that it will become dangerous if neither the manual driver nor the automated driver regard herself or himself as the ultimately responsible. Such reciprocal *underride* is therefore obviously important to reduce properly when performing the risk assessment for driving on SAE L4.

C. *Stuck in Transition*

If either the ADS or the driver is unsuccessful in executing a transition for some period of time, then this may impair the driving skills of the responsible party, thus leading to a hazard. Consider the case when the driver tries to activate, e.g., by pressing one or multiple buttons, and the ADS refuses or fails to activate itself. The driver might react to this by repeatedly pressing the buttons to activate the system. When doing so, it is a risk that the driver is *stuck in transition*, gets distracted and thus cannot drive safely.

IV. Method for Assuring Safe Transitions

In the previous section, we listed new categories of hazards to handle related to the dual driving modes when going up in automation degree to SAE L4. In the following sections, we outline a method to handle these. In Section IV-A we discuss how to define a safe handover functionality and in Section IV-B we describe how to do Hazard Analysis and Risk Assessment, HA&RA.

A. *Principles for safe handover*

Below we propose a way to define the part of a functionality (denoted *item* in ISO26262 [23] and *feature* in J3016 [2]) which transfers control of the DDT between the driver and the ADS. We remark that this section only discusses the part of the item definition which is related to transitions. A complete item/feature for an ADS will also include, e.g., how the ADS drives, i.e., performs the DDT.

We assume that both the manual driver and the ADS are capable of safe driving, as well as judging its own ability to drive safely. Being capable of safe driving also includes driving safely until a handover is completed.

The item definition seeks to be "traffic safe by definition" assuming that the ADS works as intended. This is to say that functional safety of the item/feature implies traffic safety. Consequently, only violations of the principles below, i.e., malfunctions can lead to hazards. We remark that it is possible to make a more explicit definition of the item/feature functionality, which would then require that safety of the defined functionality must be proved outside the scope of functional safety.

For a safe transition of control between manual driver and the ADS, transfer of responsibility for the DDT may only occur if the following conditions are fulfilled:

1. Driver and the ADS both accept transfer, i.e., have consensus
2. The recipient (driver or ADS) is capable to drive safely

These two points introduce a fair procedure for handover to eliminate *unfair transitions*. This means that the current responsible (driver or ADS) stays responsible until there is an agreement for a handover to a capable recipient. This also implies that both the driver and the ADS need to explicitly confirm that a transition is possible and fair to perform. Furthermore, it implies that both the driver and the ADS really are aware of what has been agreed. Thus, neither the driver nor the ADS are required to take control and thus the vehicle will be in a safe state if either of them accept to take control of the vehicle.

Note that these two principles may imply that conditions on the surrounding environment are fulfilled. Traffic situation will probably need to be "tactically simple" to hand over safely from the ADS to the driver.

The problem of *Mode confusion* can be solved by combining the safe handover procedure described above with mechanisms that handle interference from the part which is not in charge, i.e., override. To ensure safe driving between transitions, the following condition must also be fulfilled:

3. The non-responsible party (driver or ADS) must not affect vehicle motion outside the constraints set by the responsible party (ADS or driver)

This can be handled either by making the current responsible capable of ignoring the other or by avoiding interference by the non-responsible party. When the driver is responsible, we require the ADS not to interfere in such a way that the driver cannot control the motion of the vehicle. This is how ADAS are designed today.

When the ADS is responsible, the driver should then try to avoid interfering with the vehicle controls. A potential solution is not allowing the driver to have any impact on the vehicle, if not first going through a handover procedure. We then transfer part of the responsibility to the ADS by putting safety requirements on ignoring any try from the driver to control the motion of the vehicle. For means of trust and comfort, it may be advisable to allow the human operator to control, e.g., lane positioning or following distance. The range of such adjustment should then be constrained within bounds set by the ADS, similar to how adaptive cruise control contains merely a few distance settings.

To manage the *stuck-in-transition* hazard we formulate the following condition:

4. Transition sequence shall not affect the capability of the responsible party (driver or ADS) to drive safely

This will put requirements on the handover sequence to be easily managed by the driver when activating the ADS. In the other direction, the ADS must not let the deactivation sequence affect its driving.

There are many ways to define a detailed handover protocol between the driver and ADS which implement the safety principles above. For examples, see Section V.

B. *Hazard Analysis and Risk Assessment*

A Hazard Analysis and Risk Assessment (HA&RA) is needed to identify situations and driver behaviours that could lead to hazards. The driver behaviours to be analysed must also include reasonably foreseeable driver mistakes. Already today, we have a substantial amount of serious traffic accidents caused by driver lapses. There is no reason why not to regard the driver of a highly automated vehicle as prone to mistakes in any HMI, including the one for transition of responsibility.

The granularity of this analysis is a design choice. We could make a conservative assumption that all driver mistakes are common and that they will always lead to severe hazards. This makes the HA&RA simple but will most likely lead to higher ASIL on some system components compared to a more detailed HA&RA.

All hazardous events are assigned values for exposure, severity and controllability C, which together lead to an ASIL. As an example, consider the case where the ADS is driving at high speed and a malfunction in the ADS combined with a relatively frequent driver mistake leads to unintentional deactivation of the ADS. The situation is common leading to high exposure (E4). Furthermore, we assume that the driver cannot control the vehicle at unintentional deactivation (C3) and that this would have a fatal consequence (S3). Conclusion is that the system must not deactivate at high speed due to this specific driver mistake with ASIL D.

A similar analysis can be performed for any hazard and situation, e.g., single or multiple and coordinated driver mistakes. Less probable driver mistakes will result in a lower exposure and thereby lower ASIL.

A way to argue that a transition is safe with regards to all relevant driver mistakes is to check what happens if there is either a driver mistake or an E/E failure, or combination of these. This must be checked for any state in the transition protocol. For any hazardous consequence, it must be shown that the corresponding E/E failure is prevented with an appropriate safety requirement.

Note that this method also addresses the nominal function of the protocol. If a manual failure may lead to a hazardous consequence even in a fault-free case, the protocol implementation is obviously not robust enough.

For the ADS, we assume that safety requirements are allocated to all elements critical for achieving a transition in such a way that it can be considered as fair and consistently understood by both drivers. Of course, redundancy patterns may be applied allowing the ASIL D to be decomposed onto different elements of the implementation.

V. General Implementation Suggestion

This section provides some guidance on how to design and implement a protocol for safe handovers. To make a transition tolerant to any single manual mistake, there are a few different general ways to design the protocol. The

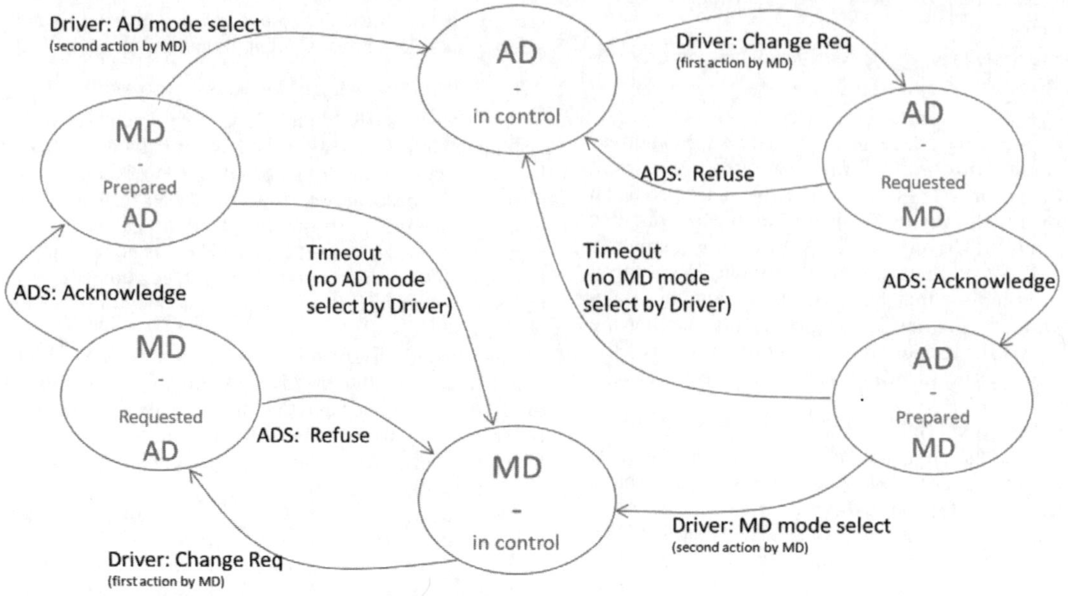

Figure 1. Example of a simple transition protocol.

redundant action from the manual driver can in general be either in time or in space, or a combination of these. By time redundancy, we mean here to request a sequence of actions where the second must follow in a certain time interval after the first one. Space redundancy is on the other hand when the manual driver is requested to apply several actions simultaneously. In both cases, the idea is that it can be argued that the set of actions is extremely unlikely to be performed by mistake.

A less conservative assumption is that a protocol should be immune against any single manual mistake. A more conservative assumption is to increase the number of mistakes a driver can perform still being conformant to the protocol. A high number of such mistakes may be argued to occur if they entire protocol sequence can be seen as an automated behaviour, being possible to execute in total by mistake. The scope of this paper is not to argue what combination of manual mistakes that are likely, but showing a general technique and illustrate this with some examples. The first examples are designed to be robust to single human mistakes, and the last one is implementing a protocol still safe in the presence of two human mistakes.

A. *Example HMI Protocol and Implementations*

As a first example in this paper, we chose to describe a protocol based on manual time redundancy. This means that we always require two actions from the driver for any transition from the mode when the driver is responsible, here denoted MD, to the mode when the ADS is responsible, here denoted AD. The same requirement on two actions by the manual driver are also valid for the reverse transition from the mode AD to the mode MD. Furthermore, we say that the second action of the manual driver defines the transition, which means that there is no requirement on the manual driver to observe the resulting outcome correctly, more than knowing what she or he is doing herself or himself. As long as the second action is fulfilled, the transition is deemed to have occurred.

In Figure 1, a general protocol is illustrated, where two coordinated actions are required from the manual driver. When implementing this it is important for the ADS HMI not to allow the driver to perform the second action, without having acknowledged the first one.

In this example, we choose the first action to be a press of a button and the second to be a change of lever position. This lever has exactly two possible positions, equal to the two modes: AD and MD. For a certain L4 feature, the journey is always to be started in MD, and the driver may change the mode after reaching the proper state in the transition protocol. We consider the lever to be locked at any other time. Furthermore, if the lever is not moved fast enough after getting acknowledge by the ADS, it will be locked again requiring the protocol to start over again to perform a transition.

This protocol is based on the assumption that it is always safe to keep the mode if nothing else is agreed. The current responsible (manual driver or ADS) should always be able to continue to take care of the vehicle in a safe manner. The exception is when the progress of the protocol execution is hindered in a way that generates the failure *stuck in transition*.

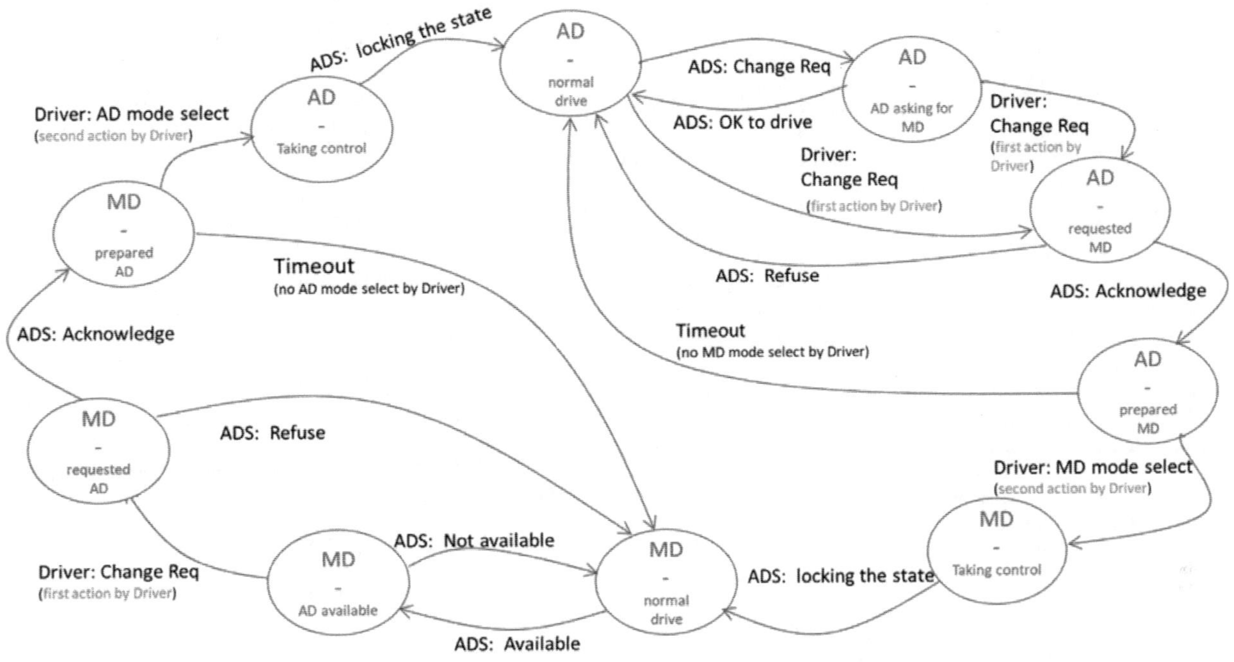

Figure 2. Example of an elaborated transition protocol.

We can extend the protocol to cover the cases where the ADS can suggest a transition, either by declaring that the ADS is ready to take over from the manual driver, or by telling the manual driver that the ADS performance is limited. Such a protocol is depicted in Figure 2.

To implement this protocol, we show two different possible implementations. In the first implementation, we chose the following HMI components:

- Tell-tale light showing the ADS view of preferred mode
- Push-button to for the manual driver to ask for mode change (first action)
- Tell-tale light showing whether the ADS is prepared for a change as requested by the manual driver
- Lever for the manual driver to select mode (second action)

Any failure mode of these four HMI components then needs to be included in the safety analysis, and this in combination by any single mistake by the manual driver.

To summarize, a fault-free uninterrupted transition from the MD mode to the AD mode in this example follow the steps:

- The manual driver drives the vehicle (MD mode)
- The ADS declares it is ready to take over by changing the preference tell-tale to AD mode available
- The manual driver asks to take over by pressing the push-button
- The ADS acknowledges that it is prepared by indicating the readiness tell-tale and unlocking the lever
- The manual driver changes the lever to AD mode position
- The ADS locks the lever, and continues to drive in AD mode

The transition from AD mode to MD mode is performed in a similar way, i.e., the manual driver may either independently, or suggested by the ADS, start by asking for a mode change. The ADS then acknowledges by indicating on the readiness tell-tale and unlocking the lever. Finally, the manual driver changes the lever to the MD mode position and starts to drive manually.

B. Safety Analysis

In the following section, the above protocol and implementation is analysed with respect to its sensitivity to any human mistake, vehicle component failure, or a combination of these. Hence, we walk through the detailed state diagram and investigate the possible failure consequences at any state. When doing the safety analysis, we document the result in Table I. The columns are:

- Protocol state
- HMI failure to investigate
- Possible driver mistake
- Consequence in words
- Consequence in terms of safe/unsafe

Each row in this table marked as unsafe in the last column, needs to be protected by a corresponding safety requirement allocated to restrict this HMI failure. If all occurrences of an unsafe consequence are protected by appropriate safety requirements, the protocol implementation is deemed safe. For the safety argumentation to be valid, it is important that the table is shown to be complete. This includes an argumentation that all possible human mistakes are considered.

C. *Safety Assessments*

As concluded from the safety analysis in Table I, there are four ways for this first example protocol implementation to fail in an unsafe way, caused by either of a manual mistake, a vehicle component failure, or a combination of these. The four failures that we need to avoid maintaining safety are:

- The ADS cannot correctly sense the mode lever position, which may cause *mode confusion.*
- The ADS cannot guarantee lock of the mode lever according to the protocol. This in combination with the manual driver moving the mode lever to AD mode, without noticing it, may cause *mode confusion* (or *unfair transition* if discovered by the manual driver).
- The ADS cannot guarantee locking of the mode lever according to the protocol. This in combination with the manual driver changing lever position from MD to AD, without getting acknowledgment of a prepared ADS, may cause *unfair transition.*
- The ADS cannot guarantee unlocking the mode lever according to the protocol. Which may cause *stuck in transition.*

TABLE I. SAFETY ANALYSIS OF TRANSITION PROTOCOL

Protocol state	HMI failure	Driver mistake	Consequence	Safe/ Unsafe
MD - normal drive	Fault in lever lock	No	MD driver not trying to touch lever. Stay in MD.	Safe
MD - normal drive	Fault in lever lock	Driver changes lever position without asking for change first.	Unfair transition.	Unsafe
MD - normal drive	Fault in preference tell-tale	Any mistake or correct behaviour	MD cannot change locked lever. Stay in MD- normal drive.	Safe
MD - AD available	Fault in lever lock	No	MD driver not trying to touch lever. Stay in MD.	Safe
MD - AD available	Fault in lever lock	Driver changes lever position without asking for change first.	Unfair transition.	Unsafe
MD - AD available	Fault in preference tell-tale	No	Stay in MD	Safe
MD - AD available	Fault preference tell-tale	Driver ignores lack of availability	Transition sequence fulfilled. Change to AD.	Safe
MD - requested AD	Fault in push-button	Any mistake or correct behaviour	No Acknowledge by AD. Lever still locked. Stay in MD.	Safe
MD - prepared AD	Fault in prepared tell-tale	Driver correct: Driver stops transition sequence	Time-out in protocol. Stay in MD.	Safe
MD - prepared AD	Fault in prepared tell-tale	Driver incorrect: Driver ignores lack of ack.	Transition sequence fulfilled. Change to AD	Safe
MD - prepared AD	Fault in lever lock	Driver correct: Driver tries but cannot fulfil transition sequence.	Stuck in transition.	Unsafe
MD - prepared AD	Fault in lever lock	Driver incorrect: Driver doesn't continue transition sequence.	Time-out in protocol. Stay in MD.	Safe
AD – taking control	Fault in lever sensor	Any mistake or correct behaviour	Mode confusion	Unsafe
AD – normal drive	Fault in lever lock	No	MD driver not trying to touch lever. Stay in MD.	Safe
AD – normal drive	Fault in lever lock	Driver changes lever position to MD without asking for change first, and without noticing what is happening.	Mode confusion. (Unfair transition, if realized later).	Unsafe
AD – normal drive	Fault in preference tell-tale	No	MD acts as in normal AD mode. Stay in AD or ask for transition.	Safe
AD – normal drive	Fault in preference tell-tale	Driver tries to change lever position but it is locked in AD position.	Stay in AD.	Safe
AD – asking for MD	Fault in lever lock	No	MD not touching lever without asking for change first. Stay in AD.	Safe
AD – asking for MD	Fault in lever lock	Driver changes lever position by mistake without noticing it in the first place, and without asking for change first.	Mode confusion (Unfair transition, if realized later).	Unsafe
AD – asking for MD	Fault in preference tell-tale	Any mistake or correct behaviour	MD can request MD mode or stay in AD mode.	Safe
AD – requested MD	Fault in push-button	Any mistake or correct behaviour	No Acknowledge by AD. Lever still locked. Stay in AD.	Safe
AD – prepared MD	Fault in prepared tell-tale	No	Driver stops transition sequence. Time-out in protocol. Stay in AD.	Safe
AD – prepared MD	Fault in prepared tell-tale	Driver ignores lack of ack.	Transition sequence fulfilled. Change to MD	Safe
MD – taking control	Fault in lever lock	Any mistake or correct behaviour	Driver tries but cannot fulfil transition sequence. Stuck in transition	Unsafe
MD – taking control	Fault in lever sensor	Any mistake or correct behaviour	Mode confusion	Unsafe

As we assume that the manual driver may make any single failure at any time, the way to argue for avoiding the above failures is to put the entire responsibility on the ADS. This implies that we put three safety requirements on the HMI of the ADS:

- ASIL D on restricting faulty lever sensor, i.e., the lever sensor needs to be always correct.
- ASIL D on restricting lever lock faulty unlocked.
- ASIL D on restricting lever lock faulty locked.

If we can guarantee that the ADS HMI is implemented according to these three safety requirements, we can claim that we make a safe transition even in the presence of an arbitrary single manual mistake. This takes care of all three aspects (*mode confusion, unfair transition* and *stuck in transition*) of a safe transition.

If ASIL D sensors and/or ASIL D locks are considered either unavailable or very expensive, we may consider redundancy implementation techniques. Instead of one sensor always telling the correct lever position with ASIL D attribute, we may consider three (sic!) sensors each with ASIL B. If at least two of the three are correct, we can stay safe. This means that we need to restrict that two of the three are failing. This shall be guaranteed with a total ASIL D, which we distribute as ASIL B on each sensor. Similarly, using ASIL A sensors would require seven times redundancy. If four out of seven are working we consider it as safe. This means that we need to restrict that four of the sensors are failing. This shall be guaranteed with a total ASIL D, which we distribute as ASIL A on each sensor.

As a second example in this paper, we use the same protocol, but chose other means of HMI components. Instead of pushing a button to initiate the AD->MD transition, the driver keeps his eyes focused on the traffic on the road for some seconds. Instead of a tell-tale on the instrument cluster to indicate to the driver that a mode change is prepared, we use a heads-up display (HUD) icon. Finally, instead of a lever for the driver to indicate the mode change, we choose a flip of some lateral steering wheel segments. These means can be argued as in-line with the idea of not distracting the driver, but making sure that while performing the transition sequence, the driver keeps attention to the driving task as well.

When we perform a similar analysis of this protocol implementation as we did for the first example in Table I, we will get exactly the same results. This means that in presence of fault-free HMI components, the implemented protocol is robust to any single driver mistakes. Furthermore, to guarantee safety in the presence of HMI component failures and any single manual mistake, we need to put safety requirements restricting failures on the steering wheel flip indicator, and on the locking mechanism of the steering wheel flipping mechanism.

Both the above examples can be argued as idiotic implementations. The idea here is not to show what is the best implementation of a protocol, but rather to illustrate the technique to investigate the failure modes of the HMI components together with the possible manual mistakes according to a certain protocol.

In the last example, we go one step further and construct a protocol tolerant to any double human mistakes. This implies that any handover sequence involves three coordinated actions by the driver (two actions could be a double failure).

The example protocol can be found by just expanding the previous one with one action from each part, as shown in Figure 3.

The chosen HMI components for the sake of the argument are the following:

- A tell-tale + sound indicating to driver that the ADS prefers to leave control to the Driver.
- A button for the Driver to push when initiating a mode change from AD to MD.
- A HUD icon asking the driver to show readiness to take over control.
- An eye tracker checking that the Driver keeps the eyes on essential parts of the road and traffic environment.
- A HUD icon telling the Driver that it is OK to take over control.
- A steering wheel with flippable lateral segments for the driver to indicate mode of driving (when compressed in AD mode; when expanded in MD mode).
- A locking mechanism, making sure the steering wheel segments only are flipped at valid moments according to the protocol.
- A HUD icon telling Driver when mode change from MD to AD is available.
- A button for the driver to press when initiating a MD to AD hand over.
- A HUD icon asking for confirmation from Driver that mode change to AD is intended.

We can now again walk through the protocol and investigate the failure modes in similar was as was done in Table I. This leads to similar result following the general pattern:

Every ADS HMI component being responsible for either of

- *not allowing the driver to (by mistake) perform such a forward transition in the protocol that makes any of the user actions unneeded to complete the transition*
- *not misinterpret the driver actions such that a forward transition in the protocol that makes any of the user actions unneeded to complete the transition*
- *not hindering the driver to perform the last action in the transition protocol, when the user should expect it to be aloud*

will get an ASIL requirement. And only those.

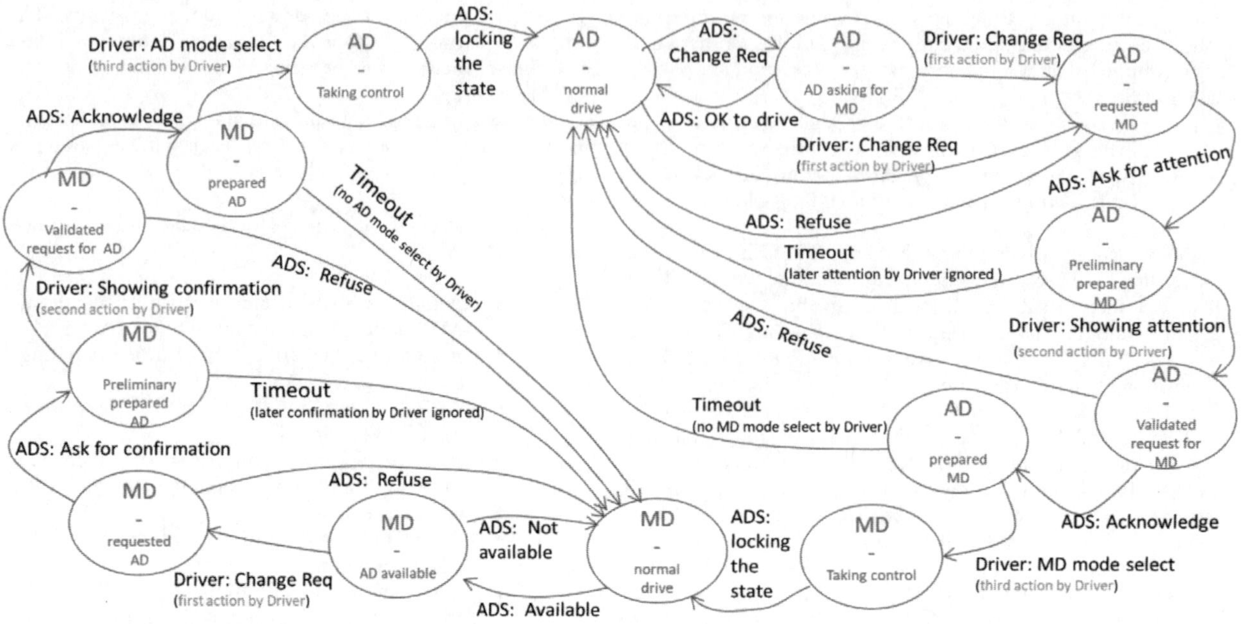

Figure 3. Example of an elaborated 3-action protocol, robust against two manual failures.

The first two conditions above are to guarantee absence of *mode confusion* and of *unfair transitions*, and the third one is for avoiding *stuck in transition*. Note that what is listed above are just the safety requirements on the HMI components. The internal logic executing the protocol is still subject to safety requirements for any failing transition.

VI. CONCLUSION

When introducing an automated driving system (ADS) according to SAE Level 4, which takes full responsibility to drive the vehicle once activated, it becomes crucial to ensure safe transitions between the manual driver and the ADS. The existence of dual driving modes brings three new sources of risk, namely *unfair transition*, *mode confusion* and *stuck in transition*.

We propose to define a safe transition as a transition where neither a (complex) manual mistake nor an E/E failure, nor combination of these, leads to an *unfair transition*, *mode confusion* or *stuck in transition*.

We do not prescribe what manual failures to consider, but rather showing a methodology how to perform safety analysis of implementations of transfer protocols. Given that we agree on what set of single, double or multiple failures by the driver to assume, we show how to argue that an appropriate set of safety requirements on the HMI components would be sufficient to deem the HMI of the ADS functionally safe.

Furthermore, we demonstrate on some system examples how to allocate safety requirements on HMI elements to ensure safe transitions, and we show how the same protocol can be implemented by different HMI components. We also show an example of a protocol and implementation designed to be robust to dual driver mistakes.

Results from this example show that it is sufficient to allocate safety requirements on the sensor of the driver action and of the lock of the mode control, to ensure a safe transition. No safety requirements are needed on visual feedback to the driver, e.g., displays. We remark that the example implementations by no means are unique or optimal solutions to the safe transitions problem, but intended to illustrate a methodology.

ACKNOWLEDGMENT

This research has been supported by the Swedish government agency for innovation systems (VINNOVA) in the ESPLANADE project (ref 2016-04268).

REFERENCES

[1] R. Johansson, J. Bergenhem, and M. Kaalhus, "Safe transitions of Responsibility in Highly Automated Driving," DEPEND 2016: The Ninth International Conference on Dependability, July 2016.

[2] SAE, "Surface Vehicle Recommended Practice – J3016 – Taxonomy and Definitions for Terms Related to Driving Automation systems for On-Road Motor Vehicles", September 2016.

[3] C. Gold, D. Damböck, K. Bengler, and L. Lorenz, "Partially Automated Driving as a Fallback Level of High Automation," 6. Tagung Fahrerassistenzsysteme. Der Wig zum Autom. Fahren., 2013.

[4] National Highway Traffic Safety Administration, "Human Factors Evaluation of Level 2 And Level 3 Automated Driving Concepts Past Research, State of Automation Technology, and Emerging System Concepts," http://www.nhtsa.gov/DOT/NHTSA/NVS/Crash%20Avoidance/Technical%20Publications/2014/812043_HF-EvaluationLevel2andLevel3AutomatedDrivingConceptsV2.pdf, retrieved: June 2016.

[5] M. H. Martens and A. P. Van Den Beukel, "The road to automated driving: Dual mode and human factors considerations," IEEE Conf. Intell. Transp. Syst. Proceedings (ITSC) , 2013, pp. 2262–2267.

[6] F. Naujoks, C. Mai, and A. Neukum, "The effect of urgency of take-over requests during highly automated driving under distraction conditions," Adv. Hum. Asp. Transp. Part I, vol. 7, July 2014, p. 431.

[7] M. Blanco, J. Atwood, H. M. Vasquez, T.E. Trimble, V.L. Fitchett, J. Radlbeck, and J. F. Morgan, "Human factors evaluation of level 2 and level 3 automated driving concepts," Report No. DOT HS 812 182, Washington, DC, National Highway Traffic Safety Administration, 2015.

[8] N. Merat, A.H. Jamson, F. F. C. H. Lai, M. Daly, and O. M. Carsten, "Transition to manual: Driver behaviour when resuming control from a highly automated vehicle," Transportation Research Part F: Traffic Psychology and Behaviour, 26, 1–9, 2014.

[9] T. Helldin, G, Falkman, M. Riveiro, and S. Davidsson, "Presenting system uncertainty in automotive UIs for supporting trust calibration in autonomous driving," In Proceedings of the 5th International Conference on Automotive User Interfaces and Interactive Vehicular Applications - AutomotiveUI '13 (pp. 210–217). New York, New York, USA: ACM Press, 2013.

[10] J. Beller, M. Heesen, and M. Vollrath, "Improving the Driver-Automation Interaction: An Approach Using Automation Uncertainty," Human Factors: The Journal of the Human Factors and Ergonomics Society, 55(6), 1130–1141, 2013.

[11] B. Seppelt, and J. Lee, "Making adaptive cruise control (ACC) limits visible," International Journal of Human-Computer Studies, 2007.

[12] S. Brandenburg and E. Skottke, "Switching from manual to automated driving and reverse: Are drivers behaving more risky after highly automated driving?," IEEE 17th Int. Conf. Intell. Transp. Syst. (ITSC), pp. 2978–2983, 2014.

[13] A. Marinik, R. Bishop, V. Fitchett, J. F. Morgan, T. E. Trimble, and M. Blanco. "Human factors evaluation of level 2 and level 3 automated driving concepts: Concepts of operation," Report No. DOT HS 812 044. Washington, DC: National Highway Traffic Safety Administration., July 2014.

[14] H. Orlady, and R. Barnes, "A Methodology for Evaluating the Operational Suitability of Air Transport Flight Deck System Enhancements," SAE Technical Paper # 975642, 1997.

[15] T. Inagaki, "Design of human–machine interactions in light of domain-dependence of human-centered automation," Cognition, Technology & Work, Volume 8, Issue 3, pp 161-167, 2006

[16] T. Lackman, "Utredning och kartläggning av tillfällen då människan räddat och förbättrat en situation där automatiken inte räckt till eller fungerat fel," Strålskerhetsmyndigheten 2011:24, ISSN 2000-0456, 2011.

[17] J. Cunningham "Break the monotony," Professional Engineering, 20(20), 33-33, 2007.

[18] D.B. Kaber, and L. J. Prinzel, "Adaptive and adaptable automation design: A critical review of the literature and recommendations for future research," NASA/TM-2006-214504, September 2006.

[19] R. Johansson, C. Bergenhem, and H. Sivencrona, "Challenges of Functional Safety in ADAS and Autonomous Functions," SAE World Congress, Detroit, April 2014.

[20] J. A. Michon, "A Critical view of driver behavior models: What do we know, what should we do?,",in L. Evans & R.C Schwing (eds.) Human behavior and traffic safety (pp. 485-520). New York: Plenum Press, 1985.

[21] R. Sukthankar, "Situation Awareness for Tactical Driving," Ph.D. thesis, Robotics Institute, Carnegie Mellon University, USA, January 1997.

[22] T. X. P. Diem and M. Pasquier, "From Operational to Tactical Driving: A Hybrid Learning Approach for Autonomous Vehicles," 10th Intl. Conf. on control, Automation, Robotics and Vision, Hanoi, Vietnam, December 2008.

[23] ISO, "International Standard 26262 Road vehicles -- Functional safety", November 2011.

Intermodal Contour Accessibility Measures Computation Using the 'UrMo Accessibility Computer'

Daniel Krajzewicz, Dirk Heinrichs, Rita Cyganski
Institute of Transport Research
German Aerospace Center
Berlin, Germany
daniel.krajzewicz@dlr.de, dirk.heinrichs@dlr.de, rita.cyganski@dlr.de

***Abstract*—Contour accessibility measures form a set of performance indicators used to value a location by the amount of accessible activities, places, or space within certain time or distance limits. They are used for evaluating a region's activity potential taking the connectivity to its surroundings into regard and act as input data for land use planning models and traffic demand models. With the availability of disaggregated data and sufficient computer power, accessibility measures can be computed at a very fine-grained level of single buildings, points of interest or areas. This approach considers single routes through the transportation network and allows for computing intermodal accessibilities which assume a usage of multiple carriers along a single way. This report presents a tool that realizes such a disaggregated computation of accessibility measures. A strong focus is put on the tool's internal computation steps for supporting a reference to potential users.**

Keywords*—*Accessibility measures; performance indicators; intermodality.

I. INTRODUCTION

In [1], we presented tool for computing so-called accessibility measures. With a raising awareness about (road) traffic's impacts on the environment and the quality of life, especially in urban areas [2], measures and incentives for supporting sustainable modes of transport become increasingly important. In conjunction, proper performance indicators are needed for determining areas that need improvements as well as for measuring the results of planned or already performed measures. One class of performance indicators for valuing a given area or location are so-called accessibility measures [3]. Briefly spoken, accessibility measures describe how well an area or a location is connected to the surrounding activity places taking into account different modes of travel.

Following Litman [4], the concept of accessibility measures introduces a paradigm shift in transport planning. Conventional mobility-based measures cover mainly the performance of the road infrastructure, including the average speed, capacity, or, when looking at traffic participants, the vehicle miles travelled. In contrary, accessibility measures "favor different strategies, including improvements to alternative modes, incentives to change travel behavior, and more accessible land use" [5]. Summarizing, in contrary to mobility-based measures, which focus on automobile traffic, accessibility measures put people into focus [5].

Meanwhile, accessibility measures are a common tool for evaluating a region's transport offer and are not only used in academic context, but also by local administrations [6][7]. Accessibility measures take into account the infrastructure, the distribution of localities and inhabitants in space, the passengers' preferences for using different modes of transport as well as their disabilities [3].

This paper presents a tool for computing so-called contour accessibility measures at the fine-grained level of detail of single buildings and the transportation network. Often, accessibility measures are used at the coarser level of so-called "travel analysis zones" (TAZ). TAZs usually divide a region such as a city or a bigger area into cells with a most possible homogenous travel behavior. So-called macroscopic demand models compute the amount of traffic between such TAZs, and macroscopic land-use models describe the attributes of locations at this level for computing the development of cities or regions. Increasingly, such macroscopic approaches are replaced by microscopic models where every single entity – household, person or vehicle in transportation context – is modelled and simulated individually. Accordingly, fine-grained "microscopic" approaches for computing accessibility are attempted.

The tool for computing accessibility measures described herein was developed for the project "Urbane Mobilität" [8][9], or "UrMo" for short, and was thereby named "UrMo Accessibility Computer", or abbreviated "UrMoAC". In the following, "UrMoAC" and "the tool" are used synonymously. The topic of the project "Urbane Mobilität" is intermodality – travelling using different modes of transport (e.g., subsequently riding a bike, using the public transport, and walking) along a single journey [10]. Accordingly, the tool described in [1] was extended by the possibility to compute intermodal accessibility measures to meet the project's scope.

Besides describing the extensions needed for computing intermodal accessibility measures, the tool's functionalities, including reading and processing input data, computing individual accessibility measures and aggregating them in spatial means as well as the generation of outputs is described in the following. The focus on the tool's internals shall support potential users with an in-depth understanding about the tool.

The remainder is structured as following. In Section II, a short overview on accessibility measures is given. Section III lists the requirements of the project. In Section IV, implementation details are given. Section V shows some use cases and visualization possibilities. This report closes with a summary and outlook in Section VI.

II. ACCESSIBILITY MEASURES

"Accessibility" is not a single, well-defined function, but rather a set of concepts, see [3][11]. One common understanding is that accessibility is a compound measure that describes how many locations can be approached within a given time from a given starting point. Compound, as accessibility consists of two parts. The first is the space that can be covered within the given limits. The second one is the existence of locations of the investigated type within this accessible space. But this is a very brief view at accessibility measures. [3] and [11] give summaries of accessibility measures' classes and distinguish between "spatial separation measures", "contour measures", "gravity measures", "competition measures", "time-space measures", "utility measures", and "network measures". One can treat this set of measurements as a class hierarchy of continuous attempts to regard new information, the prior class did not consider. Figure 1 summarizes this hierarchy, which is also briefly discussed in the following.

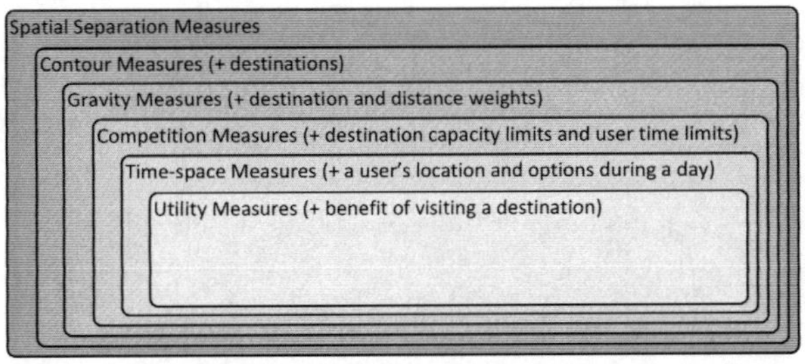

Figure 1. Hierarchy of accessibility measures.

"Spatial separation measures" describe how well (or bad) an area is connected to other areas. Here, distances or travel times are used as a basic measurand. "Contour measures" introduce the land use aspect by incorporating the number of destinations that can be accessed in a given limit, usually given by a maximum travel time. Usually, this number is the desired result of "contour measures". "Gravity measures" add a weight to the accessible destinations, usually including the respective destination's attractiveness (e.g., number of employees at a work location or the size of a shop) and a decay imposed by the distance from the source to the respective destination. "Competition measures" additionally incorporate time limits of the users as well as capacity limits of the destinations, partially also the fact that when investigating destinations of the same type, e.g., shops with the same brand, only the nearest ones are of relevance and more distant ones are neglected. "Time-space measures" look at accessible locations taking into account the changing position and the changes in availability of the transport modes that are available for a single user. Finally, "utility measures" incorporate the benefit a user gains by visiting accessible locations.

One may note that "network measures" have been listed before, yet were not discussed. Although counted as accessibility measures, network measures concentrate on the transportation network, measuring its attributes, such as connectivity, distances, and transfer times. Thereby, in contrary to the other described accessibility measures, they describe the transportation network and not locations or areas.

The inclusion of further weights, attributes and constraints into the computation of accessibilities is meant to increase the fitness of the measures to describe real-world needs and to include the anticipation of accessibility by users. Yet, one may note that these extensions raise the need for corresponding data. Representations of the transportation network as well as positions of locations as needed by contour measures are available, even as a part of publicly available data such as OpenStreetMap (OSM) [12]. But weighting functions, the users' time limits, constraints, and daily activities or the benefits of visiting a certain location can only be guessed, extrapolated from surveys, or computed using models and are thereby usually vague.

III. REQUIREMENTS AND DESIGN

In the following, the derivation of the requirements for the discussed tool will be outlined. First, the context of the project "Urbane Mobilität" the tool was developed for will be given. Then, the derived requirements are presented, followed by some design decisions.

A. *Project Context*

Besides evaluating nowadays intermodal mobility behavior, the project "Urbane Mobilität" aims at predicting the effects of measures for increasing the share of intermodality in everyday choice of transport modes to use. Three simulation models are used for this purpose: the agent-based demand model "Travel Activity PAttern Simulator" (TAPAS) [13][14], the microscopic traffic flow simulation "Simulation of Urban MObility" (SUMO) [15][16], and the location choice model "SimulAting Location Demand and Supply in Urban Agglomerations" (SALSA) [17].

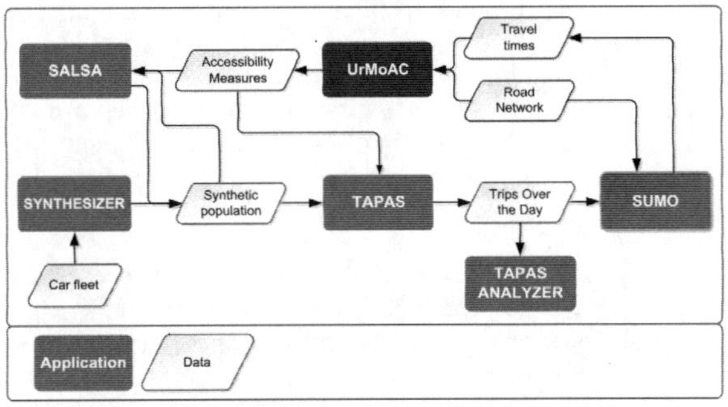

Figure 2. Coupled simulations used in project "Urbane Mobilität".

Within the project context, SALSA is applied for computing long-term mobility decisions of the population of Berlin by choosing a place of residence. TAPAS models medium- and short-term mobility decisions, mainly the selection of the transport mode, but as well the locations to visit during a day. This is done individually for each of the persons the modeled population in the analysis region consists of. Finally, SUMO simulates the traffic on the transportation network using the demand generated by TAPAS and returns travel time information. This information is given back to TAPAS and SALSA for iteratively obtaining a valid representation of the traffic in the city. The iteration ends as soon as an equilibrium state between the demand and the resulting travel times is reached. The overall workflow is presented in Figure 2. The shown "SYNTHESIZER" application is responsible for generating a disaggregated population [18].

Supporting SALSA with data about a location's accessibility was the major reason for developing an accessibility computation tool. SALSA itself is macroscopic – locations are grouped into areas at the level of so-called "Teilverkehrszellen" (TVZ, English: sub traffic analysis zone) that represent the TAZ SALSA uses. Berlin's 1223 TVZs are shown in Figure 3. Albeit being microscopic (agent-based) in its nature, also the demand model TAPAS requires matrices that describe travel time and distances between the centers of TVZ.

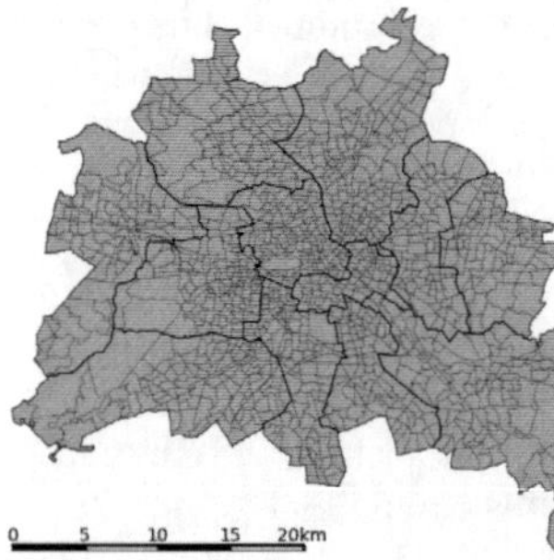

Figure 3. Segmentation of Berlin into "Teilverkehrszellen" (TVZ) as used by SALSA.

SALSA uses a large number of different measures for describing different aspects of the dwellings within a given TAZ. Besides attributes such as the average price, size, or construction year, different accessibility measures can be found among them. It is not known which measures are significant a-priori. Instead, different measures have to be computed first, and their significance has to be determined afterwards by using correlation and regression models that explain their influence in choosing the respective inhabitance area [17][19].

As a starting point, commonly found accessibility measures were defined to be tested for their relevance in household location choice. They include measures such as:

- average travel time to other zones;
- average distance to other zones;
- travel time to nearest commercial center;
- travel time to nearest railway station;
- travel time to closest grocery store (>= 200m^2);
- travel time to closest small park (>= 10000m^2);
- grocery retail floor space within 10min travel time;
- green space area within 30min travel time;
- number of jobs within 30min travel time;
- travel time to closest large park (>= 50000m^2).

One may note that the large variety of accessibility measures used by SALSA is not only a result of using different types of sources and destinations such as dwellings, job locations, shops, or parks. Instead, one may as well find different rules for limiting the investigated area, different types of aggregation, or an optional collection of a variable that is attached to the accessible destinations. The large variety can yet be simplified to the formula (1) that describe the accessibility of the area Z_i in means of a contour measure:

$$A(Z_{i,m}^{res}) = \frac{\sum_{\{O_k \in Z_i\}} \sum_{l} (g_O(O_k) \cdot g_D(D_l) \cdot f_{res}(c_{k,l,m}))}{\sum_{\{O_k \in Z_i\}} \sum_{l} (g_O(O_k) \cdot f_{res}(c_{k,l,m}))} \quad (1)$$

with:

$A(Z_{i,m}^{res})$: the accessibility of aggregation area Z_i when using the mode m, bound by the limit res

i: the index of the source aggregation area (e.g., a TAZ)

m: the used mode of transport

k: the index of a single source (e.g., building)

l: the index of a single destination

O_k: source k

D_l: destination l

$g_o(O_k)$: the weight of source O_k (e.g., the number of households)

$g_D(D_l)$: the weight of destination D_l (e.g., the number of work places)

$c_{k,l,m}$: the costs of the route (e.g., the travel time) between k and l when using mode m

$f_{res}(c_{k,l,m})$: restriction function that realizes the limits

Hereby, the different limits (nearest destination, max. number of accessible destination, maximum travel time or distance) can be realized by choosing a proper restriction function f_{res}. E.g., the following restriction formula (2) can be used for limiting the accessible destinations by a maximum travel time c_{max}:

$$f_{res}(c_{k,l,m}) = \begin{cases} c_{k,l,m} & if\ c_{k,l,m} \le c_{\max} \\ 0 & otherwise \end{cases} \quad (2)$$

The named accessibility measures have to be computed for the transport modes "walking", "bicycle", "motorized individual traffic" (MIT), and "public transport" (PT). In addition, as the project's scope is intermodality, these measures have as well to be computed for the major combinations of different transport modes, namely "bicycle and PT" and "MIT and PT". Here, one has to consider that some public transport modes allow entraining a bicycle while others do not. Private cars, of course, have always to be left at the place the public transport is entered and after leaving the public transport, the remaining way has always to be passed by foot. Using a car- or bike-sharing service for a part of the route is currently neglected.

B. Requirements Summary

All formulated accessibility measures needed by SALSA fall into the class of "contour measures". The measures needed by TAPAS belong to the class of "spatial separation measures", which are the superset of "contour measures". Thereby, the tool should be able to compute "contour measures" and cover "spatial separation measures".

For computing the needed accessibility measures, the tool shall read information about the sources and the destinations from the project's database as the underlying data used in the "UrMo" project is available in a disaggregate manner and is stored as unique tables in a database. This includes the positions of dwellings, shops and job opportunities. Accessibility measures have to be computed regarding the traffic on roads that affects the travel times. The application shall support the modes "walking", "bicycling", "motorized individual traffic", and "public transport". All of those should be routed only at the roads they are legally allowed to use. In addition, intermodal combinations of public transport with a private car or alternatively with a bike shall be supported. For modelling public transport, real-world schedules have to be used.

Albeit using disaggregated descriptions of the sources and destinations, the accessibility measures shall be computed for TAZ areas. The tool shall provide different criteria for limiting the accessible space, namely routing to the first encountered destination, routing bound by a time limit or unbound routing over the complete analyzed area. In the first and the last case, the travel times and distances shall be computed. When searching bound by the travel time, the number of accessible locations, optionally weighted by an attribute is demanded.

Neither the computation time nor the needed memory was limited as the accessibility measures are usually computed once for a given area and no iterations are needed.

C. Major Design Considerations

The major design aspect was to use disaggregated data as a starting point even though SALSA uses measures aggregated at the level of TAZ. This was motivated by the availability of disaggregated positions of sources and destinations and the attempted usage of a digital road network representation that includes the information about the allowed transport modes and velocities. This approach resembles the current development of transport and land-use models where disaggregated, microscopic models are increasingly replacing macroscopic models. A fine-grained accessibility computation makes use of available disaggregated data, should be more exact than macroscopic approaches and may come along with the inclusion of further information, such as elevators, stairs or other hindrances. Thereby, it not only fulfills the formulated requirements, but is also extensible for future research questions and tasks.

The tool was written in the Java programing language. Currently, it is a command line application what means that no graphical user interface is provided. This is surely a usability restriction, as operating applications at the command line is not common to a large number of users. Yet, besides reducing the implementation effort, command line applications may be run from external scripts or batch files more easily than ones having a graphical user interface what increases the ability to compute a large number of different accessibility measures with least manual interaction. Being a command line application, the data to read and the processing itself is controlled via command line parameters.

The tool computes accessibility measures for a defined set of sources and destinations, yet only for a single mode or intermodal mode combination and for a single route starting time at once. For comparing the accessibilities of different modes, the tool has to be rerun with different parameters. Within the scope of the "UrMo" project, usually the peak hour at 8:00am is used. When determining accessibility measures for public transport, a date must be additionally given for choosing according public transport rides.

IV. IMPLEMENTATION AND PROGRAM FLOW

The overall workflow of the application consists of reading the necessary data, preprocessing it, performing the computation, and generating the outputs. The individual steps are described detailed in the following subsections.

Albeit the used methods – mainly routing using the Dijkstra algorithm [20] – are neither novel nor complex, the overall tool is very flexible due to some simple features. They include filtering, variable limits, or weighting the sources and will be emphasized in the following subsections.

A. Input Data

While for a basic computation of accessibility measures within an investigated region only the positions of destinations and sources and a road network representation are needed, further input values may get necessary, either for defining the aggregation areas, for regarding the public transport offer, or for using travel times of the motorized individual traffic as caused by the respective traffic volume. In the following subsections, the different input data will be presented, distinguishing the description of a) the sources and the destinations, b) the road network, and c) the public transport offer.

1) Sources and Destinations

For the study area, the application first reads the positions of the sources and destinations from a database. As mentioned, different disaggregated spatial locations can be used as sources and destinations, including dwellings, public transport stops, job locations, shops, parks, etc. Figure 5 shows the first two of the named as a visual example. While some of the locations are represented as their footprints using polygons, the tool currently uses the centroids of them only.

This is surely an approximation that introduces an error. But the error is assumed to be small and better models of the access/egress to the road network could only be achieved if the positions of the dwellings' entrances would be known, what is not the case. In later investigations, the usage of CityGML [21] descriptions of buildings, which include the entrances, is planned. Locations with other geometries than polygons may be used as sources/destinations as well, as long as the geometry can be converted to simple points by the used geometry library "JTS" [22]. Besides the need for having a geometry for being allocated in space, each source and destination must have a unique numeric identifier (ID) for later reference.

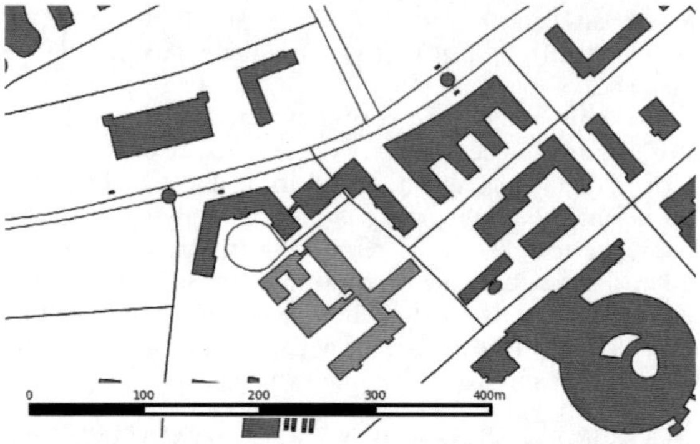

Figure 4. Examples for sources and destinations – dwellings (grey polygons) and bus stop positions (red dots) around the DLR in Berlin (light grey).

When reading sources/destinations from a database a simple filter realized as a SQL WHERE-clause can be given. For bigger datasets – e.g., the locations of all shops in a city – this can be used to select only a subset of the locations, e.g., only groceries or only shops that are bigger than a given threshold. The filter may either be applied to a column of the database table that defines the respective source/destination or be computed using a more complex query, for example using the PostGIS [23] extensions. Thereby, operations, such as filtering objects by their size are possible, even if this information is not explicitly given as an own database table column.

To both, sources and destinations, a numerical value can be attached. For sources, this value is used for weighting the individual source's influence when computing the average value by aggregation, see also Section IV.D. A possible application is weighting dwellings by the number of persons inhabiting them. For destinations, the value's semantics are kept abstract and, if given, the values of the accessible destinations are added together. Usual applications are counting the number of jobs accessible from a location or, as a more abstract measure – determining the selling space of groceries in a specific range. Similar to the filtering option described above, the numerical value may either be read directly from the database or be the result of a more complex computation as long as it is based on the values of a single row of a PostGIS database table.

In summary, the definition of a source and/or a destination consists of a set of variables, which is given in Table I. The database tables used within the project had a consistent naming of these variables. Yet, during further usage of the tool, datasets have occurred where both the ID as well as the geometry were stored under different names. To avoid changing the used database tables, the tool has been extended by possibilities to name the database columns that contain the IDs and the geometries.

TABLE I. VARIABLES OF SOURCES AND DESTINATIONS READ FROM THE DATABASE

Variable	Meaning	Type	Default Name
ID	The object's identifier	bigint	rid
Geometry	The object's location	geometry	the_geom
Value	The object's weight	real	*none (opt.)*

Besides the sources and destinations, further geometry objects may be loaded that describe the areas the computed accessibilities for single source/destination relationships shall be aggregated within. Here, the objects' geometries must be of the type polygon and – as for the sources and destinations – they must support a unique ID. A weight is not loaded. The usage of aggregation areas will be described more detailed in Section IV.D.

2) Road Network

The tool uses a specific database representation of a road network as given in Table II.

TABLE II. THE ATTRIBUTES THE EDGES OF THE READ ROAD NETWORK ARE DEFINED BY

Column	Meaning	Type
id	Edge (road) identifier	serial
oid	Original edge identifier / name	text
nodefrom	ID of the node the edge starts at	bigint
nodeto	ID of the node the edge ends at	bigint
numlanes	The number of the edge's lanes	smallint
length	The edge's length (in meters)	double
vmax	The allowed speed (in km/h)	double
street_type	Abstract street type (not used)	text
mode_walk	Is walking allowed / possible?	boolean
mode_bike	Is riding a bike allowed?	boolean
mode_pt	Are PT carriers allowed? (not used)	boolean
mode_mit	Is driving a private car allowed?	boolean
the_geom	The edge's geometry	multilinestring

Currently, three external import modules exist that generate such representations from the free OpenStreetMap data, from Navteq networks, and from PTV VISUM networks. The import of OSM networks needs some preprocessing steps, which mainly include a) the determination of intersections by selecting nodes used by more than one way, and b) the consolidation of access and one-way information for obtaining a unidirectional network with access information for different transport modes. After performing these preprocessing steps, the import script writes the road network into the database.

Please note that albeit the geometry is currently stored as a PostGIS "MultiLineString" geometry object, it in fact always consists of a single "LineString" only. It is assumed that this will be corrected in the near future. The road network of the city of Berlin as used in subsequently presented evaluations consists of 709,713 edges (roads) and 269,604 nodes. It is shown in Figure 5.

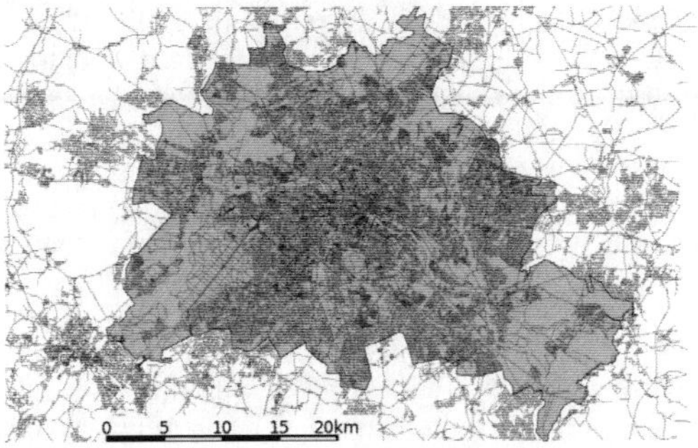

Figure 5. The used road network (black) of the city of Berlin (blue).

Nowadays, road network representations often distinguish between bi- and unidirectional roads. A road with a green space or a parking lane between both directions is usually encoded as two unidirectional roads, each with an own geometry. On the contrary, if both directions are not separated, the road is marked as bidirectional and has one geometry only. The network import tools translate this information and generate a road network representation that contains unidirectional edges only. Yet, for allowing pedestrians to use a road in both directions, the tool additionally builds an edge in the opposite direction for those edges that permit walking and for which no opposite direction exists. This additionally built edge allows walking only. The usage of a road for bicycling into a – legally forbidden – direction what may be found in real life is not supported.

As shown in Table II, the network's edges include the information about the maximum speed allowed for motorized individual traffic. Yet, this information disregards the decrease in average velocities over the day caused by a changing traffic volume. To accommodate this, additional information about the average speeds at each edge over time can be read from a database. Table III shows the structure of such tables. Within the project, the travel time information is generated from the outputs of the microscopic traffic flow simulation SUMO. An import script, which reads SUMO's edge-based traffic measures (see documentation at [16]) and stores them into the database, is supported.

TABLE III. STRUCTURE OF THE ROWS WITHIN THE EDGES' SPEED PROFILES TABLE

Column	Meaning	Type
ibegin	Begin of the time interval (in s)	real
iend	End of the time interval (in s)	real
eid	The original edge identifier / name	text
speed	The average speed (in m/s)	real

3) Public Transport Offer

Optionally, the tool additionally reads a public transport network using a database representation of a General Transit Feed Specification (GTFS) [24] data set. The database representation keeps the original GTFS format and a script for importing GTFS files into database tables is supported. "UrMoAC" itself reads the information about stops, routes, the services offered at the specified date, and the respective trip schedules. As soon as a read public transport line connects two stops, a new public transport edge that connects these stops is added to the network. Instead of the information about the allowed speed, these public transport edges hold the read connections between them, including the departure and arrival times. Using these connections during routing will be discussed in Section IV.C.3.

When computing intermodal accessibility measures, a definition of entrainment possibilities is necessary for a complete description of the intermodal transport offer. This description is again stored in an optionally read database table which has the structure as given in Table IV. For a maximum flexibility in conjunction with keeping the definition of public transport carriers as given in GTFS data, the carrier is described using two fields. One may note that time-dependent entrainment is not supported and that all lines using the same carrier will have the same entrainment constraints.

TABLE IV. THE DEFINITION OF ENTRAINMENT

Column	Meaning	Type
carrier	The name of the carrier vehicle (mode name, e.g., "pt" or "car")	character(40)
carrier_subtype	GTFS route type enum	smallint
carried	The name of the carried vehicle (mode name)	character(40)

4) Map Projection

While dealing with real-world descriptions of geospatial data, the tool has to cope with different types of geographic projections. Because the desired outputs use the metric system, usually a re-projection of the data's original coordinate system to metric measures is needed. The tool allows defining the projection to use on the command line and when reading input data, all coordinates are transformed into this target projection using native PostGIS functions.

B. Preprocessing Data After Reading

In a first step, the objects read from the database to route between are allocated on the road network. As mentioned, their centroid is computed first. For every centroid representing a source/destination, the nearest road that allows to be passed using the investigated mode of transport is determined. A direct, shortest access to this road is assumed, being usually a line normal to the road's shape at the point that is nearest to the object. Yet, in some cases, a source/destination may be located behind the nearest road's beginning or end.

A spatial index, namely the RTree [25] implementation from the Java Spatial Index library [26], is used during this process for increasing the computation speed by searching for roads in the objects' vicinities only. It should be noted that because the RTree structure stores the roads via their bounding box, obtaining the closest road for a given point is not sufficient as the road may be located at the opposite site of the bounding box than the point. Figure 6 shows the connections between sources/destinations and the road network.

Figure 6. Attaching sources/destinations to the road network; buildings (grey polygons) and public transport stations (black points) are connected to the road network (grey lines) via access paths (black lines).

A second issue to solve when allocating objects to roads is the identification of the correct road direction. As mentioned, bidirectional roads are often represented by a single "multiline", a sequence of lines, with no geometrical distinction between both directions. Thereby, both directions have the same distance to the source's/destination's position and an arbitrary one of them would be chosen. This ambiguity is solved by determining the road direction and mapping it onto the direction the source/destination is located right to. The direction is computed as given in formula (3).

$$dir=(x_{le}-x_{lb})(y_p-y_{lb})-(x_p-x_{lb})(y_{le}-y_{lb}) \quad (3)$$

with:

dir: direction (right if negative, left if positive)

x_A: the x-coordinate of point A

y_A: the y-coordinate of point A

where A is one of the following points:

lb: begin of the line nearest to the point

le: end of the line nearest to the point

p: the point (location position)

Usually, sources and destinations are located besides a road. Yet, in some cases, the access to bigger, areal locations (e.g., parks) has to be computed. Such amenities can be usually approached from different directions and are often crossed by roads. In such cases, it does not make sense to allocate them at a single road. Instead, they have to be assigned to all edges that surround and/or cross them. Yet, this is a matter of future extensions.

Optionally read positions of public transport stops have to be assigned to the previously read road graph as well. This is done in a similar way as for the sources/destinations. For each position of a public transport stop, the nearest road is determined and the stop is mapped onto it. Both directions of the road are used if the road was originally bidirectional. Albeit OSM partially includes detailed information about paths across a station or a hub, stations are allocated at the road network via their centroids only. In contrast to sources/destinations, the edge(s) a stop is located at is split at the position of the stop. To this new node, pathways that connect the respective stop and allow to be passed using the modes "walking" and "bicycle" are added. This forms a connection between the original road network and the public transport stops.

C. *Processing*

In its basics, the process of computing accessibility measures is very straightforward. The application iterates over the read sources. For each, the road network is scanned using the Dijkstra algorithm, taking the available and allowed modes of transport and the respective travel times into account. Yet, the wish to compute fine-grained accessibility measures including public transport and intermodal mobility as well as supporting variable routing limits made several extensions necessary, which will be described in the following.

1) Approaching a Destination

One major extension is needed due to the allocation of the sources/destinations along a unidirectional edge. When approaching a destination that is located at the opposite road site, the router would need to move along the current edge to the next intersection (node) to change the moving direction by entering the opposite edge for finally approaching the respective destination. For avoiding this behavior, the router assumes that the edge may be crossed at the position of the destination. Figure 7 visualizes the difference per example.

To implement the functionality of "crossing the road", the router starts in both directions of the edge the respectively processed source is located at. In addition, when approaching an edge, not only the destinations at this edge, but also those that are located at the opposite edge, if given, are collected. One may note that this makes a post-processing of the collected destinations necessary, as discussed later in Section IV.C.4. In case of edges where both directions are separated, e.g., by a green space, crossing (both) is assumed to be not possible.

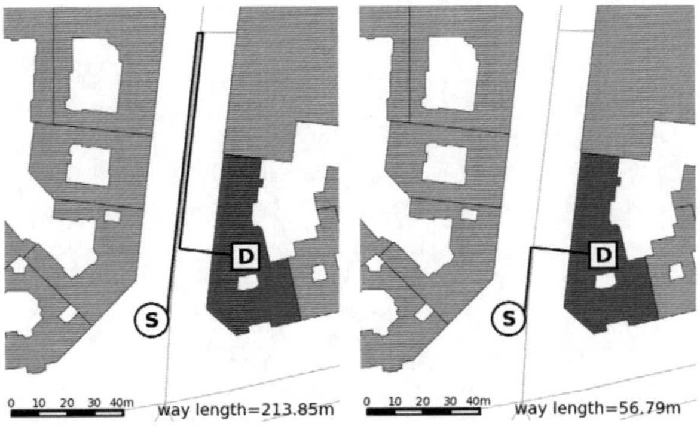

Figure 7. Difference in approaching a public transport stop (S) from a dwelling (D) if crossing the road is not possible (left) or possible (right).

2) Travel Times

The travel speed used for determining the travel time needed to pass an edge mainly depends on the chosen travel mode. The tool uses the speeds as given in Table V. As shown, an edge's speed restrictions are only regarded for motorized individual traffic and bicycling. Having a low velocity, walking is "naturally" bound to the roads' speed limits.

TABLE V. SPEEDS OF THE MODELLED MODES

Mode	Speed
walking	5km/h
bicycling	15km/h
MIT	minimum of 200km/h and the road's speed limit; the latter optionally replaced by read travel time timelines
PT	time schedule (from GTFS)

It should be noted that using the length of edges and the travelling speed for computing the travel time of motorized traffic is not correct as in this case, additional travel time delays posed by traffic lights and other traffic participants are neglected. This issue is solved by additionally reading speed time lines for the loaded edges, as outlined in Section IV.A.2. When entering an edge, these loaded time lines are scanned for finding a time span that matches the time the edge was entered at. The speed stored for this time span is used. There is an additional workaround in case the loaded speed is equal to zero, what e.g., may happen due to grid locks within the simulation that was used to compute the speed timelines. In this case, the half of the allowed velocity is used as travelling speed.

Public transport connections are treated in a different way. When encountering a public transport stop, the available connections to next stations are regarded, for each line operating at this stop. The router chooses the connection with the earliest departure time that is higher than or equal to the arrival time at the stop and returns the time difference between the time of the arrival at the subsequent stop and the time the current stop was approached at.

3) Changing the Mode and Intermodality

The tool is called with a list of available modes of transport as a command line option. When starting the routing, the first of those is selected for being the currently used mode of transport. Yet, the available modes are kept for later routing steps.

When approaching an edge, modes not allowed to be used at this edge are removed from the list of available modes. The mode of transport to switch to is chosen by selecting the mode from the remaining available ones that is the fastest one for passing the edge. The priority queue of the extended Dijkstra algorithm holds not only the visited nodes, but as well the remaining available modes when approaching them. Given this, the consecutive competition of modes and mode combinations along the route is maintained while progressing through the road network.

Public transport stops are connected to the remaining network using edges that allow the modes "walking" and "bicycling". Other modes of transport are therefore abandoned when approaching a public transport stop. Up to now, no penalties for leaving a car or for parking a car are regarded. Allowing using a bike when approaching a stop may be wrong as often one has to dismount and walk. But, as discussed in Section IV.B, no fine-grained information about the access paths from the road network to the public transport stops are given. The stops are only connected to the road network using a shortest line. Allowing to approach a stop by cycling seems therefore to be a good solution for keeping the bike as an available travelling mode for simulating the entrainment of bikes in public transport.

Whether the bike can be entrained between two stops or not is stored in the respective connection between those stops and is based on the information about the carrier used between these stops and the read entrainment table.

4) Variable Limits

One of the tool's strengths is the capability to use different limits for routing. The search for destinations ends as soon as one of the following limits that has to be specified at the command line is reached:

- maximum travel time: stops as soon as the given travel time is exceeded;
- maximum distance: stops as soon as all objects in the given distance have been visited;
- maximum number: stops as soon as the given number of destinations has been visited;
- maximum variable sum: stops as soon as the sum of the variable attached to the destinations is above the given number;
- shortest: stops as soon the first destination is reached.

It must be noted that the determination of the accessible destinations does not end as soon as the limit was reached for the first time. Because the destinations are allocated along the edges, the edges' length cannot be used as a proxy for the search depth in Dijkstra. Even when searching for a nearest destination and finding one at the starting edge, the travel time between the current source and the found destination may be higher than that to a destination located at a different edge. Thereby, the identified destinations have to be temporarily stored and the search limit has to be adapted to be at least the same as the distance to the farthest destination found so far. Storing found destinations temporarily is also necessary as they are collected from both, the travelled edge as well as an optionally given opposite edge during the routing process. The correct set of destinations that fulfills the limits can be only determined by post-processing the destinations collected during routing. Thereby, after finishing the search with adapted limits, the collected results are sorted by their travel time and those exceeding the limit are removed from the collection.

5) Routing Results

For each source, the result of the routing process consists of a set of edges with assigned destinations that are accessible in given limits. For each edge, the travel time, the distance, the used and the available modes, the PT line in case PT was used as well as the information whether this edge was on the opposite side of the originally travelled one are given. Furthermore, the edge information contains a pointer to the predecessor edge for reconstructing the complete route.

The so obtained distinct paths between a single source and the accessible destinations are given to aggregators and output generators discussed in the following section.

D. Aggregation and Output Generation

Given the results for single source/destination relationships, the tool supports several outputs and is capable to apply different kinds of aggregation. Both will be discussed individually in the following.

1) Generated Measures

The results for each source/destination are given to so-called "measurement generators" first. These measurement generators process the routing results and transform them into measurements of different kinds. This kind of post-processing offers some benefits, such as the possibility to generate only the desired outputs or the reduction of needed memory by avoiding keeping unnecessary information. The currently available measurements generators are described in the following. All outputs can be either written to a file or into a database table generated by the tool.

The "n:m output" computes the basic accessibility measures, namely the distance, the travel time, the number of accessed destinations, and their weight. When using an aggregation option, these numbers represent average values, optionally weighted by the sources' weights. The given IDs of the source (fid) and the destination (sid) either name the source / destination itself or, in case of aggregating them by areas they are located within, the ID of the respective aggregation area. If the aggregation option "all" is set for sources and/or destinations, the respective field contains the value -1. The structure of an "n:m output" database table is given in Table VI.

TABLE VI. THE STRUCTURE OF THE "N:M OUTPUT"

Column	Meaning	Type
fid	The id of the source (or source aggregation area)	bigint
sid	The id of the destination (or destination aggregation area)	bigint
avg_distance	The (average when aggregating) distance between the source and the destination in meters	real
avg_tt	The (average when aggregating) travel time between the source and the destination in seconds	real
avg_num	The (average when aggregating) number of seen destinations	real
avg_value	The (average when aggregating) weight of seen destinations	real

The "extended n:m output" extends the "n:m output" by further measurements that can only be computed by traversing each path between a source and a destination. The additional measures include the personal energy needed for the trip, the trip's price, the generated amount of CO_2 emissions, and the list of used modes. The structure of the table is given in Table VII.

TABLE VII. THE STRUCTURE OF THE "EXTENDED N:M OUTPUT"

Column	Meaning	Type
fid	See Table VI	bigint
sid	See Table VI	bigint
avg_distance	See Table VI	real
avg_tt	See Table VI	real
avg_v	The (average when aggregating) velocity between the source and the destination in meters per second	real
avg_num	See Table VI	real
avg_value	See Table VI	real
avg_kcal	The (average when aggregating) personal energy consumption in kcal	real
avg_price	The (average when aggregating) price of the trip/ride in Euro	real
avg_co2	The (average when aggregating) CO_2 emission in g	real
modes	The modes used during the trip	text

The mode-dependent constants for the generated measurements are given in Table VIII. The CO_2 emission is based on information from the German federal environment agency [27]. ADAC's (Germany's major automotive club) price list for passenger vehicles was used for determining the costs of using MIT while the price for using PT is based on the assumption of the availability of an annual pass and the usage of PT three times a day within 20 working days per month. The values for personal energy consumption were collected and cross-checked using different web sites, e.g., http://gesuender-abnehmen.com/. The work in [28] explains the derivation of these constants in more detail.

TABLE VIII. CONSTANTS USED FOR COMPUTING EXTENDED TRIP MEASURES

Mode	CO_2	Personal Energy Consumption	Price
walking	0g/km	280kcal/h	0€/km
bicycling	0g/km	300kcal/h	0€/km
MIT	150g/km	85kcal/h	0.45€/km
PT	75g/km	170kcal/h	0.95€/trip

In addition, the tool supports a so-called "interchanges output" that writes information about the usage of interchanges. Both, public transport interchanges as well as the points (nodes) at which the mode of transport is changed are counted. For each interchange, the ID of the PT stop / network node the interchange took place at, the mode or public transport line the node was approached by, and the one used to leave the node are given. In addition, the number of interchanges at this stop between these modes is given. The structure of this output is given in Table IX.

TABLE IX. THE STRUCTURE OF THE "INTERCHANGES OUTPUT"

Column	Meaning	Type
fid	See Table VI	bigint
sid	See Table VI	bigint
halt	The ID of the described public transport stop or road network node	text
line_from	The mode or line used to approach the stop / node	text
line_to	The mode or line used to leave the stop / node	text
num	The number of interchanges at this node of the given type	bigint

1) *Aggregation*

Another major feature of the tool is the capability to perform different kinds of aggregation. For both, the sources and the destinations, additional aggregation areas (e.g., TAZ) can be read from the database. If given for the sources, the measures collected by routing from individual sources within an aggregation area are averaged. When being applied to the destinations, the values of all destinations within a given aggregation area that are accessible in the given limits will be joined and averaged. Additionally, an "aggregate all" option is available for joining the measures for all sources or respectively destinations. Not all of the possible aggregation combinations are meaningful.

Subdivision of a city into abstract areas, such as TAZ, can be found quite often when dealing with the urban development of a single city or regarding the needs of single districts or quarters. Yet, for a better comparability between different cities or areas, aggregation areas of similar size and shape are of benefit. In such cases, so-called fishnet- or hexagon-grids are used. The tool itself does not compute such grids, yet they can be generated a-priori and loaded as aggregation areas.

V. USE CASES AND VISUALISATION

In the following, some examples for using the tool are given, focusing on showing the tool's capabilities and on pointing out some findings on using accessibility measures.

A. *Isochrones*

Isochrones are a prominent method for visualizing a single source's accessibility. The tool is capable to compute isochrones by limiting the number of sources to one and searching for destinations within a given time limit. Given the list of destinations with assigned travel times needed to access them, isochrones can be visualized using, e.g., the "contourf" method from matplotlib [29], a visualization library for the Python programming language. An example for an isochrones generated this way is shown in Figure 8 for the area accessible within half an hour when starting at the Institute of Transport Research in Berlin Adlershof at 8:00am and using public transport in combination with bicycling. The figure shows the typical accessibility "islands" occurring when using fast public transport connections between distant locations.

Figure 8. Simple isochrones representation; isochrones for using the public transport and a bicycle, starting at Berlin Alexanderplatz at 8:00am.

When investigating intermodal mobility, one may be interested in visualizing the gain of using public transport in addition to another mode of transport. Figure 9 shows the isochrones when using a bicycle only (light blue) and combining it with public transport (purple).

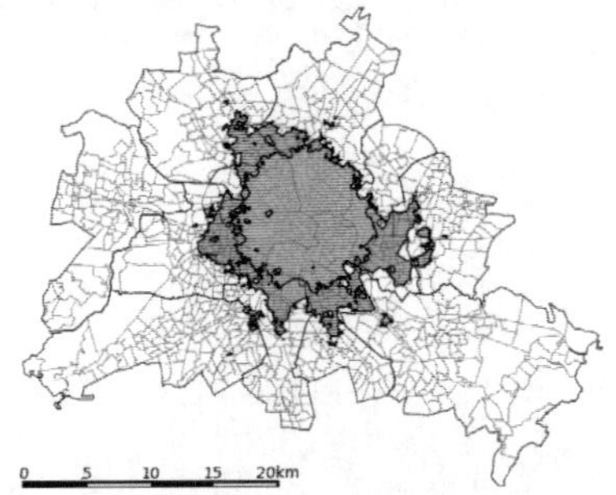

Figure 9. A comparison between the area accessible within half an hour by bike only (light blue) and when combining biking with public transport (purple), starting at Berlin Alexanderplatz at 8:00am.

B. Contour Measures

One often used accessibility measure is the distance or travel time to the next public transport stop. When visualizing the results, one may note that showing disaggregated data (e.g., dwellings) within a bigger area and coloring them is not meaningful, because they vanish due to their small size in comparison to the region and the vacant land. Thereby, an aggregation should be performed. Figure 10 demonstrates this by showing the travel times to the next metro or city rail station for every dwelling individually (top) and aggregated by TAZ (bottom).

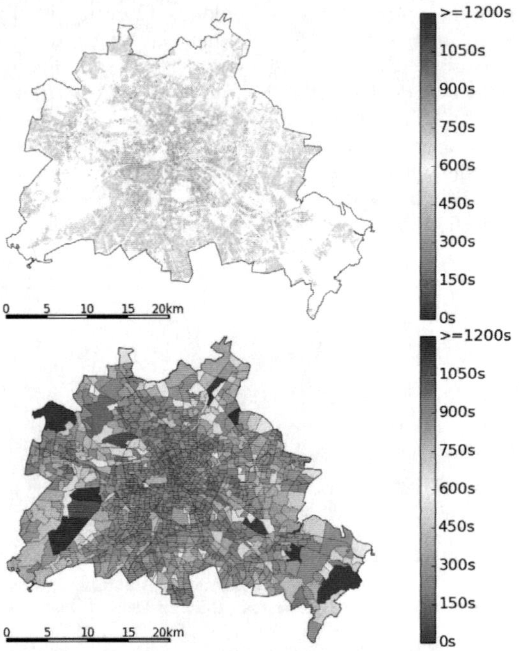

Figure 10. Differences when aggregating accessibility measures.

Using the same example, the influence of weighting sources is shown in Figure 11, which displays the difference between weighted by household number and unweighted travel times from dwellings to the next city rail or metro station aggregated by TAZ.

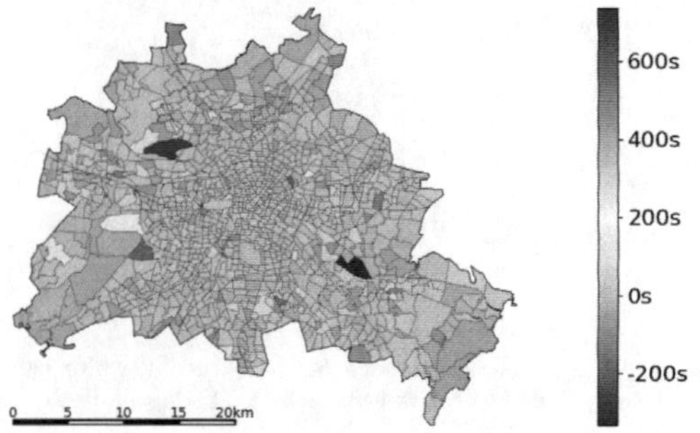

Figure 11. Difference in the access time between a weighted and an unweighted computation.

As visible, neglecting the weight yields in significant deviations.

C. Beyond Travel Time

While intermodality is often appraised to generate less pollution and to be healthier than the monomodal usage of motorized vehicles due to incorporating active modes of transport, only few quantitative evaluations exist. In [29], the performance of intermodality was quantified in means of the personal energy consumption, travel time, price, CO_2 emissions, and the number of accessible places. For this purpose, the number of accessible work places when starting at selected locations in Berlin was computed. The "extended n:m output" was used, and no aggregation was applied. This was done for all implemented modes and mode combinations. The so obtained statistics about mono- and intermodal routes were then evaluated by different means. As an example, Figure 12 shows the performance of the intermodal combination of bicycling and using the public transport against driving a passenger car. The shown lines display the progress when using the respective average velocity. A detailed explanation is given in [28]. Still, one may note that the combination of public transport and bicycling even outperforms the usage of a passenger car.

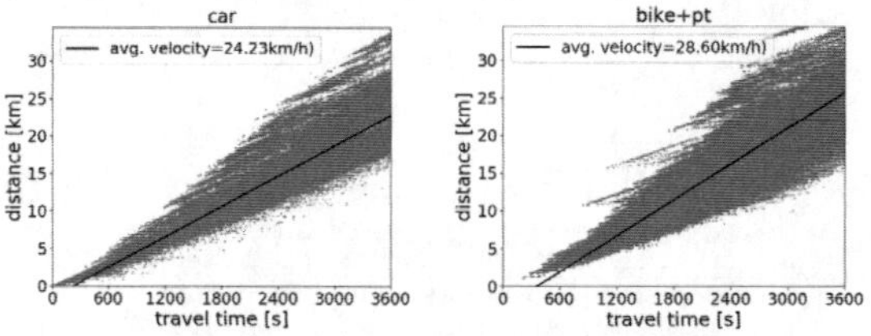

Figure 12. Performance of the intermodal combination of bicycling and using public transport in comparison to driving a passenger car.

Of course, such a disaggregated representation is hard to interpret and raises the amount of needed figures. A summarizing view at the modelled modes' performance in terms of the speed and the number of work places accessible within one hour is given in Figure 13.

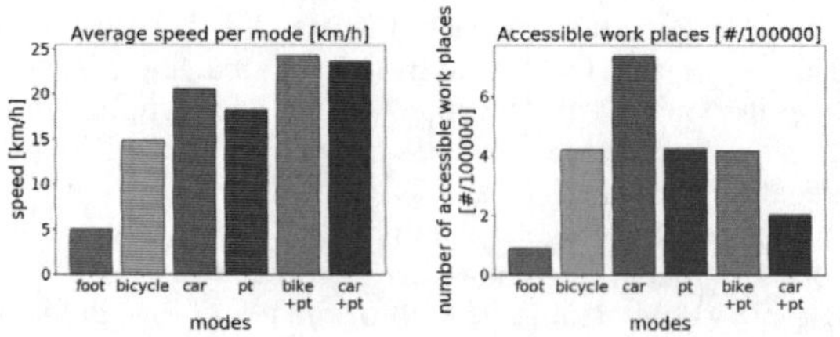

Figure 13. The performance of the mono- and intermodal modes of transport in terms of average speed (left) and the number of accessible work places (right).

One may note that albeit intermodal mode combinations are faster, the number of accessible work places is the same or even lower than for the unimodal modes, especially the car. The reason is that especially when looking at the combination of public transport and a passenger car, only few destinations are approached faster when combining the modes, even though the combination covers bigger distances. This is already visible in the spread of accessibilities when combining public transport with a bicycle as shown in Figure 12, right. As shown, near work places are missing, because it does not make sense to use the public transport to access them when the direct path using a bicycle is already faster.

As mentioned, other measures than speeds were computed for this study, using the "extended n:m-output". Figure 14 shows the average price, the average CO_2 emissions, and the average personal energy consumption for using the modelled modes and mode combinations. In summary, the results prove that intermodal mode combinations outperform the monomodal usage of a car in terms of health, pollutant emission, price, and travel times.

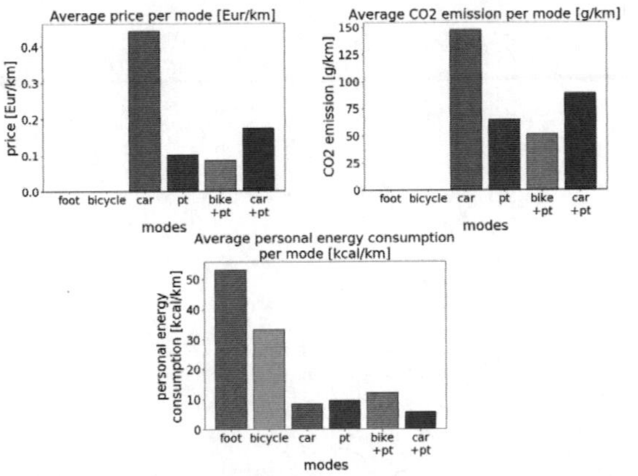

Figure 14. Further performance measures of the mono- and intermodal modes of transport.

VI. SUMMARY AND OUTLOOK

This report presents a tool for computing accessibility measures that can be used for benchmarking areas and for generating measures needed by land use planning models and traffic demand models. The tool follows a fine-grained approach to compute accessibility measures by routing between individual sources and destinations, mainly dwellings, shops, bus stop positions and other man-made objects.

Albeit contour accessibility measures come in many different variations, only some simple methods seem to be sufficient for enabling the tool to compute a large amount of them, fulfilling the requirements given by the "UrMo" project. One important feature are flexible limits, including a maximum travel time, distance, or the possibility to abort the search when a first destination was seen. Another one is the possibility to aggregate the individual sources' accessibility values into averages for bigger areas, including variable aggregation areas and a variable weighting of the individual sources. Reading sources and destinations from a database and supporting a pre-filtering when doing so has proved to be valuable as well. Finally, attaching values to the destinations is required for computing some of the needed accessibility measures and was accordingly implemented.

Some approaches for computing accessibility measures choose only subsets of sources and destinations for estimating accessibility. But the experiences with the tool described herein do not prove the necessity for reducing the amount of data to process.

While being usable as-is, some improvements to the tool and the data it uses seem to have the capacity to improve the results and enable investigations of further research questions. As mentioned, the currently used representation of sources and destinations via their centroids introduces an error in the paths between the respective source/destination and the road network. Using the nearest position to the road network from a given source's/destination's polygon would be possible. Still, this does not regard the positions of a building's doors or entrances. Routing itself should be extended by approaches for a more realistic person routing, which considers slopes, barriers, elevators, and the possibility to walk across free places. Finally, the user friendliness could be increased by adding a graphical interface to the tool.

Summarizing, it is surprising how much flexibility a very small and simple application can achieve. The release of the tool under an open source license is planned for the near future.

REFERENCES

[1] D. Krajzewicz and D. Heinrichs, "UrMo Accessibility Computer - A tool for computing contour accessibility measures," in: SIMUL 2016, The Eighth International Conference on Advances in System Simulation, pp. 56-60, ISBN 978-1-61208-501-2, ISSN 2308-4537, 2016.

[2] UN Habitat, "Planning and Design for Sustainable Urban Mobility: Global Report on Human Settlements 2013," Global Report on Human Settlements Series, 978-92-1-132568-3, 2013.

[3] K. T. Geurs and B. van Wee, "Accessibility evaluation of land-use and transport strategies: review and research directions," in: Journal of Transport Geography, Volume 12, Issue 2, pp. 127-140, ISSN 0966-6923, doi:10.1016/j.jtrangeo.2003.10.005, 2004.

[4] T. A. Litman, "Evaluating Quality of Accessibility for Transportation Planning," in: Transportation Research Board 87th Annual Meeting. No. 08-0495. 2008.

[5] T. A. Litman, "Evaluating Accessibility for Transportation Planning: Measuring People's Ability to Reach Desired Goods and Activities," Victoria Transport Policy Institute, 2016.

[6] M. Pitot, T. Yigitcanlar, Tan, N. Sipe, and R. Evans, "Land Use and Public Transport Accessibility Index (LUPTAI) tool: the development and pilot application of LUPTAI for the Gold Coast," 29th Australasian Transport Research Forum, 2006.

[7] A. Dahlgren, "Geographic Accessibility Analysis - Methods and Application," Real Estate Science, Department of Technology and Society, Lund University, 2008.

[8] L. Gebhardt et al., „Intermodal urban mobility: users, uses, and use cases," in: Transport Research Arena, Elsevier Ltd. Selection and peer-review. Transport Research Arena (TRA), Warsaw, Poland, 2016.

[9] DLR, "Urbane Mobilität" project web pages, http://www.urmo.info/, 2017, last visited on 11th of December 2017.

[10] W. B. Jones, C. R. Cassady, and R. O. Bowden, "Developing a Standard Definition of Intermodal Transportation," in: Transportation Law Journal 27 (3), pp. 345-352, 2000.

[11] J. Scheurer and C. Curtis, "Accessibility Measures: Overview and Practical Applications," URBANET working paper No. 4, Curtin University of Technology, 2007.

[12] OpenStreetMap contributors, OpenStreetMap project pages, http://www.openstreetmap.org/, 2017, last visited on 11th of December 2017.

[13] M. Heinrichs, D. Krajzewicz, R. Cyganski, and A. von Schmidt, "Introduction of car sharing into existing car fleets in microscopic travel demand modelling," in: Personal and Ubiquitous Computing, pp. 1-11, Springer. DOI: https://doi.org/10.1007/s00779-017-1031-3, ISSN 1617-4909, 2017.

[14] DLR, TAPAS web page, http://www.dlr.de/vf/en/desktopdefault.aspx/tabid-2974/1445_read-29381/, 2017, last visited on 11th of December 2017.

[15] D. Krajzewicz, J. Erdmann, M. Behrisch, and L. Bieker, "Recent Development and Applications of SUMO - Simulation of Urban Mobility," in: International Journal On Advances in Systems and Measurements, 5 (3&4), pp. 128-138, 2012, ISSN 1942-261x.

[16] DLR, SUMO web pages, http://sumo.dlr.de/, 2017, last visited on 11th of December 2017.

[17] B. Heldt, K. Gade, and D. Heinrichs, "Challenges of Data Requirements for Modelling Residential Location Choice: the Case of Berlin, Germany," European Transport Conference 2014, 2014.

[18] A. von Schmidt, R. Cyganski, and D. Krajzewicz, „Generierung synthetischer Bevölkerungen für Verkehrsnachfragemodelle - Ein Methodenvergleich am Beispiel von Berlin," in: HEUREKA'17 - Optimierung in Verkehr und Transport, pp. 193-210, FGSV-Verlag, ISBN 978-3-86446-177-4, 2017.

[19] B. Heldt, K. Gade, and D. Heinrichs, "Determination of Attributes Reflecting Household Preferences in Location Choice Models," in: Transportation Research Procedia, 19, Elsevier B.V., pp. 119-134, doi: 10.1016/j.trpro.2016.12.073, ISSN 2352-1465, 2016.

[20] E. W. Dijkstra, "A note on two problems in connexion with graphs," in: Numerische Mathematik 1, pp. 269–271. 1959, doi:10.1007/BF01386390.

[21] 3D Geoinformation group at TU Delft, CityGML homepage, https://www.citygml.org/, last visited on 11th of December 2017.

[22] Location tech (earlier: Vivid Solutions), JTS homepage, https://www.locationtech.org/projects/technology.jts, last visited on 11th of December 2017.

[23] PostGIS PSC, PostGIS homepage, http://postgis.net/, last visited on 11th of December 2017.

[24] Google, General Transit Feed Specification pages, https://developers.google.com/transit/gtfs/, 2017, last visited on 11th of December 2017.

[25] A. Guttman, "R-Trees: A Dynamic Index Structure for Spatial Searching," in: Proc. ACM SIGMOD International Conference on Management of Data, pp. 47-57, 1984, doi:10.1145/602259.602266

[26] JSI contributors, JSI (Java Spatial Index) RTree Library web pages, http://jsi.sourceforge.net/, 2017, last visited on 11th of December 2017.

[27] Umweltbundesamt, "CO_2-Emissionsminderung im Verkehr in Deutschland," available at: https://www.umweltbundesamt.de/sites/default/files/medien/461/publikationen/3773.pdf, 2010.

[28] L. Gebhardt, D. Krajzewicz, and R. Oostendorp, "Intermodality – key to a more efficient urban transport system?" in: Proceedings of the 2017 ECEEE Summer Study, pp. 759-769, ISBN 978-91-983878-1-0 (online)/978-91-983878-0-3 (print) ISSN 2001-7960 (online)/1653-7025 (print), 2017.

[29] The Matplotlib development team; matplotlib web site, https://matplotlib.org/, last visited on 11th of December 2017.

Pesticides Free Spectrophotometric Filters Creation For Pesticides Quantification in Various Vegetables

Umberto Cerasani
CERAGOS Electronics and Nature
Sophia Antipolis, France
Email: umbertocera@gmail.com

Safa Boudrai
CERAGOS Electronics and Nature
Sophia Antipolis, France
Email: safa.boudrai@gmail.com

Ennio Cerasani
CERAGOS Electronics and Nature
Sophia Antipolis, France
Email: cerasani@ceragos.org

Oumy Diop
Antibes, France,
Email : diop.oumydiop@gmail.com

***Abstract*— A method for estimation of food contaminants, including pesticides, is further described in this document. First, Visible Near InfraRed spectrometric measures were performed on various food samples with different levels of pollution, including pesticides free foods. Methodology and data extraction were meticulously addressed. Based on pesticides free food spectral data, pesticides free filters were created. These filters permitted pesticides isolation without the need of complex chemical procedures from foods natural occurring compounds. The removal of the natural occurring compounds in foods from their artificial counterparts was the initial step, before applying precise pesticides estimation procedures to the remaining spectral data. To accurately quantify foods pesticides contamination, two methods were developed: (1) standard Beer-lambert's concentration law and (2) linear regression. The pesticides contamination evidenced by these two methods were very closed, with less than 3µg/mL of difference. Finally, implementation of these quantification methods in an embedded device, communicating with smartphone application is discussed allowing users to monitor food contaminants.**

Keywords*—*pesticides; Vis NIR spectroscopy; Beer-Lambert's law; Linear Regression Analysis; Microspectrometer

I. Introduction

Pesticides are widely used in agriculture to protect crops and seeds and may have contributed to improvement in society health and economy [1]. At the same time, widespread use of pesticides has led to serious harm on the environment and human health [2] [3] [4]. With the increasing demand for a high quality agricultural products, new quality and safety control devices are being investigated. Because pesticides damaging effects are invisible and cannot be directly warned by visible observation or simple testing, pesticides estimation in soil or in foods prior to their consumption, requires complex techniques and remains very challenging [5-7].

A number of analytical methods, including mass spectroscopy gas and liquid chromatography gas chromatography–mass spectrometry (GC-MS), have been reported to detect various pesticides contamination in foods and these methods are very sensitive and reliable [5]. However, these classical analytical approaches are usually confined to a laboratory environment and require costly, long sample preparation time, solvent wasting, and hazardous samples contact [5, 8, 9]. Additional disadvantages of these methods include the restricted database mapping of pesticides analysis and the possibility of false negatives in the results [10].

Biosensors provides a promising alternative for the detection of pesticides [11-15]. Biosensors convert the signal produced by the immobilized biological element that detect the analyte into an electrically detectable signal and can be classified from their signal transduction techniques into electrochemical, optical, piezoelectric and mechanical biosensors [16]. Many biosensors designed for pesticides detection are based on the inhibition reaction or catalytic activity of several enzymes after pesticides contact [17]. Electrochemical transducers are usually simple to design, small and affordable making them candidate of choices for portable pesticides detection [16]. For instance, Enzyme-Linked ImmunoSorbent Assays (ELISA) have grown rapidly as tools for pesticide measurement, although still challenged [17]. Since a number of pesticides have a similar mode of action affecting the activity of the same enzyme, most of ELISA based biosensors suffer poor individual pesticide specificity although improper to detect total pesticide content. On the other hand, immunosensors are biosensors that senses specific pesticides using antibodies (Ab) or antigens (Ag) taking advantage of the newest development of Ab technologies, targeted against pesticide molecules. Immunosensors are therefore able to provide concentration-dependent results in a certain range [17, 18]. For instance in [19], Triazines were assayed using florescent antibodies (conjugated with with fluoresceine isothiocyanate binding to the fibre surface). After contact with the pesticide Triazines the fluorescence signal decreased since less antibodies were binding to the fibre. The detection limit using this immunosensor was very satisfying (around 0.1 ng/ml) [19]. However, there is a time gap between current status in the field and the most recent created immunosensors [17]. In addition, immunosensors usually requires specific testing procedures and have low reusability capacity without loss of sensitivity for most of them [20-22].

Due to the great amount of pesticides currently being used, there is an augmented concern in the investigation and creation of rapid and non-destructive methods for pesticides detection [23]. In the last few years, advanced in optical instruments allowed the residuals of insecticides detection from agricultural samples [10]. Detection of hydrophobic organic pollutants via UV, Raman, and IR spectroscopic methods directly at solid sorbent phases are usually reported to be less sensitive than conventional chromatographic analysis, but permit on-site pollution measurements [9].

Near Infrared spectroscopy (NIR) is a well described method to assess the composition and quality of products in the food industry [24-28], since it has the capability to analyze organic substances rapidly and cost-effectively, although suffering of low spectral resolution for samples in aqueous solutions due to strong water infrared absorption. As an example, a model for the quality control of herbicide Diuron in intact olives with 85.9% of accuracy using reflectance NIR spectroscopy is presented in [29]. Peppers are a frequent object of food safety alerts in various member states of the European Union since they frequently contain unauthorised pesticide residues. Near Infrared Reflectance Spectroscopy (NIRS) for the measurement of pesticide residues in peppers using commercially available spectrophotometers and demonstrating satisfying results is proposed in [30]. Spectral information in the ranges 1644–1772 and 2014–2607 nm without baseline correction and Partial Least Squares (PLS) model interpretation were used to detect Buprofezin, Diuron and Daminozide without any sample pre-treatment and sample destruction in [31].

Diuron determination in pesticide formulations was also analyzed after its extraction with acetonitrile and subsequent transmittance NIR measurements (2021 and 2047 nm). Diuron limit of detection reached 0.013 $mg.g^{-1}$ with this methodology which was 10 times higher than that the results obtained by Liquid Chromatography (LC), making NIR vibrational method appropriate for the quality control of pesticide commercial formulations [32]. Fourier transform near infrared (FT-NIR) spectroscopy is also of value for the determination of pesticides in agrochemicals. Following previous extraction of the active principles and transmission measurements were performed on Chlorsulfuron, Metamitron, Iprodione, Pirimicarb, Procymidone and Tricyclazole, leading to detection values limits ranging from 0.004 to 0.17 $mg.g^{-1}$, 10 times faster than chromatography analysis [33]. Chlopyrifos residue detection in white radish, based on NIR spectroscopy and PLS regression is proposed in [34]. PLS was mainly permitted the determination of the optimum wave number range.

Field portable NIR spectrometer (from 360 to 1690 nm) was able to determine nutrient composition of beef feedlot manure in [35]. On the basis of analysis of dried mannure samples, the field-portable NIR spectrometer allowed fast determination of Carbon, Nitrates, and several other parameters [35]. Field portable pesticides detectors, based on NIR spectrometry could be therefore considered for pesticides detection using a similar procedure.

Infrared (IR) spectroscopy provides a rapid, low cost and highly reproducible diagnostic screening tool. IR spectroscopy is currently employed for soil surveillance systems, crops health and water quality assessment [36]. For instance, soil absorption over the Visible/Near-InfraRed (Vis/NIR) wavelength regions (350–2500 nm) is mostly associated with (1) the vibrational energy transitions of the dominant molecular bonds of Fe-oxides (which have absorptions over the visible (350–780 nm) and short-wave NIR (780–1100 nm) spectral regions), (2) clay minerals (which have absorption over the long-wave NIR (1100–2500 nm) regions), (3) water (which has strong absorption features over Vis/NIR regions, most visibly near 1400 and 1900 nm), and (4) organic matter (which has distinct absorption features over the Vis/NIR, due to the various complex chemical bonds) [37]. Under certain conditions, such as very high concentration in soil, some transition elements (including Ni, Cu, Co) may also exhibit absorption features in the Vis/NIR spectral regions [37], permitting direct soil characterization and estimation of pesticides utilization in fields. A Vis/NIR mobile soil sensor was developed in [38] composed by optical unit to detect soil extractable phosphorous (305 and 1711 nm in reflectance mode).

Vis/NIR spectroscopy also permits pesticides and other food contaminants detection [37, 39]. It may be particularly suited for free space measurement and field studies [40]. Internal and external pesticides damage detection of various fruits in Korea and Japan were detected using non damaging methods, such as Vis/NIR Spectroscopy [41].

Many aromatic pesticides are either naturally fluorescent or photodegrade into fluorescent byproducts and are hence suited for fluorescent spectroscopy detection [42]. For example, Polycyclic Aromatic Hydrocarbons (PAHs), pesticides are naturally fluorescent in aqueous solutions and allows for trace elements detection without previous pesticides concentration procedures [42]. Portable fluorometers are now available on market in a single portative device and with fiber-optic probes that permit remote observations [42].

Progress in Raman spectroscopes and in embedded computation equipment have enabled Raman spectroscopy to be used as an analytical tool for both solid samples and aqueous solutions, offering information permitting to determine the internal content in samples [5]. Because Raman spectrum of compound can furnish narrow and highly resolved bands it contains more complete vibrational information than IR spectrum. It may not require stabilizing materials and needs no chemical or mechanical pretreatment and allows nondestructive extraction of physical information [5, 10].

Raman spectroscopic techniques mostly gathers dispersive Raman spectroscopy, Fourier transform Raman spectroscopy and Surface Enhanced Raman Spectroscopy (SERS) [5]. Because conventional Raman spectroscopy is limited to a small scattering cross section and requires large amount of specimen and strong incident light, the employment of SERS greatly enhances the sensitivity of the conventional Raman spectroscopy and offers more elevated measurement speed and sensitivity [10].

In food industry, spectroscopy has been satisfactorily used to monitor food quality and safety. For instance Raman spectroscopy was applied to discriminate between transgenic and normal crops in various breeding such as tobacco. Different Raman spectrum were obtained between the transgenic tobacco and the wild type, since for transgenic tobacco, the expression of cinnamyl alcohol dehydrogenase was greatly depleted after cinnamaldehyde lignin incorporation [5]. In addition, Raman spectroscopy was successfully used to distinguish the Brassica napus ‘Drakkar’ from the new genetically modified line [5].

Furthermore, the use of Raman spectroscopy permitted carotenoids content quantification in fruits and vegetables [5]. Other antioxidant quantification such as lycopene could be obtained by NIR-FT-Raman spectroscopy method [5]. FT-Raman spectroscopy method in conjunction with Hierarchical Cluster Analysis (HCA) may accurately assess the energetic value and total carbohydrates, protein, and fat of powdered milk infant formulas [5].

Raman spectroscopic techniques are not only applied in quality control but also in safety control of various beverages, most specifically for microorganisms contamination and adulterants adjunction [43-48]. The identification of oil adulteration is of great importance from both market and health perspectives in the olive oil industry [49-55]. Unsaturation of oil Free Fatty Acids (FFA) and total degree of unsaturation could be estimated using spectroscopy measures [5]. Since Raman spectroscopy has been successfully applied to organic compounds detection in food and beverage, its employment for pesticides detection is particularly adequate. Most particularly identification and detection of large family of sulfur-containing pesticide residues at various fruit peels was performed utilizing the shell thickness-dependent Raman enhancement of silver-coated gold nanoparticles [56].

Transmittance spectroscopy is particularly suited for free space measurements without sample preparation and can be applied to pesticides detection. For example, using a transmittance spectroscopy (in the 550 and 980 nm region), insect infested cherries within a tart cherry fruit were detected with accuracy varying from 82% to 87% [57].

Data clustering analysis following spectroscopy data is often required to distinguish food contaminants. Spectroscopy such as SERS coupled with clustering analysis has been shown to enable the trace-level detection of various pesticides [58]. For instance, cluster analysis, following Wavelength Dispersive X Rays Fluorescence Spectroscopy may permit classification of black tea and green tea from tea mineral elements [59]. Clustering algorithms often requires variable fitting or selection methods. Most commonly employed methods are: Stepwise Regression Analysis, Uninformative Variable Elimination, Interval Partial Least Squares (IPLS) regression, Clonal Selection Feature Selection algorithm [23]. As an example improving PLS regression models, used in spectrum data post-processing, may hence result in more specific database inquiries and sample chemical identification.

In this paper, we quantified food pesticides contamination using Vis-NIR reflectance spectroscopy. Since there are several thousand of different active pesticide molecules reported [60, 61], current pesticides detection is limited to few types of pesticides chemical and does not ascertain pesticides free products. We worked from another perspective by comparing the spectral information obtained from pesticides free and pesticides contaminated foods, irrespective of the pesticide types. We searched for particular traces in the spectroscopy spectrum that could be characteristic of pesticides contamination. Mostly two cases could be found: (1) the spectra of foods grown with pesticides contains additional traces which could be related with pesticides own spectral characteristics or modified endogenous food proteins [62-64], (2) oppositely the absence of spectral components in particular wavelength in pesticides contaminated foods compared to organic or totally natural foods (grown without pesticides addition) may also be used as a spectral indicator of food purity since certain food proteins may not be expressed when pesticides are utilized [65-68].

The measured pesticides free foods spectral data were used as filters to isolate the additional non-natural constituents of foods. Pesticides contamination quantification was hence performed on these additional non-natural food components spectral data, avoiding the need of pesticide chemical isolation from the food natural components to increase measures reliability. Transmission spectroscopy was performed for 3 pesticides commonly employed in agriculture: (1) Dicofol, (2)

Thiamethoxam and (3) Malathion and their respective absorption spectral data were computed. Since the concentration of the tested pesticides was known, peaks in absorption spectral data permitted to calculate the Dicofol, Thiamethoxam and Malathion absorption coefficients at 791 nm, 774 nm and 475 nm respectively. Pesticides estimation was realized for different foods category from different suppliers, including a market gardener claiming to produce pesticides free foods, an organic food producer and two supermarkets. Pesticides contamination for each food was computed using: (1) the standard concentration law applied at pesticides characteristic wavelength and (2) linear regression model solved with Non Negative Classical Least Squares. Very closed pesticides levels were obtained by both methods, although there were applied to foods of different category and different suppliers.

Finally, algorithm implementation inside a portative device with an embedded spectrometer, as depicted in Figure 1, allows pesticide estimation for non-specialized users. For easier user data reading, a wireless communication device (Bluetooth module) is integrated in the embedded system for user's smartphone communication. A specific smartphone application was created for embedded spectrometer results monitoring. To diminish the costs of the overall device, sunlight is used as spectroscopic light source, limiting device utilization in bright areas.

Our document will be organized into 3 main sections: first, the methodology of our experiment will be introduced with the devices used, then, the Vis-NIR spectroscopy results are reported and analyzed, finally a conclusion is drawn with possible future work direction propositions.

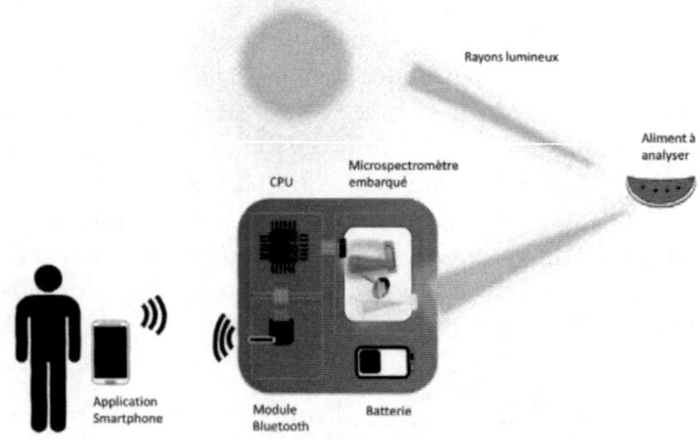

Figure 1. User centric based device for food pesticides monitoring

II. Methods

Measurements detailed information and equipment used are presented in this Section.

A. *Food samples variety*

We tested 3 different food categories: tomatoes, zucchini and potatoes. The precise variety of vegetable tested is reported in Table I. Food were bought directly from (1) a market gardener that did not used any pesticides or chemical contaminant, (2) an organic store and from 2 famous French supermarket brands, where we assumed that plants were grown using pesticides ((3) and (4)). Although several pesticides are contained in the vegetable peel, we decided to perform the measure on the decorticated vegetable to avoid peel color bias. Each vegetable was tested in 3 different areas.

TABLE I. VEGETABLE TYPES AND VARIETIES USED FOR THE EXERIMENT

Food Variety (botanical name)	**Food suppliers**			
	Market gardener (pesticides free)	**Organic shop**	**Supermarket 1**	**Supermarket 2**
Tomatoes	*Lycopersicon escubentum*	*Lycopersicon escubentum, Solanum lycopersicum*	*Lycopersicon escubentum Lycopersicon esculentum*	*Lycopersicon escubentum Lycopersicon esculentum*
Zucchini	*Cucurbita moschata, Cucurbita pepo ´De Nice à fruit ronds´*	*Cucurbita pepo ´Verte non coureuse´*	*Cucurbita pepo ´Verte non coureuse´*	*Cucurbita pepo ´Verte non coureuse´*
Poataoes	*Solanum tuberosum ´Charlotte´ (yellow), Solanum tuberosum ´Desiree´ (red),*	*Solanum tuberosum ´Charlotte´ (yellow)*	*´Cherie´*	*´Cherie´*

B. *Test system description:*

Reflectance spectroscopy measures were performed using the test bench described in Figure 2. We used the Ocean Optics kit including the ECOVIS Krypton Lightsource, the USB-650 Red Tide Spectrometer (preconfigured in the 350-1000 nm wavelength range), a 200 µm Bifurcated Fiber (Vis-NIR) and the OceanView software. The results were then extracted and manipulated with Matlab software. The distance between the bifurcated fiber and the sample to measure was fixed to 5mm, and the reflectance robe was positioned at an angle of 90° to the flat surface of the sample to analyze.

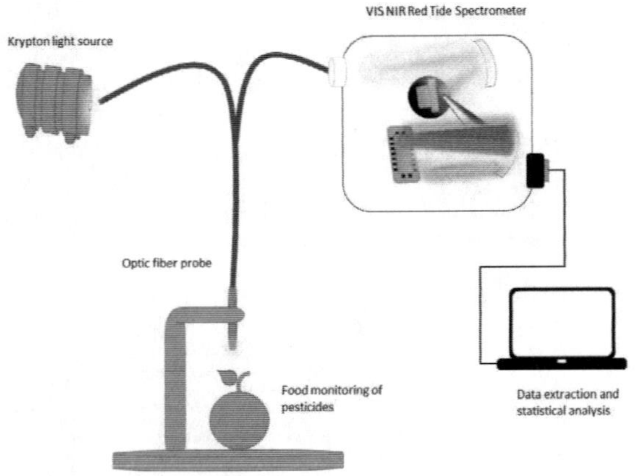

Figure 2. Test bench diagram used for Vis-NIR spectroscopy measurements in various vegetables

C. Absorption spectrum determination

Fresnel's equations are valid in non-near field spectrophotometric analysis and describe the light behavior when moving between media of differing refractive indices. We use reflective Vis-NIR spectroscopy to analyze opaque solutions (foods), which did not necessitate particular sample preparation. On the other hand, transmission spectroscopy was selected to study transparent media of the pesticides Dicofol, Thiamethoxam and Malathion. The three pesticides studied, which are described in Table II, were added to a cuvette of 1 square centimeter area, specifically designed for transmission spectroscopy.

TABLE II. ANALYZED PESTICIDES PHYSICAL CHARACTERISTICS

Pesticides	Concentration (Mole/L)	Density (g/mL)	Molar mass (g/Mole)
Dicofol	*0.75e-3*	*1.23*	*370*
Thiamethoxam	*0.36e-3*	*0.998*	*291*
Malathion	*1.9e-3*	*1.27*	*330*

From the food reflection spectra, the corresponding absorption spectra were immediately determined by noticing that the transmission light was inexistent since the foods were opaque at the considered Vis-NIR wavelengths range (400nm – 850nm).

Secondly the absorption spectra of the pesticides were directly deduced from the pesticides transmission spectra since there was no reflected light (light source was perpendicular to the cuvette containing the analyzed solutions).

To establish the foods absorption spectra and the pesticides absorption spectra, we used the ECOVIS Krypton Light source as the incident reference light and we further removed the light background and electronic device noises. Finally, the absorption spectra were shifted to avoid negative absorption values.

D. Beer Lambert's concentration law

Beer lambert's law (reported in eq. (1)) correlates the solution absorbance to the concentration of the solution and to the thickness of the material sample [69, 70]:

$$-\log_{10}(I_{transmitted}/I_{incident}) = \varepsilon * c * l \qquad (1)$$

where $I_{transmitted}$ is the transmitted light source spectrum, $I_{incident}$ is the incident light source spectrum, c the solution concentration, ε is the absorption coefficient and l is the length of the cuvette. Therefore, the concentration of a solution is directly proportional to the absorbance measurements obtained using a spectrophotometer [71]. Traditional solution concentration determination using Beer Lambert's law is restricted to a single wavelength, corresponding to the absorption spectrum peak. In fact the absorption coefficient (ε) is related to the complex index of refraction (n'') and to the "peak" wavelength (λ), as described in eq. (2) (rewritten from [72]):

$$\varepsilon = 4n''/\lambda \qquad (2)$$

Absorption spectra are additive meaning that absorption spectra of a mixture is the sum of absorption spectra of each mixture components, measured separately.

In many cases absorption calibration curve deviates from this ideal straight behavior. Deviations from linearity are divided into three categories: (1) fundamental which gather the deviations in absorptivity coefficients at high concentrations (>0.01 Moles) due to electrostatic interactions between molecules in close proximity and the changes in refractive index at high analyte concentration, (2) chemical, mainly due to shifts in chemical equilibria as a function of concentration, and (3) instrumental which originate from non-monochromatic radiation and light scattering [70, 73]. In consequence, spectrophotometric study of pesticides concentration using the linear Beer-lambert's law is restricted to a given concentration interval, above the minimum pesticides concentration detection limit.

E. Multiwavelength spectrophotometric analysis

The spectroscopic analysis of mixtures, when the spectra of the components overlap considerably, can be performed using multiple linear regression analysis, which can be solved by Least Squares methods [74]. First, measurement of absorption spectra of each mixture component at a particular concentration permit to determine the absorption coefficient sensitivity (φ) for all the considered Vis-NIR wavelengths interval.

Given the variable of interest c (scalar vector corresponding to the concentration of each component in the mixture), linear regression methods aim to model and estimate the relationship between a scalar dependent variable c and a vector of explanatory variable A (representing the absorption spectrum at the considered wavelength) through the linear relation described in eq. (3):

$$A_\lambda = \varphi_{n,\lambda} \cdot c_n \quad (3)$$

where n represent the number of different components in the mixture and λ the wavelength (also referred as regressors in linear regression models). The classical linear regression model with "standard assumptions", can be solved using the Least Squares principle, which minimizes the sum-squared error in the reproduction of the values of A, using only the concentration vector c, over all j wavelengths, as expressed in eq. (4):

$$\sum_j (Error)^2 = \sum_j (A_j - \sum_i \varphi_{ij} * c_i)^2 \quad (4)$$

In the special case of error functions, equating the first order derivative of the squared sum of errors to 0 with respect to the concentrations c_i, results in determination of the concentrations c_i which minimize the differences between the measured absorption spectrum and the reconstituted spectrum. Alternatively, the equations can be converted into matrix expressions, permitting to determine the concentrations c_i of each individual components of the mixture, as described in eq. (5) [74-76]:

$$c_n = (\varphi_{n,\lambda}^T * \varphi_{n,\lambda})^{-1} * \varphi_{n,\lambda}^T * A_\lambda \quad (5)$$

For multiple component analysis, we preferred the use of non negative Least Squares, resulting in non negative concentrations c_i estimation of the components forming the analyzed mixture.

The use of multicomponent analysis was however restricted to experimentation purposes and not directly implemented in the created embedded spectrophotometer.

F. *Algorithms implementation*

For embedded device pesticides detection, the choice of the algorithm for pesticides detection was limited by several elements, mainly: (1) spectrophotometer accuracy, (2) the computational resources, (3) simplicity of implementation allowing machine portability, (4) real time computation requirements.

Given these strong restrictions, we decided to select monowavelength Beer-Lambert's concentration determination, with predetermined absorption coefficients, for samples contamination quantification.

Figure 3 depicts the measurement procedure we followed to extract the absorption coefficient associated with each pesticide, from the measured transmission spectrum. The procedure for pesticides quantification in foods is indicated in Figure 4.

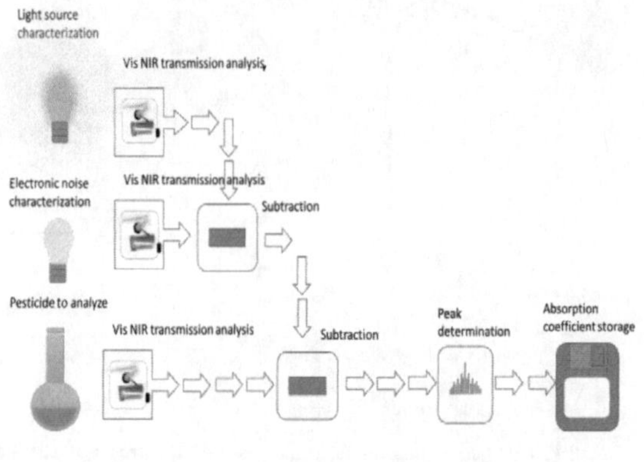

Figure 3. Pesticide absorption coefficient determination procedure

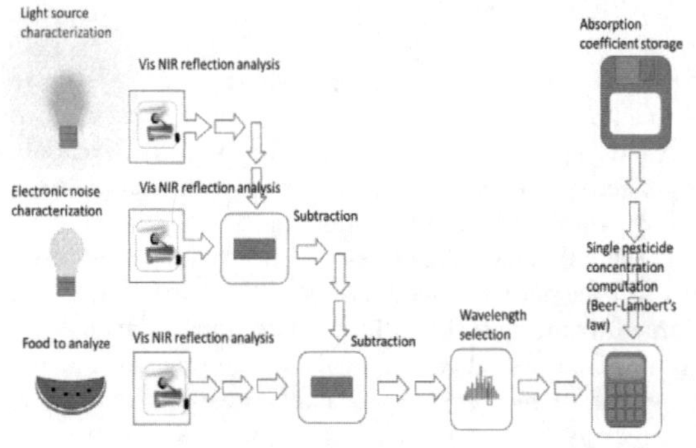

Figure 4. Food analysis procedure using the Vis-NIR reflected spectrum and the Beer-Lambert's concentration law

III. RESULTS

A. *Additional spectral traces comparison*

Tomatoes spectroscopic measures from different supplier's origin are presented in Figure 5, after division by their respective Area Under Curve, to remove the light intensity drift differences between samples. Each line represents the spectral measurements realized on tomatoes from a market gardener that did not used any pesticides or chemical contaminant (blue line), an organic store (green line) and from 2 famous French supermarket brands, where we assumed that plants were grown using pesticides (red and pink lines respectively). For each different tomatoes supplier, measures were performed on several vegetable samples to decrease the samples intervariability bias and the mean value was computed and reported on the figures. As an example, the green line in Figure 5 outlines the mean relative light intensity of organic tomatoes sample and the magenta lines in the same figure outlines the mean relative light intensity of the Supermarket 2 tomatoes sample.

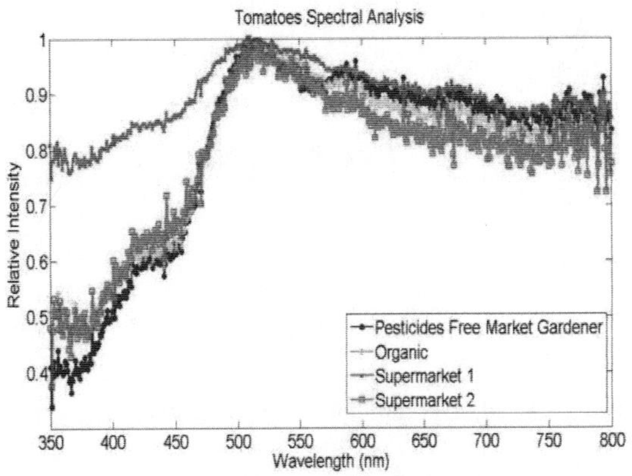

Figure 5. Tomatoes spectral analysis comparison (mean samples values).

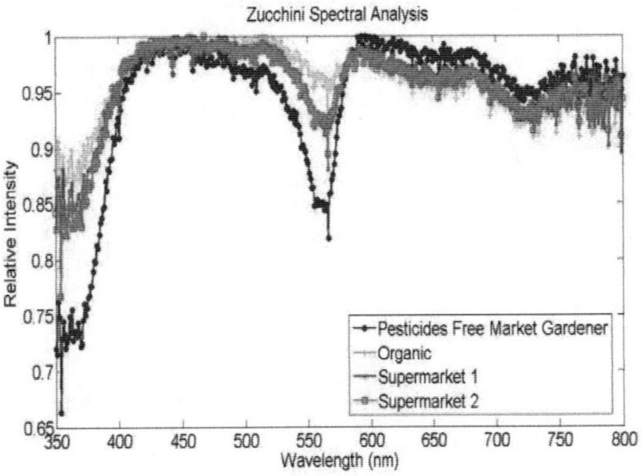

Figure 6. Zucchini spectral data comparison (mean samples values).

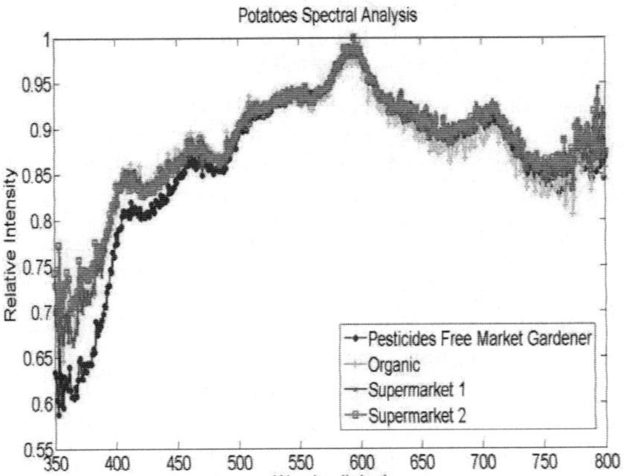

Figure 7. Potatoes spectral data comparison (mean samples values).

Figure 6 and Figure 7 depict the spectral measures associated with zucchini and potatoes from different food supplier's origin respectively. For easier data interpretation, light intensity drift was removed. The mean relative light intensity values of the pesticides free zucchini and potatoes are both reported in blue thick lines in each figure. Similarly, to the previous figure results, each different color line describes the spectral measurements associated with the 4 different origins of the food under study (pesticide free market gardener, organic store, supermarket 1 and supermarket 2).

B. Spectral filters creation

Chemical manipulations mostly precede spectrophotometric pesticides analysis to isolate the pesticide from its containing solution. Such manipulations often demand material and expertise. The spectrum of pesticides free foods was extracted for different food category. This spectrum when subtracted to the spectrum of foods grown with pesticides, split each pesticide grown food spectrum into (1) the natural components composing the food spectrum from (2) the extra artificial components of foods spectra (mostly non-naturals adulterants). Supplementary components of foods include airborne pollutants, pesticides, dust, etc. It was assumed that the main supplementary components, following foods mechanical cleansing are mainly the pesticides and conservatives.

Analyzing pesticides content on the spectrum additional non-natural constituents, remove the need of pesticides chemical extraction. The creation of pesticides free Vis-NIR filters is hence of capital importance in food pesticides estimation, provided that the filters created corresponds to the same food category and variety that the food under study.

Reflective spectroscopy spectral data from organic shop (green line), supermarket 1 (red line) and supermarket 2 (pink line) were subtracted to reflective spectral data of pesticides free food of similar variety to obtain the additional non natural components contained in the foods studied. These supplementary artificial compounds for tomatoes, zucchini and potatoes are respectively presented in Figure 8, Figure 9 and in Figure 10.

Figure 8 shows that spectral relative intensity in the 350 nm – 400 nm region is particularly characteristic of the tomatoes added chemicals. Other spectral rays (435 nm, 587 nm, 672 nm, 781nm, 791 nm, etc.) deserve extended analysis and database characterization.

Although characterization of food additives or pesticides contaminants for zucchini seems straightforward with two large peaks at 374 nm and 570 nm compared to pesticides free zucchini (Figure 9), the analysis may be more complex. In fact, as presented in Table I, the zucchini variety of the organic shop, supermarket 1 and supermarket 2 (*Cucurbita pepo 'Verte non coureuse'*) is not exactly the same as the one proposed by the pesticide free market gardener (*Cucurbita moschata* and *Cucurbita pepo 'De Nice à fruit ronds'*). Modification in chromophore molecules between these two varieties of zucchini may explain the large results variation. For more conclusive analysis, data obtained from organic zucchini should be used for spectral filter construction, although we further noted that in these wavelength areas, data obtained from organic stores also differ from the ones associated from the two supermarkets. Of particular interest seems to be the spectral rays of 715 nm, 774 nm, 450 - 456 nm area and need deeper investigation.

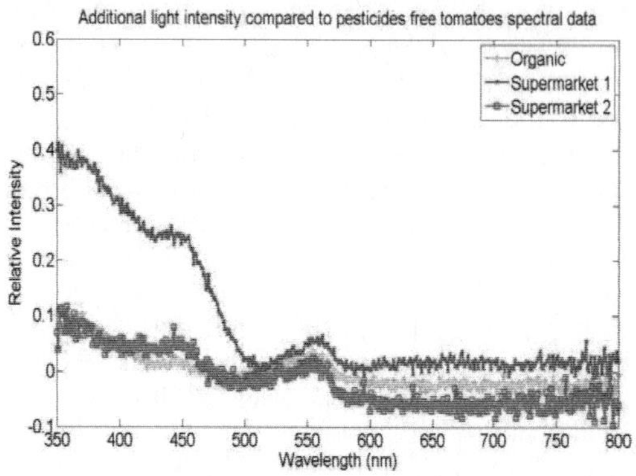

Figure 8. Additional relative light intensity compared to pesticides free tomatoes spectral data

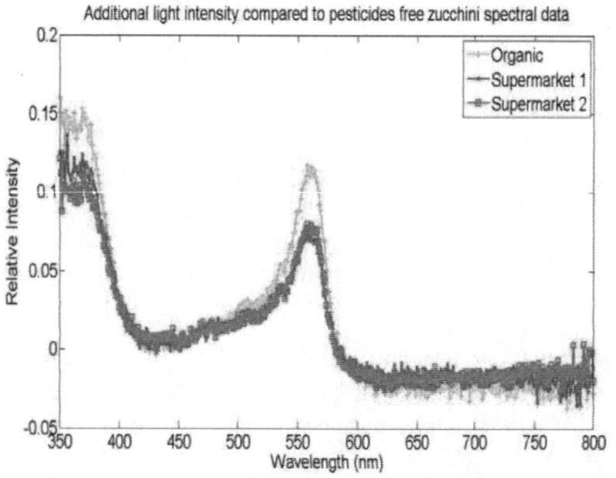

Figure 9. Additional relative light intensity compared to pesticides free zucchini spectral data

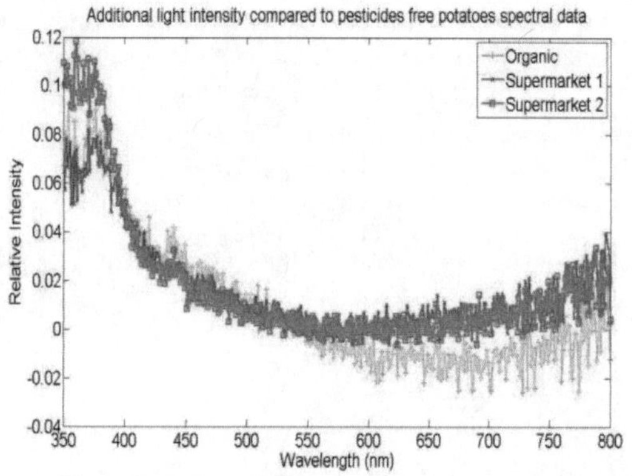

Figure 10. Additional relative light intensity compared to pesticides free potatoes spectral data

Filtration of spectral data from organic shop (green line), supermarket 1 (red line) and supermarket 2 (pink line) with spectral data of potatoes pesticides free mean value is described in Figure 10. Except in the 350 nm - 450 nm and the 600 – 750 nm regions, spectral data obtained from the two supermarkets (red and pink curves) seems to be closer to the pesticide free spectrum. Several explanations may exist. Like for zucchini, not the same potato varieties were compared, explaining the discrepancies between results. A second explanation is the presence of specific food additional substances, possibly pollutants, in organic food compared to supermarket ones (organic foods are not entirely devoid of pesticides, since pesticides from natural sources are allowed in organic gardening [77]).

C. *Dicofol, Thiamothexame and Malathion pesticides spectrophotometric characterization*

The three pesticides Dicofol, Thiamethoxam and Malathion were studied and since they were almost transparent, transmission measured were performed to determine their corresponding absorption spectrum, reported in

Figure 11.

In [78], a spectrophotometric method for the determination of Malathion is proposed, involving the decomposition of Malathion in the presence of alcoholic KOH, further reacting with Ammonium meta vanadate in Nitric acid to form a blue color. The absorbance maximum of the Malathion solution was observed at 760 nm and it was shown that the Beer-Lambert's law was obeyed in the 0.5-11 µg/mL interval [78]. Another selective spectrophotometric method developed in [79] for the determination of Malathion required Gention Violet addition. First alkaline hydrolysis of Malathion in presence of sodium ethoxide formed sodium dimethyl dithiophosphate (Na-DMDTP), then the obtained solution was complexed with the cationic dye Gention Violet, before chloroform extraction. The color of the organic layer was measured at 587 nm and the concentration law was respected in the 0.1-10 µg/mL interval. Other authors proposed a cost-effective method for determination of Malathion using spectrophotometric measures with absorbance peak around 520 nm (Amaranth dye titration) [80]. Spectrophotometric organophosphates detection methods require mainly three steps: (1) the reaction of Malathion with an excess of oxidant in acid medium to specifically select Malathion component from the containing solution, followed by (2) the addition of a reacting dye and finally (3) the spectrophotometric measure of the reactive dye variation when added to Malathion, since the reacting dye has notable absorption peaks well characterized [80].

Similar procedures permitted the extraction of concentration's law for Dicofol, with an absorption peak in the UV range (232 nm) [81]. A spectrophotometric method for the determination of Dicofol is described in [82] and based on the Fujiwara reaction (Alkaline hydrolysis of Dicofol, reaction with pyridine to produce red color, addition of glacial acetic acid and final reaction with 4-aminoacetanilide to give an orange-red dye, further extracted in 3-methyl-1-butanol). The extracted dye shows absorption maximum at 525 nm. Beer's law was obeyed in the range of 0.025–0.25 µg mL^{-1} using this method as discussed in [82].

Statistical analysis using UV spectroscopy showed that there was a significant linear relationship between the concentration of Thiamethoxam in tea and the absorbance at 250 nm in the UV spectra of the mixture [83].

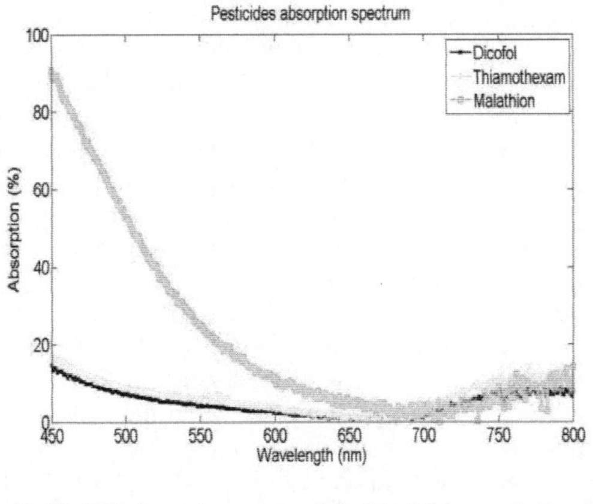

Figure 11. Vis NIR absorption spectra of the Dicofol (concentration: 0.75e-3 Mole/L), Thiamethoxam (concentration: 0.36e-3 Mole/L) and Malathion (concentration: 1.9e-3 Mole/L).

Without the use of the coloring dye and based only on the Vis-NIR absorption spectra measured (reported in Figure 11), each pesticide we studied most probably has absorption peaks in the UV and IR regions. We retained the 475 nm (Blue region), 774 nm (NIR region) and 791nm (NIR region) as Malathion, Thiamethoxam and Dicofol respective absorption peaks, further used to determine absorption coefficients for pesticides concentration estimation. Because the absorption peaks were possibly non optimal absorption peaks, the concentration range for pesticide detection was reduced compared to other literature studies [70]. Avoiding using the wavelengths associated with the colors green (approximatively 550 nm), and red (approximatively 650 nm) but contrarily using wavelengths in the Blue or NIR area permit to avoid any influence of the food maturation or common food color change due to various natural processes. These wavelengths were used to extract the absorption coefficients according to Beer Lambert's concentration law, since the concentration of the tested pesticides was known.

TABLE III. DICOFOL, THIAMETHOXAM AND MALATHION PESTICIDES CONCENTRATION IN DIFFERENT FOODS CATEGORY OBTAINED FROM DIFFERENT SUPPLIERS

	Dicofol (mg/mL)	**Thiamethoxam (mg/mL)**	**Malathion (mg/mL)**
Peak wavelengths (nm)	*791*	*774*	*475*
Absorption Coefficient (Mole/L)	*9.8e5*	*3.3e6*	*3.8e6*
PESTICIDES CONCENTRATION (MG/ML)			
Organic tomatoes	0,014	0,005	0,003
Supermarket1 tomatoes	0,082	0,017	0,002
Supermarket 2 tomatoes	0,057	0,013	0,008
Organic zucchini	0,167	0,038	0,029
Supermarket 1 zucchini	0,113	0,026	0,019
Supermarket 2 zucchini	0,119	0,026	0,017
Organic potatoes	0,016	0,005	0,003
Supermarket 1 potatoes	0,0099	0,005	0,004
Supermarket 2 potatoes	0,0089	0,002	0,004

To directly estimate the foods pesticide contamination without previous chemical manipulation and dye addition, the main problem to address was to isolate the pesticide contribution from other factors at the selected pesticide wavelength. Although not perfectly accurate the filtering of the food reflection spectra with the corresponding food spectrum obtained from the pesticide free market gardener, permitted to isolate the non-natural added substances. This method is hence an alternative solution to avoid food sample chemical adulteration and dye addition, before spectrophotometric analysis. To further increase the accuracy of the measures, multiple wavelengths can be considered when computing the Beer Lambert's concentration relation and the mean concentration among these multiple wavelengths can be selected instead, for each pesticide. The concentrations of the studied pesticides among each food category studied after pesticides free market gardener food spectra removal is reported in Table III.

Dicofol, Thiamethoxam and Malathion pesticides contamination is markedly lower in tomatoes obtained from organic farming than in tomatoes from supermarkets. Very surprisingly, higher Dicofol, Thiamethoxam and Malathion pesticides traces were found in organic farming zucchini. Difference in variety between market gardener pesticides free zucchini and organic farming zucchini may partially explain their higher absorption coefficients. Another possible hypothesis to interpret these unpredicted results is that the pesticides studied are not the commonly used in foods farming but are rather more adapted for flowers farming and could easily be transported by wind.

Besides, since the foods were bought in a single organic store and in 2 different supermarkets, they are not representative of respectively organic agriculture or conventional agriculture.

D. Non Negative Classical Least Squares analysis

Vis-NIR spectrum of a solution composed of multiple components, knowing the spectrum of each component can be approximated using multiple linear regression models. Multiple linear regression equations can be solved using Least Squares developments. The main idea with multiple linear regression models is to express a function in a different base: from the wavelength base (old base or regressor basis) to a new base (base of concentration). This can be simply performed by multiplying the analyzed function with the inverse transfer matrix. Transfer matrix is used to transform the old base (wavelength or regressor base) into the new base (concentration base). Least Squares is the mathematical method selected to accomplish this operation, permitting to reduce the squared error between the analyzed function expressed in the old base compared to the analyzed function expressed in new base. Because the dimensions in the old base (number of wavelength) is usually much larger than the dimensions in the new base (number of different concentrations of the pesticides studied), direct transfer matrix inversion is most of the time not permitted. It finally results that the foods studied are described with the relative concentrations of the pesticides studied.

Similarly, to the pesticide concentration determination in foods using the previously described method, it is necessary to isolate the pesticide spectrum from the entire foods spectra. Consequently, pesticides free filters determined for each food category were applied before any pesticides concentration estimation, highlighting the importance of the created filters.

The reconstruction of the additional non natural components foods absorption spectra using the Non Negative Least Squares analysis are reported in Figure 12 for organic tomatoes, Figure 13 for organic zucchini and Figure 14 for organic potatoes. These spectra reconstruction was based on the product of (1) the concentration coefficients obtained by the Non Negative Least Squares analysis, (2) by their corresponding pesticides absorption spectra. It should be noted that Non Negative Least Squares algorithm, mainly permitted to obtain the Thiamethoxam pesticides concentration in foods, since only positive concentration coefficients determination were allowed.

In the reconstructed spectrum using the Non Negative Least Squares algorithm for organic tomatoes (Figure 12), only the 470 – 530 nm and the 730 – 800 nm wavelengths regions were correctly modeled. Wavelength regions correctly modeled from the reconstructed spectrum using the Non Negative Least Squares algorithm were further reduced for organic zucchini (Figure 13), with mostly the 520 – 530 nm and the 740 – 800 nm wavelengths regions precisely reproduced. The reproduction of the organic potatoes additional non natural components spectrum from analyzed pesticides spectra using the same algorithm (Figure 14) was very restricted with only few wavelengths correctly replicated (490 – 500 nm and 730 – 740 nm). Obviously the additional non natural components spectra of the various foods did not only contain the three studied pesticides but many other constituents, explaining the reconstruction divergences. Besides the three pesticides studied absorption spectra have a very similar mathematical description (Gaussian distribution with peaks at close wavelengths), impeding correct reconstruction in other wavelengths area. In a general way, stronger are the similarities between the reconstruction from pesticides spectra and the foods spectra, stronger is the validity of the concentration coefficient obtained by the Non Negative Least Squares algorithm.

The algorithm implemented increased the proximities of the solutions at the regressors (wavelengths) maximum and minimum values, corresponding to the wavelength regions of the pesticides spectral apex. However, these wavelength regions are the most corrupted by measurement noise. It is also interesting to mention that to avoid strong boundary noises the Least Squares method can be weighted by the reflectance spectra of the pesticides, leading to better foods spectra reconstruction [74].

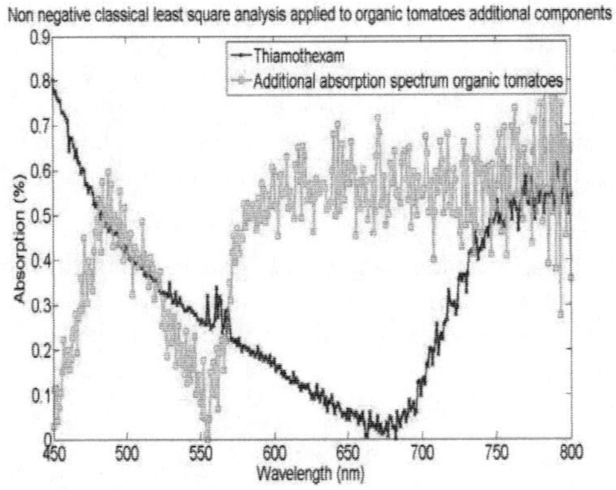

Figure 12. Organic tomatoes additional artificial components spectrum reconstructed from Non Negative Classical Least Squares analysis using the pesticides Dicofol, Thiamethoxam and Malathion spectra.

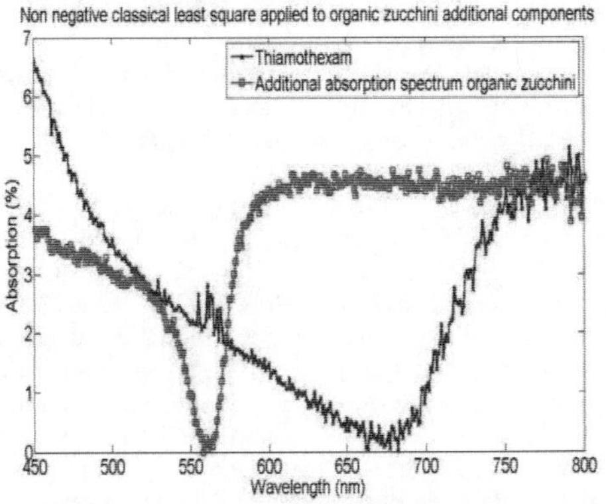

Figure 13. Organic zucchini additional artificial components spectrum reconstructed with Non Negative Classical Least Squares analysis using the pesticides Dicofol, Thiamethoxam and Malathion spectra.

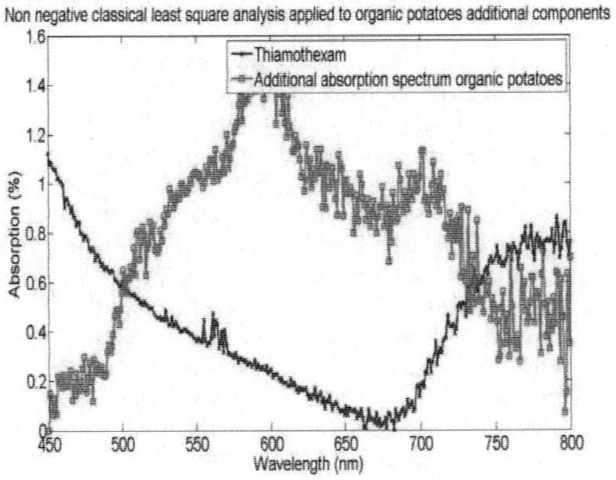

Figure 14. Organic potatoes additional artificial components spectrum reconstructed with Non Negative Classical Least Squares analysis using the pesticides Dicofol, Thiamethoxam and Malathion spectra.

Table IV depicts the comparison between the Thiamethoxam pesticides concentration in various foods categories obtained with the Beer-Lambert procedure or with the Non Negative Least Squares procedure. Both methods permit to obtain very close concentration values with less than 3µg/mL maximum errors.

TABLE IV. THIAMETHOXAM PESTICIDE CONCENTRATION COMPARAISON BETWEEN SINGLE WAVELENGTH CONCENTRATION LAW AND USING NON NEGATIVE LEAST SQUAREs ANALYSIS

	Beer-Lambert's concentration law	**Non Negative Least Squares**
THIAMETHOXAM PESTICIDE CONCENTRATION (MG/ML)		
Organic tomatoes	0.005	0.005
Supermarket1 tomatoes	0.017	0.014
Supermarket 2 tomatoes	0.013	0.016
Organic zucchini	0.038	0.040
Supermarket 1 zucchini	0.026	0.028
Supermarket 2 zucchini	0.026	0.026
Organic potatoes	0.005	0.007
Supermarket 1 potatoes	0.005	0.006
Supermarket 2 potatoes	0.002	0.005

IV. CONCLUSION AND FUTURE WORK

Due to their wide use and toxicity, pesticides quantification in foods are measured by several methods including Liquid Chromatography with Mass Spectrometry (LC-MS), Gas Chromatography (GC), High Performance Liquid Chromatography (HPLC), Voltammetry, Atomic Absorption Spectrophotometry (AAS) and spectrophotometry [80].

Spectrophotometry analysis of pesticides often requires chemical manipulations such as pesticides extraction with solvents and dye addition before dye quantification by spectrophotometric measures. Such manipulations are difficult to reproduce in outside measures and often requires specific material and expertise. In order to directly estimate the pesticides concentration in foods extract using the Beer-Lambert's concentration law, pesticides extraction from foods should be realized first. Avoiding using chemicals for pesticides extraction is therefore a very challenging part, that we partially solved in this document. By performing spectrophotometric measures on food devoid of pesticides contamination and repeating the measures to different foods variety and category, the spectra of pesticides free foods were extracted. These pesticides free foods spectra were used to extract the foods genuine spectra from the added constituents such as pesticides and conservatives. Therefore, we propose an innovative method based on Vis-NIR spectroscopy for detecting food contaminants using spectral filters constructed from pesticides free food samples data.

Our methodology choices were mainly dictated by the currently restricted number of contaminants analyzed using spectrophotometric measures, since pesticides extraction experimental procedures are limited and complex. In contrast, we used the Vis-NIR spectral trace of additional atypical constituents in foods, obtained after application of adequate pesticides free foods filters. The creation of these filters required first the laborious finding of a certified market gardener pesticides free food supplier. Then pesticides free foods spectral data were measured using reflective spectroscopy and used as pesticides free filters. Vis-NIR spectral data of three categories of foods from different food suppliers were compared to the corresponding pesticides free foods spectral data and Vis-NIR spectral traces of contaminants were extracted. We further discussed the most likely wavelengths in the Vis-NIR spectral range associated with pesticides chemicals.

For more rigorous pesticides contamination quantification, we compared two different methods of spectrophotometric pesticides detection: one based on the standard Beer-Lambert's concentration law and the second based on Non Negative Least Squares algorithm. The pesticides of interest were Dicofol, Thiamethoxam and Malathion and their respective absorption spectra were measured. We further extracted the absorption coefficients of these pesticides at appropriate wavelengths.

Measurement of the additional components of the various foods categories in the Vis-NIR spectral trace permitted: (1) the estimation of the pesticides contamination at precise wavelengths (791 nm for Dicofol, 774 nm for Thiamethoxam and 475 nm for Malathion) using the standard Beer-Lambert's law and (2) the estimation of Thiamethoxam food contamination principally, using all the wavelengths (Non Negative Least Squares algorithm). The pesticides concentration results were very similar among the two methods for each category of food with less than 3µg/mL of difference between the two methods.

Globally and from early conclusion, our method is promising, easy to implement and directly permits to interpret pesticides food pollution. Confrontation of the obtained pesticides concentration with another recognized pesticide concentration estimation method such as Liquid Chromatography with Mass Spectrometry is the next step to validate these encouraging results. The use of pesticides free spectral filters and the quantification of pesticides using linear regression models are particularly innovative and should facilitate non-invasive pesticides testing procedures.

The main constraint in the developed method is that meticulous data should be obtained first for numerous pesticide free food variety and category studied, possibly stored in a database.

Astonishingly, when applying the method we developed to foods from different suppliers, it resulted that foods from organic farming were not always the less contaminated with pesticides.

Finally, the implementation of such algorithm in an embedded platform with a microspectrometer module may allow convenient device user estimation of foods chemical contaminants.

REFERENCES

[1] O. Diop and U. Cerasani, "Light Reflection Spectrum Comparison of Pesticides Free Foods, Organic Foods and Conventional Farming Foods for VIS NIR Filter Creation," in *The Ninth International Conference on Advances in Human-oriented and Personalized Mechanisms, Technologies, and Services (CENTRIC 2016)*, Rome, 2016.

[2] D. Pimentel, "Environmental and economic costs of the application of pesticides primarily in the United States," *Environment, development and sustainability,* vol. 7, pp. 229-252, 2005.

[3] N. J. Osborne, R. Cairns, A. H. Dawson, K. M. Chitty, and N. A. Buckley, "Epidemiology of coronial deaths from pesticide ingestion in Australia," *International journal of hygiene and environmental health,* vol. 220, pp. 478-484, 2017.

[4] M. Sarwar, "The dangers of pesticides associated with public health and preventing of the risks," *International Journal of Bioinformatics and Biomedical Engineering,* vol. 1, pp. 130-136, 2015.

[5] D. Yang and Y. Ying, "Applications of Raman spectroscopy in agricultural products and food analysis: A review," *Applied Spectroscopy Reviews,* vol. 46, pp. 539-560, 2011.

[6] B. B. Dzantiev, N. A. Byzova, A. E. Urusov, and A. V. Zherdev, "Immunochromatographic methods in food analysis," *TrAC Trends in Analytical Chemistry,* vol. 55, pp. 81-93, 2014.

[7] G. Marrazza, "Piezoelectric biosensors for organophosphate and carbamate pesticides: a review," *Biosensors,* vol. 4, pp. 301-317, 2014.

[8] D. Lee, S. Lee, G. H. Seong, J. Choo, E. K. Lee, D.-G. Gweon, *et al.*, "Quantitative analysis of methyl parathion pesticides in a polydimethylsiloxane microfluidic channel using confocal surface-enhanced Raman spectroscopy," *Applied spectroscopy,* vol. 60, pp. 373-377, 2006.

[9] M. Karlowatz, M. Kraft, and B. Mizaikoff, "Simultaneous quantitative determination of benzene, toluene, and xylenes in water using mid-infrared evanescent field spectroscopy," *Analytical chemistry,* vol. 76, pp. 2643-2648, 2004.

[10] K. Wong-Ek, M. Horprathum, P. Eiamchai, P. Limnonthakul, V. Patthanasettakul, P. Chindaudom, *et al.*, "Portable surface-enhanced Raman spectroscopy for insecticide detection using silver nanorod film fabricated by magnetron sputtering," in *SPIE BiOS*, 2011, pp. 791108-791108-11.

[11] W. Zhang, A. M. Asiri, D. Liu, D. Du, and Y. Lin, "Nanomaterial-based biosensors for environmental and biological monitoring of organophosphorus pesticides and nerve agents," *TrAC Trends in Analytical Chemistry,* vol. 54, pp. 1-10, 2014.

[12] S. Hassani, S. Momtaz, F. Vakhshiteh, A. S. Maghsoudi, M. R. Ganjali, P. Norouzi, *et al.*, "Biosensors and their applications in detection of organophosphorus pesticides in the environment," *Archives of toxicology,* pp. 1-22, 2017.

[13] M. Stoytcheva, V. Gochev, and Z. Velkova, "Electrochemical biosensors for direct determination of organophosphorus pesticides: a review," *Current Analytical Chemistry,* vol. 12, pp. 37-42, 2016.

[14] L. M. Nollet and H. S. Rathore, *Handbook of pesticides: methods of pesticide residues analysis*: CRC press, 2016.

[15] M. Mutlu, *Biosensors in food processing, safety, and quality control*: CRC Press, 2016.

[16] A. Sassolas, B. Prieto-Simón, and J.-L. Marty, "Biosensors for Pesticide Detection: New Trends," *American Journal of Analytical Chemistry,* pp. 210-232, 2012.

[17] X. Jiang, D. Li, X. Xu, Y. Ying, Y. Li, Z. Ye, *et al.*, "Immunosensors for detection of pesticide residues," *Biosensors and Bioelectronics,* vol. 23, pp. 1577-1587, 2008.

[18] C. R. Suri, M. Raje, and G. C. Varshney, "Immunosensors for pesticide analysis: antibody production and sensor development," *Critical reviews in biotechnology,* vol. 22, pp. 15-32, 2002.

[19] F. Bier, W. Stöcklein, M. Böcher, U. Bilitewski, and R. Schmid, "Use of a fibre optic immunosensor for the detection of pesticides," *Sensors and Actuators B: Chemical,* vol. 7, pp. 509-512, 1992.

[20] M.-I. Baraton, *Sensors for Environment, Health and Security: Advanced Materials and Technologies*: Springer Science & Business Media, 2008.

[21] M. Ferrari, M. Ozkan, and M. Heller, *BioMEMS and Biomedical Nanotechnology: Volume II: Micro/Nano Technologies for Genomics and Proteomics* vol. 2: Springer Science & Business Media, 2007.

[22] O. Tigli, *Novel SAW devices in CMOS for biosensor applications: design, modeling, fabrication and characterization*: ProQuest, 2007.

[23] L. Xue, J. Cai, J. Li, and M. Liu, "Application of particle swarm optimization (PSO) algorithm to determine dichlorvos residue on the surface of navel orange with Vis-NIR spectroscopy," *Procedia Engineering,* vol. 29, pp. 4124-4128, 2012.

[24] J. T. Alander, V. Bochko, B. Martinkauppi, S. Saranwong, and T. Mantere, "A review of optical nondestructive visual and near-infrared methods for food quality and safety," *International Journal of Spectroscopy,* vol. 2013, 2013.

[25] Y.-Z. Feng, G. ElMasry, D.-W. Sun, A. G. Scannell, D. Walsh, and N. Morcy, "Near-infrared hyperspectral imaging and partial least squares regression for rapid and reagentless determination of Enterobacteriaceae on chicken fillets," *Food Chemistry,* vol. 138, pp. 1829-1836, 2013.

[26] E. J. N. Marques, S. T. de Freitas, M. F. Pimentel, and C. Pasquini, "Rapid and non-destructive determination of quality parameters in the 'Tommy Atkins' mango using a novel handheld near infrared spectrometer," *Food chemistry,* vol. 197, pp. 1207-1214, 2016.

[27] M. Manley, "Near-infrared spectroscopy and hyperspectral imaging: non-destructive analysis of biological materials," *Chemical Society Reviews,* vol. 43, pp. 8200-8214, 2014.

[28] H. Huang, L. Liu, and M. O. Ngadi, "Recent developments in hyperspectral imaging for assessment of food quality and safety," *Sensors,* vol. 14, pp. 7248-7276, 2014.

[29] L. Salguero-Chaparro, A. J. Gaitán-Jurado, V. Ortiz-Somovilla, and F. Peña-Rodríguez, "Feasibility of using NIR spectroscopy to detect herbicide residues in intact olives," *Food control,* vol. 30, pp. 504-509, 2013.

[30] M. T. Sánchez, K. Flores-Rojas, J. E. Guerrero, A. Garrido-Varo, and D. Pérez-Marín, "Measurement of pesticide residues in peppers by near-infrared reflectance spectroscopy," *Pest management science,* vol. 66, pp. 580-586, 2010.

[31] S. Armenta, S. Garrigues, and M. de la Guardia, "Partial least squares-near infrared determination of pesticides in commercial formulations," *Vibrational Spectroscopy,* vol. 44, pp. 273-278, 2007.

[32] J. Moros, S. Armenta, S. Garrigues, and M. de la Guardia, "Near infrared determination of Diuron in pesticide formulations," *Analytica chimica acta,* vol. 543, pp. 124-129, 2005.

[33] J. Moros, S. Armenta, S. Garrigues, and M. de la Guardia, "Univariate near infrared methods for determination of pesticides in agrochemicals," *Analytica chimica acta,* vol. 579, pp. 17-24, 2006.

[34] Y. Zhou, B. Xiang, Z. Wang, and C. Chen, "Determination of chlorpyrifos residue by near-infrared spectroscopy in white radish based on interval partial least square (iPLS) model," *Analytical Letters,* vol. 42, pp. 1518-1526, 2009.

[35] D. Malley, C. McClure, P. Martin, K. Buckley, and W. McCaughey, "Compositional analysis of cattle manure during composting using a field-portable near-infrared spectrometer," *Communications in Soil Science and Plant Analysis,* vol. 36, pp. 455-475, 2005.

[36] K. D. Shepherd and M. G. Walsh, "Infrared spectroscopy—enabling an evidence-based diagnostic surveillance approach to agricultural and environmental management in developing countries," *Journal of Near Infrared Spectroscopy,* vol. 15, pp. 1-19, 2007.

[37] T. Shi, Y. Chen, Y. Liu, and G. Wu, "Visible and near-infrared reflectance spectroscopy—An alternative for monitoring soil contamination by heavy metals," *Journal of hazardous materials,* vol. 265, pp. 166-176, 2014.

[38] M. Maleki, A. Mouazen, H. Ramon, and J. De Baerdemaeker, "Optimisation of soil VIS–NIR sensor-based variable rate application system of soil phosphorus," *Soil and Tillage Research,* vol. 94, pp. 239-250, 2007.

[39] M. Kamruzzaman, Y. Makino, and S. Oshita, "Non-invasive analytical technology for the detection of contamination, adulteration, and authenticity of meat, poultry, and fish: a review," *Analytica chimica acta,* vol. 853, pp. 19-29, 2015.

[40] G. Rateni, P. Dario, and F. Cavallo, "Smartphone-Based Food Diagnostic Technologies: A Review," *Sensors,* vol. 17, p. 1453, 2017.

[41] S.-H. Noh and K.-H. Choi, "Nondestructive quality evaluation technology for fruits and vegetables," in *International Seminar on Enhancing Export Competitiveness of Asian Fruits, Bangkok, Thailand*, 2006.

[42] R. D. JiJi, G. A. Cooper, and K. S. Booksh, "Excitation-emission matrix fluorescence based determination of carbamate pesticides and polycyclic aromatic hydrocarbons," *Analytica Chimica Acta,* vol. 397, pp. 61-72, 1999.

[43] A. Kwiatkowski, M. Czerwicka, J. Smulko, and P. Stepnowski, "Detection of denatonium benzoate (Bitrex) remnants in noncommercial alcoholic beverages by raman spectroscopy," *Journal of forensic sciences,* vol. 59, pp. 1358-1363, 2014.

[44] E. Ali and H. G. Edwards, "The detection of flunitrazepam in beverages using portable Raman spectroscopy," *Drug testing and analysis,* vol. 9, pp. 256-259, 2017.

[45] K. Ilaslan, I. H. Boyaci, and A. Topcu, "Rapid analysis of glucose, fructose and sucrose contents of commercial soft drinks using Raman spectroscopy," *Food Control,* vol. 48, pp. 56-61, 2015.

[46] G. G. Buyukgoz, A. G. Bozkurt, N. B. Akgul, U. Tamer, and I. H. Boyaci, "Spectroscopic detection of aspartame in soft drinks by surface-enhanced Raman spectroscopy," *European Food Research and Technology,* vol. 240, pp. 567-575, 2015.

[47] C. A. F. Penido, M. T. T. Pacheco, I. K. Lednev, and L. Silveira, "Raman spectroscopy in forensic analysis: identification of cocaine and other illegal drugs of abuse," *Journal of Raman Spectroscopy,* vol. 47, pp. 28-38, 2016.

[48] C. Martin, J.-L. Bruneel, F. Guyon, B. Médina, M. Jourdes, P.-L. Teissedre, *et al.*, "Raman spectroscopy of white wines," *Food chemistry,* vol. 181, pp. 235-240, 2015.

[49] T. O. Mendes, R. A. da Rocha, B. L. Porto, M. A. de Oliveira, V. d. C. dos Anjos, and M. J. Bell, "Quantification of extra-virgin olive oil adulteration with soybean oil: a comparative study of NIR, MIR, and Raman spectroscopy associated with chemometric approaches," *Food analytical methods,* vol. 8, pp. 2339-2346, 2015.

[50] V. O. Clavero, A. Weber, W. Schröder, D. Curticapean, N. Javahiraly, and P. Meyrueis, "Monitoring of the molecular structure of lubricant oil using a FT-Raman spectrometer prototype," in *Optical Sensing and Detection III*, 2014, p. 91411W.

[51] K. Czamara, K. Majzner, M. Z. Pacia, K. Kochan, A. Kaczor, and M. Baranska, "Raman spectroscopy of lipids: a review," *Journal of Raman Spectroscopy,* vol. 46, pp. 4-20, 2015.

[52] P. Vandenabeele, H. Edwards, and J. Jehlička, "The role of mobile instrumentation in novel applications of Raman spectroscopy: archaeometry, geosciences, and forensics," *Chemical Society Reviews,* vol. 43, pp. 2628-2649, 2014.

[53] S. Feng, F. Gao, Z. Chen, E. Grant, D. D. Kitts, S. Wang, *et al.*, "Determination of α-Tocopherol in vegetable oils using a molecularly imprinted polymers–surface-enhanced raman spectroscopic biosensor," *Journal of agricultural and food chemistry,* vol. 61, pp. 10467-10475, 2013.

[54] R. S. Uysal, I. H. Boyaci, H. E. Genis, and U. Tamer, "Determination of butter adulteration with margarine using Raman spectroscopy," *Food chemistry,* vol. 141, pp. 4397-4403, 2013.

[55] C. A. Nunes, "Vibrational spectroscopy and chemometrics to assess authenticity, adulteration and intrinsic quality parameters of edible oils and fats," *Food Research International,* vol. 60, pp. 255-261, 2014.

[56] B. Liu, G. Han, Z. Zhang, R. Liu, C. Jiang, S. Wang, *et al.*, "Shell thickness-dependent Raman enhancement for rapid identification and detection of pesticide residues at fruit peels," *Analytical chemistry,* vol. 84, pp. 255-261, 2011.

[57] J. Xing and D. Guyer, "Detecting internal insect infestation in tart cherry using transmittance spectroscopy," *Postharvest biology and technology,* vol. 49, pp. 411-416, 2008.

[58] B. Saute, R. Premasiri, L. Ziegler, and R. Narayanan, "Gold nanorods as surface enhanced Raman spectroscopy substrates for sensitive and selective detection of ultra-low levels of dithiocarbamate pesticides," *Analyst,* vol. 137, pp. 5082-5087, 2012.

[59] G. Chunhui, Z. Guoqiang, G. Liangquan, L. Jun, and W. Ziqiang, "Determination of trace elements in tea by wavelength dispersive X-ray fluorescence spectroscopy," *Nuclear Techniques,* vol. 36, 2013.

[60] L. R. Goldman, "Managing pesticide chronic health risks: US policies," *Journal of agromedicine,* vol. 12, pp. 67-75, 2007.

[61] Centers, for, Disease, Control, and, and Prevention. (2013). *CDC - Pesticide Illness & Injury Surveillance - NIOSH Workplace Safety and Health Topic.* Available: http://www.cdc.gov/

[62] S. Parvez and S. Raisuddin, "Protein carbonyls: novel biomarkers of exposure to oxidative stress-inducing pesticides in freshwater fish Channa punctata (Bloch)," *Environmental Toxicology and Pharmacology,* vol. 20, pp. 112-117, 2005.

[63] J. Dorts, F. Silvestre, H. T. Tu, A.-E. Tyberghein, N. T. Phuong, and P. Kestemont, "Oxidative stress, protein carbonylation and heat shock proteins in the black tiger shrimp, Penaeus monodon, following exposure to endosulfan and deltamethrin," *Environmental toxicology and pharmacology,* vol. 28, pp. 302-310, 2009.

[64] J. J. Fortunato, G. Feier, A. M. Vitali, F. C. Petronilho, F. Dal-Pizzol, and J. Quevedo, "Malathion-induced oxidative stress in rat brain regions," *Neurochemical research,* vol. 31, pp. 671-678, 2006.

[65] S. B. Ceyhun, M. Şentürk, D. Ekinci, O. Erdoğan, A. Çiltaş, and E. M. Kocaman, "Deltamethrin attenuates antioxidant defense system and induces the expression of heat shock protein 70 in rainbow trout," *Comparative Biochemistry and Physiology Part C: Toxicology & Pharmacology,* vol. 152, pp. 215-223, 2010.

[66] R. M. Johnson, J. D. Evans, G. E. Robinson, and M. R. Berenbaum, "Changes in transcript abundance relating to colony collapse disorder in honey bees (Apis mellifera)," *Proceedings of the National Academy of Sciences,* vol. 106, pp. 14790-14795, 2009.

[67] H. T. Hogberg, A. Kinsner-Ovaskainen, T. Hartung, S. Coecke, and A. K. Bal-Price, "Gene expression as a sensitive endpoint to evaluate cell differentiation and maturation of the developing central nervous system in primary cultures of rat cerebellar granule cells (CGCs) exposed to pesticides," *Toxicology and applied pharmacology,* vol. 235, pp. 268-286, 2009.

[68] M. Collotta, P. Bertazzi, and V. Bollati, "Epigenetics and pesticides," *Toxicology,* vol. 307, pp. 35-41, 2013.

[69] J. D. Ingle Jr and S. R. Crouch, "Spectrochemical analysis," 1988.

[70] J. Clack and G. Gunawardena. (Updated in February 2017). *The Beer-Lambert Law (Chemistry LibreTexts ed.).* Available: https://chem.libretexts.org/Core/Physical_and_Theoretical_Chemistry/Spectroscopy/Electronic_Spectroscopy/Electronic_Spectroscopy_Basics/The_Beer-Lambert_Law

[71] University of California, Los Angeles. (Accesses February 2017). *Colorimetric Analysis (Beer's law or Spectrophotometric Analysis).* Available: http://www.chem.ucla.edu/~gchemlab/colorimetric_web.htm

[72] Andor, Oxford, Instruments, and Company. (Accessed in February 2017). *Absorption, Transmission and Reflection Spectroscopy* Available: http://www.andor.com/learning-academy/

[73] B. M. Tissue. (Accessed in February 2017). *Beer-Lambert Law.* Available: http://www.tissuegroup.chem.vt.edu

[74] T. C. O'Haver. (Accessed in February 2017). *Curve fitting B: Multicomponent Spectroscopy.* Available: https://terpconnect.umd.edu/~toh/spectrum/CurveFittingB.html

[75] C.-M. Kuan, "Classical Least Squares Theory," in *National Taiwan University, Department of Finance & CRETA*, 2010.

[76] H. Mark and J. Workman, "Classical Least Squares, Part I: Mathematical Theory," 2010.

[77] B. P. Baker, C. M. Benbrook, E. G. III, and K. L. Benbrook, "Pesticide residues in conventional, integrated pest management (IPM)-grown and organic foods: insights from three US data sets," *Food Additives & Contaminants,* vol. 19, pp. 427-446, 2002.

[78] N. Venugopal and B. Sumalatha, "Spectrophotometric determination of malathion in environmental samples," *Journal of Chemistry,* vol. 9, pp. 857-862, 2012.

[79] K. Reddy, K. Suvardhan, K. S. Kumar, D. Rekha, and P. Chiranjeevi, "Extractive spectrophotometric determination of malathion in environmental samples using Gention violet," *Journal of Chemistry,* vol. 2, pp. 187-192, 2005.

[80] A. A. Gouda, A. S. Amin, R. El-Sheikh, and M. A. Akl, "Sensitive spectrophotometric methods for determination of some organophosphorus pesticides in vegetable samples," *Chemical Industry and Chemical Engineering Quarterly,* vol. 16, pp. 11-18, 2010.

[81] A. Bouhaouss, A. Bensaoud, M. El Azzouzi, C. Perrin-Ganier, and M. Schiavon, "Etude par spectroscopie ultraviolet et infrarouge de l'adsorption des pesticides par les apatites," *Phys. Chem. News,* vol. 1, pp. 115-118, 2001.

[82] G. P. Pandey, A. K. Singh, L. Deshmukh, and A. Asthana, "Determination of dicofol in various environmental samples by spectrophotometric method using chromogenic reagent," *Synthesis and Reactivity in Inorganic, Metal-Organic, and Nano-Metal Chemistry,* vol. 45, pp. 1199-1205, 2015.

[83] J. Zhang, Z. Zhao, L. Wang, X. Zhu, L. Shen, and Y. Yu, "Two-Dimensional UV Absorption Correlation Spectroscopy as a Method for the Detection of Thiamethoxam Residue in Tea," *Journal of Applied Spectroscopy,* vol. 82, pp. 311-315, 2015.

Enhanced 4T Loadless SRAM Comparison With Selected Volatile Memory Cells

Karol Niewiadomski and Dietmar Tutsch
University of Wuppertal
Chair of Automation and Computer Science
Wuppertal, Germany
Email: {niewiadomski, tutsch}@uni-wuppertal.de

Abstract—**The adaptiveness of Field Programmable Gate Arrays is a key aspect in many mobile applications. Modern vehicles contain up to 100 "Electronic Control Units" in order to implement all necessary functions for autonomous driving. Due to the limited power resources of mobile applications, an appropriate implementation of power reduction measures is crucial for achieving an acceptable amount of power savings. However, effective power reduction mechanisms have to be applied to the backbone of each Field Programmable Gate Array: the look-up table. In this paper, we describe the implementation and comparison of various Static Random Access Memory cells and the related characteristics which are used as a benchmark. All Static Random Access Memory cells have been analyzed in order to evaluate feasible modifications for the sake of lowering leakage currents and modified for minimizing static and dynamic power consumption. The trade-off between low-power use cases, a fast response time and area considerations as well as yield after manufacturing has to be carefully analyzed. Therefore, further aspects like signal to noise ratio and area increase due to additional, required transistors are deliberated about whether the additional efforts delivers desired results. Since speed in terms of a high operating frequency is demanded by many applications, we analyze each design upon its capabilities to run at their maximum speed.**

Keywords–Field Programmable Gate Array; Static Random Access Memory cell optimization; low-power; signal to noise ratio; max. operating frequency; signal propagation delay.

I. INTRODUCTION

During the last years, the number of classic desktop computers used in domestic homes has constantly decreased. The reason behind this phenomenon is the rising number of mobile devices such as smartphones and tablets, taking over most of the functionalities provided by desktop computers before [1]. Furthermore, upcoming features like highly automated driving cars or fully autonomous vehicles require a high demand for computing power. Whilst the computing performance of mobile devices is improved constantly to face the challenges of complex applications like video processing for adaptive cruise control on long distance highway drives, the capacities of batteries providing the needed energy resources have not been extended in the same way. A modern, upper-class vehicle contains more than 70 electronic control units (ECUs) to provide all features desired by consumers these days [2]. Onboard communication networks like Controller Area Network (CAN), FlexRay and ethernet ensure the communication between these devices, but also introduce a remarkable amount of additional weight of approximately up to 30% (depending on the used technology). In order to counter the limits set by power consumption and overall weight, a significant reduction of the ECU number would be an efficient approach. This could lead to the application of more powerful processors, taking over many of the functionalities from the large number of slower ECUs used before. The downside of this approach would be a higher power consumption due to higher clock frequencies. A more comprehensive approach focuses on the massive usage of FPGAs in mobile applications. Field Programmable Gate Arrays (FPGAs) offer various advantages compared to processors and Application Specific Integrated Circuits (ASICs). Being fully configurable, FPGAs are well-suited for the execution of various functions which have been spread over several ECUs before, either purely by hardware implementations or software execution running on a softcore processor implemented on the FPGA's fabric. However, FPGAs do not offer similar power saving mechanisms implemented on microprocessors and lack of of a substantial power management system. Power consumption saving mechanisms shall be applied to series production passenger cars, which is a cost-sensitive market, hence we choose the Xilinx Spartan-3 low-cost FPGA as a baseline architecture for all further considerations [3]. FPGAs play a major role for the realization of adaptive systems. Partial, dynamic reconfiguration [4], supported by various FPGA designs, offer a vast potential for fast adaption of the implemented functional range within a vehicle, e.g., realizing a requested function by the driver and disengaging a previously implemented vehicle function which is not required any more [5].

In this paper, we evaluate selected Static Random Access Memory (SRAM) cell designs on their suitability for a low-leakage look-up table (LUT) implementation, which are the elementar computational elements. Since the overhead of reconfigurability leads to unused parts within the FPGA, both static and dynamic power consumption are analyzed for each cell design. In Section II, we give an overview about a selection of existing designs and our motivation for improvements. In Section III, we describe a number of leakage reduction techniques and evaluate the feasible adaption on current designs. In Section IV, we investigate the SRAM cell designs on their assets and drawbacks and compare the simulation results. In Section V, circuit improvement methods for standby and active currents reduction are introduced. All investigated SRAM cells are enhanced with these additional improvements and compared again. In Section VI, we use each modified SRAM cell to implement a 4-input LUT reference design and explore the power consumption during the idle and active state. The advantages of reasonable SRAM cell design modifications are presented based upon the simulation results. In Section VII, further timing considerations are described. In Section VIII, all previous discussions are summarized and concluded.

II. RELATED WORK

Various SRAM cell designs have been under research over the years. Compared to dynamic RAM (DRAM), which is widely used as main memory in many applications, SRAM offers numerous advantages like quick read & write-cycles, cell stability, data retention without refresh cycles, differential outputs and many more. During the pre-Complementary Metal-Oxide-Semiconductor (CMOS) era, the 4T cell [6] was commonly used for cache memories. Considering the additional effort in terms of process variations for implementing the resistor load and weaker signal to noise (SNM) margin, this cell type was replaced by the 6T cell [7]. This design depicts the mostly used approach for combining reliable functionality with a proven in use fabrication process due to its CMOS structure. Being the starting point for benchmarking, cell variations like the 5T SRAM [6] design were developed to eliminate the parasitic capacitance penalties of two bitlines. Further derivations like the 7T cell implementation [8] inherit the characteristics of the reference 6T design and provide power savings by exploiting an effective writing mechanism, putting no further requirements on adaptions to auxiliary circuitry. Features like soft error rate robustness during low-power operation have been explored in a 10T design variation [9]. All of these cell types have been designed during research without applying additional, commonly used power reduction measures. LUT designs have been evaluated and improved on architectural level [10] for power reduction by power gating mechanisms. New FPGA designs were presented and compared to commercial products, by adding structural improvements [11].

Our approach goes one step further and is based on circuit level improvements to a LUT by reasonable selection of a suitable SRAM cell design and substantial modification of the cell circuitry to achieve better leakage reduction and power savings. The improvements achieved on that level are essential for important leakage current suppression and are an inevitable step to be combined with architectural amendments.

III. LEAKAGE REDUCTION

Three major components of leakage currents can be identified for a Metal-Oxide-Semiconductor (MOS) transistor of gate lengths in nanometer scales:

- Subthreshold leakage
- Direct tunneling gate leakageshown in
- Reverse biased p-n BTBT leakage

Whilst the band-to-band tunneling (BTBT) leakage currents can be neglected for devices exceeding 50nm gate lengths, subthreshold and direct tunneling gate leakage currents come into consideration for our design. Tunneling electrons through gates oxides can be countermeasured by carefully setting an adequate oxide thickness of each transistor. This dependency can be seen in (1):

$$J_{DT} \propto A(\frac{V_{ox}}{T_{ox}})^2 \tag{1}$$

$$A = \mu_o C_{ox} \frac{W}{L_{eff}} (\frac{kT}{q})^2 e^{1.8}$$

By increasing the oxide thickness T_{ox}, the direct tunneling current density J_{DT} can be efficiently lowered to a minimum stage [12]. Increasing the gate length L_{eff} would have a similar effect, but lead to higher effort in the manufacturing process due to a change in one of the basic technology parameters like the gate length of a transistor. Therefore, this option should be avoided. However, the usage of multi-oxide thicknesses is a technology dependent parameter and requires awareness for the selection of a suitable multi-oxide technology.

Subthreshold currents can be expressed by the following equation:

$$I_{sub} \propto \frac{W}{L_{eff}} e^{(V_{GS} - V_{t0} - \gamma V_{SB} + \eta V_{DS})/nV_t)(1 - e^{-\frac{V_{DS}}{V_t}})} \tag{2}$$

Equation (2) shows the parameters which contribute to the overall weak-inversion current, flowing below the threshold voltage V_{th} of each MOS transistor in the circuit. Several leakage reduction measures can be applied by utilizing these parameters to design a low leakage circuit:

- W: setting the width of a transistor as small as possible leads to a higher resistance of it and therefore to smaller leakage currents
- V_{gs}: Gate biasing is done by applying a V_{gs} voltage lower than Gnd, which turns the transistor deeply off
- V_{sb}: Body biasing by tweaking the body voltage of a turned off transistor
- V_{dd}: Lowering the supply voltage mitigates or even completely removes the DIBL (drain-induced barrier lowering) effect, represented by η in (2)

In general, we can distinguish between two classes of leakage reduction techniques [13]. Some can be applied during the design, whereas others can be used during operation time of the circuit. A reasonable extract of these techniques is shown in Table I.

TABLE I. LEAKAGE REDUCTION TECHNIQUES

Design leakage reduction	*Static leakage reduction*	*Active leakage reduction*
Dual-V_{th}	Stacking	DVS
Multi-V_{dd}	Sleep mode	
	VTCMOS	DVTS

Energy efficient circuits should feature multiple supply voltages and at least a dual threshold approach. As shown in Table I, these characteristics need to be added during the development phase. Furthermore, additional techniques working during operation of the circuit can help to continuously reduce the overall power consumption. Dynamic (threshold) voltage scaling (DVS & DVTS), as well as variable threshold CMOS (VTCMOS) circuitry are powerful methods to overcome the side-effects like subthreshold leakage due to progressive scaling to smaller technology nodes.

We analyze the techniques listed in Table I on their careful combination and application to volatile (SRAM) memory cells and therefore automatically to LUTs.

IV. SRAM Cell designs

The backbone of each computational activity within an FPGA is the LUT [14]. Typically an FPGA consists of a sea of tiles which contain the necessary logic in terms of LUTs and interconnection circuitry, shown in Figure 1. Two different groups of logic can be identified: Configurable Logic Block (CLB) and switch matrix. A CLB is used for ensuring the feature of adaptiveness due to the built-in LUTs, therefore it contains the LUTs and additional components, e.g., flip-flops, multiplexers and basic logic gates. On the other hand, the switching matrix is used for providing all necessary interconnections to other tiles / LUTs in case that more complex functions are requested to be implemented and require a combination of multiple CLBs.

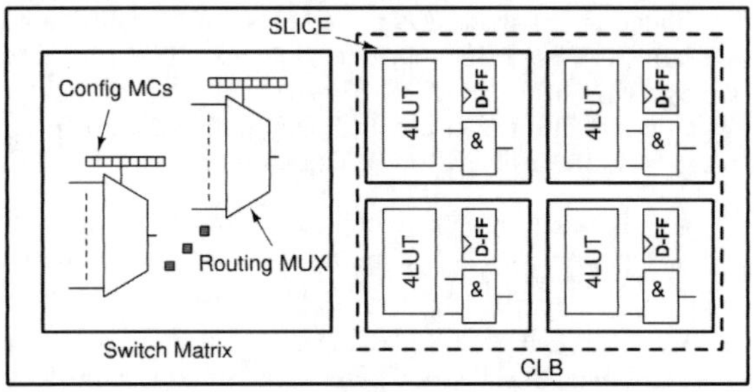

Figure 1. Simplified 'Tile' of an FPGA

By putting a higher focus on the optimization of the configuration RAM cells, these efforts serve not only improving the power balance of the CLBs, but also to decrease the switch matrices standby leakage currents. For communication with peripheral logic General Purpose Input Output (GPIOs) blocks are implemented, which can be used for bidirectional data. However, switch matrices and GPIOs are not subject matter of this paper and will be discussed in later publications.

Depending on the number of the LUT's inputs, a LUT can contain numerous SRAM cells. For example, in case of a 4-input LUT, 16 SRAM cells are necessary for the realization of all possible input value combinations. An exemplary illustration of a LUT is shown in Figure 2.

Since the memory cells are used for configuration, they are also called configuration RAM (CRAM). Once configured during the start-up phase, the content of these memory cells would not be changed until the next reconfiguration cycle. In consequence, the static leakage current reduction is of higher significance for the overall power consumption.

The selection of a low-power SRAM cell design is crucial for an appropriate energy-efficient implementation of integrated circuits. Many memory cell designs have been introduced in the past. The common 6 transistor cell can be found in most FPGAs nowadays [15]. In principle, this memory cell consists of two cross-coupled inverter and two access transistors, connecting the inverters to the bitlines, as shown in Figure 3.

As long as $M5$ and $M6$ are in cut-off mode, the cross-coupled inverters are isolated from the bitlines and store the

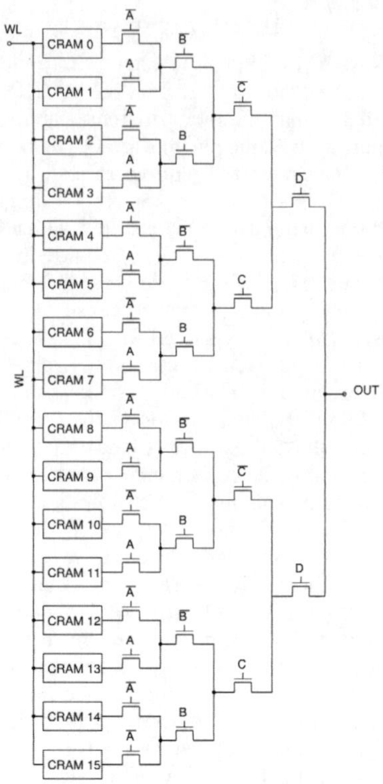

Figure 2. Simplified 4-input LUT

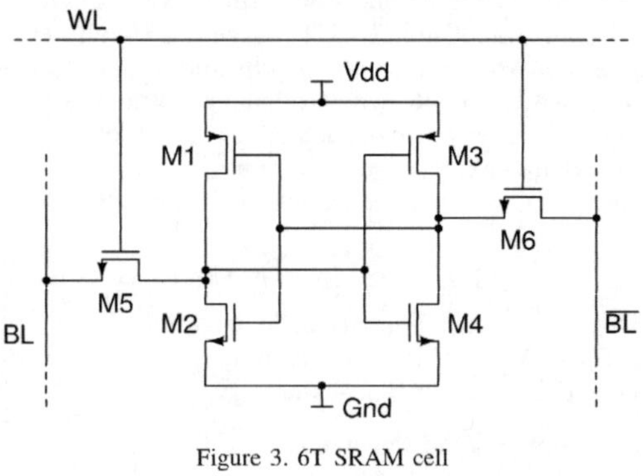

Figure 3. 6T SRAM cell

complementary data value at the output nodes of each inverter. Data retention is ensured as long as a sufficient supply voltage V_{dd} is applied. Before reading the stored data, both bitlines BL and $\overline{BL}$ are precharged to V_{dd} by a special precharge circuit and the access transistors $M5$ and $M6$ are turned on. One of the bitlines will be discharged to Gnd, whereas the other bitline will remain on V_{dd}. The voltage drop between BL and $\overline{BL}$ will be sensed and evaluated by a sense amplifier. For writing data into the cell, one of the bitlines is kept at V_{dd}, whereas the other bitline is kept at Gnd. By turning the access transistors on, the desired value is written. For this purpose, a suitable bitline driver circuit is needed to ensure the propoer execution of the writing cycle. Careful transistor sizing is required for avoiding the cell to flip during, e.g., a read cycle. This cell design is well-elaborated and used for years in integrated circuits. Its stability and reliability is well-known and therefore used in various applications. However, the power consumption of the 6T SRAM cell can be further optimized by some modifications resulting in the SRAM cells described in the following paragraphs:

1) 4T SRAM cell: A typical implementation of a four transistor SRAM cell is shown in Figure 4. In comparison to the 6T cell, a smaller are of approximately 30% can be achieved [16]. Due to the replacement of all pMOS transistors by polysilicon resistors, only nMOS transistors are used for the pure functionality of this cell. Despite of the space-savings, which could lead to a higher yield after the manufacturing process, the realization of high-resistivity polysilicon resistor adds additional technological steps to the manufacturing process, resulting in higher costs.

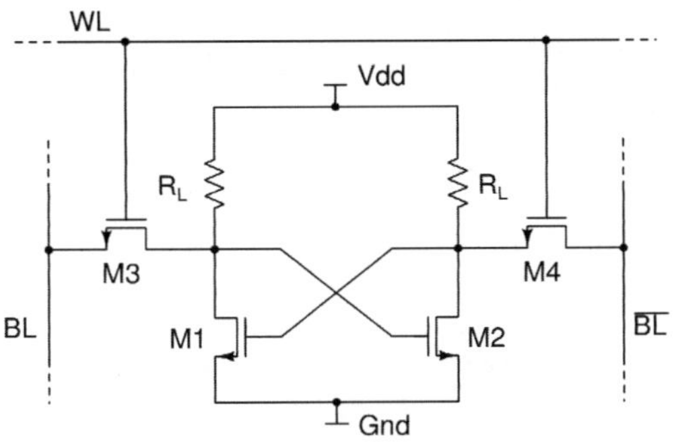

Figure 4. 4T SRAM cell

The 4T (polysilicon) SRAM is a predecessor of all CMOS-based SRAM cells. Lower stability, lower tolerance against soft-errors and a more technically demanding manufacturing process exclude this cell type from further considerations [6].

2) 5T SRAM cell: The circuitry of a five transistor SRAM cell is shown in Figure 5. The advantage of this cell design compared to the 6T reference cell is the availability of just one access transistor $M5$ and therefore only one bitline BL [17]. The connecting bitlines in each slice of an FPGA add undesired parasitic capacitances, which underly the process of charging and discharging during each read- and write-cycle and lead subsequently to higher power consumption. A cell design working with just one access transistor adds space-savings. For a proper and stable functionality of this cell, asymmetric transistor sizing is required, which may complicate the manufacturing process and to modifications of auxiliary circuitry like sense amplifiers, precharge circuits, etc..

3) 7T SRAM cell: The seven transistor SRAM cell is shown in Figure 6, which enhances the 6T reference cell design by an additional feedback transistor $M7$ and 2 signal lines R and W. The idea behind this design is a write mechanism, which depends only on one of the two bitlines in order to execute a write operation. This can be also expressed in equation (3) [12].

While the activity factor α equals 1 in conventional memory cells, the 7T SRAM cell reduces this factor to less than 0.5 by exploiting the fact, that most of the bits in memories and caches are zeros [8]. The main asset of this implementation is

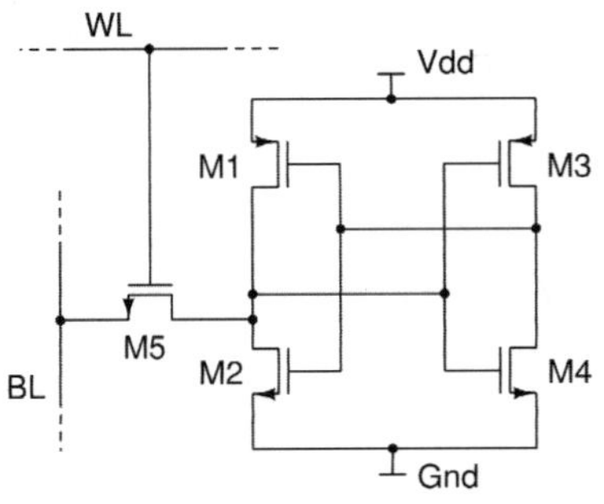

Figure 5. 5T SRAM cell

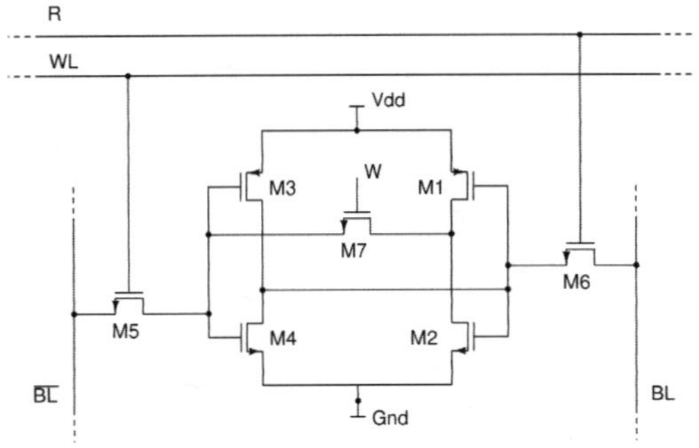

Figure 6. 7T SRAM cell

the reduction of the switching activity and therefore a reduction of charging and discharging cycles of parasitic capacitances. The drawback is the required additional control logic and the loopback transistor, which lead to higher complexity and required space.

$$P = \alpha C_{BL} V^2 F_{write} \tag{3}$$

V. SRAM Cell design modifications

The simulation results showed that the choice of a suitable SRAM cell design leads to a significant impact on power consumption of a LUT. In this section we present further improvements on each cell design in order to achieve even better power savings in this essential component. Since Xilinx' Spartan 3(A) is manufactured in a 90nm process and has a recommended internal supply voltage of $1.2V$, we choose a 90nm TSMC technology library at an comparable operating voltage of $1.2V$.

Coming back to the proposed cell designs in Section IV, we refer to the 4T SRAM cell since its compact design is of interest for further considerations and performance comparison to other design. The major drawback of the 4T SRAM cell is the high-resistive polysilicon resistor, which should be replaced or completely omitted in an improved cell. A possibility how to bypass this drawback is shown in Figure 7.

The previous pull-down network (PDN) consisting of two nMOS transistors is replaced by a pull-up network of two pMOS $M1$ and $M2$ transistors [18]. In combination with both nMOS access transistors $M3$ and $M4$ a stable and power saving functionality is achieved. Instead of precharging both

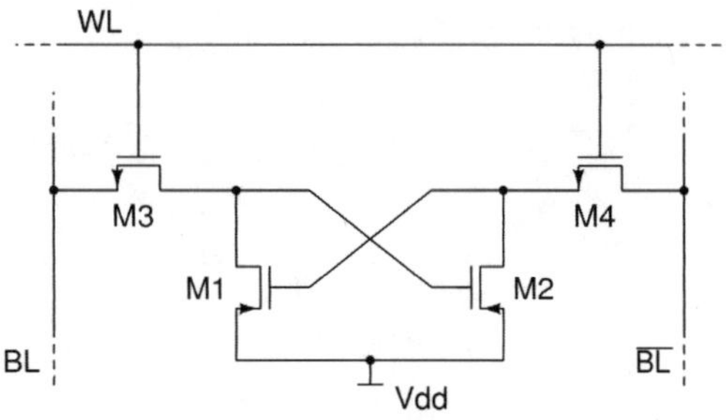

Figure 7. 4T loadless SRAM cell

bitlines to V_{dd} as a pre-step of the reading-phase, the bitlines are "precharged" to Gnd, due to the fact that pMOS transistor are used as drivers in this cell. This saves power and ensures compatibility with CMOS logic processes. Nevertheless, minor adaptions to the auxiliary circuitry around the cell have to be done, e.g., modifying the bitline drivers.

A. Test results

All SRAM cells have been designed and simulated by usage of the Cadence toolchain and a 90*nm* technology provided by TSMC at an ambient temperature of 27°C. The main challenge to achieve comparable results was to develop suitable bitline drivers, precharge circuitry and a sense amplfier. Careful design of the bitline drivers is crucial for avoiding the cell to flip during a read cycle. All simulations are performed with a clock frequency of 200*MHz* and a load of 600*aF*. Configuration memory cells used in a LUT are not supposed to be written and read at high frequencies, like, e.g., memory arrays in a microprocessor's cache (up to 4*GHz*). Therefore, we choose a lower frequency, nevertheless all cells have also been successfully tested with a higher clock frequency of 500*MHz*. All cell designs have been applied to the test circuit in Figure 8.

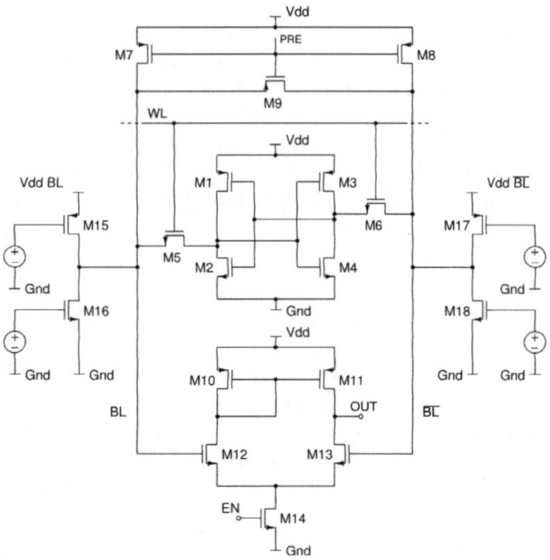

Figure 8. Test circuit

Figure 8 shows a 6T SRAM cell as DUT (design under test), the precharge circuit consisting of transistors $M7$, $M8$ and an equalizing transistor $M9$, two bitline drivers ($M15$, $M16$ and $M17$, $M18$) a sense amplifier. For the first step, the determination of the best SRAM cell design in terms of power consumption without any further improvements, is done. The simulation results of the 6T cell design are shown in Figure 9.

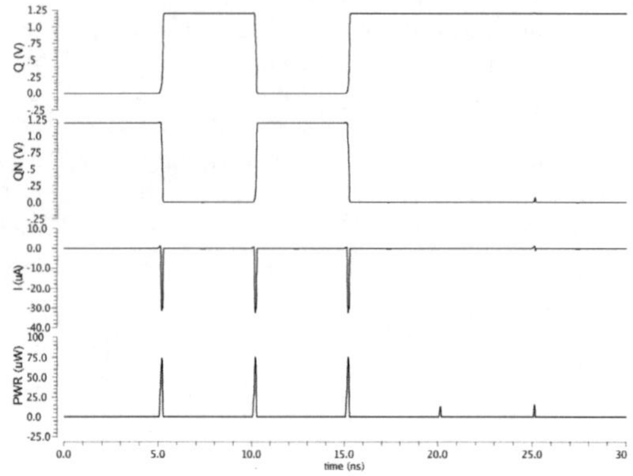

Figure 9. Power dissipation and I_{Leak} of 6T SRAM cell

The average power consumption, the maximum and minimum power consumption during simulation time were traced and summarized in Table II.

TABLE II. SIMULATION RESULTS WITHOUT MODIFICATIONS

SRAM cell	*Average Power nW*	*Max. Power uW*	*Min. Power pW*
4T	334.5	35.07	161.7
5T	587.2	61.26	217.34
6T	927	75.39	250.8
7T	491	49.19	221.7

Compared to the other designs, Table II shows clearly the drawbacks of the reference 6T SRAM cell. Substantial power savings can be achieved by the choice of alternative cell design. For example, the average power consumption of the 6T SRAM reference cell design is 927*nW* and about 3 times higher than the average power consumption of the 4T loadless SRAM cell, which is only $334.5nW$. That results in power savings of approximately 65%.

B. Dual Threshold CMOS

Further optimizations can be achieved by the introduction of high threshold voltage (V_{th}) transistors. High V_{th} transistors require a higher V_{GS} voltage at the gate in order to turn the transistor on, which can lead to an increase of the propagation delay within a signal path. Therefore, high V_{th} should be only used in applications which are not timing-critical. However, the SRAM cells in a LUT are used as configuration RAM (CRAM) and are pertinent for use with high threshold voltage transistors. All cell designs have been modified and the simulations were performed again. These modifications are limited to the core cell only, the precharge circuitry, the sense amplifier and the bitline drivers have not been modified. The results are summed up in Table III.

TABLE III. SIMULATION RESULTS WITH HIGH THRESHOLD VOLTAGE TRANSISTORS (hvt)

SRAM cell	*Average Power nW*	*Max. Power uW*	*Min. Power pW*
4T hvt	324	31.83	74.99
5T hvt	541.78	54.9	130.5
6T hvt	695.1	64.46	158.3
7T hvt	427	36.21	161.9

In comparison to the reference design of the 6T SRAM cell, the introduction of the high V_{th} transistors adds power savings of about 25%. The performance of the high V_{th} 4T loadless SRAM cell is slightly improved and leads to energy savings of approximately $10nW$. In general, we can say that this modification improves both, the maximum and minimum energy consumption of all introduced cells. For illustration purposes, these improvements are shown in Figure 10 and Figure 11.

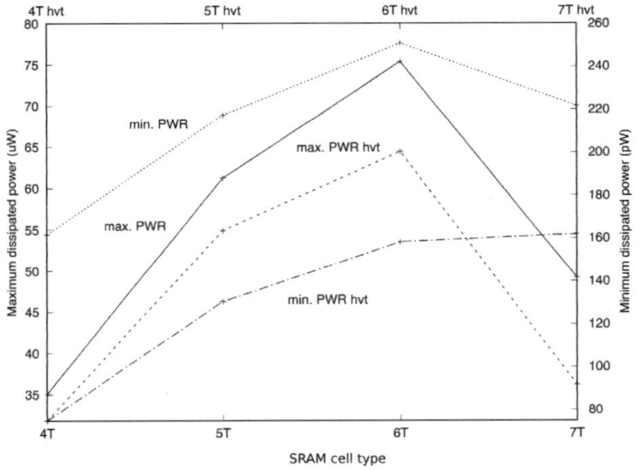

Figure 10. Comparison of minimum and maximum PWR dissipation between standard and high V_{th} designs

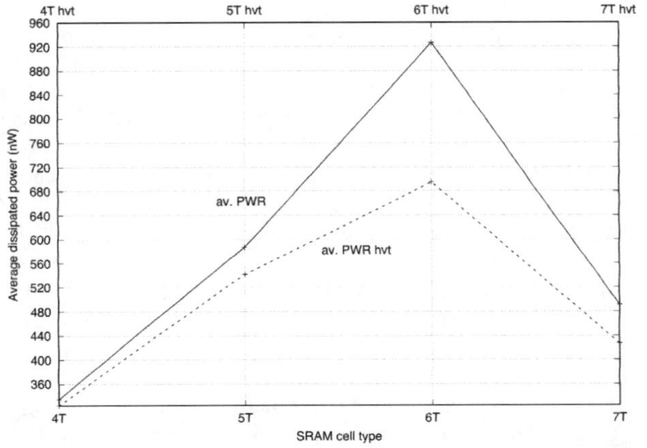

Figure 11. Comparison of average PWR dissipation between standard and high V_{th} designs

Since the 4T loadless SRAM cells offers an excellent out of the box power balance, the strongest impact of the first optimizing steps can be primarily noticed on all previously already existing designs, especially the 6T SRAM cell. Independent from the respective implementation, each exploited measurement is positively influenced by the modification done in a step before.

C. Transistor Stacking

Transistor stacking, shown in Figure 12, which is also known as self-reverse biasing, is a strong technique to reduce subthreshold leakage current by raising the voltage at the source terminal of each transistor. By constantly increasing the source voltage V_S and keeping the gate voltage V_G at the same level, V_{GS} becomes negative at a certain point of time, which leads the transistor into super cut-off mode and turns it deeply off. Subthreshold currents are exponentially reduced.

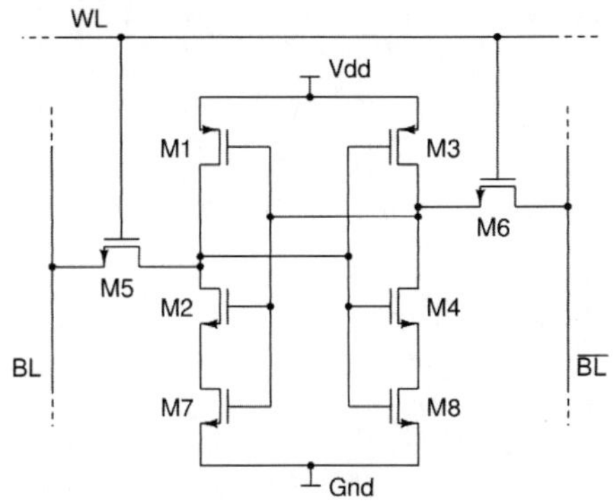

Figure 12. 6T SRAM cell with stacking

At the same time, the body to source potential V_{SB} also becomes negative, since the body terminal of a nMOS transistor is usually kept at Gnd. In consequence, the body effect is intensified, thus V_{th} is tuned by that effect to a higher level. This fact can be further exploited by continuing stacking transistors in series, but the effect of subthreshold current reduction becomes diminished with a rising number of transistors. This technique implies a trade-off between power savings and size ratio of the chip. Despite the gradual technology shrink up to $16nm$ FinFET, on-chip space is not an unlimited resource and should be used carefully. Therefore, we choose to add two stacking transistors only in order to have a reasonable compromise between leakage current reduction and size-ratio of the cells. The simulation results are shown in Table IV and Table V.

TABLE IV. SIMULATION RESULTS WITH STANDARD TRANSISTORS AND STACKING

SRAM cell	*Average Power nW*	*Max. Power uW*	*Min. Power pW*
4T	346.8	35.31	137.6
5T	327.4	25.1	189.4
6T	826.6	72.05	274
7T	540.4	31.64	168.3

If the used manufacturing process does not support dual-threshold CMOS technology, Table IV shows that a noteworthy reduction of leakage currents within the 4T SRAM cell is achieved by approximately 90%. Even the standard 6T SRAM

TABLE V. SIMULATION RESULTS WITH hvt TRANSISTORS AND STACKING

SRAM cell	*Average Power nW*	*Max. Power uW*	*Min. Power pW*
4T hvt	336.6	32.79	70.42
5T hvt	327.4	25.1	189.4
6T hvt	672.4	61.28	167.4
7T hvt	461.8	30.84	523.9

cell features important amendments in terms of power savings ($\approx 12\%$) and leakage currents.

The combination of both techniques, dual-threshold CMOS and transistor stacking, puts additional improvements to the overall power savings parameters. Since most of the currently available technologies feature dual-threshold CMOS, the feasibility of this combination is high.

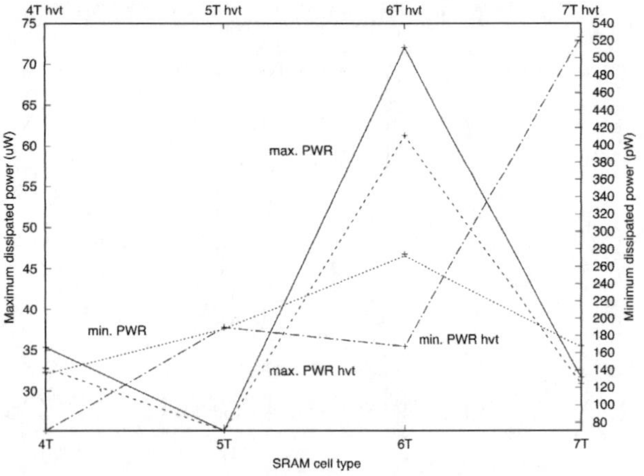

Figure 13. Comparison of minimum and maximum PWR dissipation between standard and high V_{th} designs with stacking

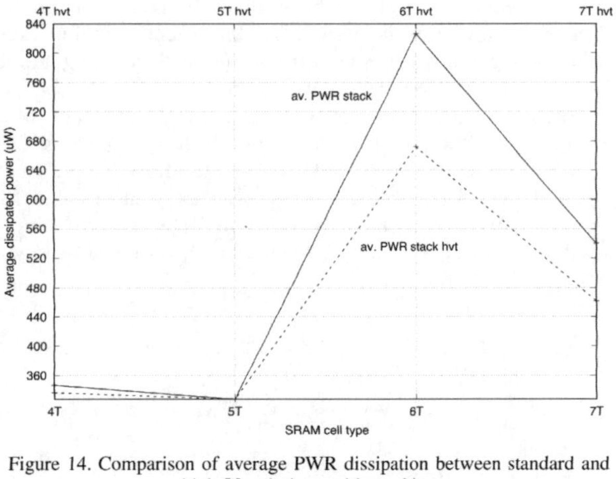

Figure 14. Comparison of average PWR dissipation between standard and high V_{th} designs with stacking

Figure 13 and Figure 14 display different characteristics of the consumed power by referring to the values of Table IV and V. The 5T SRAM offers a slight advantage compared to the 4T loadless SRAM design due higher active and standby intrinsic power consumption of less transistors when applying stacking to a logic design. Nevertheless, the 4T loadless SRAM cell still performs better than the remaining memory circuits. Another interesting aspect to be considered is the signal to noise ratio, which gives a benchmark about the margin between the transferred signal or stored data inside a memory cell and the influence of background noise on the signal lines, which can not be neglected. This factor is even of higher significance when volatile memory cells are equipped with high V_{th} transistors, replacing their standard V_{th} counterparts. To investigate potential undesirable side effects on the intended functionality, Figure 15 shows the butterfly plots of two 6T SRAM implementations, each realized with high and standard V_{th} transistors. It can be seen that this modification has a small impact on the signal to noise margin, but this is still acceptable due to predominant benefits in terms of power savings.

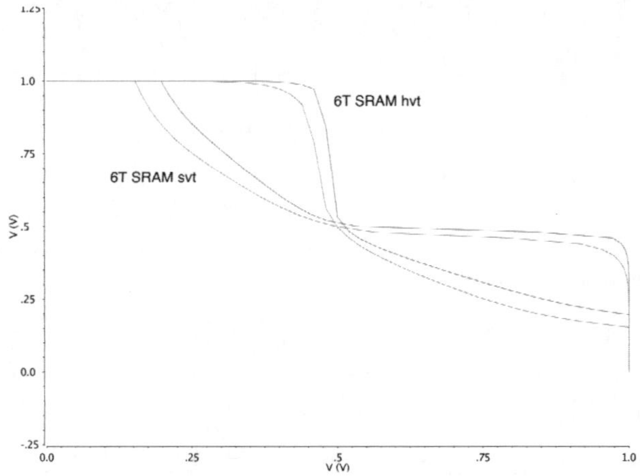

Figure 15. Butterfly plots of 2 different 6T SRAM implementations

D. Dynamic Voltage Scaling

The higher the supply voltage is, the faster the operation of the integrated circuit will be, since high V_{dd} allows fast charging and discharging of parasitic capacitances. In case of low demand on performance such as for CRAMs, the supply voltage can be lowered while still ensuring data retention within the cell. Dynamic voltage scaling (DVS) depends usually at least on an operating system and a regulation loop to recognize the circuit speed and to cover a wide range of operating voltages. Our approach simplifies this principle by introducing two additional transistors, shown in Figure 16.

Both transistors $M9$ and $M10$ are used to connect the SRAM cell to two different supply voltages, V_{dd} and V_{ddL}, whereas V_{dd} equals the primary $1.2V$. On the one hand, the prerequisite of this method is a dual-V_{dd} setup, representing a simple alternative to the mentioned operating system driven regulation loop, and on the other hand, a modified power gating approach is implemented. Since the 4T SRAM cell has no connection to Gnd in its core, power gating is achieved by the possibility to fully cut-off the supply voltage, if needed. However, power gating should be introduced at a coarse-grain level, e.g., by powering or switching off groups of cells at a higher abstraction layer. By lowering the supply voltage to V_{ddL}, which equals $1V$, we can further reduce leakage

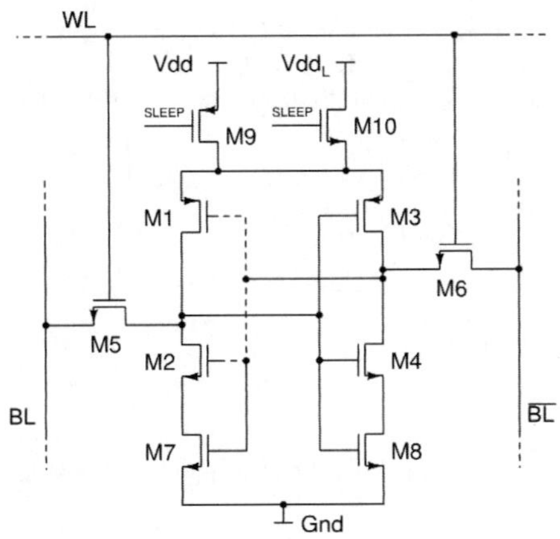

Figure 16. 6T SRAM cell with hvt transistors, stacking and DVS

power consumption. Experimental results have shown that data retention will still be ensured at supply voltages down to $400mV$. A combination of all three power saving mechanisms in a 6T SRAM cell is shown in Figure 16.

TABLE VI. SIMULATION RESULTS WITH hvt TRANSISTORS, STACKING AND DVS

SRAM cell	*Average Power nW*	*Max. Power uW*	*Min. Power pW*
4T hvt	232.9	21.27	49.59
5T hvt	327.4	25.1	189.4
6T hvt	458.7	44.67	166.1
7T hvt	368.3	26.53	167

In order to achieve an average power consumption of $232.9nW$ at a clock requency of $200MHz$ and full data retention like shown in Table VI, we combined all three power saving methods introduced in the chapters before with careful transistor sizing of an efficient memory cell design. We present the modified, loadless 4T SRAM cell in Figure 17.

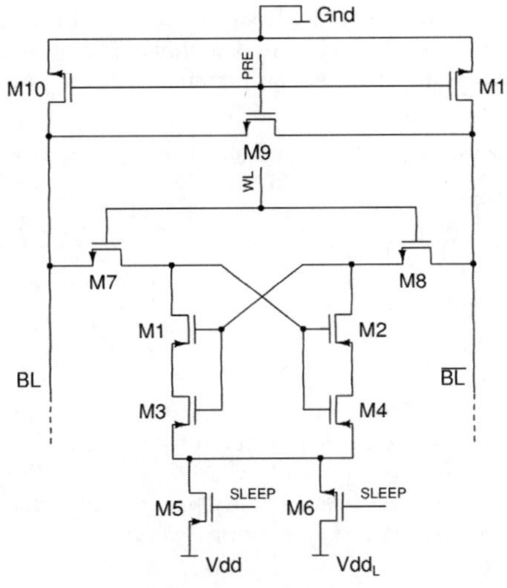

Figure 17. Modified 4T SRAM cell

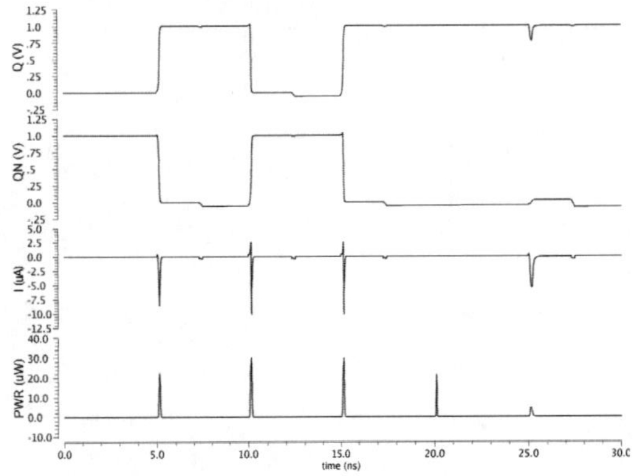

Figure 18. Power dissipation and I_{Leak} of a modified 4T SRAM cell

The simulation was done by injecting a $1 \rightarrow 0 \rightarrow 1$ sequence and one read cycle at the end of the simulation time, which can be seen in Figure 18. By comparing the results of Figure 18 with the outputs shown in Figure 9, we see a reduction in both, power and current spikes. Looking back on the continuous improvements added to each cell type, we see the benefits in reduction of average power consumption in Figure 19.

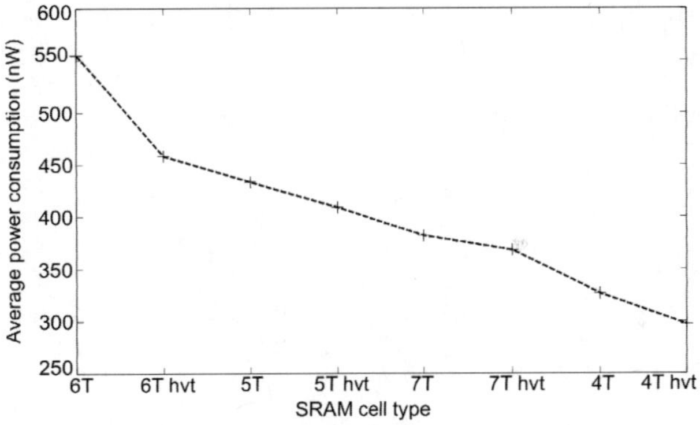

Figure 19. Power dissipation reduction

Analogue to the previous sections and in terms of a good overview, all results from Table VI are displayed in Figure 20. For highlighting the effects of all applied modifications, the simulation plots of all original designs are added to the same Figure.

Figure 20 and Figure 21 underline the numbers in Table VI. Both illustrations, especially Figure 21, clearly depict the advantages of combining an SRAM cell design with inherent power efficiency and appropriate modifications for even better energy savings in applications with limited resources.

VI. LUT SIMULATIONS

The LUT was implemented with each cell type investigated in the previous chapters. In order to achieve an equal distribution of bits, all memory cells have alternating bits stored and are not connected to the bitlines by switching off all access transistors. As a matter of lucidity, we present a comparison

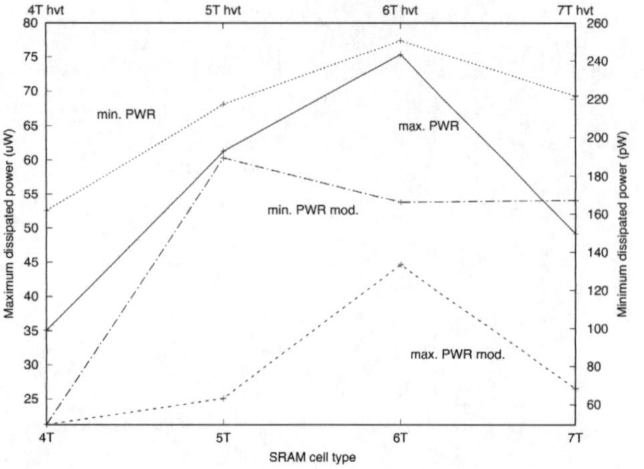

Figure 20. Comparison of minimum and maximum power dissipation between original and modified cell designs

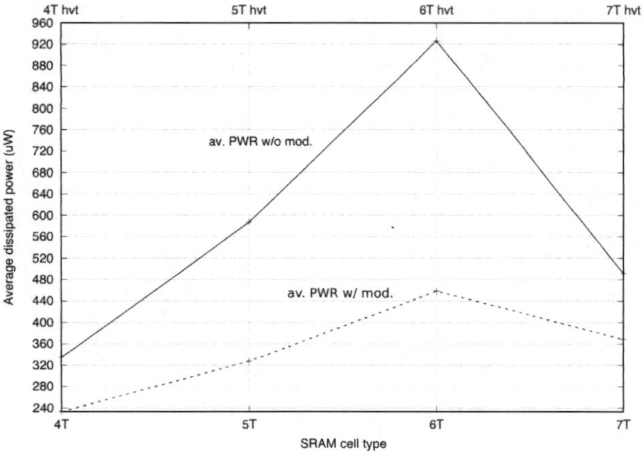

Figure 21. Comparison of average power dissipation between original and modified cell designs

between the 6T SRAM- and 4T SRAM LUT implementation. As expected, the 4T SRAM cell design shows a better performance in terms of power savings and leakage current reduction than the 6T SRAM cell design does. By comparing a LUT implementation with a standard 6T SRAM cell and our modified 4T SRAM design, Table VII summarizes the results and highlights the improvements in power dissipation, which equals power savings of approximately 16%. Figure 22 shows the related leakage current of the 4T SRAM based LUT.

TABLE VII. LUT COMPARISON

SRAM cell	*Average PWR nW*	*Max. PWR uW*	*Min. PWR nW*	*Energy aJ*
4T hvt	424.2	40.94	0.24	127
6T	500	42.99	2.8	150

It should be mentioned that either the precharge circuit nor the sense amplifier have been optimized for power efficiency. Optimizing these parts will lead to even better results and raise the duration of a battery charge, independent of the target application. Further optimization can be achieved by coarse-grain power gating of CRAM blocks within the LUT architecture. Unused CRAMs should be completely powered off by adding additional, thick-oxide transistors, cutting off the cell from V_{dd} and Gnd.

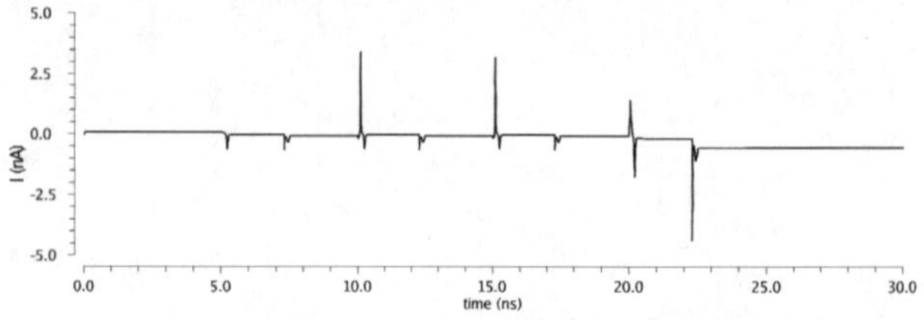

Figure 22. Leakage current of an improved 4T SRAM based LUT

The modified 4T memory cell design introduced in Figure 17 is superior in terms of low power aspects compared to all other investigated cell designs. However, this solution requires additional space, since it requires at least four additional transistors to achieve its intended power-efficient functionality.

VII. Timing Considerations

Despite the fact that timing aspects play a minor role for volatile memory cells used for configuring LUTs, a closer investigation of, e.g., the maximum operating frequency f_{max} is helpful to sound the limits of these circuits for their intended usage. In special cases like critical real time calculations, fast reconfigurability of an programmable logic device may be a inevitable requirement. This maximum operating frequency can be determined by (4):

$$f_{max} = \frac{1}{t_{HL} + t_{LH}} \quad (4)$$

The summands t_{HL} and t_{LH} display the time necessary for a *HIGH* $\rightarrow$ *LOW* and *LOW* $\rightarrow$ *HIGH* transition respectively. Figure 23 shows a typical $1 \rightarrow 0$ switching event with additional measurement marks at 90% and 10% of the supply voltage V_{dd}, including the Δ of time, which is considered to be t_{HL}. All considered SRAM cells have been investigated upon these characteristics and compared against each other. The correspondent results are summarized in Table VIII.

TABLE VIII. TRANSITION TIMES AND MAXIMUM OPERATION FREQUENCY

SRAM cell	*time LH ps*	*time HL ps*	*Max. freq. GHz*
4T hvt	40.22	38.74	12.66
5T hvt	58.24	132.41	5.25
6T hvt	102.53	60.7	6.12
7T hvt	62.47	380.87	2.25

The results reveal the superior performance of the 4T loadless SRAM in terms of elapsed time for both t_{HL} and t_{LH}. In direct comparison to the reference 6T SRAM cell, we achieve an improvement of $\approx 60\%$ for the *LOW* $\rightarrow$ *HIGH* transition. The improvement for the complementary operation *HIGH* $\rightarrow$ *LOW* is less, but energy savings of $\approx 36\%$ are still noteworthy.

For having a better overview about the different slew rates and maximum operating frequencies, all results were visualized in Figure 24. The 4T loadless SRAM cell outperforms the

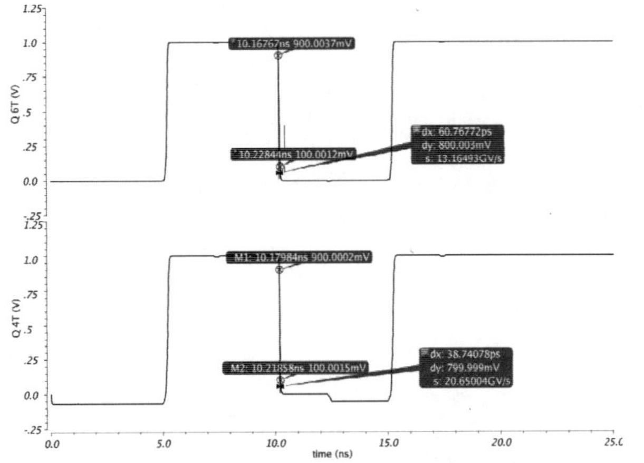

Figure 23. 4T & 6T SRAM HIGH LOW transition

other cells in each considered aspects. The maximum operating frequency gives an impression about the capabilities of this newly developed cell to be used for calculations in critical real time environments. It should be mentioned, that this designed was not optimized for short channel effect suppression. The recent proceedings in process technology lead to a continuous design shrink, which come along with a significantly higher yield in manufacturing. The downside of these achievements are undesirable physical effects, e.g., the short channel effect. The smaller the channel length becomes, the higher leakage currents in standby mode will be, due to tunneling effects of electrons from drain to source even without establishing a steady voltage $V_{GS} > V_{th}$ at the gate of a transistor.

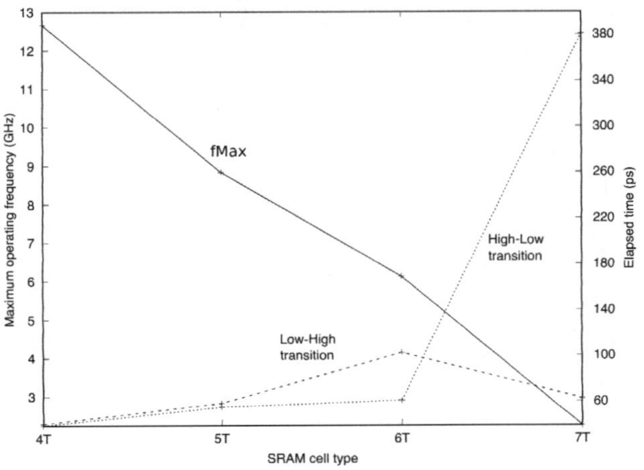

Figure 24. Slew rates and f_{max}

VIII. Conclusion

We analyzed a typical LUT structure of an FPGA in terms of power dissipation and leakage current. Our approach was to integrate power savings mechanisms at the basic circuit level before heading for further optimizations on architectural level. Different SRAM cell structures have been investigated on their power characteristics in order to evaluate the best design for implementing a LUT, which features inherent low-power characteristics. Simulations have shown that the 4T loadless SRAM cell features the required properties. We applied various low-power techniques and enhanced this cell for standby leakage current mitigation. Hence, we presented a modified 4T loadless SRAM cell design. By combining dedicated techniques during design time and during operating time, we achieved a reduction of the average power consumption within the LUT of 16% during simulation time. Subsequently, this leads to overall energy savings of $127aJ$ compared to the origin $150aJ$ of a 6T SRAM cell based LUT implementation. The leakage current I_{leak} is reduced dramatically from $1.741nA$ to approximately $0.2nA$, showing the strong impact of leakage reduction methods on power-critical circuitry. On the other hand, the 4T loadless SRAM design offers very fast reconfiguration capabilities due to its remarkably high top operating frequency f_{max} above $12GHz$, which outperforms the alternative designs significantly. This goes back to a good slew rate for each of both transitions during signal processing. The overall performance of this design could be further enhanced be careful adaption of the gate length to catch up disadvantages in terms of short channel effects. It can be predicted that this measure would further decrease standby leakage current I_{leak}, but it would automatically lead to increasing the width of the transistors to avoid any penalties in speed. This would be acceptable if area considerations do not play a role, which is rather unlikely due to a preferable high yield at the end of a semiconductor manufacturing process. All identified and investigated pros come along at the cost of certain adaptions to peripheral circuitry, e.g., the sense amplifier, which needs to be redesigned for the usage with this newly developed memory design. Additional wiring for the DVS transistors is required which is synonymous with more parasitic capacitances and area consumption. These challenges have to be faced during layout phase after synthesis and strongly depend on the chosen process node. Since registers and GPIOs occupy a large amount of area in FPGAs, further power savings can be achieved by adapting the architecture of these circuits. This will be addressed in future publications.

FPGAs support adaptiveness of whole systems by re-configuration abilities on demand of the respective application. The presented low-power cell design reduces power consumption significantly during the charging and discharging cycles of re-configuration tasks within an FPGA and delivers an overall good performance leading to an appropriate suitability for mobile low power applications.

Acknowledgment

The authors thank Amit Majumdar, from Xilinx, for his support and interesting discussions on FPGA architectures. Also, we want to give credit to Ray Chiang, from TSMC, for his explanations and suggestions on the used technology. We are grateful to Andreas Ullrich, from University of Wuppertal, for his restless dedication in PDK compilation and tool maintenance.

REFERENCES

[1] K. Niewiadomski, C. Gremzow, and D. Tutsch, "4t loadless srams for low power fpga lut optimization," in Proceedings of the 9th International Conference on Adaptive and Self-Adaptive Systems and Applications (ADAPTIVE 2017), February 2017, pp. 1–7.

[2] S. Fürst, "Challenges in the design of automotive software," in Proceedings of the Conference on Design, Automation and Test in Europe, ser. DATE '10. 3001 Leuven, Belgium, Belgium: European Design and Automation Association, 2010, pp. 256–258, last accessed on 2017-11-13. [Online]. Available: http://dl.acm.org/citation.cfm?id=1870926.1870987

[3] XA Spartan-3A Automotive FPGA Family Data Sheet, Xilinx, 04 2011, rev. 2.0.

[4] M. Ullmann, M. Hübner, B. Grimm, and J. Becker, "An fpga run-time system for dynamical on-demand reconfiguration," in Parallel and Distributed Processing Symposium, 2004. Proceedings. 18th International. IEEE, 2004, p. 135.

[5] R. Anthony, A. Rettberg, D. Chen, I. Jahnich, G. de Boer, and C. Ekelin, "Towards a dynamically reconfigurable automotive control system architecture," in Embedded System Design: Topics, Techniques and Trends. Springer, 2007, pp. 71–84.

[6] A. S. Pavlov, "Design and Test of Embedded SRAMs," Ph.D. dissertation, University of Waterloo, Ontario, May 2005.

[7] J. P. Uyemura, CMOS Logic Circuit Design. Norwell, MA, USA: Kluwer Academic Publishers, 1999.

[8] R. E. Aly, M. I. Faisal, and M. A. Bayoumi, "Novel 7t sram cell for low power cache design," in Proceedings 2005 IEEE International SOC Conference, Sept 2005, pp. 171–174.

[9] S. M. Jahinuzzaman, D. J. Rennie, and M. Sachdev, "A soft error tolerant 10t sram bit-cell with differential read capability," IEEE Transactions on Nuclear Science, vol. 56, no. 6, Dec 2009, pp. 3768–3773.

[10] A. Lodi, L. Ciccarelli, D. Loparco, R. Canegallo, and R. Guerrieri, "Low leakage design of lut-based fpgas," in Proceedings of the 31st European Solid-State Circuits Conference, 2005. ESSCIRC 2005., Sept 2005, pp. 153–156.

[11] T. Tuan, S. Kao, A. Rahman, S. Das, and S. Trimberger, "A 90nm low-power fpga for battery-powered applications," in Proceedings of the 2006 ACM/SIGDA 14th international symposium on Field programmable gate arrays. ACM, 2006, pp. 3–11.

[12] J. M. Rabaey, A. Chandrakasan, and B. Nikolic, Digital integrated circuits- A design perspective, 2nd ed. Prentice Hall, 2004.

[13] C. Piguet, Low-power processors and systems on chips. CRC Press, 2005.

[14] C. Maxfield, The Design Warrior's Guide to FPGAs: Devices, Tools and Flows, 1st ed. Newton, MA, USA: Newnes, 2004.

[15] K. Itoh, VLSI Memory Chip Design, ser. Springer Series in Advanced Microelectronics. Springer Berlin Heidelberg, 2001, last accessed on 2017-11-13. [Online]. Available: https://books.google.de/books?id=p2FsQgAACAAJ

[16] A. Bellaouar and M. I. Elmasry, Low-Power Digital VLSI Design Circuits and Systems, 1st ed., J. Allen, Ed. Norwell, MA, USA: Kluwer Academic Publishers, 1995.

[17] I. Carlson, S. Andersson, S. Natarajan, and A. Alvandpour, "A high density, low leakage, 5t sram for embedded caches," in Solid-State Circuits Conference, 2004. ESSCIRC 2004. Proceeding of the 30th European, Sept 2004, pp. 215–218.

[18] J. Yang and L. Chen, "A new loadless 4-transistor sram cell with a 0.18 m cmos technology," in 2007 Canadian Conference on Electrical and Computer Engineering, April 2007, pp. 538–541.

Insights on a Low-Cost Recursive Least-Squares Algorithm for Adaptive Noise Cancellation

Roxana Mihăescu, Cristian Stanciu, Cristian Anghel, Lucian Stanciu
Politehnica University of Bucharest, Romania
Email: roxana.2010.mihaescu@gmail.com
{cristian, canghel, lucians}@comm.pub.ro

***Abstract*—Adaptive Noise Cancellation (ANC) belongs to the interference cancellation class. It employs an adaptive filter to estimate a perturbation signal, which corrupts a primary acoustic source. In most of the corresponding applications, the goal is to imitate an original speech signal. This paper proposes the use of a low-complexity recursive least-squares (RLS) adaptive algorithm for the ANC procedure. The combination between the RLS method and the dichotomous coordinate descent (DCD) iterations offers good performance with acceptable arithmetic costs. Simulation results are provided in order to demonstrate the validity of the ANC system based on the RLS-DCD adaptive algorithm.**

Keywords: adaptive noise cancellation; recursive least-squares; dichotomous coordinate descent.

I. Introduction

Modern technology allows the deployment of telecommunication networks in challenging environments, which frequently introduce strong acoustic interference. The high-quality communication performed in extremely noisy surroundings, such as airplane cockpits or social gatherings, requires the real-time estimation of corrupted acoustic signals (usually speech sequences).

With the development of adaptive algorithms, the field of Adaptive Noise Cancellation (ANC) has also been the subject of intensive study [1]-[3]. The workhorse of signal processing systems employing adaptive methods is the Least Mean Squares (LMS) family [2]-[6]. Although the classical LMS adaptive algorithms were improved to a certain degree, their performances are limited when working with highly correlated signals. A new generation of efficiently implementable adaptive systems is required in order to increase the noise cancellation capabilities.

The standard recursive least-squares (RLS) adaptive methods have attractive convergence properties [2]-[6]. However, the classical solutions for directly solving the corresponding matrix inversion problem have high arithmetic complexities and require large amounts of computational resources. Moreover, the implementations employing the traditional RLS algorithms suffer from occasional numeric instability caused by higher order arithmetical operations, such as divisions. Although the Fast RLS (FRLS) [5] considerably reduces the arithmetic effort, it is not stable when working with nonstationary signals, such as speech.

In [7]-[9], the prohibitive nature of the RLS methods was approached using the combination with the dichotomous coordinate descent (DCD) iterations. The DCD part of the algorithm replaces the classical matrix inversion problem with an auxiliary system of equations, which is solved using only additions and bit-shifts. The solution is based on the statistical properties of the input signals and reduces the overall arithmetic complexity to a value proportional to L, which is used to denote the adaptive filter's length. The resulting RLS-DCD algorithm is a numerically stable alternative, offering comparable results in terms of adaptation speed and precision, with a considerably reduced computational effort [7]-[11]. By comparison, the classical RLS method has a complexity of $O(L^3)$, which can be reduced using Woodburry's identity to $O(L^2)$ – both methods are considered unaffordable for practical applications [2][5].

The original RLS-DCD solution was rarely tested with colored signals, such as speech sequences [8], [9]. It was later effectively applied for stereophonic acoustic echo cancelation (SAEC) setups requiring the estimation of multiple unknown systems [10]. This paper proposes the use of the RLS-DCD method for ANC systems employed in real-time recovery of speech signals. A theoretical model is presented and tested using different types of acoustic interference, with low Signal-to-Noise Ratio (SNR). Although the number of adaptive filter coefficients associated with ANC applications is lower than the case of acoustic echo cancellation (AEC) scenarios, the reduction in terms of arithmetic workload (in comparison to the classical RLS) is valuable for mobile devices (i.e., headphones, mobile phones, etc.). As a consequence, the compromise between arithmetic complexity and performance is analyzed, and a comparison is performed with the standard RLS.

The paper is organized as follows. In Section II, the theoretical model of the ANC setup is defined. Section III describes a new approach on the theory associated with RLS adaptive algorithms and Section IV introduces a low-complexity RLS-type method, which is suitable for acoustic applications, such as the ANC. The performances of the proposed adaptive method are demonstrated using simulations in Section V. The standard RLS adaptive algorithm is employed as a reference. Finally, in Section VI, a few conclusions are stated regarding the compromise between arithmetic complexity and the performance of the ANC system using a low-complexity RLS method.

II. System Model

Figure 1 illustrates the ANC scheme. By using the notation n for the discrete time index, we denote the *desired* signal $d(n)$ as the accumulation between the relevant signal $s(n)$ and the corrupting sequence $q(n)$ (also called the *interference* signal). The *input* of the adaptive algorithm $x(n)$ is a *reference* signal, which is linearly correlated with the interference $q(n)$. In literature, the relation between $x(n)$ and $q(n)$ is usually modelled through a finite impulse response (FIR) filter, which generates $q(n)$ using $x(n)$ as the input. In practical ANC applications, the samples corresponding to $x(n)$ and $d(n)$ are available through microphones [3]. The influence of the physical distance between the two acoustic sensors is represented in Figure 1 through the delay factor D, which is associated with the length of the mentioned FIR filter.

The purpose of the ANC system is to generate an estimate $y(n)$ of $q(n)$ (using the adaptive filter) and subtract it from the desired signal. Consequently, the error signal $e(n)$ is an estimate of s(n), i.e., $e(n) \rightarrow s(n)$. The *error* of the adaptive algorithm is used to adjust the coefficients of the adaptive filter in order to minimize the noise interference. In an optimal situation, $e(n)$ is composed of the signal $s(n)$, free of the noise interference $q(n)$.

For the theoretical model of the adaptive algorithm we denote by $\hat{\mathbf{h}}(n)$ the L x 1 vector comprising the adaptive filter's variable coefficients at time index n, i.e.,

$$\hat{\mathbf{h}}(n) = \left[h_0(n), h_1(n), ..., h_{L-1}(n)\right]^T, \tag{1}$$

where ^{T} is the transpose of a matrix/vector. The output of the filter $y(n)$ is generated by performing the convolution between $\hat{\mathbf{h}}(n-1)$ and the L dimensional vector $\mathbf{x}(n)$ formed with the most recent input samples:

$$\mathbf{x}(n) = \left[x(n), x(n-1), ..., x(n-L+1)\right]^T. \tag{2}$$

Consequently, the error signal can be expressed as:

$$e(n) = d(n) - y(n) = d(n) - \hat{\mathbf{h}}^T(n-1)\mathbf{x}(n). \tag{3}$$

The core of the ANC system presented in Figure 1 is the adaptive algorithm. The usual methods employed for the update of $\hat{\mathbf{h}}(n)$ are the LMS-type adaptive algorithms, which have reduced performance when working with highly correlated input signals. In the ANC case, the samples of signal $x(n)$ can be associated with speech, music, engine noise or other (highly correlated) acoustic signals. In such circumstances, the RLS-based systems can generate superior performance (in comparison to the LMS class) through their de-correlation properties. Despite the attractive features of the RLS algorithms, the classical versions employ arithmetically costly methods for computing the corresponding matrix inverse and solving the associated system of equations. Consequently, excessive workloads are imposed on signal processing chips, which usually handle multiple tasks.

III. A Different Approach on the RLS Algorithm

The RLS-DCD adaptive algorithm was proposed as a stable alternative for other low-complexity RLS versions (such as the FRLS). Initially, the method was mostly employed for processing weakly correlated signals and later for the identification of long unknown acoustic systems (e.g., the AEC/SAEC scenarios) [7]-[11]. The corresponding least-squares cost function is defined as:

$$J(n) = \sum_{i=0}^{n} \lambda^{n-i}\left[d(i) - \hat{\mathbf{h}}^T(n)\mathbf{x}(i)\right]^2, \tag{4}$$

where we denote by λ $(0 << \lambda < 1)$ the forgetting factor associated with the memory of the algorithm [1]. The minimization of $J(n)$ requires the solution to the normal equations [2], [3]:

$$\mathbf{R}_x(n)\hat{\mathbf{h}}(n) = \mathbf{p}_{xd}(n), \tag{5}$$

where $\mathbf{R}_x(n)$ is the L x L correlation matrix of the input signal and $\mathbf{p}_{xd}(n)$ is an L x 1 vector. The matrix $\mathbf{R}_x(n)$ and vector $\mathbf{p}_{xd}(n)$ are known for every iteration of the adaptive filter and can be expressed recursively using the forgetting factor:

$$\mathbf{R}_x(n) = \sum_{i=0}^{n} \lambda^{n-i}\mathbf{x}(i)\mathbf{x}^T(i) = \lambda\mathbf{R}_x(n-1) + \mathbf{x}(n)\mathbf{x}^T(n), \tag{6}$$

$$\mathbf{p}_{xd}(n) = \sum_{i=0}^{n} \lambda^{n-i}\mathbf{x}(i)d(i) = \lambda\mathbf{p}_{xd}(n-1) + d(n)\mathbf{x}(n). \tag{7}$$

The direct computation of the solution associated with (5) has an arithmetic complexity of $O(L^3)$ and is considered an impossible task even for the most advanced signal processing chips. In [7], [8] a new approach was proposed by transforming the normal equations (5) into an auxiliary system, which is solved using iterative methods. The goal is to express (5) as:

$$\mathbf{R}_x(n)\left[\hat{\mathbf{h}}(n-1) + \Delta\hat{\mathbf{h}}(n)\right] = \mathbf{p}_{xd}(n), \tag{8}$$

where $\Delta\hat{\mathbf{h}}(n) = \hat{\mathbf{h}}(n) - \hat{\mathbf{h}}(n-1)$ is regarded as the new

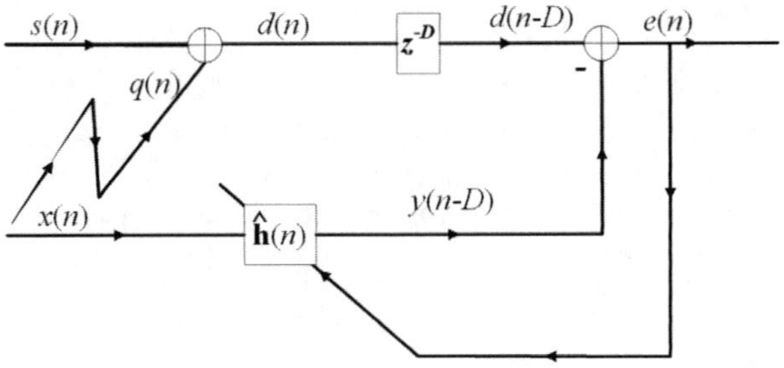

Figure 1. The ANC scheme

unknown (or *solution*) vector, which is used to update the adaptive filter through accumulation.

Considering that the solution for (5) is approximately known at time index n-1, a residual vector can be defined as [7], [8]:

$$\mathbf{r}(n-1)=\mathbf{p}_{xd}(n-1)-\mathbf{R}_x(n-1)\hat{\mathbf{h}}(n-1). \quad (9)$$

Additionally, the changes between consecutive iterations, corresponding to the elements in (5), can be denoted as:

$$\Delta\mathbf{R}_x(n)=\mathbf{R}_x(n)-\mathbf{R}_x(n-1), \quad (10)$$
$$\Delta\mathbf{p}_{xd}(n)=\mathbf{p}_{xd}(n)-\mathbf{p}_{xd}(n-1). \quad (11)$$

The auxiliary system of linear equations can be obtained by using (9), (10) and (11) to extract $\mathbf{R}_x(n)\Delta\hat{\mathbf{h}}(n)$ from (8) and to setup $\Delta\hat{\mathbf{h}}(n)$ as the new unknown vector:

$$\begin{aligned}\mathbf{R}_x(n)\Delta\hat{\mathbf{h}}(n)&=\mathbf{p}_{xd}(n)-\left[\mathbf{R}_x(n-1)+\Delta\mathbf{R}_x(n)\right]\hat{\mathbf{h}}(n-1)\\&=\mathbf{p}_{xd}(n-1)+\Delta\mathbf{p}_{xd}(n)-\\&-\mathbf{R}_x(n-1)\hat{\mathbf{h}}(n-1)-\Delta\mathbf{R}_x(n)\hat{\mathbf{h}}(n-1)\\&=\mathbf{r}(n-1)+\Delta\mathbf{p}_{xd}(n)-\Delta\mathbf{R}_x(n)\hat{\mathbf{h}}(n-1)\\&=\mathbf{p}_0(n). \quad (12)\end{aligned}$$

Although the solution of (12) would require the inverse of the same matrix $\mathbf{R}_x(n)$ as in the case of (5), the reduction in arithmetic complexity is determined by the few values of $\Delta\hat{\mathbf{h}}(n)$, which can be computed for any time index n in order to achieve good convergence properties. It can also be noticed that (12) requires the residual vector corresponding to the n-1 time index. After several computations are performed, the values comprising $\mathbf{r}(n)$ can be expressed using the elements of the auxiliary system of equations [7], [8]:

$$\begin{aligned}\mathbf{r}(n)&=\mathbf{p}_{xd}(n)-\mathbf{R}_x(n)\hat{\mathbf{h}}(n)\\&=\mathbf{p}_{xd}(n-1)+\Delta\mathbf{p}_{xd}(n)\\&-\mathbf{R}_x(n-1)\left[\hat{\mathbf{h}}(n-1)+\Delta\hat{\mathbf{h}}(n)\right]-\Delta\mathbf{R}_x(n)\hat{\mathbf{h}}(n)\\&=\mathbf{r}(n-1)+\Delta\mathbf{p}_{xd}(n)-\mathbf{R}_x(n-1)\Delta\hat{\mathbf{h}}(n)-\Delta\mathbf{R}_x(n)\hat{\mathbf{h}}(n)\\&=\mathbf{p}_0(n)-\mathbf{R}_x(n-1)\Delta\hat{\mathbf{h}}(n)-\Delta\mathbf{R}_x(n)\Delta\hat{\mathbf{h}}(n)\\&=\mathbf{p}_0(n)-\mathbf{R}_x(n)\Delta\hat{\mathbf{h}}(n). \quad (13)\end{aligned}$$

In accordance with (6) and (7), after some algebra the values of $\mathbf{r}(n)$ can also be determined in a recursive manner, i.e.,

$$\mathbf{r}(n)=\lambda\mathbf{r}(n-1)+e(n)\mathbf{x}(n). \quad (14)$$

The approach described in the current section re-states the least-squares problem by targeting the computation of the variation associated with the adaptive filter's coefficients between two consecutive time indexes. Therefore, the number of significant values in $\Delta\hat{\mathbf{h}}(n)$ is considerably smaller than the entire set of coefficients corresponding to $\hat{\mathbf{h}}(n)$, which is directly computed in the classical RLS versions. A major reduction in arithmetic complexity can be achieved when using the DCD iterations.

IV. The RLS-DCD Adaptive Algorithm

The symmetric positive-definite property of the matrix $\mathbf{R}_x(n)$ makes possible the combination between the RLS algorithm and the DCD method [7]-[10]. We propose to use the resulting algorithm (i.e., the RLS-DCD - presented in Table I) for real time retrieval of speech signals in ANC scenarios.

In step 1 of the adaptive method the correlation matrix is updated by exploiting its transpose property, i.e., $\mathbf{R}_x(n)=\mathbf{R}_x^T(n)$. The modification is performed by copying the upper-left L-1 x L-1 block of $\mathbf{R}_x(n-1)$ to the lower-right L-1 x L-1 submatrix of $\mathbf{R}_x(n)$, and by computing only the first column [8]-[10]. Consequently, the complexity associated with step 1 is reduced to a value proportional to the length of the adaptive filter [8], [10]. The main diagonal of $\mathbf{R}_x(n)$ is initialized using the identity matrix $\mathbf{I}_L$ and the constant value δ, in order to avoid processing a singular matrix in the initial stages of the adaption course.

TABLE I. THE RLS-DCD ALGORITHM

Initialization	$\hat{\mathbf{h}}(0)=\mathbf{0},\ \mathbf{r}(0)=0,\ \mathbf{R}_{\mathbf{x}}(0)=\delta\mathbf{I}_L$	x	+
for n = 1, 2, …			
Step 1	$\mathbf{R}_{\mathbf{x}}^{(1)}(n)=\lambda\mathbf{R}^{(1)}(n-1)+x(n)\mathbf{x}(n)$	L	$2L$
Step 2	$e(n)=d(n)-\hat{\mathbf{h}}^T(n-1)\mathbf{x}(n)$	L	L
Step 3	$\mathbf{r}(n)=\lambda\mathbf{r}(n-1)+e(n)\mathbf{x}(n)$	L	$2L$
Step 4 (DCD)	$\mathbf{R}_x(n)\Delta\hat{\mathbf{h}}(n)=\mathbf{r}(n)\Rightarrow\Delta\hat{\mathbf{h}}(n),\mathbf{r}(n)$	0	$2N_uL+$ $+L+M_b$
Step 5	$\hat{\mathbf{h}}(n)=\hat{\mathbf{h}}(n-1)+\Delta\hat{\mathbf{h}}(n)$	0	L

After determining the error of the filter in step 2, the DCD portion of the algorithm is processed in stages 3 and 4. The residual vector $\mathbf{r}(n)$ is updated using the forgetting factor in the sense of correlating $e(n)$ with the input vector $\mathbf{x}(n)$. The classical system of equations is replaced by an auxiliary problem. Although, the same matrix requires an inversion, the statistical properties of the new model allow for much simpler operations. For each of the *maximum number of allowed* (or *successful*) *updates* (denoted by N_u), the DCD performs a search and an update for a value of the solution vector, which is initialized with zero. Considering that only the main diagonal of $\mathbf{R}_x(n)$ comprises contributions of squared numbers (positive numbers), then it is safe to assume that (statistically) the rest of the matrix has negligible quantities regarding the *decision process*. Accordingly, the choice of performing an update to $\Delta\hat{\mathbf{h}}(n)$ is based on finding the maximum absolute value in the residual vector and comparing it to the corresponding number (situated on the same position) on the main diagonal of $\mathbf{R}_x(n)$, which is scaled using half of the *step size*, denoted by α. If the first term of the comparison is larger, then an update is performed on the corresponding position of $\Delta\hat{\mathbf{h}}(n)$ and the residual vector is also modified to reflect the newest change in the solution vector. The values comprising $\Delta\hat{\mathbf{h}}(n)$ and $\hat{\mathbf{h}}(n)$ are considered to be represented using a fixed-point format with M_b bits.

Table II describes the behavior of the DCD iterations with a *leading element* [7]-[11]. The name of the method is associated to its *greedy* manner of searching the most probable locations where updates could be performed. The DCD is employed at step 4 in Table I, i.e., for each time index n. The key factor associated with the reduction in arithmetic workload is the choice of the step size α. The selection starts with the parameter H, which is the maximum expected amplitude of the values comprising the solution vector, i.e., the numbers in $\Delta\hat{\mathbf{h}}(n)$ are expected to be in the interval ($-H$, H). Correspondingly, the value of α can be initialized with $H/2$ and is halved for each time a comparison fails to lead to a successful update. By choosing H as a power of 2, any multiplication with α can be performed on signal processing chips as a bit-shift. Moreover, the smaller the step size becomes, the closer to the Least Significant Bit (LSB) is the contribution added in $\Delta\hat{\mathbf{h}}(n)$ (the update operation can have positive or negative contributions). The complete update procedure is presented in Table II (the end of each *for iteration*). It comprises an adjustment performed for one the solution vector values and an entire residual vector modification. The values of $\mathbf{r}(n)$ tend to become smaller as the DCD produces updates to $\Delta\hat{\mathbf{h}}(n)$.

The DCD portion of the algorithms ends when one of two conditions is met [7]. Firstly, if N_u updates are performed, then the planned arithmetic effort is finished and the current values of $\mathbf{r}(n)$ and $\Delta\hat{\mathbf{h}}(n)$ are considered to be the produced results. Otherwise, if enough comparisons are unsuccessful, then the value of the step size becomes too small (i.e., the value of m corresponds to a value greater than the position of the LSB) and the DCD is stopped. Although in the last mentioned case the algorithm stops when $m>M_b$ and the number of performed updates is smaller than the planned value N_u, $\mathbf{r}(n)$ and $\Delta\hat{\mathbf{h}}(n)$ are still considered valid results and used by the RLS-DCD.

In any DCD ending situation, step 5 in Table I uses the determined solution vector to modify the adaptive filter coefficients $\hat{\mathbf{h}}(n-1)$ and generate the new vector corresponding to the adaptive algorithm, i.e., $\hat{\mathbf{h}}(n)$. It is important to mention that because $\Delta\hat{\mathbf{h}}(n)$ is altered for a maximum number of times equal to N_u, only several coefficients are really modified (for any given time index n), as the other remain with their initial values. However, the invested arithmetic effort is enough to generate sufficient performance, as already shown in [7]-[10] for AEC and SAEC scenarios.

Relevant information about arithmetic complexity is also displayed in Table I. It can be noticed that the DCD method uses no multiplications or divisions. The corresponding computational effort is influenced by the length of the adaptive filter L, by the number of *successful iterations* N_u (which is usually smaller than 10) and by the number of bits M_b used to represent the values comprising $\Delta\hat{\mathbf{h}}(n)$. The leading DCD employs only bit-shifts of the operands and no more than $(2N_u+1)L+M_b$ additions [7]-[9]. Considering that we propose to use the RLS-DCD algorithm for ANC scenarios, the value of L is expected to be comparable to N_u and M_b.

The overall complexity of the RLS-DCD can be further reduced by choosing the forgetting factor as $\lambda=1-1/(KL)$, where K and the filter length L are positive integers, powers of 2. Therefore, any multiplication with λ can be replaced by a bit-shift and one subtraction. The total amount of arithmetic operations corresponding to the algorithm described in Table I is represented by $3L$ multiplications and less than $6L+2N_uL+M_b$ additions for every time index n [8].

TABLE II. THE DCD WITH A LEADING ELEMENT

Initialization	$\Delta\hat{\mathbf{h}} = \mathbf{0}$, $\alpha = H/2$, $m = 2$
for k = 1, 2, …N	
$[val,\ poz] = \max\{\lvert r_0(n)\rvert, \lvert r_1(n)\rvert \dots \lvert r_{L-1}(n)\rvert\}$ $v = val;\ p = poz;$	
while $\left(\left(v \le (\alpha/2)R_{x;\,p,p}(n)\right)$ *and* $\left(m \le M_{\mathrm{b}}\right)\right)$ $m = m+1;\ \alpha = \alpha/2;$ ***end***	
if *(m>M)* ***exit DCD***	
$\hat{h}_p(n) = \hat{h}_p(n) + sign\{r_p(n)\}\alpha$ $\mathbf{r}(n) = \mathbf{r}(n) - sign\{r_p(n)\}\alpha\mathbf{R}_x^{(p)}(n)$	
end for iteration	

We notice that the value of M_b has a limited influence on the number of arithmetic operations. However, the parameter is relevant for their complexity.

V. SIMULATIONS

Simulations results are presented for the context illustrated in Figure 1, using the RLS-DCD and RLS adaptive algorithms. The performance of the ANC system is analyzed using time domain plots and spectrograms with 256 points Fourier Transforms for the generated error signals. The reference RLS method employs Woodburry's identity to estimate the inverse of the correlation matrix and to solve the classical least-squares system of equations.

The acoustic test signals are sampled with a frequency of 8 kHz, using 16 bits/sample. The goal is to recover interference-free speech sequences available in the $s(n)$ waveforms [12]. The desired signal is generated by filtering the interference $x(n)$ with a Matlab generated low-pass filter and adding the output $q(n)$ to $s(n)$. The Matlab filter is a *fir1* impulse response with 13 coefficients and a cut-off frequency of 0.475 of the sampling frequency.

The length of the adaptive filter is L=25 and the corresponding forgetting factor is set to $\lambda = 1 - 1/(16L)$. Correspondingly, the L values comprising the RLS-DCD solution vector are represented in the numerical interval $(-H, H)$=(-1,1) using M_b bits. The parameter M_b directly influences the precision of the ANC system and is varied in order to study the compromise between the performance and complexity. Furthermore, $\Delta\hat{\mathbf{h}}(n)$ is updated for a maximum number of N_u=4 times per every time index n.

The first simulation compares the performance of the RLS-DCD and RLS algorithms using Gaussian noise as acoustic interference. The $s(n)$ and $q(n)$ signals have the same power (i.e., the corresponding SNR has the value 0 dB). It can be noticed in Figure 2 that increasing the number of bits used for the representation of the adaptive filter coefficients leads to better estimates of interference samples and a better reduction in noise level. Additionally, the comparison performed with the RLS spectrogram indicates

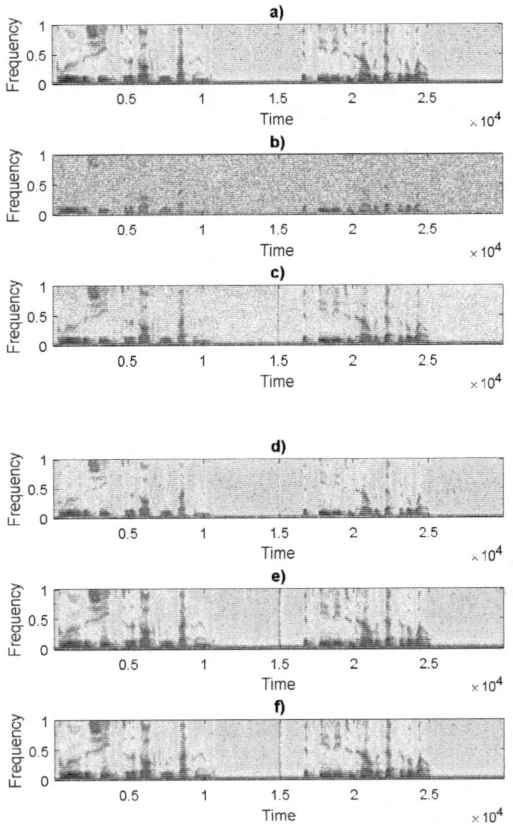

Figure 2. Spectrograms with 256 Fourier Transforms – the interference is Gaussian noise (SNR=0 dB): a) The speech sequence to be recovered; RLS-DCD error signal with b) M_b=3, c) M_b=6, d) M_b=8, e) M_b=16; f) RLS error signal

that higher values of the parameter M_b provide similar performance from the RLS-DCD method, with lower arithmetic effort. Figures 3 and 4 provide results in the time domain for the scenario. The original speech is compared to the corrupted signal (Figure 3) and the recovered sequences (i.e., the error signals) are displayed for the RLS method, respectively the RLS-DCD algorithm with M_b=16 (Figure 4). Both plots in Figure 4 indicate an obvious reduction in noise level.

For the second simulation (Figure 5), the interference signal $x(n)$ is acoustic engine noise. The same value is used for the SNR (0 dB). In comparison to the previous scenario, it can be noticed that the settings M_b=8 and M_b=16 do not provide the same performance rating anymore. The properties of the second interference type require more precision in order to generate similar results between the RLS-DCD and the RLS methods. The time domain signals illustrated in Figures 6 and 7 also demonstrate that the RLS-DCD algorithm can provide similar performance with the RLS using considerably less arithmetic resources.

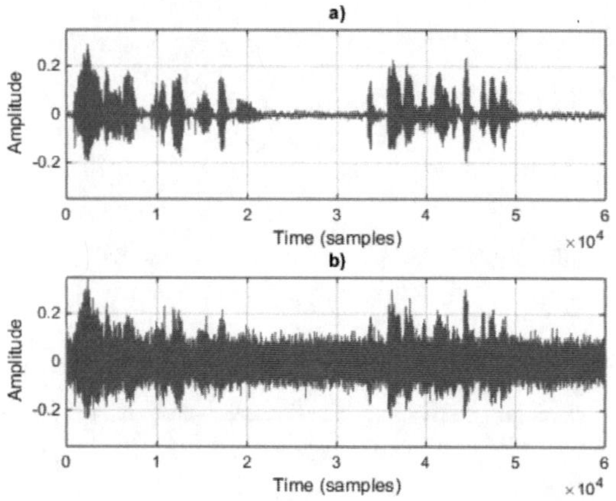

Figure 3. Acoustic signals in the time domain: a) The speech sequence to be recovered; b) Corrupted speech signal: Gaussian noise with SNR=0 dB

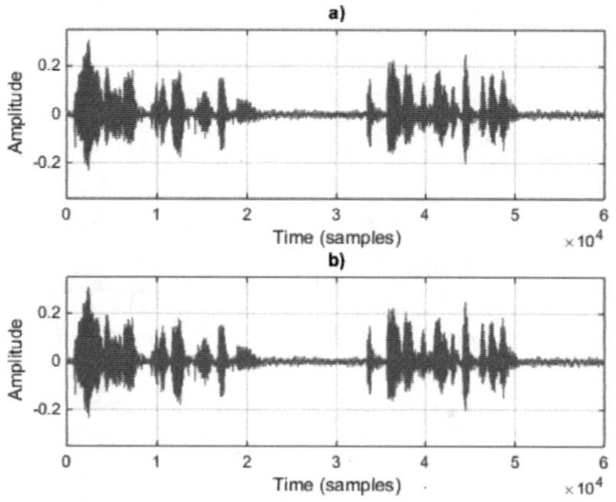

Figure 4. Acoustic signals in the time domain; Gaussian noise interference (SNR=0 dB) a) The recovered speech signal using RLS-DCD with M_b=16; b) The recovered signal using RLS

The spectrograms corresponding to a third experiment are illustrated in Figure 8. The speech $s(n)$ is corrupted for the first half of the simulation by engine sound, which is afterwards replaced by music. The SNR is set to -10 dB for the entire scenario. The change in interference produces a spike in each error spectrogram and the adaptive algorithms require an adaptation period. It can also be noticed that the music is harder to eliminate from the desired signal (the corresponding interference leaves easier noticeable traces in the error signal). As a consequence, the correlation properties of the interference signals have an important influence on the performance of the adaptive algorithms.

The performance of the adaptive filter is also illustrated in the time domain (Figures 9 and 10), for scenario 3. The change in interference type [see Figure 9.b)] generates short spikes in the error signals plotted in Figure 10. It can be noticed that the reaction time of the RLS-DCD adaptive method is similar to the RLS.

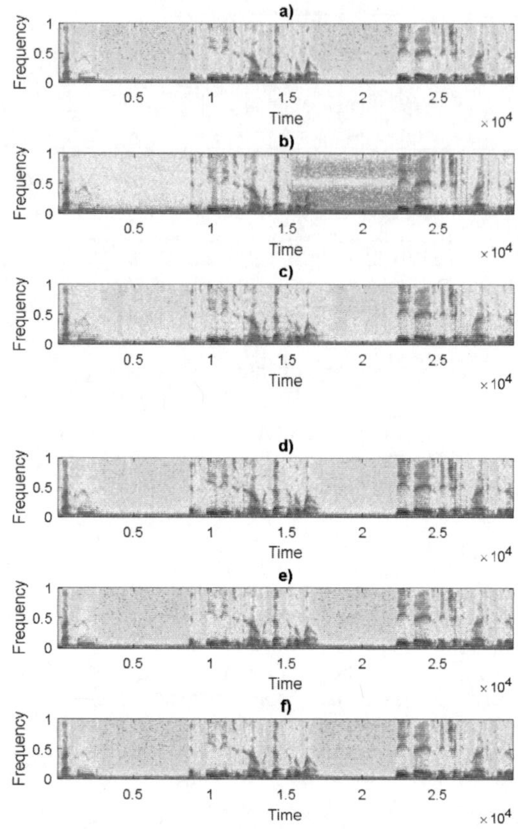

Figure 5. Spectrograms with 256 Fourier Transforms – the interference is engine noise (SNR=0 dB): a) The speech sequence to be recovered; RLS-DCD error signal with b) M_b=3, c) M_b=6, d) M_b=8, e) M_b=16; f) RLS error signal

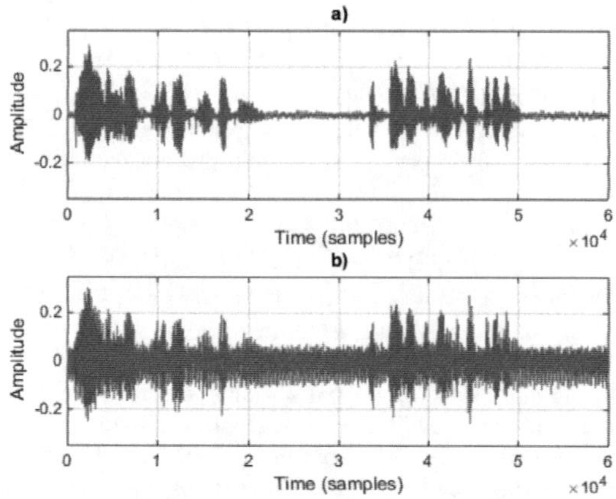

Figure 6. Acoustic signals in the time domain: a) The speech sequence to be recovered; b) Corrupted speech signal: engine noise with SNR=0 dB

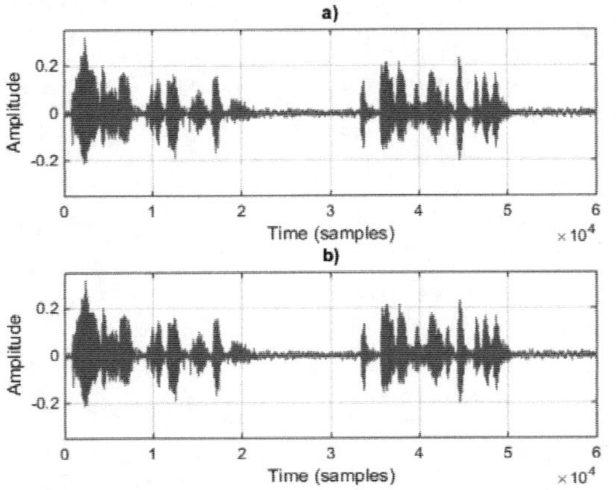

Figure 7. Acoustic signals in the time domain; engine noise interference (SNR=0 dB) a) The recovered speech signal using RLS-DCD with M_b=16; b) The recovered signal using RLS

VI. CONCLUSIONS

This paper has presented a low-complexity RLS algorithm for ANC scenarios. The RLS-DCD adaptive method is based on a reinterpretation of the classical least-squares problem and replaces the standard system of linear equations with an auxiliary system. The new unknown vector (i.e., the solution vector) represents the changes of the adaptive filter between consecutive iterations. The model favors low-complexity solutions, such as the leading DCD iterations, which computes a low number of values for the update stage of the filter's coefficients.

The DCD method exploits the statistical properties of the correlation matrix associated with the input signal and solves the proposed auxiliary system using only bit-shifts and additions. Moreover, the overall combination between the RLS and the DCD requires no divisions and the multiplication volume can be drastically reduced by choosing an appropriate value for the forgetting factor. The RLS-DCD is also a stable alternative, which has comparable performance with the RLS method implemented using Woodburry's identity.

Simulations have been performed in order to analyze the behavior of the proposed system. The results indicate that the RLS-DCD has attractive performance when working with correlated signals, such as speech. The computational efficiency of the proposed adaptive algorithm recommends it as a suitable candidate for ANC implementations on signal processing chips for mobile devices.

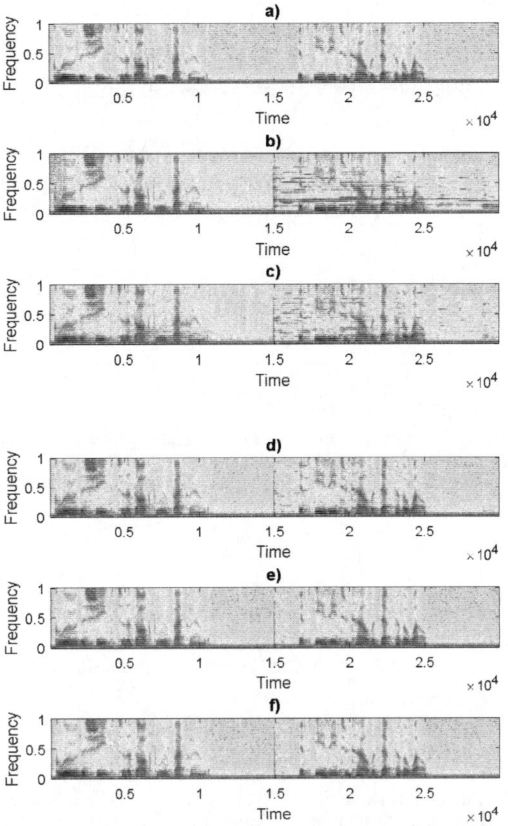

Figure 8. Spectrograms with 256 Fourier Transforms - the interference is engine noise, which changes to music at time index 15000 (SNR=-10 dB): a) The speech sequence to be recovered; RLS-DCD error signal with b) M_b=3, c) M_b=6, d) M_b=8, e) M_b=16; f) RLS error signal

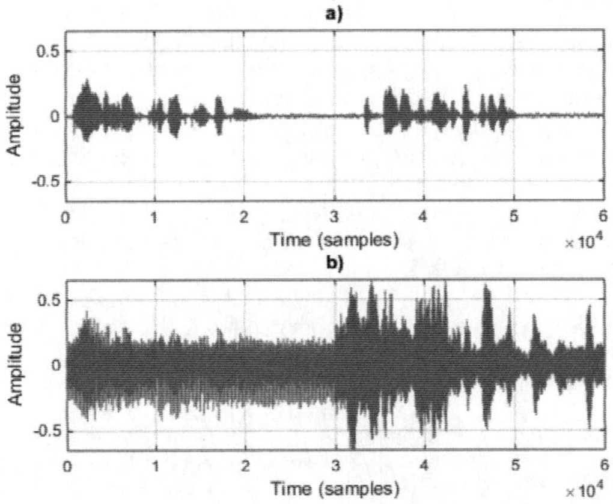

Figure 9. Acoustic signals in the time domain: a) The speech sequence to be recovered; b) Corrupted speech signal: engine noise (first half) and music (second half); SNR=0 dB

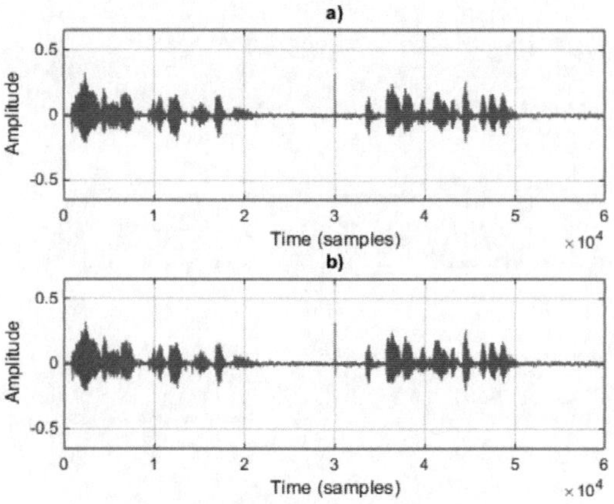

Figure 10. Acoustic signals in the time domain; interference: engine noise (first half) and music (second half); SNR=0 dB a) The recovered speech signal using RLS-DCD with M_b=16; b) The recovered signal using RLS

ACKNOWLEDGMENT

This work was supported by European Space Agency under Grant no. 4000121222/17/NL/CBi and University Politehnica of Bucharest under Grant no. 18/05.10.2017.

REFERENCES

[1] C. Stanciu, L. Stanciu, and R. Mihăescu, "Low Complexity Recursive Least-Squares Algorithm for Adaptive Noise Cancellation," in *Proc. ICN*, 2017, pp. 102–106.

[2] S. Haykin, *Adaptive Filter Theory*. Fourth Edition, Upper Saddle River, NJ: Prentice-Hall, 2002.

[3] E. Hänsler and G. Schmidt, *Acoustic Echo and Noise Control – A Practical Approach*. John Wiley & Sons, Inc., Hoboken, New Jersey, 2004.

[4] A. H. Sayed, *Adaptive Filters*. New York, NY: Wiley, 2008.

[5] J. Benesty, C. Paleologu, T. Gänsler, and S. Ciochină, *A Perspective on Stereophonic Acoustic Echo Cancellation*, Springer-Verlag, Berlin, Germany, 2011.

[6] B. Farhang-Boroujeny, *Adaptive Filters - Theory and Applications*. Second Edition, John Wiley & Sons, Inc., Hoboken, New Jersey, 2013.

[7] Y. V. Zakharov and T. C. Tozer, "Multiplication-free iterative algorithm for LS problem," *IEE Electronics Lett.*, vol. 40, pp. 567–569, Apr. 2004.

[8] Y. V. Zakharov, G. P. White, and J. Liu, "Low-complexity RLS algorithms using dichotomous coordinate descent iterations," *IEEE Trans. Signal Processing*, vol. 56, pp. 3150–3161, July 2008.

[9] J. Liu, Y. V. Zakharov, and B. Weaver, "Architecture and FPGA design of dichotomous coordinate descent algorithms," *IEEE Trans. Circuits and Systems I: Regular Papers*, vol. 56, pp. 2425–2438, Nov. 2009.

[10] C. Stanciu, J. Benesty, C. Paleologu, T. Gänsler, and S. Ciochină, "A widely linear model for stereophonic acoustic echo cancellation," *Signal Processing*, vol. 93, pp. 511–516, Feb. 2013.

[11] C. Stanciu and C. Anghel, "Numerical of the DCD-RLS Algorithm for Stereo Acoustic Echo Cancellation," in *Proc. COMM*, 2014, pp.65–68.

[12] The Open Speech Repository, http://www.voiptroubleshooter.com/open_speech/ [last accessed: 02.09.2017].

Development of MOX Sensors for Low VOCs Concentrations Detection: Responses Comparison for WO_3, SnO_2, and ZnO Sensitive Layers with Interfering Gases as CO and CO_2

Short Paper

Frank James, Tomas Fiorido, Marc Bendahan, Khalifa Aguir
Aix Marseille Univ, Univ Toulon CNRS, IM2NP, Marseille, France
e-mail: khalifa.aguir@im2np.fr

Abstract—**N-type Metal Oxide sensors was developed to detect Volatile Organic Compounds at low concentration level. Sensitive layers like SnO_2, ZnO and WO_3 were deposited by reactive RF sputtering method. The sensors is based on a heater and a MOX sensitive layer on a silicon substrate. Gas sensing properties have been investigated toward isobutylene, as a typical VOC and benzene. The optimum working temperature was experimentally determined at 285°C for this study. This work highlights the detection of VOCs with interfering gases by MOX sensor at low level. Gas like CO and CO_2 can be interfering gas for VOCs detection. This study was focused on the detection of isobutylene and benzene from 50 ppb to 500 ppb. The low selectivity is in fact a well-known problem of these sensors but we made a comparison between these MOX sensors at the same temperature in order to have a simple sensor array on the same chip in the future. This system will be used for a real time indoor air monitoring.**

Keywords- gas sensor; MOX sensor; isobutylene; benzene carbon dioxyde; carbone monoxyde.

I. INTRODUCTION

In the last decades, an increasing demand for the monitoring of several parameters allowing to guarantee the safety and quality products and environment represents a wide market for chemical sensors. Responses comparison between sensors allows to choose specific systems for a target gas [1]. In different fields, like environmental monitoring, home security, and safety, the detection and evaluation of gaseous emissions is strongly required [2].Volatile organic compounds (VOCs) are emitted to the atmosphere from various industrial and natural sources. The concentration of VOCs is much higher in indoors compared to outdoors, which not only pollutes the environment but also affects human health through breathing and skin contamination. VOCs are present in several household products such as paints, disinfectants, wood preservatives and automotive products. All these products contribute to indoor air pollution. There is a need to develop fast, sensitive, and cost-effective gas sensors for the detection of VOCs.

Gas sensing applications require continuous and direct exposition of gas sensors to environment to be analyzed with interferers. The most common gas sensing technology for sensing applications is metal oxide (MOX) gas sensors. The development of transducers for metal –oxide gas sensors has been reported lately [3].

MOX sensors in particular is still the most promising class of sensing materials, thanks to easy fabrication methods and chemical stability. In our case, MOX sensors are investigated in order to detect VOCs thanks to their miniaturization and real-time monitoring capabilities. These sensors need to be heated to elevated temperature to make them gas sensitive and to allow them to respond rapidly to the momentary gas concentration levels in the ambient air.

The sensitive layers have been obtained by Radio Frequency Magnetron Sputtering. Great attention was dedicated to the control of the film thickness. An appropriate choice of the materials for a particular gas is very important, and some materials are suitable for each type of gas detection. Considering that metal oxides are very good sensitive layer candidates, the analysis of various parameters including electro-physical properties and structural properties is important for the choice of an effective sensor. It is also necessary to pay attention to the performances towards interfering gases. An interesting approach to obtain enhanced selectivity consists in operating the sensors with variable temperature profiles or light modulation [4] [5]. Many different shapes and periods of the sensor temperature profiles have been proposed in the literature depending also on the particular structure of the sensors used [6]. Nevertheless, if different materials are on the same chip, the right choice have to be made in order to select the more sensitive layer for the gas at a working temperature.

Isobutylene, which is a typical VOC is one of our target gas because it is easy to detect. It is also easy to realize a concentration calibration with a photoionization detector for example. We will start with this gas then we will try to detect benzene which is more dangerous for human health. Benzene exposure can cause leukemia and permissible exposure limits have been set up. This two VOCs will help us to estimate how selective can be a system with our different sensors.

In this work, we have chosen three main n-type metal oxides used in this field: SnO_2 [7], WO_3 [8] [9], and ZnO [10]. The aim of the comparison between the performances of these sensitive materials is to find the best sensitive layer for our low VOCs concentrations sensors and to evaluate the effect of interfering gases like CO and CO_2. These interferences can be a problem when the detection system is too sensitive towards these gases.

II. SENSITIVE LAYER

A. *Deposition Method*

The three sensitive thin layers (~50nm) under study were deposited by reactive magnetron RF sputtering. So, the metal oxide films were grown by reactive R.F. magnetron sputtering of pure metal by means of a plasma of argon as carrier gas and oxygen as reactive gas. The experimental set-up was a conventional capacitive coupled R.F. magnetron sputtering chamber with a water-cooled cathode target. The deposition chamber was first pumped down to high vacuum conditions (10^{-7} mbar). Under a dynamic strangling pumping through a valve, pure oxygen was then introduced into the chamber and the partial pressure of oxygen was adjusted to the desired value (10^{-3} mbar) by means of a mass flow controller. Pure argon was afterwards introduced bringing the total working dynamic pressure up to 20 x 10^{-3} mbar. The R.F. forward input power was maintained at 100 W with a reflected power rendered minimum (almost zero) by means of an impedance matching. The corresponding self-bias voltage was around -100 V. These conditions were kept constant during the whole films depositions process. Only several parameters as the oxygen pressure and the deposition time were changed and studied to obtain the right oxide. Magnetron Sputtering is a low cost and easy control method for layer growth. Finally, the materials were annealed at 450°C during 1h30 to improve their nano-crystallization and the stability of the sensors response.

B. *Structural charatherizations*

X-ray diffraction (XRD) measurements were made using a Philips X'Pert MPD. The angular range was between 20° and 60° for 2θ. Data were collected with an angular step of 0.02°, 3 s per step. The Cu X-ray source was operated with a high intensity ceramic sealed tube (3 kW).

Fig. 1 shows the XRD patterns of the three thin film. All the diffraction peaks show tetragonal rutile structure for SnO_2, monoclinic structure for WO_3 and hexagonal structure for ZnO (JCPDS cards No 72-1147, 41-1445, 36-1451 respectively). The grains size of these materials was around 20 nm for each one high porosity (Fig. 2).

Under isobutylene, the reducing molecules will react with the adsorbed oxygen ions and release the trapped electrons back to the metal oxide conduction band. This reaction leads to the decrease of electron depletion barrier and to increase the electrical conduction of the metal oxide. The same reaction happened under benzene.

The sensitive layer is the main part of the gas sensor. The right choice have to be made about this material in order to obtain the best response possible. All these materials have to be studied for each VOCs.

The material characterization was also carried out by using scanning electron microscopy (SEM). A SEM image of one the SnO2 film is shown in Fig. 2 to appreciate the morphology. All these materials shown the same surface properties that have helped us to compare them.

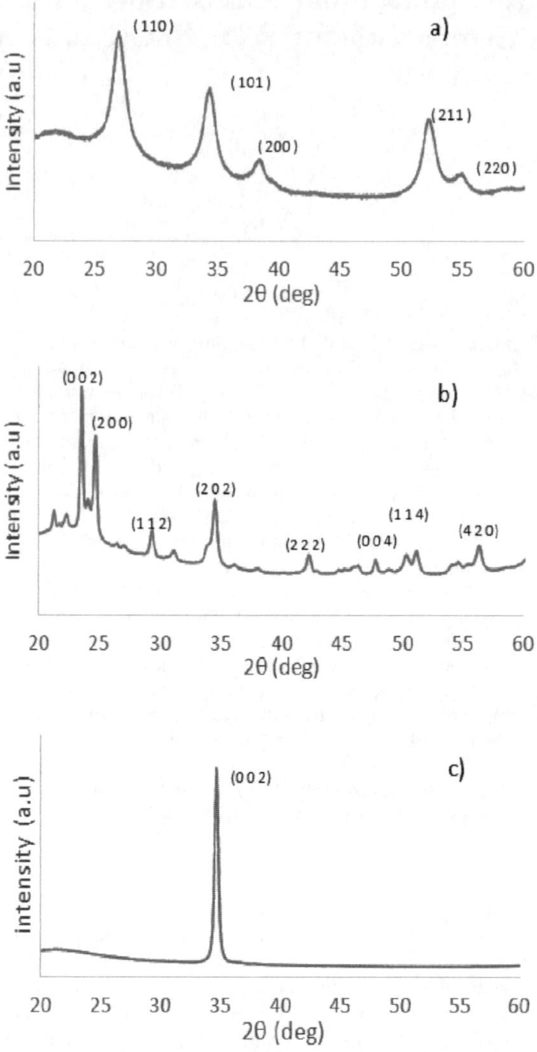

Figure 1. XRD patterns of a) SnO_2, b)WO_3 and c) ZnO made by reactive RF sputtering

The material characterization was also carried out by using scanning electron microscopy (SEM). A SEM image of one the SnO_2 film is shown in Fig. 2 to appreciate the morphology. All these materials shown the same surface properties that have helped us to compare them. The grain size was around 20 nm, with homogeneous shapes.

These layers are the main part of the detection system and their structural characterization was decisive to identify them and understand their behavior under gases. We looked for a simple deposit method and characterization methods to demonstrate the feasibility of the process on an industrial scale.

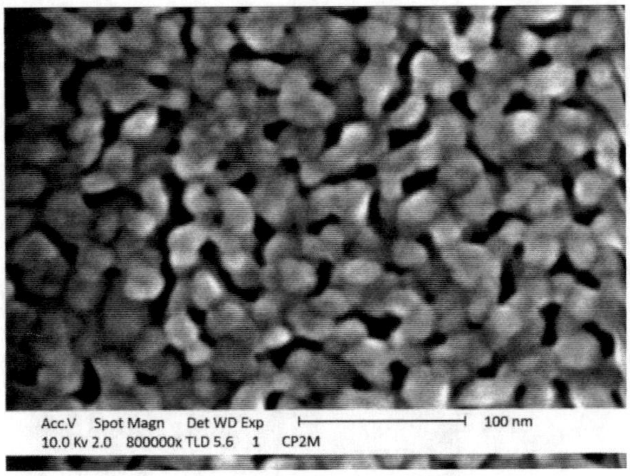

Figure 2. SEM of a SnO_2, layer

C. *Chip gas sensor*

The gas sensors fabricated with SnO_2, WO_3 and ZnO layers as sensitive material is presented in Fig. 3. It was made of Si/SiO_2 substrate with Ti/Pt interdigitated electrodes. The sensitive layer was deposited on and between the electrodes by reactive magnetron RF sputtering. These materials were the sensitive layers which will interact with isobutylene in this case. This chip was on a hotplate that allowed us to reach temperature of 285°C. The temperature was monitoring thanks to a K type thermocouple.

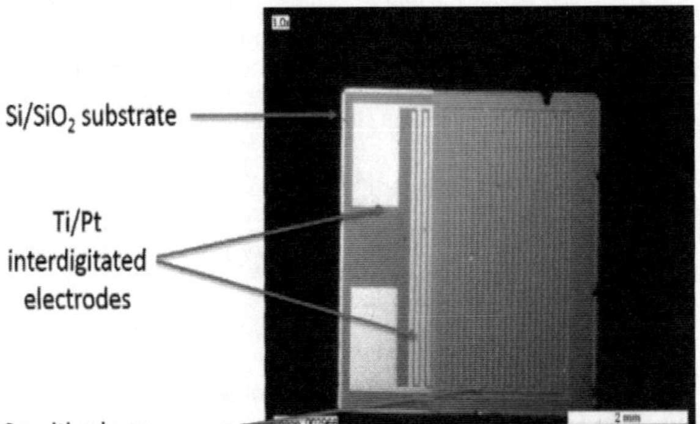

Figure 3. MOX Sensor with Si/SiO_2 substrate

So, three sensors with the different layers were made to obtain the same thickness and the same grain size. These sensors were made with the same conditions in order to elaborate them on the same chip in the future, for a sensors array. This is the first version of the chip. The final device could have the three materials on the same chip at the same temperature. Particular attention should be given on the test conditions to realize the comparison between the sensors.

III. Methods

A. *Gas test bench*

This device has been tested with an automated gas bench (Fig. 4) with isobutylene, benzene, carbon monoxide and dioxide. We used a power supply to control the operating temperature and a source meter for the data acquisition. This target gas was injected into a dilution system with or without interfering compounds. The outline was connected to a thermo-regulated test chamber. For each concentration, the sensor was exposed to gas for 1 min then to dry air during 10 min. The sensors were maintained at the nominal heating voltage in dry air until the baseline was obtained to reach the response [11] under a flow rate of 500 sccm.

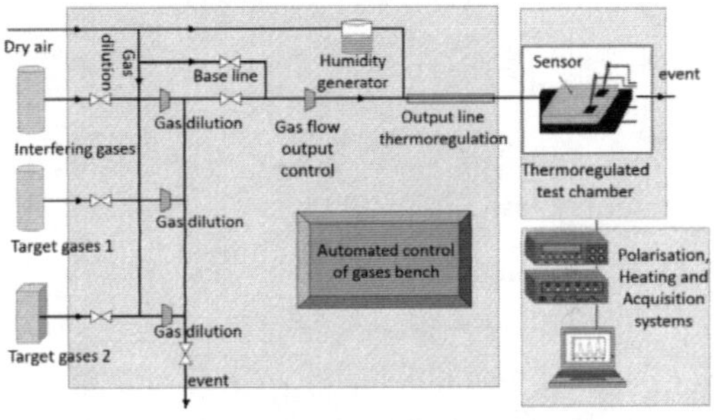

Figure 4. Gas measurement experiment set-up

The device electrical resistance was recorded by forcing 0.1 V as the polarisation using a Keithley system. We had measured the current I to obtain the polarization resistance. The data acquisition is controlled by a PC via a Labview program and stored for futher analysis.

The target gas includes two VOCs including isobutylene and benzene, and two interfering gases as carbon monoxyde and dioxyde. All of them are reducing gases diluted in synthetic air at different concentrations with a constant total flow of 500 sccm. These devices have been tested at room temperature.

B. *Tested vapours*

Isobutylene is a typical VOCs, currently used for concentration calibration. We also used calibrated concentrations of benzene by using a permeation tube. All the concentration were checked with a photoionization detector. The outline was heated to prevent a gas condensation and it was connected to a thermo-regulated test chamber. The test were realized without humidity in order to characterize the influence of the interfering gases alone at stationarity temperature regime.

IV. Results

A. *Response to isobutylene*

Many authors have characterized oxygen adsorption state on metal oxide and discovered four species: O_2, O^{2-}, O^- and O_2.

The oxidation of isobutylene on the oxide surface can lead to a change of the resistance material. When this reducing gas is oxidized by the oxygen ions on the metal oxide surface, an electron is given back to the oxide. Then the resistance of the gas sensor decreases.

Fig 5 shows a typical responses with a wide range of detection from 50 ppb to 500 ppb of isobutylene at 285°C. WO_3 and ZnO sensors seem to be the best devices for isobutylene. We have reached the highest responses from the three sensitive layers with low concentrations.

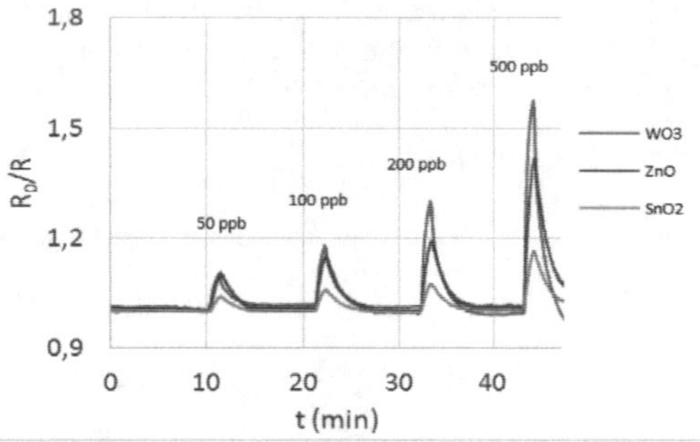

Figure 5. Sensors response for isobutylène concentrations, from 50 ppb to 500 ppb.

These results show fast response to isobutylene at 285°C. We reached a response of 1.6 with WO_3 although we reached 1.15 with SnO_2. These two results will allow us to have a specific response for isobutylene from our system.

B. *Response to benzene*

The oxidation of benzene on oxide surface can also lead to the generation of electrons .Fig. 6 shows lower responses for benzene than isobutylene with the range of detection from 50 ppb to 500 ppb of isobutylene. The working temperature was the same as the previous test.

ZnO and SnO_2 sensors are the best devices for benzene. We can noticed that the WO_3 sensor has the worst response for this gas. So, we will be able to compare the responses for each VOCs and improve the selectivity of our future system with three sensors.

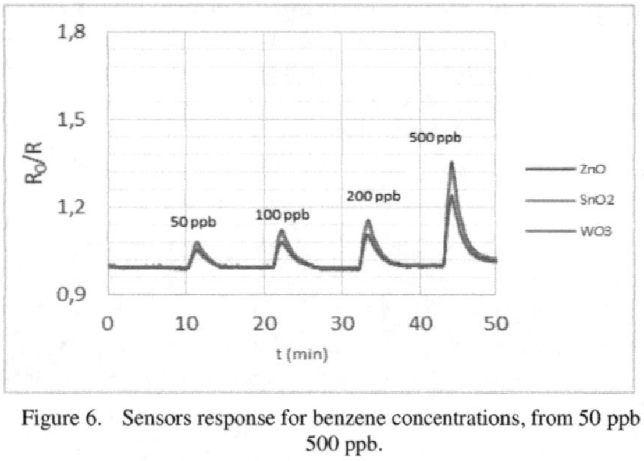

Figure 6. Sensors response for benzene concentrations, from 50 ppb to 500 ppb.

C. *Influence of interfering gases*

We have chosen 10 ppm of CO and 1% CO_2 as interfering gases concentrations. These are the type of concentration we can meet in ambient air. The Fig. 7 shows the comparison of the responses of the three materials and for the two gases.

Sensors were exposed to this interfering concentration with the same conditions as isobutylene i.e., 1 min exposition time then 10 min of dry air at 500 sccm.

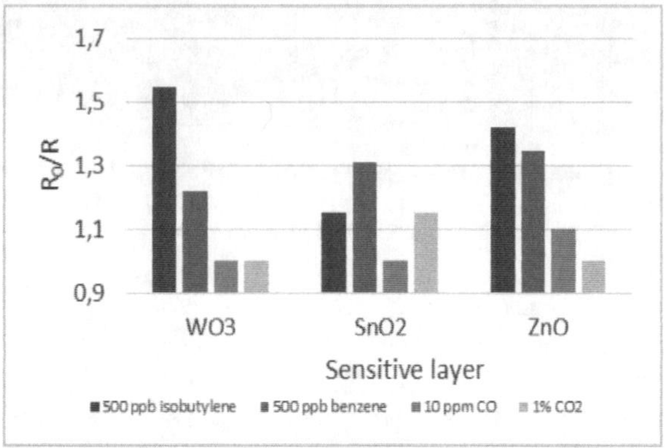

Figure 7. Sensor response under isobutylene and interferring gases

WO_3 and SnO_2 show low responses towards CO and CO_2 despite the better response for the target gases. With tests under the same experimental conditions (Fig. 7) we can classify the right metal oxide for a target gas like isobutylene in presence of interfering gases.

A system based on metal oxide gas sensor array [12] [13] and pattern recognition algorithms could give an identification for each gas according to the sensors response. The temperature modulation could also help to obtain better selectivity.

V. CONCLUSION

A set of sensors of single metal oxide has been selected to detect isobutylene and benzene. An array of sensors was then obtained at the same temperature. In the background of realistic concentrations of CO and CO_2 showed high selectivity to VOCs.

According to these results, the gas measurement showed fast response / recovery times towards isobutylene and benzene. The best sensitive layers are WO_3 and ZnO for isobutylene because we have the highest responses for this gas and the weakest influence towards gases like CO and CO_2. The best sensors for benzene are ZnO and SnO_2 for the same reasons. This is the first step for air gas monitoring. We want to improve the selectivity towards others VOCs. On the other hand, and after identifying the appropriate sensitive materials, we plan to study the improvement of the selectivity of these sensors. This array could be being used with test procedure applied to an isotherm mode. Also, this study can be the beginning of a study of detection of VOCs with three sensitive materials on the same chip.

ACKNOWLEDGMENT

The authors would like to thank Antoine Dumas from EcologicSense Rousset – France, a company specialized in Diagnostics & Monitoring environments, SATT Sud Est a technology transfer accelerator company and Mr. A. Combes for his technical support in this work.

REFERENCES

[1] F. James, T. Fiorido, M. Bendahan, K. Aguir, "Comparison between MOX sensors for low VOCs concentration with interfering gases", Allsensors 2017 : The Second Internaltional Conference on Advances in Sensors, Actuators, Metering end Sensing, IARIA, Mar 2017, pp. 39-40, ISBN: 978-1-61208-543-2.

[2] B. Firtat, C. Moldovan, C. Brasoveaunu, G. Muscalu, M. Gartner, "Miniaturised MOX bases sensors for polluant and explosive gases detection", Sens. Actuators B 249, pp. 647-655, 2017.

[3] E. Comini, C. Baratto, I. Concina, G. Faglia, M. Falasconi, "Metal oxide nanoscience and nanotechnology for chemical sensors", Sens. Actuators B 179, pp. 3-20, 2013.

[4] K. A. Ngo, P. Lauque, K. Aguir, "High performance of a gas identification system using sensor array and temperature modulation", Sens. Actuators B 124, pp. 209-216, 2007.

[5] Q. Deng, S. Gao, T. Lei, Y. Ling, S. Zhang, "Temperature & light modulation to enhance the selectivity of Pt modified zinc oxide gas sensor", Sens. Actuators B 247, pp. 903-915, 2017.

[6] Z. Tang, G. Jiang, P. C. H. Chan, J. K. O. Sin, S. S. Lau, "Theory and experiments on r.f. sputtered tin oxide thin-films for gas sensing applications", Sens. Actuators B 43, pp.161-164, 1997.

[7] M. Schweizer-Berberich, M. Zdralek, U. Weimar, W. Gopel, T. Vidal, D. Martinez, A. Peyre-Lavigne, "Pulsed mode of operation and artificial neural networks evaluation for improving the CO selectivity of SnO_2 gas sensors", Sens. Actuators B 65, pp. 91–93, 2000.

[8] M. Bendahan, R. Boulmani, J.L. Seguin, K.Aguir, "Characterization of ozone sensors based on WO_3 reactively sputtered films: influence of O_2 concentration in the sputtering gas and working temperature", Sens. Actuators B 100, pp. 320-324, 2004.

[9] K. Aguir, C. Lemire, D. Lollman, "Electrical properties of reactively sputtered WO_3 thin films as ozone gas sensor", Sens. Actuators B 84, pp. 1–5, 2002.

[10] V. Senay, S. Pat, S. Korkmaz. T. Aydoğmuş, S. Elmas, S. Özen, N. Ekem, M. Z. B Balbağ, "ZnO thin film synthesis by reactive radio frequency magnetron sputtering", Applied Surface Science vol. 318, pp. 2-5, 2014.

[11] C. Wang, L. Yin, L. Zang, D. Xiang, R. Gao, "Metal oxide gas sensors: Sensitivity and influencing factors", Sensors, vol. 10, pp. 2088-2106, 2010.

[12] D.S. Lee, Y.T. Kim, J.S. Huh, D.D. Lee, "Fabrication and characteristics of SnO_2 gas sensor array for volatile organic compounds recognition", Thin Solid Films 416, pp. 271–278, 2002.

[13] D.S. Lee, J.K. Jung, J.W. Lim, J.S. Huh, D.D. Lee, "Recognition of volatile organic compounds using SnO_2 sensor array and pattern recognition analysis", Sens. Actuators B 77, pp. 228–236, 2001.

Examination of Best-time Estimation for Each Tourist Spots by Interlinking using Geotagged Tweets

Masaki Endo, Shigeyoshi Ohno
Division of Core Manufacturing
Polytechnic University, Japan
e-mail: endou@uitec.ac.jp, ohno@uitec.ac.jp

Daiju Kato
BI Quality Assurance Division
WingArc1st Inc.
e-mail:kato.d@wingarc.com

Masaharu Hirota
Department of Information Science, Okayama University of Science, Japan
e-mail: hirota@mis.ous.ac.jp

Hiroshi Ishikawa
Graduate School of System Design
Tokyo Metropolitan University, Japan
e-mail: ishikawa-hiroshi@tmu.ac.jp

Abstract—**Numerous studies have been conducted to analyze social media data in real time and to extract events occurring in the real world. A benefit of analysis using data with position information is that it can accurately extract an event from a target area to be analyzed. However, because data with position information are scarce among all social media data, the amount to analyze is insufficient for almost all areas: we cannot fully extract most events. Therefore, efficient analytical methods must be devised for accurate extraction of events with position information, even in areas with few data. For this study, we estimate the time of biological season observation in areas and sightseeing spots with interlinkage of tweet location information. Herein, we explain the analysis results obtained using information from interpolation and analysis of cherry blossoms in Japan in 2016.**

Keywords–trend estimation; phenological observation; Twitter

I. Introduction

This paper is an extended version of earlier published work [1]. After improvement of our algorithm, this report describes more accurately estimated best times for viewing organisms at tourist spots using interlinking.

In recent years, because of the wide dissemination and rapid performance improvement of various devices such as smart phones and tablets, diverse and vast data are generated on the web. Particularly, social networking services (SNSs) have become popular because users can post data and various messages easily. Twitter [2], an SNS that provides a micro-blogging service, is used as a real-time communication tool. Numerous tweets have been posted daily by vast numbers of users. Twitter is therefore a useful medium to obtain, from a large amount of information posted by many users, real-time information corresponding to the real world.

Sightseeing has come to be regarded as an extremely important growth field in Japan for revival of its powerful economy [3]. Tourism, with its strong economic ripple effects, is expected to produce benefits from regional revitalization and employment opportunities by accommodating world tourism demand, including that from rapidly growing Asia. In addition, people around the world can discover and disseminate the charm of Japan and can promote mutual understanding with other countries.

In addition to the promotion of tourism to Japan, the progress of domestic travel is important. A nation with modern tourism must build a community society that serves regional economies well, attracting tourists widely. Moreover, it is necessary to cultivate tourist areas full of individuality and to promote their charm positively.

According to a survey reported in the Inbound Landing-type Tourism Guide [4] by the Ministry of Economy, Trade and Industry (METI), tourists want real-time information and local unique seasonal information posted on websites. Current websites provide similar information in the form of guidebooks. Nevertheless, the information update frequency of that medium is low. Because each local government, tourism association, and travel company independently provides information about travel destination locales, it is difficult for tourists to collect information for "now" tourist spots. Therefore, providing current, useful, real-world information for travelers by capturing changes of information in accordance with the season and relevant time period of the tourism region is important for the travel industry. As described herein, we define "now" information as information that travelers require for tourism and disaster prevention such as best flower-viewing times, festivals, and local heavy rains. As one might expect, the period estimated for disaster prevention information would be an estimate of the "worst" time instead of the best time.

We consider a method for estimating the best time for tourists to make phenological observations, such as the best time for viewing cherry blossoms and autumn leaves in various regions by particularly addressing phenological observations assumed for "now" in the real world. We define "now" as information for tourism and disaster prevention required by travelers during travel, such as the best flower-viewing times, interesting festivals, and the likelihood of locally heavy rains.

Tourist information for best times requires a peak period, which means that the best time is neither a period after or before falling flowers, but a period to view blooming flowers. Furthermore, the best times differ among regions and locations. Therefore, for each region and location, it is necessary to estimate the best time for phenological observations. Estimating best-time viewing periods requires the collection of large amounts of information having real-time properties. For this study, we use Twitter data obtained from many users throughout Japan. We use Twitter, a typical microblogging service, and also use geotagged tweets that include position information sent in Japan to ascertain the best time (peak period) for biological season observation by region. We proposed a low-cost estimation method [5]. Using this method, prefectures and municipalities showing a certain number of tweets with geotags can be estimated with a relevance rate of about 80% compared to the flowering day / full bloom day of cherry blossoms observed by the Japan Meteorological Agency. The geotagged tweets that are used with this method are useful as social indicators that reflect real-world circumstances. They are a useful resource supporting a real-time regional tourist information system in the tourism field. Therefore, our proposed method might be an effective means of estimating the best time to view events other than biological seasonal observations.

However, to analyze the information of each region from Twitter data, it is necessary to specify the location from tweet information. Because geotagged tweets can identify places, they are effective for analysis. However, because geotagged tweets account for a very small proportion of the total information content of tweets, it is not possible to analyze all regions. For this research, we propose a method of estimating the best time by tourist spot by performing interlinkage using geo-tagged tweets. We conducted experiments to estimate the position around areas not identified by locations based on the amounts of regional information.

The remainder of the paper is organized as follows. Section II presents earlier research related to this topic. Section III describes our proposed method for estimating the best-time of phenological observation through interlinkage using regional amounts. Section IV describes experimentally obtained results obtained using our proposed method, along with a discussion of the results. Section V presents a summary of the contributions and future work.

II. RELATED WORK

The amounts of digital data are expected to increase greatly in the future because of the spread of SNSs. Numerous reports describe studies of the effective use of these large amounts of digital data. Some studies use microblogs to conduct real-world understanding and prediction by analyzing information transmitted from microblogs. Kleinberg [6] describes detection of a "burst" of keywords signaling a rapid increase in time-series data. Sakaki et al. [7] explain their proposal of a method to detect events such as earthquakes and typhoons based on a study estimating real-time events from Twitter. Kaneko et al. [8] propose a method of detecting an event using geotagged non-photo tweets and non-geotagged photo tweets, as well as geotagged photo tweets. Yamagata et al. [9] propose a real-time urban climate monitoring method using geographically tagged tweets, demonstrating the effectiveness of tweets for urban risk management. Consequently, various methods for extracting event and location information have been discussed. Nevertheless, although event detection has been done in earlier studies, no discussion of the event validity period has been reported. As described herein, after proposing a method for extracting such information, we estimate "now" in relation to tourism information, such as the full bloom period of phonological observations. Additionally, we address an important difficulty related to geotagged content analysis: what amount of data is effective for an analyzed area?

Next, along with rising SNS popularity, real-time information has increased. Analysis using real time data has become possible. Many studies have examined efficient methods for analyzing large amounts of digital data. Some studies have been conducted to predict real world phenomena using large amounts of social big data. Phithakkitnukoon et al. [10] analyze details of traveler behavior using data from mobile phone GPS location records such as departure place, destination, and traveling means on a personal level. Mislove et al. [11] develop a system that infers a Twitter user's feelings from the tweet text and visualizes changes of emotion in space–time. After research to detect events such as earthquakes and typhoons, Sakaki et al. [7] propose a method to estimate real-time events from Twitter tweets. Cheng et al. [12] estimate Twitter users' geographical positions at the time of their contributions, without the use of geotags, by devoting attention to the geographical locality of words from text information in Twitter posted articles. Although various studies have analyzed spatiotemporal data, research to estimate the viewing period using interlinkage is a new field.

III. OUR PROPOSED METHOD

This section presents a description of an analytical method for target data collection. It presents best-time estimation to obtain a guide for phenological change from Twitter data in Japan. Our proposal is portrayed in Figure 1.

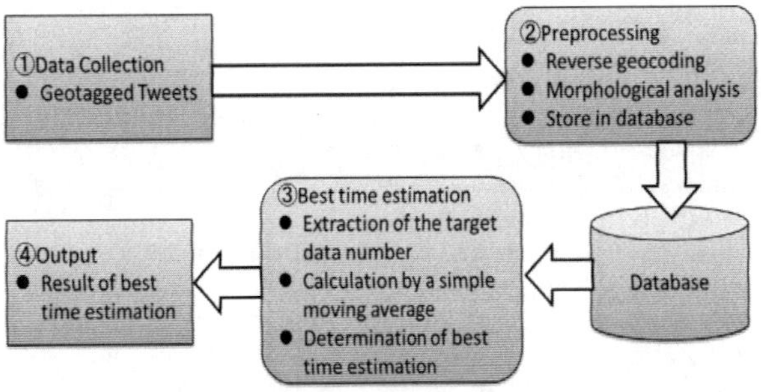

Figure 1. Our proposal.

We describe the best-time estimation method of organisms by analysis using a moving average method for geotagged tweets that include organism names. The best-time estimation in this paper is to estimate the period of time during which the creatures at the tourist spots are useful for sightseeing. Such information can be useful reference information when visiting tourist spots. The information supports estimation of the period during which a tourist can enjoy the four seasons by viewing cherry blossoms and autumn leaves. Hereinafter, Section III.A describes collection of geotagged tweets to be analyzed. Section III.B describes preprocessing for conducting analysis. Section III.C explains the best-time estimation method. In our proposed method up to now, the numbers of geotagged tweets have been small. It is possible to estimate the best time in a prefecture unit or municipality, but finely honed analyses have not been possible. Estimating the best time to visit sightseeing spots with finer granularity is possible using the method with interlinkage proposed in this paper. We propose two improvements of the best estimation method using interlinkage based on the best-time estimation method without interlinkage using the moving average method we have proposed. Section III.C.1 presents interlinkage using Kriging. Section III.C.2 presents interlinking using the average of regional amounts. Section III.D describes the output of the estimation result.

A. Data collection

This section presents a description of the Method of (1) data collection presented in Figure 1. Geotagged tweets sent from Twitter are a collection target. The range of geotagged tweets includes the Japanese archipelago (120.0°E – 154.0°E, and 20.0°N – 47.0°N) as the collection target. The collection of these data was done using a streaming API [13] provided by Twitter Inc.

Next, we describe the number of collected data. According to a report presented by Hashimoto et al. [14], among all tweets originating in Japan, about 0.18% are geotagged tweets: they are rare among all data. However, the geotagged tweets we collected are an average of 500 thousand tweets per day. We use about 250 million geotagged tweets from 2015/2/17 through 2017/5/13. We calculated the best time for flower viewing, as estimated using the processing described in the following sections using these data.

B. Preprocessing

This section presents a description of the method of (2) preprocessing shown in Figure 1. Preprocessing includes reverse geocoding and morphological analysis, as well as database storage for data collected through the processing described in Section III.A.

From latitude and longitude information in the individually collected tweets, reverse geocoding is useful to identify prefectures and municipalities by town name. We use a simple reverse geocoding service [15] available from the National Agriculture and Food Research Organization in this process: e.g., (latitude, longitude) = (35.7384446°N, 139.460910°E) by reverse geocoding becomes (Tokyo, Kodaira City, Ogawanishi-cho 2-chome).

Morphological analysis divides the collected geo-tagged tweet morphemes. We use the "Mecab" morphological analyzer [16]. By way of example, "桜は美しいです" (in English "Cherry blossoms are beautiful.")" is divided into "(桜 / noun), (は / particle), (美しい / adjective), (です / auxiliary verb), (。 / symbol)".

Preprocessing accomplishes the necessary data storage for best-time viewing, as estimated based on results of the processing of the data collection, reverse geocoding, and morphological analysis. Data used for this study were the tweet ID, tweet post time, tweet text, morphological analysis result, latitude, and longitude.

C. Estimating best-time viewing

This section presents a description of the method of (3) best-time estimation presented in Figure 1. Our method for the best-time viewing processes the target number of extracted data and calculates a simple moving average, yielding an inference of the best time to view the flowers. The method defines a word related to the best-time viewing: the target word. Table I shows that the target word is a word including Chinese characters, hiragana, and katakana, which represents an organism name and a seasonal change.

TABLE I. TARGET WORD EXAMPLES

Items	Target Words	In English
さくら	桜, さくら, サクラ	Cherry blossoms
かえで	楓, かえで, カエデ	Maple
いちょう	銀杏, いちょう, イチョウ	Ginkgo
こうよう	紅葉, 黄葉, こうよう, もみじ, コウヨウ, モミジ	Autumn leaves

A 7-day moving average is based on one week because a tendency exists for tweets to be more numerous on weekends than on weekdays. In addition, the phenological observations which are the current experiment subjects are targeting "events" that happen once a year (e.g., appreciation of cherry blossoms, viewing of autumn leaves, moon viewing). Such events are therefore based on a one-year moving average.

Next, we describe the simple moving average calculation, which uses a moving average of the standard of the best-time viewing judgment. A simple moving average is calculated on a daily basis using aggregate data by the target number of data extraction described above. Figure 2 presents an overview of the simple moving average of the number of days.

We calculate the simple moving average in formula (1) using the number of data going back to the past from the day before the estimated date of the best-time viewing.

$$X(Y) = \frac{P_1 + P_2 + \cdots + P_Y}{Y} \quad (1)$$

$X(Y)$: Y day moving average
P_n : Number of data of n days ago
Y : Calculation target period

The standard lengths of time we used for the simple moving average are 7 days and one year. A 7-day moving average is based on one week as the criterion of the estimated period of full bloom because, as shown in Table II, geotagged tweets of the increases tend to be more numerous on weekends than on weekdays. In addition, the phenological observations which are on the basis of the moving average of best-time the current experiment subjects are targeting "events" that happen once a year (e.g., appreciation of cherry blossoms, viewing estimated in prior years because many such "viewing" events occur every year: cherry blossom viewing, of autumn leaf viewing, and even leaves, moon viewing). Such events are therefore based on a one-year moving average.

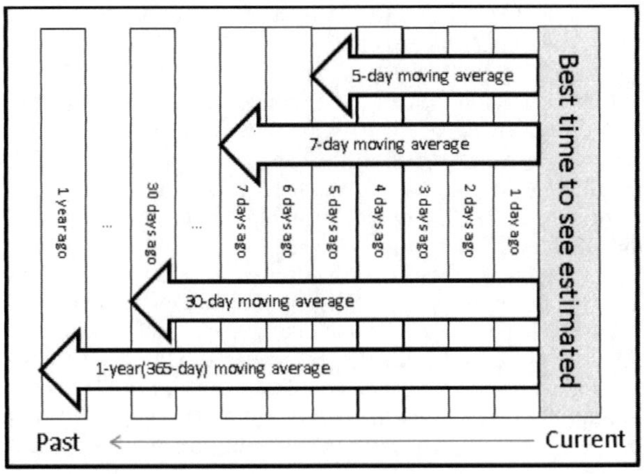

Figure 2. Number of days simple moving average.

TABLE II. TRANSITION OF GEOTAGGED TWEETS (2015/5/9 – 6/3)

Date (Day of the week)	Volume [tweet]	Date (Day of the week)	Volume [tweet]
5/9 (Sat)	117,253	5/22 (Fri)	92,237
5/10 (Sun)	128,654	5/23 (Sat)	55,590
5/11 (Mon)	91,795	5/24 (Sun)	72,243
5/12 (Tue)	87,354	5/25 (Mon)	82,375
5/13 (Wed)	67,016	5/26 (Tue)	83,851
5/14 (Thu)	88,994	5/27 (Wed)	83,825
5/15 (Fri)	89,210	5/28 (Thu)	85,024
5/16 (Sat)	116,600	5/29 (Fri)	121,582
5/17 (Sun)	126,705	5/30 (Sat)	119,387
5/18 (Mon)	89,342	5/31 (Sun)	81,431
5/19 (Tue)	83,695	6/1 (Mon)	76,364
5/20 (Wed)	87,927	6/2 (Tue)	76,699
5/21 (Thu)	86,164	6/3 (Wed)	78,329

Next, we describe a simple moving average of the number of days specified for each organism to compare the 7-day moving average and the one-year moving average. In this study, the best time to view the period varies depending on the specified organism, the individual organism, and the number of days from the biological period.

As an example, we describe cherry blossoms. The Japan Meteorological Agency [17] carries out phenological observations of "Sakura," which yields two output items of the flowering date and the full bloom date observation target. The "Sakura flowering date" [18] is the first day on which blooming of 5–6 or more wheels of flowers occurs on a specimen tree. The "Sakura in full bloom date" is the first day on which about 80% or more of the buds are open in the specimen tree. In addition, "Sakura" is the number of days from general flowering until full bloom: about five days. Therefore, "Sakura" in this study uses a 5-day moving average, which is standard.

Next, we describe an estimated judgment of the best-time for viewing, as calculated using the simple moving average (7-day moving average, one-year moving average, and another biological moving average). It specifies the two conditions as a condition of an estimated decision for the best-time for viewing. Condition 1 is the number of data one day before expression. Formula (2) is a simple moving average, which is greater than that of the estimated best-time to view date. Condition 2 is a case that follows formulas (3) ((*A*) / (2)) or more. The short number of days by comparison of the 7-day moving average and another biological moving average is A. A long number of days is B.

$$P_1 \geqq X(365) \tag{2}$$

$$X(A) \geqq X(B) \tag{3}$$

Finally, an estimate is produced from conditions 1 and 2. Using the proposed method, a day satisfying both condition 1 and condition 2 is estimated for best-time viewing.

The method presented above is the conventional method we have proposed. However, when interlinkage is not used, it is difficult to estimate the optimum position with fine granularity. Therefore, we propose a method using the following information 1) and 2). Then, interlinkage using 1) or 2) is used to estimate the best viewing time.

1) Interlinkage using Kriging

This section presents the first method of interlinkage, for which we used Kriging [19], an estimation method used for estimating values for points where information was not acquired. We ascertain the distribution of information in the whole space in geostatistics.

Next, the granularity for estimation is shown. For an estimate for Japan as a whole, prefecture units are assumed and acquired by reverse geocoding. However, when conducting more detailed analyses, a difficulty arises: it is impossible to estimate the number of geotagged tweets for each city or town or village or tourist spot. Therefore, based on latitude and longitude information of collected tweets, data are accumulated for each division of land using tertiary mesh data provided by the Land Numerical Information download service of the Ministry of Land, Infrastructure, and Transport [20]. The tertiary mesh is a section of about 1 km square. We attempted estimation through interlinkage using data aggregated for each section of tertiary mesh data. The estimated value of the target data at a certain point S0 is represented in formula (4) as a weighted average of the measured values $Z(S_i)$ (i = 1, 2..., N) at N points S_i existing around point S_0. As described in this paper, we experimentally assigned a +1 weight for 'full bloom' and 'beautiful', and assigned -1 on 'still' or 'falling'. Then we assigned value Z to tweets including the target word and Z. Here, N represents the 30 nearby targeted tweets. λ

represents a spherical model that decreases the influence as the distance increases.

$$\hat{z}(S_0) = \sum_{i=1}^{N} \lambda_i Z(S_i) \qquad (4)$$

$Z(S_i)$: Measurement value at i-th position
λ_i : Unknown weighting of measured value at i-th position
S_0 : Predicted position
N : Number of measurements

2) Interlinkage using regional quantity

In this section, we explain the interlinkage method using regional quantities of tweets of city, town, and village units. Conventionally, the best optimum time was estimated using the moving average value without interlinkage using estimation judgment, as described later. As a result, for the analysis of a wide area such as prefecture unit, the R_value can be estimated as about 80%. However, with an estimate of granularity such as by a sightseeing spot, the inability to estimate the viewing period from scarce data is difficult. Therefore, we propose a method of using regional quantities that newly use interlinkage to compensate for the lack of data volume. The proposed method uses the result of reverse geocoding obtained during preprocessing in the previous section. Tweets that were judged as originating from the same municipality by reverse geocoding are summed for each day by city, town, or village. Then, considering the characteristic that the tweets move on a weekly basis, we obtain a 7-day moving average and set the 7-day moving average of the municipalities as the regional quantity of each region. To estimate the best time for viewing, use the value obtained by adding the regional quantity of the municipality where the sightseeing spot is located to the tweet amount of the sightseeing spot to be estimated.

D. Output

This section presents a description of the method of (4) output presented in Figure 1. Output can be visualized using a best-time viewing result, as estimated from processing explained in the previous section. A time-series graph presents the inferred results for best-time viewing. The graph presents the number of data and the date, respectively, on the vertical axis and the horizontal axis. We are striving to develop useful visualization techniques for travelers.

IV. EXPERIMENTS

This section presents a description of an experiment to estimate the best-time viewing for cherry blossoms using the method described in Section III. An experiment is conducted to infer the best time to view flowers for the proposed method described in Section III. Section IV.A describes the dataset used for optimal time reasoning to see flowers in full bloom. As an estimation result by sightseeing spot, Section IV.B presents the estimation result without using interlinkage, and the best estimation result obtained using interlinkage in Section IV.C. Section IV.D presents a comparison of the experiment results from Section IV.B and Section IV.C.

A. Dataset

Datasets used for this experiment were collected using streaming API, as described for data collection in Section III.1. The data, which include about 250 million items, are geotagged tweets from Japan during 2015/2/17 – 2017/5/13.

The estimation experiment conducted to ascertain the best-time viewing of cherry blossoms uses the target word "cherry blossom," which is "桜" and "さくら" and "サクラ" in Japanese. We analyzed tweet texts that included the target word. About 100,000 tweets during in the experiment period included the subject word.

The subject of the experiment was set as tourist spots in Tokyo. In this report, we describe "Takao Mountain," "Showa Memorial Park," "Shinjuku gyoen," and "Rikugien." Figure 3 presents the target area locations. A, B, C, and D in the figure respectively denote "Takao Mountain," "Showa Memorial Park," "Rikugien," and "Shinjuku Gyoen." A and B are separated by about 16 km straight-line distance. B and C are about 32 km apart. C and D are about 6 km apart. In this experiment, about 30,000 tweets including the target word in Tokyo were found. In this experiment, all tweets made by the same user are also used as analysis targets if they are tweets including the target word.

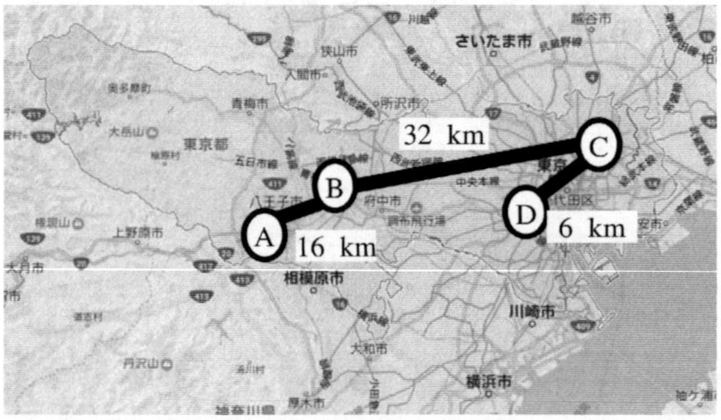

Figure 3. Position of the target area.

We use these datasets to estimate the optimum time for the sightseeing spots in Tokyo using experiments without interlinkage. We conducted experiments of the following two kinds. The first is an experiment using the number of tweets including the target word and the sightseeing spot name without interlinkage. This experiment uses the conventional method we proposed. This experiment was compared as Baseline to confirm the usefulness of interlinkage proposed in this paper. The second is an experiment using interlinkage. In this experiment, we used two methods: interlinkage using Kriging of Section III.C.1) and interlinkage using regional quantity described in Section III.C.2).

B. Estimation experiment for best-time viewing without interlinkage

This section presents experimentally obtained results for estimating the best time without using interlinkage from tweets containing a target word and sightseeing spot name. Figure 4 presents results for the estimated best-time viewing in 2016 using the target word 'cherry blossoms' in the target tourist spots. The dark gray bar in the figure represents the number of tweets. The light gray part represents best-time viewing as determined using the proposed method. Additionally, the solid line shows the 5-day moving average. The dashed line shows the 7-day moving average. The dotted line shows the one-year moving average.

At tourist spots targeted for the experiment in 2016, as portrayed in Figure 4, many data were obtained for C and D. The maximum number of tweets per day was about 30. These results confirmed that some estimation can be accomplished using near-site estimation method without interpolation. However, best-time viewing cannot be done in A and B because of the very small number of tweets.

This difficulty applies to many sightseeing spots in Japan. In fact, a difficulty exists by which it is impossible to estimate the best-time to see the sightseeing spots and other fine-grain sight by simply using the number of geotagged tweets. This experimentally obtained result clarified that the method we proposed previously cannot be predictive for detailed areas such as sightseeing spots. This result is attributable to the lack of information volume.

C. Estimation experiment for best-time viewing with interlinkage

In this section, the results of interlinkage using Kriging of Section III.C.1, which is the method proposed in this paper, and interlinkage using the region quantities of Section III.C.2 are shown in Section IV.C.1 and Section IV.C.2.

1) Estimation experiment for best-time viewing by interlinkage using Kriging

Figure 5 portrays an experimentally obtained result from interlinking results for a tertiary mesh including the tourist spots we examined. The notation is the same as that presented in Figure 4.

Apparently, A and B were able to produce an estimate using the proposed method by increasing the number of tweets using interlinkage with surrounding tweets. For C and D, there are days when it can be determined more accurately by interpolating the number of tweets. However, because tweets of negative judgments exist such as "still" or "scattered" among surrounding tweets, in some cases, interpolation excluded the day determined as the best time in Experiment 1. Therefore, the judgment condition of the tweet is subject to further study. These results confirmed the possibility of estimating the peak period, even for an area without tweets, using data interpolation and overall tweet number interpolation.

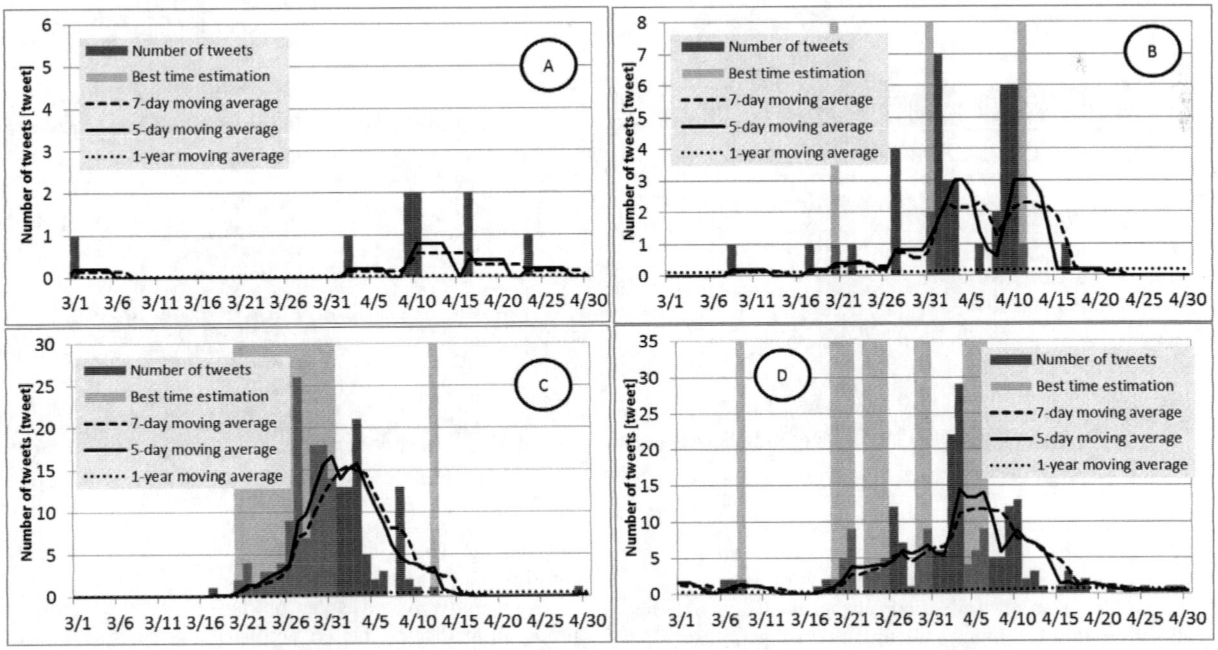

Figure 4. Experimental results obtained using tweets including the target word and the tourist spot name.

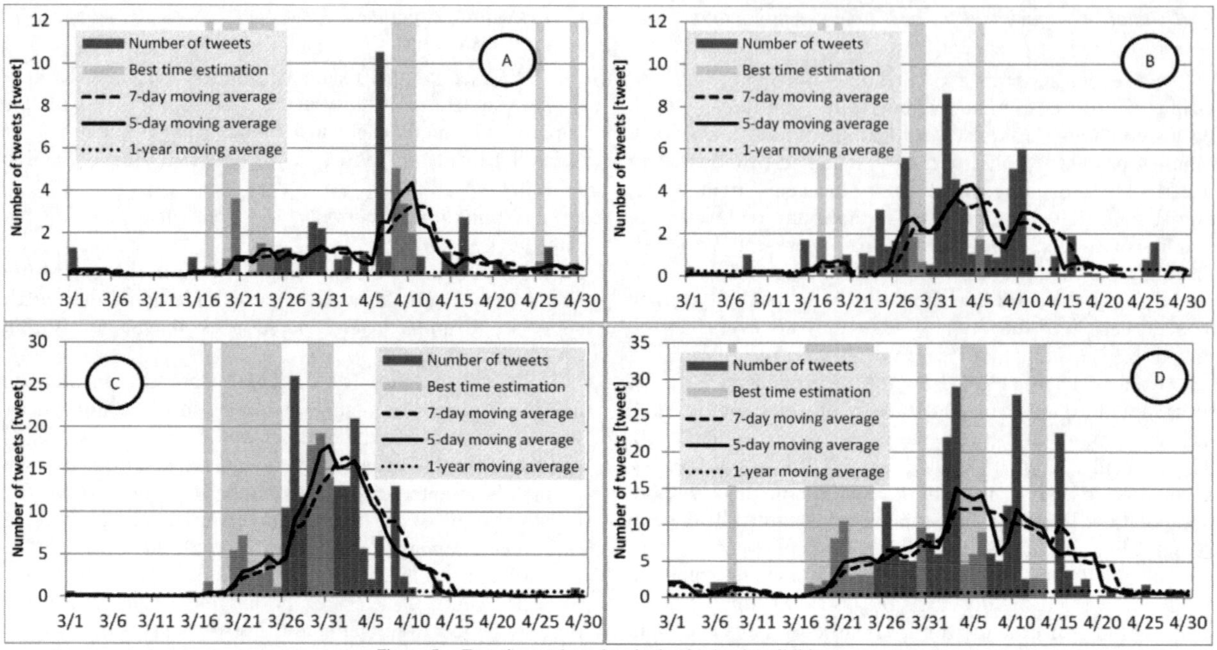

Figure 5. Experimental results obtained using interlinking.

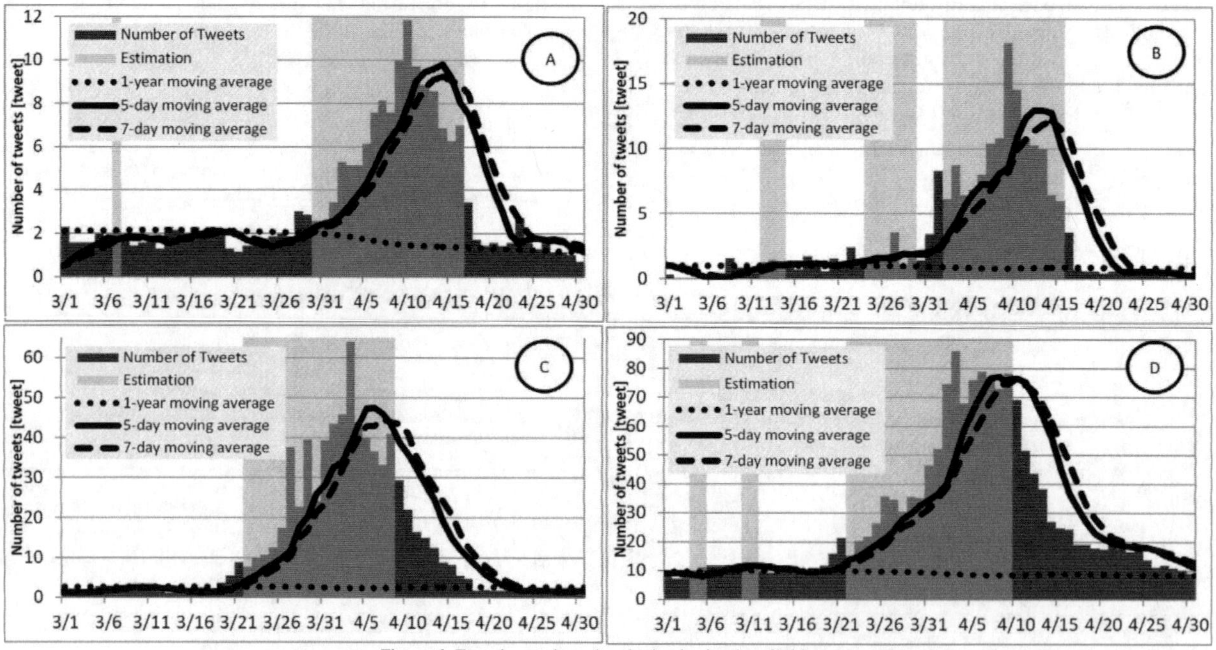

Figure 6. Experimental results obtained using interlinking.

2) Estimation experiment for best-time viewing by interlinkage using regional quantities

In this section, we explain experimentally obtained estimation results obtained using interlinkage of regional quantities. Figure 6 presents results obtained using interlinking. The notation is the same as the notation used for Figure 3 in the previous section.

Apparently, A and B can produce an estimate using the proposed method by increasing the number of tweets using interlinkage with surrounding tweets. For C and D, there are days that can be determined more accurately by interpolating the number of tweets. These results demonstrate the possibility of first resolving the difficulty of insufficient information when using sightseeing spot tweet data of the tourist spot area along with interpolation, and then estimating the peak period for each tourist spot.

Furthermore, even given the same area of Tokyo, the times estimated for A and B are later than those of C and D. These later results is attributable to the fact that A and B are at higher altitudes than either C or D. Flowers can be expected to bloom later in the year there.

Therefore, using interlinkage, one can confirm differences in surroundings even within one prefecture. More detailed analysis becomes possible with interlinkage using the proposed method.

D. Comparing estimations and observed data for best times for viewing

This section presents a comparison between experimentally obtained results and observation data. An estimation result obtained without using interlinkage was taken as the Baseline. Then, the experiment using interlinkage with Kriging of Section IV.C.1 was taken as experiment 1. Experiment 2 was based on interlinkage using the regional quantity of Section IV.C.2.

1) Comparison of observation data with best time of viewing estimation using interlinkage with Kriging

Table III presents results of the optimal time for viewing in 2016, as estimated using Kriging. The baseline examination used co-occurring words in tweets including the sightseeing spot name coexisting with the target word "Sakura." Experiment 1 used interlinkage on a tertiary mesh including sightseeing spots. The numerical values in the table are the numbers of tweets including the target word and co-occurrence word in the Baseline. Experiment 1 uses the sum of the number of tweets in the Baseline plus the numerical values by obtained using interpolation. The light gray area shows the date when the fullness prediction was made using the proposed method.

Confirming the flowering day and full bloom period of each sightseeing spot using JMA data is difficult, but this experiment evaluating SNS data for flowering is valid also for use by weather forecasting companies [21] and public service organizations [22] to ascertain the optimum times for viewing based on services and blogs that are used. Arrows indicating the flowering time can be checked manually at tourist sites. Recall and precision using the observed data and the best time to view estimated results are calculated respectively for target areas for 2016 for 3/1 – 4/30 using formula (5) and formula (6). We used the R_value as the recall rate using the proposed method, and the P_value and R_value, respectively, as the relevance rate and recall rate when using the proposed method.

$$P\_value = \frac{Number\ of\ days\ to\ match\ the\ observed\ data}{Number\ of\ days\ in\ best\ time\ to\ see\ estimated} \quad (5)$$

$$R\_value = \frac{Number\ of\ days\ to\ match\ the\ observed\ data}{Number\ of\ days\ of\ observation\ data} \quad (6)$$

TABLE III. COMPARISON RESULTS FOR BASELINE AND EXPERIMENT 1

	Takao mountain		Showa Memorial park		Rikugien		Shinjuku gyoen	
	Exp. 1	Exp. 2	Exp. 1	Exp. 2	Exp. 1	Exp. 2	Exp. 1	Exp. 2
3/1	1	1.27	0	0.40	0	0.58	0	0.28
3/2	0	0.00	0	0.00	0	0.00	0	0.00
3/3	0	0.00	0	0.00	0	0.00	0	0.00
3/4	0	0.00	0	0.00	0	0.00	1	1.00
3/5	0	0.00	0	0.00	0	0.00	0	0.00
3/6	0	0.00	0	0.00	0	0.00	2	2.00
3/7	0	0.00	0	0.00	0	0.00	2	2.00
3/8	0	0.00	1	1.00	0	0.00	2	2
3/9	0	0.00	0	0.00	0	0.00	0	0.00
3/10	0	0.00	0	0.00	0	0.00	0	0.00
3/11	0	0.00	0	0.00	0	0.00	0	0.00
3/12	0	0.00	0	0.00	0	0.00	0	0.00
3/13	0	0.00	0	0.00	0	0.00	0	0.00
3/14	0	0.00	0	0.00	0	0.00	0	0.00
3/15	0	0.84	0	1.68	0	0.41	0	0.24
3/16	0	0.00	0	0.00	0	0.00	0	0.00
3/17	0	0.40	1	1.85	1	1.67	1	1.85
3/18	0	-0.51	0	-0.43	0	0.02	2	1.64
3/19	0	0.78	0	0.49	0	0.22	2	2.30
3/20	0	3.61	1	1.00	2	5.42	5	8.18
3/21	0	0.00	0	-4.81	4	7.16	9	10.49
3/22	0	0.14	1	1.06	1	2.93	0	2.97
3/23	0	1.51	0	0.93	3	2.70	3	3.06
3/24	0	0.84	0	3.13	3	5.11	3	3.00
3/25	0	1.06	0	1.40	4	1.00	5	5.00
3/26	0	1.27	0	1.67	9	10.41	12	13.14
3/27	0	-0.08	4	5.57	26	26.00	7	7.00
3/28	0	0.94	0	1.85	7	11.74	1	5.19
3/29	0	2.50	0	0.66	18	17.83	5	5.00
3/30	0	2.21	0	0.52	18	19.18	9	9.62
3/31	0	0.00	2	4.13	14	14.00	6	8.82
4/1	0	0.74	7	8.60	13	13.00	6	6.00
4/2	1	0.91	3	4.56	13	13.00	22	22.00
4/3	0	0.00	3	3.30	21	21.00	29	29.00
4/4	0	1.12	0	1.05	5	5.62	4	4.55
4/5	0	0.00	0	1.73	2	2.00	6	6.00
4/6	0	10.52	1	1.00	3	7.05	9	9.00
4/7	0	0.89	0	0.88	0	0.33	5	6.06
4/8	0	5.05	2	2.00	13	13.00	5	5.00
4/9	2	3.37	6	5.05	2	2.29	12	12.62
4/10	2	2.00	6	6.00	1	1.00	13	27.88
4/11	0	0.88	1	1.00	0	0.00	2	2.47
4/12	0	0.00	0	0.00	1	-0.24	3	2.61
4/13	0	-0.50	0	0.02	0	1.79	1	2.55
4/14	0	1.11	0	0.95	0	-0.67	0	-0.37
4/15	0	0.51	0	0.12	0	0.00	1	22.54
4/16	2	2.75	1	1.91	0	0.60	3	3.63
4/17	0	0.00	0	0.00	0	0.42	1	1.54
4/18	0	0.14	0	0.17	0	0.36	2	2.51
4/19	0	-0.34	0	0.13	0	0.30	0	0.07
4/20	0	0.66	0	-0.43	0	-0.20	0	0.21
4/21	0	0.58	0	0.58	0	0.00	1	1.00
4/22	0	0.00	0	0.00	0	0.00	0	0.00
4/23	1	0.43	0	-4.08	0	0.00	1	1.19
4/24	0	0.00	0	0.00	0	0.00	0	0.00
4/25	0	0.68	0	0.76	0	0.64	1	1.75
4/26	0	1.33	0	1.61	0	-1.03	0	-0.26
4/27	0	0.00	0	0.00	0	0.00	0	0.00
4/28	0	-0.25	0	-0.34	0	0.19	1	1.11
4/29	0	0.60	0	0.00	1	1.00	1	1.00
4/30	0	0.00	0	0.09	0	0.00	0	0.00
P_value	0.26	0.38	0.72	0.75	0.89	0.89	0.84	0.75
R_value	0.00	0.20	0.11	0.22	0.67	0.61	0.56	0.50

TABLE IV. COMPARISON RESULTS FOR BASELINE AND EXPERIMENT 2

	Takao Mountain		Showa memorial park		Rikugien		Shinjuku gyoen	
	Baseline	Exp.2	Baseline	Exp.2	Baseline	Exp.2	Baseline	Exp.2
3/1	1	2.29	0	0.40	0	0.58	0	7.57
3/2	0	1.57	0	0.00	0	0.00	0	7.14
3/3	0	1.57	0	0.00	0	0.00	0	7.29
3/4	0	1.57	0	0.00	0	0.00	1	9.86
3/5	0	2.00	0	0.00	0	0.00	0	11.29
3/6	0	1.86	0	0.00	0	0.00	2	11.86
3/7	0	2.14	0	0.00	0	0.00	2	11.86
3/8	0	1.71	1	1.00	0	0.00	2	12
3/9	0	1.43	0	0.00	0	0.00	0	11.86
3/10	0	1.57	0	0.00	0	0.00	0	11.71
3/11	0	1.71	0	0.00	0	0.00	0	10.71
3/12	0	1.29	0	0.00	0	0.00	0	9.86
3/13	0	2.29	0	0.00	0	0.00	0	9.14
3/14	0	2.14	0	0.00	0	0.00	0	10.14
3/15	0	2.00	0	1.68	0	0.41	0	9.43
3/16	0	2.29	0	0.00	0	0.00	0	8.86
3/17	0	2.00	1	1.85	1	1.67	1	10.14
3/18	0	2.00	0	1.00	0	1.86	2	10.57
3/19	0	2.00	0	0.57	0	3.57	2	11.86
3/20	0	1.29	1	1.57	2	5.43	5	16.00
3/21	0	1.14	0	1.14	4	8.86	9	21.43
3/22	0	1.43	1	2.43	1	7.57	0	15.43
3/23	0	1.43	0	1.43	3	10.00	3	20.43
3/24	0	1.71	0	1.57	3	10.71	3	21.86
3/25	0	1.86	0	1.43	4	12.57	5	26.57
3/26	0	2.00	0	1.71	9	17.43	12	35.86
3/27	0	1.86	4	3.57	26	37.57	7	34.71
3/28	0	3.00	0	1.14	7	22.71	1	30.57
3/29	0	2.86	0	2.14	18	39.43	5	35.57
3/30	0	2.57	0	1.43	18	24.14	9	35.29
3/31	0	2.57	2	3.43	14	39.29	6	46.57
4/1	0	3.43	7	8.29	13	43.57	6	52.14
4/2	1	5.29	3	6.14	13	45.86	22	74.71
4/3	0	5.14	3	8.71	21	64.00	29	86.00
4/4	0	5.14	0	6.43	5	44.00	4	68.00
4/5	0	6.14	0	6.86	2	40.00	6	76.00
4/6	0	7.57	1	8.00	3	36.57	9	79.00
4/7	0	8.14	0	10.43	0	33.14	5	76.86
4/8	0	7.57	2	10.86	13	41.00	5	73.14
4/9	2	10.00	6	18.14	2	29.29	12	78.43
4/10	2	11.86	6	14.57	1	22.00	13	69.29
4/11	0	9.71	1	10.86	0	16.43	2	51.57
4/12	0	8.86	0	10.29	1	15.00	3	43.71
4/13	0	8.57	0	10.00	0	12.43	1	38.29
4/14	0	6.86	0	6.43	0	8.86	0	27.00
4/15	0	6.29	0	6.00	0	8.29	1	24.86
4/16	2	7.00	1	3.57	0	5.43	3	24.43
4/17	0	3.43	0	0.71	0	4.71	1	19.14
4/18	0	1.71	0	0.57	0	1.71	2	19.14
4/19	0	1.43	0	0.57	0	1.86	0	17.86
4/20	0	1.57	0	0.43	0	1.71	0	17.57
4/21	0	1.43	0	0.57	0	1.71	1	20.00
4/22	0	1.57	0	0.57	0	1.71	0	17.71
4/23	1	2.71	0	-4.08	0	0.00	1	16.71
4/24	0	1.57	0	0.00	0	0.00	0	18.14
4/25	0	1.29	0	0.76	0	0.64	1	13.86
4/26	0	1.57	0	1.61	0	-1.03	0	11.29
4/27	0	1.14	0	0.00	0	0.00	0	12.00
4/28	0	1.14	0	-0.34	0	0.19	1	11.00
4/29	0	1.00	0	0.00	1	1.00	1	10.29
4/30	0	0.71	0	0.09	0	0.00	0	9.14
P_value	0.26	0.77	0.72	0.74	0.89	0.84	0.84	0.82
R_value	0.00	0.58	0.11	0.44	0.67	0.58	0.56	0.83

Experimental results confirmed the tendency by which the relevance ratio and the R_value become higher for tourist spots with fewer tweets. Therefore, we can present the possibility of estimating sightseeing sites with few tweets using interlinkage. However, because the interpolation information amount is insufficient in the current method, it is necessary to improve the interlinking method further. Furthermore, because sightseeing spots with many tweets are affected by tweets of negative judgments in the surroundings, the accuracy is lower than in the Baseline. However, one might be able to estimate more details, such as the start time, using interpolation.

2) Comparison of observation data with best time of viewing estimation using interlinking with regional quantities

Table IV presents results of the optimal time for viewing in 2016, as estimated using regional quantities. Experimentally obtained results confirmed the tendency by which the relevance ratio and the R_value became higher in Experiment 2 than in the Baseline. In addition, A and B, which are at higher altitudes than either C or D, demonstrated regional features: the best viewing time occurs later. These results confirmed the usefulness of the proposed method for best-time estimation for sightseeing spots using interlinkage along with regional data. Using this proposed method, information can be interpolated according to the sightseeing spot. One can obtain better estimation with finer granularity than that available with the conventional method.

Additionally, comparison with Experiment 1 of Section IV.D.1 is good because, in Experiment 1, the tweet contents are analyzed and interpolation is performed using tweets including specific information. Therefore, the tweet number used for interlinkage is less than that in Experiment 2. By contrast, in Experiment 2, the moving average value using all tweets included in the same area judged as the same municipality by reverse geocoding is used without analyzing the tweet contents. Experiment 2 is useful at the present stage, but it seems that the possibility exists that improving Experiment 1 to analyze tweet contents might improve the estimation accuracy.

V. CONCLUSION

As described herein, to improve best-time estimation accuracy and thereby enhance tourist information related to phenological observation, we proposed an interlinking method.

For the first proposed method, information was interpolated using neighbor-weighted tweets on a tertiary mesh including sightseeing spots, thereby indicating the optimum time to view flowers at sightseeing spots. The results of cherry blossom experiments conducted at sightseeing spots in Tokyo in 2016 confirm the tendency for improvement of the estimation accuracy using interlinking. The proposed method using interlinkage for tweets related to organism names might improve the accuracy of estimating the best time in the real world. We confirmed the possibility of applying this proposed method to estimation of the viewpoint and line of sight in areas and sightseeing spots with few tweets and little location information. However, analysis of the contents of tweets is an experimentally obtained result obtained using few words. Effective interlinking cannot be established. Therefore, future research with manual experimental weighting and geotagged tweets is expected to facilitate further improvements to overcome insufficiencies in the measured values used for interpolation. Additionally, we expect to reconsider the viewing angle estimation conditions.

The second proposed method showed optimal times to see flowers at sightseeing spots by interpolating information using the 7-day moving average of the number of tweets of municipalities, including those of sightseeing spots. This method can estimate the best time for sightseeing spots with fine granularity, yielding predictions in units required for sightseeing.

The results of cherry blossom experiments conducted for tourist spots in Tokyo in 2016 using the proposed method confirmed improvement of the estimation accuracy when using interlinking. The proposed method using interlinkage for tweets related to named organisms (sakura trees) might improve the real-world accuracy of estimating the best times. We confirmed the possibility of applying this proposed method to estimation of viewpoints and lines of sight in areas and sightseeing spots with few tweets and little location information. The proposed method interpolated information and yielded highly accurate estimation, perhaps because of the fact that cherry blossoms bloom with short-term changes and because public interest is high. Therefore, future studies can be conducted to verify whether similar results are obtainable using other biological season observations.

Future studies must also assess the automatic extraction of target words and methods to make future predictions in real time. Eventually, this system might be extended to a system for travelers to obtain travel-destination-related event information and disaster information in real time.

ACKNOWLEDGMENTS

This work was supported by JSPS KAKENHI Grant Nos. 16K00157 and 16K16158, and by a Tokyo Metropolitan University Grant-in-Aid for Research on Priority Areas "Research on Social Big Data."

REFERENCES

[1] M. Endo, S. Ohno, M. Hirota, Y. Shoji, and H. Ishikawa, "Examination of Best-time Estimation using Interpolation for Geotagged Tweets," MMEDIA 2017 Proceeding of The Ninth International Conference on Advances in Multimedia, pp. 38-43, 2017.

[2] Twitter. *It's what's happening*. [Online]. Available from: https://Twitter.com/ [retrieved: September 2, 2017]

[3] Japan Tourism Agency. *Tourism Nation Promotion Basic Law*. [Online]. Available from: http://www.mlit.go.jp/kankocho/en/kankorikkoku/index.html [retrieved: April 14, 2017]

[4] Ministry of Economy, Trade and Industry. *Inbound Landing-Type Tourism Guide*. [Online]. Available from: http://www.mlit.go.jp/common/001091713.pdf [retrieved: November 10, 2017] (in Japanese).

[5] M. Endo, Y. Shoji, M. Hirota, S. Ohno, and H. Ishikawa, "On best time estimation method for phenological observations using geotagged tweets," International Workshop on Informatics 2016 (IWIN2016), 2016.

[6] J. Kleinberg, "Bursty and hierarchical structure in stream," In Proc. of the Eighth ACM SIGKDD International Conference on Knowledge Discovery and Data Mining, pp. 1–25, 2002.

[7] T. Sakaki, M. Okazaki, and Y. Matsuo, "Earthquake shakes Twitter users: real-time event detection by social sensors," WW W 2010, pp. 851–860, 2010.

[8] T. Kaneko and K. Yanai, "Visual Event Mining from the Twitter Stream," WWW '16 Companion Proceedings of the 25th International Conference Companion on World Wide Web, pp. 51–52, 2016.

[9] Y. Yamagata, D. Murakami, G. W. Peters, and T. Matsui, "A spatiotemporal analysis of participatory sensing data "tweets" and extreme climate events toward real-time urban risk management," arXiv preprint arXiv:1505.06188, pp. 1–34, 2015.

[10] S. Phithakkitnukoon, T. Teerayut Horanont, A. Witayangkurn, R. Siri, Y. Sekimoto, and R. Shibasaki, "Understanding tourist behavior using large-scale mobile sensing approach: A case study of mobile phone users in Japan," Pervasive and Mobile Computing, 2014.

[11] A. Mislove, S. Lehmann, Y.Y. Shn, and J. Kleinberg, "Bursty and hierarchical structure in stream," In P. Onnela, and Rosenquist, Understanding the Eighth ACM SIGKDD Demographics of Twitter Users, Proceedings. Fifth International AAAI Conference on Knowledge Discovery, Weblogs and Data Mining, Social Media (ICWSM'11), pp. 1–25, 2002. 133-140, 2011.

[12] Z. Cheng, J. Caverlee, and K. Yanai, "Visual Event Mining from the Twitter Stream," WWW '16 CompanionLee, You are where you tweet: a content-based approach to geo-locating twitter users, Proceedings of the 25th 19th ACM International Conference Companion on World Wide Web, pp. 51–52, 2016.on Information and Knowledge Management, 2010.

[13] Twitter Developers. *Twitter Developer official site*. [Online] Available from: https://dev.twitter.com/ [retrieved: April 2, 2017]

[14] Y. Hashimoto and M. Oka, "Statistics of Geo-Tagged Tweets in Urban Areas (<Special Issue>Synthesis and Analysis of Massive Data Flow)," JSAI, vol. 27, no. 4, pp. 424–431, 2012 (in Japanese).

[15] National Agriculture and Food Research Organization. *Simple reverse geocoding service*. [Online]. Available from: https://www.finds.jp/rgeocode/index.html.ja [retrieved: November 18, 2017]

[16] MeCab. *Yet Another Part-of-Speech and Morphological Analyzer*. [Online]. Available from: http://taku910.github.io/mecab/ [retrieved: November 10, 2017]

[17] Japan Meteorological Agency. *Disaster prevention information XML format providing information page*. [Online]. Available from: http://xml.kishou.go.jp/ [retrieved: April 5, 2015]

[18] Japan Meteorological Agency. *Observation of Sakura*. [Online]. Available from: http://www.data.jma.go.jp/sakura/data/sakura2012.pdf [retrieved: April 5, 2015]

[19] M. A. Oliver, "Kriging: A Method of Interpolation for Geographical Information Systems," International Journal of Geographic Information Systems vol. 4, pp. 313–332, 1990.

[20] Ministry of Land, Infrastructure and Transport. *Land Numerical Information download service*. [Online]. Available from: http://nlftp.mlit.go.jp/ksj-e/index.html [retrieved: April 5, 2015]

[21] Weathernews Inc. *Sakura information*. [Online]. Available from: http://weathernews.jp/sakura [retrieved: May 10, 2017]

[22] Japan Travel and Tourism Association. *Whole country cherry trees*. [Online]. Available from: http://www.nihon-kankou.or.jp/sakura/ [retrieved: November 14, 2017]

On Line Visibility-Based Trajectory Planning in 3D Dynamic Environments Using Local Point Clouds Data

[1,2]Oren Gal and [2]Yerach Doytsher

[1]Department of Marine Technologies
University of Haifa
Haifa, Israel
e-mail: orengal@technion.ac.il

[2]Mapping and Geo-information Engineering
Technion - Israel Institute of Technology
Haifa, Israel
e-mail:doytsher@technion.ac.il

Abstract - **In this paper we present an efficient and fast visible trajectory planning for unmanned vehicles in a 3D urban environment based on local point clouds data. Our trajectory planning method is based on a two-step visibility analysis in 3D urban environments using predicted visibility from point clouds data. The first step in our unique concept is to extract basic geometric shapes. We focus on three basic geometric shapes from point clouds in urban scenes: planes, cylinders and spheres, extracting these geometric shapes using efficient RANSAC algorithms with a high success rate of detection. The second step is a prediction of these geometric entities in the next time step, formulated as states vectors in a dynamic system using Kalman Filter (KF). Our planner is based on the optimal time horizon concept as a leading feature for our greedy search method for making our local planner safer. We demonstrate our visibility and trajectory planning method in simulations, showing predicted trajectory planning in 3D urban environments based on real LiDAR point clouds data.**

Keywords- Visibility; 3D; Urban environment; Spatial analysis.

I. Introduction and Related Work

In this paper we study an efficient and fast visible trajectory planning for unmanned vehicles in a 3D urban environment, based on local point clouds data. Recently, urban scene modeling has become more and more precise, using Terrestrial/ground-based LiDAR on unmanned vehicles for generating point clouds data for modeling roads, signs, lamp posts, buildings, trees and cars. Visibility analysis in complex urban scenes is commonly treated as an approximated feature due to computational complexity.

Our trajectory planning method is based on a two-step visibility analysis in 3D urban environments using predicted visibility from point clouds data. The first step in our unique concept is to extract basic geometric shapes. We focus on three basic geometric shapes from point clouds in urban scenes: planes, cylinders and spheres, extracting these geometric shapes using efficient RANSAC algorithms with a high success rate of detection. The second step is a prediction of these geometric entities in the next time step, formulated as states vectors in a dynamic system using Kalman Filter (KF).

Visibility analysis based on this approximated scene prediction is done efficiently [1], based on our analytic solutions for visibility boundaries. Based on this capability, we present a local on-line planner generating visible trajectories, exploring the most visible and safe node in the next time step, using our predicted visibility analysis, which is based on local point clouds data from the unmanned LiDAR vehicle. Our planner is based on the optimal time horizon concept as a leading feature for our greedy search method for making our local planner safer.

For the first time, we propose a solution to the basic limitation of the Velocity Obstacle (VO) search and planning method, i.e., when all the dynamic available velocities for the next time step are blocked in the velocity space and there is no legal node at the next time step of the greedy search. The computation of the minimum time horizon is formulated as a minimum time problem that generates optimal trajectories in near-time time to the goal, exploring the most visible and safest node in the next time step. We demonstrate our visibility and trajectory planning method in simulations showing predicted trajectory planning in 3D urban environments using real LiDAR data from Ford Campus Project [2].

The main challenge in motion planning is reaching the goal while searching and selecting only safe maneuvers. While reaching the goal cannot be guaranteed with an on-line planner, one can reduce the state space search to only safe states, i.e., states outside obstacles from which at least one other safe state is reachable.

Generally, we distinguish between local and global planners. The local planner generates one step, or a few steps, at every time step, whereas the global planner uses a global search toward the goal over a time-spanned tree. We can divide this work into global and local (reactive) planners. The global planners generate complete trajectories to the goal in static [3] and dynamic [4,5] environments.

Visibility problem has been extensively studied over the last twenty years, due to the importance of visibility in GIS and Geomatics, computer graphics and computer vision, and robotics. Accurate visibility computation in 3D environments is a very complicated task demanding a high computational effort, which could hardly have been done in a very short time using traditional well-known visibility methods [23]. The exact visibility methods are highly complex, and cannot be used for fast applications due to their long computation time. Previous research in visibility computation has been devoted to open environments using DEM models, representing raster data in 2.5D (Polyhedral model), and do not address, or suggest solutions for, dense built-up areas. Most of these works have focused on approximate visibility computation, enabling fast results using interpolations of visibility values between points, calculating point visibility with the Line of Sight (LOS) method [24]. Other fast algorithms are based on the conservative Potentially Visible Set (PVS) [25]. These methods are not always completely accurate, as they may render hidden objects' parts as visible due to various simplifications and heuristics.

A vast number of algorithms have been suggested for speeding up the process and reducing computation time. Franklin [26] evaluates and approximates visibility for each cell in a DEM model based on greedy algorithms. Wang et al. [27] introduced a Grid-based DEM method using viewshed horizon, saving computation time based on relations between surfaces and the line of sight (LOS method). Later, an extended method for viewshed computation was presented, using reference planes rather than sightlines [28].

II. Visibility Analysis from Point Clouds Data

As we mentioned, visibility analysis in complex urban scenes is commonly treated as an approximated feature due to computational complexity. Recently, urban scene modeling has become more and more exact, using Terrestrial/ground-based LiDAR generating dense point clouds data for modeling roads, signs, lamp posts, buildings, trees and cars. Automatic algorithms detecting basic shapes and extraction have been studied extensively, and are still a very active research field [34].

In this part, we present an unique concept for predicted and approximated visibility analysis in the next attainable vehicle's state at a one-time step ahead in time, based on local point clouds data, which is a partial data set.

We focus on three basic geometric shapes in urban scenes: planes, cylinders and spheres, which are very common and can be used for the majority of urban entities in modeling scenarios. Based on point clouds data generated from the current vehicle's position in state k-1, we extract these geometric shapes using efficient RANSAC algorithms [35] with high success rate detection tested in real point cloud data.

After extraction of these basic geometric shapes from local point clouds data, our unified concept, and our main contribution, focus on the ability to predict and approximate urban scene modeling at the next view point V_k, i.e., attainable location of the vehicle in the next time step. Scene prediction is based on the geometric entities and Kalman Filter (KF) which is commonly used in dynamic systems for tracking target systems [36,37]. We formulate the geometric shapes as states vectors in a dynamic system and predict the scene structure the in the next time step, k.

Based on the predicted scene in the next time step, visibility analysis is carried out from the next view point model [38], which is, of course, an approximated one. As the vehicle reaches the next viewpoint V_k, point clouds data are measured and scene modeling and states vectors are updated, which is an essential procedure for reliable KF prediction.

Our concept is based on RANSAC and KF, both real-time algorithms, which can be integrated into autonomous mapping vehicles that have become very popular. This concept can be applicable for robot trajectory planning generating visible paths, by analyzing local point clouds data and predicting the most visible viewpoint in the next time step from among several options.

A. Concept's Stages

Our methodology can be divided into three main sub-problems:

1) Extract basic geometric shapes from point clouds data (using RANSAC algorithms)

2) Predict scene modeling in the next viewpoint (using KF)

3) Approximated visibility analysis of a predicted scene

Each of the following stages is done after the other, where the last stage also includes updated measurement of point clouds data validating KF for the next viewpoint analysis.

B. Shapes Extraction

1) Geometric Shapes:

The urban scene is a very complex one in the matter of modeling applications using ground LiDAR, and the generated point clouds is very dense. Due to these inherited complications, feature extraction can be made very efficient by using basic geometric shapes. We define three kinds of geometric shapes planes, cylinders and spheres, with a minimal number of parameters for efficient time computation.

Plane: center point (x,y,z) and unit direction vector from center point.

Cylinder: center point (x,y,z), radius and unit direction vector of the cylinder axis.

Sphere: center point (x,y,z), radius and unit direction vector from center point.

2) RANSAC:

The RANSAC [39] paradigm is a well-known one, extracting shapes from point clouds using a minimal set of shape's primitives generated by random drawing in point clouds set. Minimal set is defined as the smallest number of points required to uniquely define a given type of geometric primitive.

For each of the geometric shapes, points are tested and approximate the primitive of the shape (also known as "score of the shape"). At the end of this iterative process, extracted shapes are generated from the current point clouds data.

Based on the RANSAC concept, the geometric shapes detailed above can be extract from a given point clouds data set. In order to improve the extraction process and reduce the number of points validating shape detection, we compute the approximated surface normal for each point and test the relevant shapes.

Given a point-clouds $P = \{p_1..p_N\}$ with associated normals $\{n_1..n_N\}$, the output of the RANSAC algorithm is a set of primitive shapes $\{\delta_1..\delta_N\}$ and a set of remaining points $R = P \setminus \{p_{\delta_1}..p_{\delta_N}\}$.

In this part we briefly introduce the main idea of plane, sphere and cylinder extraction from point clouds data. An extended study of RANSAC capabilities can be found in [35].

Plane: A minimal set in the case of a plane, can be found by just three points $\{p_1, p_2, p_3\}$, without considering normals in the points. Final validation of the candidate plane is computed from the deviation of the plane's normal from $\{n_1, n_2, n_3\}$. A plane is extracted only in cases where all deviations are less than the predefined angle α.

Sphere: A sphere is fully defined by two points with corresponding normal vectors. The sphere center is defined from the midpoint of the shortest line segment between the two lines given by the points and their normals.

A sphere counts as a detected shape in cases where all three points are within a distance of ε from the sphere and their normals do not deviate by more than α degrees.

Cylinder: A cylinder is set by two points and their normals, where the cylinder axis direction is the projected cross product of the normals, and a center point is calculated as the intersection of parametric lines generated from points and points' normal. A cylinder is verified by applying the thresholds ε and α to distance and to normal deviation of the samples.

C. Predicted Scene – Kalman Filter

In this part, we present the global Kalman Filter approach for our discrete dynamic system at the estimated state, k, based on the defined geometric shapes formulation defined in the previous sub-section.

Generally, the Kalman Filter can be described as a filter that consists of three major stages: Predict, Measure, and Update the state vector. The state vector contains different state parameters, and provides an optimal solution for the whole dynamic system [36]. We model our system as a linear one, with discrete dynamic model:

$$x_k = F_{k,k-1} x_{k-1} \tag{1}$$

where x is the state vector, F is the transition matrix and k is the state.

The state parameters for all of the geometric shapes are defined with shape center $\vec{s}$, and unit direction vector $\vec{d}$, of the geometric shape, from the current time step and viewpoint to the predicted one.

In each of the current states k, geometric shape center $\vec{s_k}$, is estimated based on the previous update of shape center location $\vec{s}_{k-1}$, and the previous updated unit direction vector $\vec{d}_{k-1}$, multiplied by small arbitrary scalar factor c:

$$\vec{s}_k = \vec{s}_{k-1} + c\vec{d}_{k-1} \tag{2}$$

Direction vector $\vec{d}_k$ can be efficiently estimated extracting the rotation matrix T, between the last two states k, k-1. In case of an inertial system fixed on the vehicle, a rotation matrix can be simply found from the last two states of the vehicle translations:

$$\vec{d}_k = T\vec{d}_{k-1} \tag{3}$$

The 3D rotation matrix T tracks the continuous extracted plans and surfaces to the next viewpoint V_k, making it possible to predict a scene model where one or more of the geometric shapes are cut from current point clouds data in state k-1. The discrete dynamic system can be written as:

$$\begin{bmatrix} \vec{s}_{x_k} \\ \vec{s}_{y_k} \\ \vec{s}_{z_k} \\ \vec{d}_{x_k} \\ \vec{d}_{y_k} \\ \vec{d}_{z_k} \end{bmatrix} = \begin{bmatrix} 1 & 0 & 0 & c & 0 & 0 \\ 0 & 1 & 0 & 0 & c & 0 \\ 0 & 0 & 1 & 0 & 0 & c \\ 0 & 0 & 0 & T_{11} & T_{12} & T_{13} \\ 0 & 0 & 0 & T_{21} & T_{22} & T_{23} \\ 0 & 0 & 0 & T_{31} & T_{32} & T_{33} \end{bmatrix} \begin{bmatrix} \vec{s}_{x_{k-1}} \\ \vec{s}_{y_{k-1}} \\ \vec{s}_{z_{k-1}} \\ \vec{d}_{x_{k-1}} \\ \vec{d}_{y_{k-1}} \\ \vec{d}_{z_{k-1}} \end{bmatrix} \tag{4}$$

where the state vector x is 6×1 vector, and the transition squared matrix is $F_{k,k-1}$. The dynamic system can be extended to additional state variables representing part of the geometric shape parameters such as radius, length etc. We define the dynamic system as the basic one for generic shapes that can be simply modeled with center and direction vector. The sphere radius and cylinder Z boundaries are defined in additional data structure of the scene entities.

III. Fast and Approximated Visibility Analysis

In this section, we present an analytic analysis of visibility boundaries of planes, cylinders and spheres for the predicted scene presented in the previous sub-section, which leads to an approximated visibility. For the plane surface, fast and efficient visibility analysis was already presented in [38].

In this part, we extend the previous visibility analysis concept [38] and include cylinders as continuous curves parameterization $C_{\text{clnd}}(x, y, z)$.
Cylinder parameterization can be described as:

$$C_{\text{Clnd}}(x, y, z) = \begin{pmatrix} r\sin(\theta) \\ r\cos(\theta) \\ c \end{pmatrix}_{r=const}$$

$$\begin{aligned} &0 \le \theta \le 2\pi \\ &c = c+1 \\ &0 \le c \le h_{peds\_\max} \end{aligned} \quad (5)$$

We define the visibility problem in a 3D environment for more complex objects as:

$$C'(x, y)_{z_{const}} \times (C(x, y)_{z_{const}} - V(x_0, y_0, z_0)) = 0 \quad (6)$$

where 3D model parameterization is $C(x, y)_{z=const}$, and the viewpoint is given as $V(x_0, y_0, z_0)$. Extending the 3D cubic parameterization, we also consider the cylinder case. Integrating equation (5) to (6) yields:

$$\begin{pmatrix} r\cos\theta \\ -r\sin\theta \\ 0 \end{pmatrix} \times \begin{pmatrix} r\sin\theta - V_x \\ r\cos\theta - V_y \\ c - V_z \end{pmatrix} = 0 \quad (7)$$

$$\theta = \arctan\left(-\frac{-r - \frac{\left(-vy\, r + \sqrt{vx^4 - vx^2 r^2 + vy^2 vx^2}\right) vy}{vx^2 + vy^2}}{vx}, -\frac{-vy\, r + \sqrt{vx^4 - vx^2 r^2 + vy^2 vx^2}}{vx^2 + vy^2} \right) \quad (8)$$

As can be noted, these equations are not related to Z axis, and the visibility boundary points are the same for each *x-y* cylinder profile.

The visibility statement leads to complex equation, which does not appear to be a simple computational task. This equation can be solved efficiently by finding where the equation changes its sign and crosses zero value; we used analytic solution to speed up computation time and to avoid numeric approximations. We generate two values of θ generating two silhouette points in a very short time computation. Based on an analytic solution to the cylinder case, a fast and exact analytic solution can be found for the visibility problem from a viewpoint.

We define the solution presented in equation (8) as x-y-z coordinates values for the cylinder case as Cylinder Boundary Points (CBP). CBP are the set of visible silhouette points for a 3D cylinder, as presented in Figure 1:

$$CBP_{i=1..N_{PBP\_bound}=2}(x_0, y_0, z_0) = \begin{bmatrix} x_1, y_1, z_1 \\ x_{N_{PBP\_bound}}, y_{N_{PBP\_bound}}, z_{N_{PBP\_bound}} \end{bmatrix} \quad (9)$$

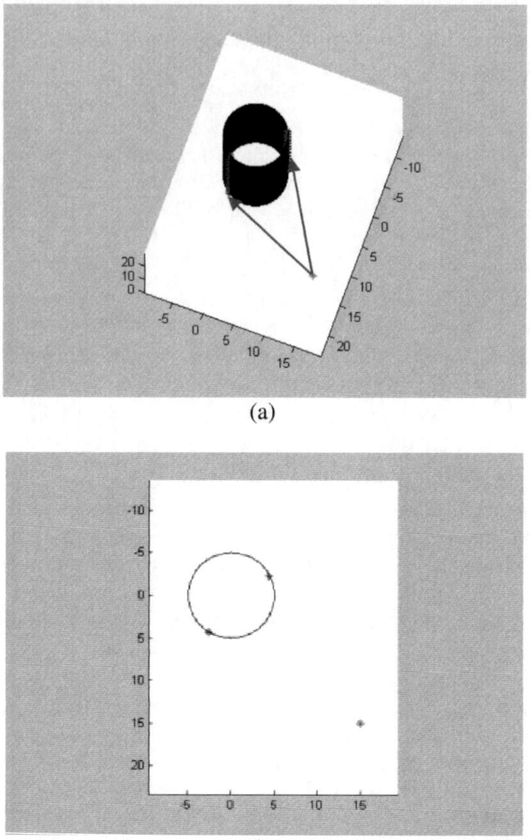

Figure 1. Cylinder Boundary Points (CBP) using Analytic Solution marked as blue points, Viewpoint Marked in Red: (a) 3D View (Visible Boundaries Marked with Red Arrows); (b) Topside View.

In the same way, sphere parameterization can be described as:

$$C_{Sphere}(x, y, z) = \begin{pmatrix} r\sin\phi\cos\theta \\ r\sin\phi\sin\theta \\ r\cos\phi \end{pmatrix}_{r=const}$$

$$\begin{aligned} &0 \le \phi < \pi \\ &0 \le \theta < 2\pi \end{aligned} \quad (10)$$

We define the visibility problem in a 3D environment for this object as:

$$C'(x,y,z) \times (C(x,y,z) - V(x_0,y_0,z_0)) = 0 \quad (11)$$

where the 3D model parameterization is $C(x,y,z)$, and the viewpoint is given as $V(x_0,y_0,z_0)$. Integrating eq. (10) to (11) yields:

$$\theta = \arctan\left(\frac{r\sin(\phi)}{v\_y} - \frac{1}{v\_y\,(v\_y^2 + v\_x^2)}\left(v\_x\left(r\sin(\phi)\,v\_x - \sqrt{-v\_y^2 r^2 \sin(\phi)^2 + v\_y^4 + v\_x^2 v\_y^2}\right)\right), \frac{r\sin(\phi)\,v\_x - \sqrt{-v\_y^2 r^2 \sin(\phi)^2 + v\_y^4 + v\_x^2 v\_y^2}}{v\_y^2 + v\_x^2} \right) \quad (12)$$

where r is set from sphere parameter, and $V(x_0,y_0,z_0)$ is changes from visibility point along Z axis. The visibility boundary points for a sphere, together with the analytic solutions for planes and cylinders, allow us to compute fast and efficient visibility in a predicted scene from local point cloud data, that being updated in the next state.

This extended visibility analysis concept, integrated with a well-known predicted filter and extraction method, can be implemented in real time applications with point clouds data.

IV. Fast Visible Trajectory Planning

Our planner is a local one, generating one step ahead at every time step reaching toward the goal, which is a depth first A* search over a tree. We extend previous planners, which take into account kinematic and dynamic constraints [16] and present a local planner for an omni-directional robot, with these constraints mounted with LiDAR in a constant Z point. As far as we know, for the first time this planner generates fast and exact visible trajectories based on an optimal analytic time horizon solution handling blocked states where all future states are inside VO, and approximates visibility based on local point clouds data for the next time step based on incomplete data. The fast and efficient visibility analysis of our method [38], extended in Section II for spheres and cylinders, allows us to generate the most visible trajectory from a starting state to the goal state in 3D urban environments, based on local decision-making capabilities, and demonstrates our capability, which can be extended to real performances in the future.

We assume incomplete data of the 3D urban environment model as mentioned in Section II, and use an extended Velocity Obstacles (VO) method with analytic optimal time horizon.

A. *Analytic Optimal Time Horizon – Escaping Mode*

The time horizon plays an important role in selecting feasible avoidance maneuvers. It allows considering only those maneuvers that would result in a collision within a specified time interval and efficiently searching for safe maneuvers in the velocity space. Setting the time horizon too high would be too prohibitive, as it would mark as dangerous maneuvers resulting in collision at a distant time; selecting a too-small time horizon would permit dangerous maneuvers that are too close and at too high speeds to avoid the obstacle.

It is essential that the proper time horizon ensures that a safe maneuver, even if temporarily pointing toward the obstacle, is selected.

The main significance of the time horizon parameter using VO was first introduced in [21]. For each obstacle, time horizon is calculated as the minimum between stopping and passing time, as approximations to the exact optimization problem. Numeric solutions of the optimal time horizon for point mass model with cubic control constraints were presented in [21], based on external trajectories generated from the boundary of the control effort. This formulation of time horizon defines approximation of VO as the boundary of ICS without analytic solution escaping VO, in a case of bounded velocity space.

B. *Analytic Optimal Time Horizon - Examples*

In this part, we focus on the efficiency of our analytic time horizon solution via classic VO demonstrated in simulations. The analytic solution extends the traditional VO planner search method and defines the strategy search in cases of blocked attainable velocity space for the next time step in velocity space.

We use a planner similar to the one presented by [21] with the same cost function, and the Omni-directional robot model mentioned above. The search is guided by a cost function planner applying the safest maneuver at every time step. Unsafe states ahead in time are recognized before the robot enters into unsafe states, also called ICS. For one obstacle, our planner can ensure safety, but the planner is not a complete one. By using an analytic search, the planner computes near-time optimal and safe trajectory to the goal.

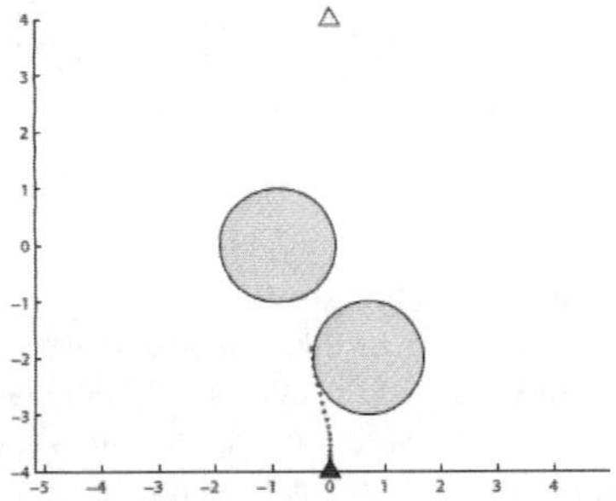

Figure 2. Avoiding Two Obstacles Using Analytic Time Horizon.

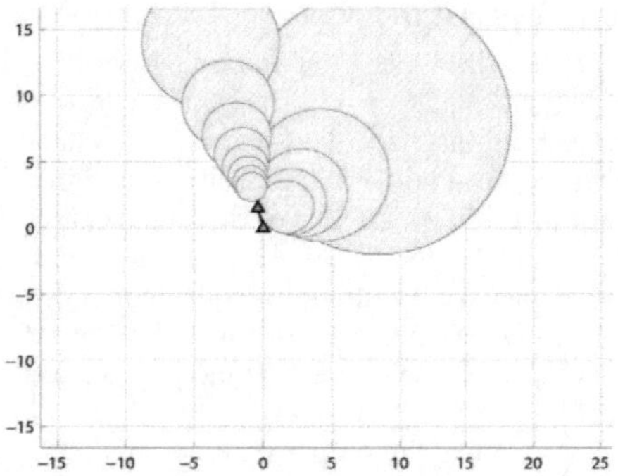

Figure 3. Blocked Velocity Space Avoiding Two Obstacles.

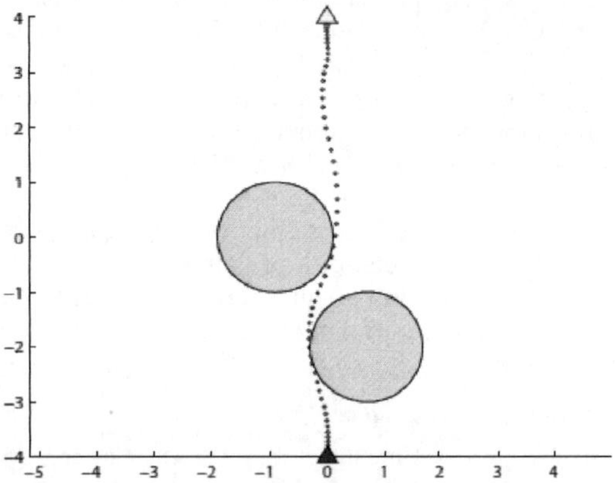

Figure 4. Final Trajectory Avoiding Two Obstacles Using Analytic Time Horizon.

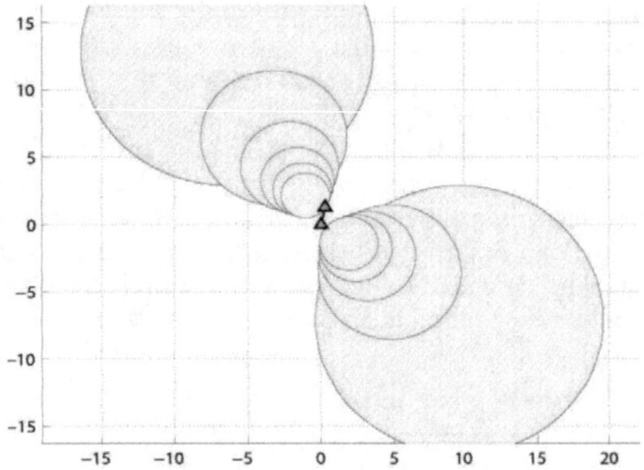

Figure 5. Escaping Blocked Velocity Space Using Analytic Time Horizon.

The main contribution of this section is to demonstrate cases of blocked nodes in the velocity space in the search tree for the next time step. In cases of blocked nodes, i.e., all of the nodes located inside the VO, the planner choose the node that leads outside VO as soon as possible, avoiding collision and formulated as analytic time horizon based search. Without using analytic time horizon formulation, there is no safe and legitimate option for the next node to be explored. As a result, conservative trajectories are computed, and in some cases safe trajectory to the goal cannot be found and collision eventually occurs.

In a two-obstacles case shown in Figure 2, the robot, represented by a point, starts near point (0,-4) at zero speed, attempting to reach the goal at point (0,4) (marked by a yellow triangle) at zero speed, while avoiding two static obstacles. The trajectory is dotted with a red dot representing the current position of the robot. The bounded velocity space, representing velocity obstacles as yellow cycles and velocity vector (with green triangles), can be seen in Figure 3, relating to the state space position as shown in Figure 2.

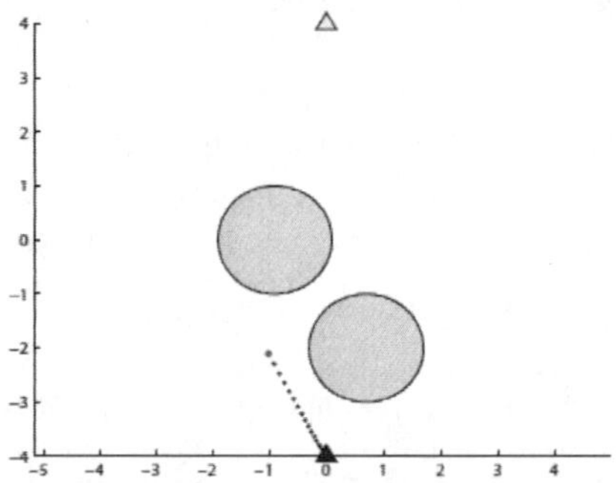

Figure 6. Conservative Solution of Avoiding Two Obstacles Using Constant Time Horizon: Blocked Velocity Space Caused to Conservative Trajectory Turning Left vs. Sliding on their Edges and Passing Between them.

Clearly, there is no gap to enter between VO's in Figure 3 and the velocity vector is bounded in the velocity space. The trivial VO, with a conservative and constant time horizon, cannot find the ultimate solution in such a case, and as a result, a conservative trajectory will be computed. The robot avoids the obstacles to the left with high time horizon values, as shown in Figure 6. Moreover, in some other cases of dense and bounded velocity space, no solution will be available at all. By using an analytic time horizon, the robot escapes velocity obstacles and searches for a safe maneuver in state space, as shown in Figure 4, and velocity space, respectively, as shown in Figure 5.

C. The Planner

By using RANSAC algorithm, at each time step point clouds data are extracted into three possible objects: plane, cylinder and sphere. The scene is formulated as a dynamic system using KF analysis for objects' prediction. The objects are approximated for the next time step, and each safe attainable state that can be explored is set as candidate viewpoint. The cost for each node is set as the total visible surfaces, based on the analytic visibility boundary, where the optimal and safe node is explored for the next time step.

At each time step, the planner computes the next Attainable Velocities (AV). The safe nodes not colliding with objects such as cubes, cylinders and spheres, i.e., nodes outside Velocity Obstacles are explored. Where all nodes are inside VO, a unified analytic solution for time horizon is presented, generating an escape option for these radical cases without considering visibility analysis. The planner computes the cost for these safe nodes based on predicted visibility and chooses the node with the optimal cost for the next time step. We repeat this procedure while generating the most visible trajectory.

1) Attainable Velocities

The set of maneuvers that are dynamically feasible over a time step is represented by AV. At each time step during the trajectory planning, we map the attainable velocities that the robot can choose under the effort control envelope.

Attainable Velocities, $AV(t+\Delta t)$, are integrated from the current state (x_1, x_2) by applying all admissible controls $u(t) \in U$. The geometric shape of AV depends on system dynamics. In our case,as described in (13):

$$\dot{x_1} = x_2$$
$$\dot{x_2} = u \qquad (13)$$

where $x_1, u \in R^2$.

$$AV(t+\Delta t) = \{v | v = v(t) + \Delta t u, u \in U\}$$

The attainable velocities at time $t+\Delta t$ apply to the position $x(t+\Delta t)$. Thus, the attainable velocities, when intersected with VO that correspond to the same position, would indicate those velocities that are safe if selected at time $t+\Delta t$.

2) Cost Function

Our search is guided by minimum invisible parts from viewpoint V to the approximated 3D urban environment model in the next time step, $t+\Delta t$, set by KF after extracting objects from point clouds data using the RANSAC algorithm. The cost function for each node is a combination of IRV and ISV, with different weights as functions of the required task.

The cost function presented in (14) is computed for each safe node, i.e., node outside VO, considering the robot's future location at the next time step $(x_1(t+\Delta t), x_2(t+\Delta t))$ as viewpoint:

$$w\big(x(t+\Delta t)\big) = \alpha \cdot ISV(x(t+\Delta t)) + \beta \cdot IRV(x(t+\Delta t)) \quad (14)$$

where $\propto, \beta$ are coefficients, affecting the trajectory's character. The cost function $w(x(t+\Delta t)$ produces the total sum of invisible parts from the viewpoint to the 3D urban environment, meaning that the velocity at the next time step with the minimum cost function value is the most visible node in our local search, based on our approximation.

We divide point invisibility value into Invisible Surfaces Value (ISV) and Invisible Roofs Value (IRV). This classification allows us to plan delicate and accurate trajectories upon demand. We define ISV and IRS as the total sum of the invisible roofs and surfaces (respectively). Invisible Surfaces Value (ISV) of a viewpoint is defined as the total sum of the invisible surfaces of all the objects in a 3D environment, as described in (15):

$$ISV(x_0, y_0, z_0) = \sum_{i=1}^{N_{obj}} IS_{VP_i^{j=1..N_{bound}-1}}^{VP_i^{j=1..N_{bound}-1}} \qquad (15)$$

In the same way, we define Invisible Roofs Value (IRV) as the total sum of all the invisible roofs' surfaces, as described in (16):

$$IRV(x_0, y_0, z_0) = \sum_{i=1}^{N_{obj}} IS_{VP_i^{j=N_{bound}}}^{VP_i^{j=N_{bound}}} \qquad (16)$$

Extended analysis of the analytic solution for visibility analysis for known 3D urban environments can be found in [37].

V. Simulations

We have implemented the presented algorithm and tested some urban environments on a 1.8GHz Intel Core CPU with Matlab. We computed the visible trajectories using our planner, with real raw data records from LiDAR as part of the Ford Campus Project.

Point clouds data are generated by Velodyne HDL-64E LiDAR [39]. Velodyne HDL-64E LiDAR has two blocks of lasers, each consisting of 32 laser diodes aligned vertically, resulting in an effective 26:8 Vertical Field Of View (FOV). The entire unit can spin about its vertical axis at speeds up to 900 rpm (15 Hz) to provide a full 360 degree azimuthal field of view. The maximum range of the sensor is 120 m and it captures about 1 million range points per second. We captured our data set with the laser spinning at 10 Hz.

Due to these huge amounts of data, we planned a limited trajectory in this urban environment for a limited distance. In Figure 7, point clouds data from the start point can be seen, also marked as start point "S" in Figure 10. Planes extracted by RANSAC can be recognized. As part of the Ford Project, these point clouds are also projected to the panoramic camera's systems, making it easier to understand the scene, as seen in Figure 8.(34)

As described earlier, at each time step the planner predicts the objects in the scene using KF. In Figure 9(a), objects in the scene are presented from a point clouds data set. These point clouds predicted using KF, and predicted to the next time step in Figure 9(b).

Figure 7. Point Clouds Data set at Start Point.

Figure 8. Point Clouds Data Projected to Panoramic Camera Set at Start Point.

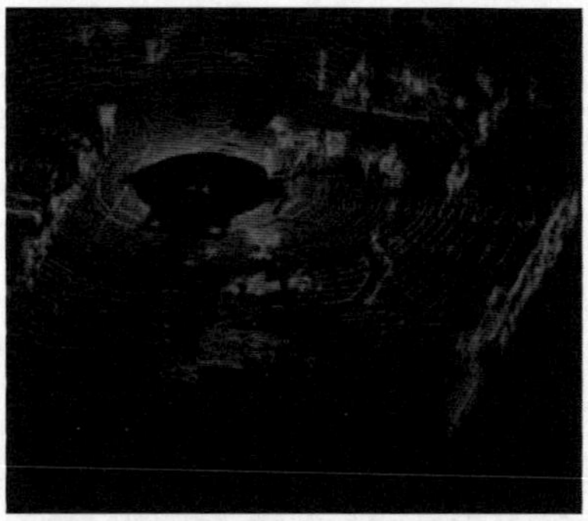

(a)

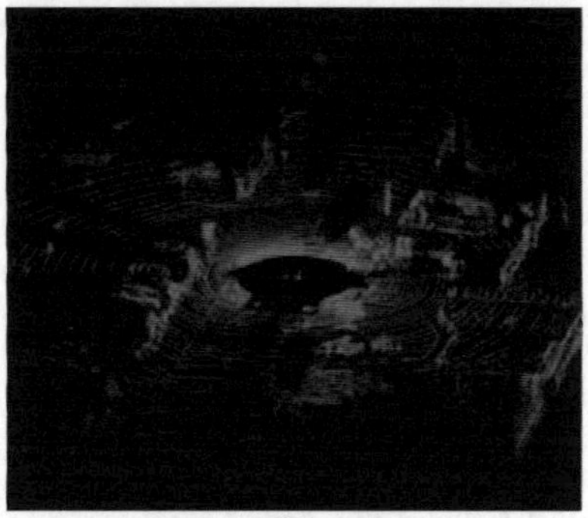

(b)

Figure 9. (a) Objects in point clouds data set. (b) Predicted objects using KF in the next time step.

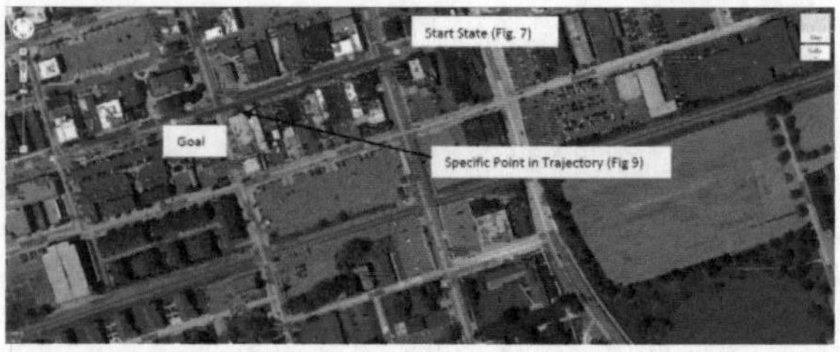

Figure 10. Vehicle Planned Trajectory Colored in Purple.

The planned trajectory presented in Figure 10 with a purple line. The starting point, marked as "S", presented in Figure 10, where the cloud points in this state are presented in Figure 8. An arbitrary state during the planned trajectory, which is marked with an arrow, is also presented in Figure 10, where point clouds prediction using KF in this state are presented in Figure 9. For this trajectory, $\propto = 1, \beta = 1$, robot velocity is set to $v_a = 10\left[\frac{km}{hr}\right]$. In this case, the robot avoided two other cars, without handling cases of analytic optimal time solution for deadlocks with bounded velocity space.

VI. Conclusion and Future Work

In this research, we have presented an efficient trajectory planning algorithm for visible trajectories in a 3D urban environment for an Omni-directional model, based on an incomplete data set from LiDAR, predicting the scene at the next time step and approximating visibility.

Our planner is based on two steps visibility analysis in 3D urban environments using predicted visibility from point clouds data. The first step is to extract the basic geometric shapes: planes, cylinders and spheres, using RANSAC algorithms. The second step is a prediction of these geometric entities in the next time step, formulated as states vectors in a dynamic system using the Kalman Filter (KF).

We extend our analytic visibility analysis method to cylinders and spheres, which allows us to efficiently set the visibility boundary of predicted objects in the next time step, generated by KF and RANSAC methods. Based on these fast computation capabilities, the on-line planner can approximate the most visible state as part of a greedy search method.

As part of our planner, we extended the classical VO method, where the velocity space is bounded and the robot velocity cannot escape from the velocity obstacles in the current state. We presented an escape mode based on an analytic time-optimal minimization problem which, for the first time, defines time horizon for these cases.

The visible trajectory is an approximated one, allowing us to configure the type of visible objects, i.e., roof or surfaces visibility of the trajectory, and can be used for different kinds of applications.

Further research will focus on advanced geometric shapes, which will allow precise urban environment modeling, facing real-time implementation with on-line data processing from LiDAR.

VII. REFERENCES

[1] O.Gal, Y.Doytsher, Fast Visible Trajectory Spatial Analysis in 3D Urban Environments Based on Local Point Clouds Data, GeoProcessing 2017.

[2] G.Pandey, J.R. McBride and R.M. Eustice, Ford campus vision and lidar data set. International Journal of Robotics Research, 30(13):1543-1552, November 2011.

[3] J.-C. Latombe, Robot Motion Planning. Kluwer Academic Publishers, 1990.

[4] M. Erdman and T. Lozano-Perez, On multiple moving objects, Algorithmica, vol. 2, pp. 447–521, 1987.

[5] K. Fugimura and H. Samet, A hierarchical strategy for path planning among moving obstacles, IEEE Transactions on Robotics and Automation, vol. 5, pp. 61–69, 1989.

[6] L. Ulrich and J. Borenstien, Vfh+: Reliable obstacle avoidance for fast mobile robots, in Proceedings of the IEEE International Conference on Robotics and Automation, pp. 1572–1577, 1998.

[7] N. Ko and R. Simmons, The lane-curvature method for local obstacle avoidance, in International Conference on Intelligence Robots and Systems, pp. 1615–1621, 1998.

[8] J. Minguez and L. Montano, Nearest diagram navigation. a new real-time collision avoidance approach, in International Conference on Intelligence Robots and Systems, pp. 2094–2100, 2000.

[9] T. Fraichard, Planning in dynamic workspace: a state-time space approach, Advanced Robotics, vol. 13, pp. 75–94, 1999.

[10] H. R. K. J.-C. Latombe and S. Rock, Randomized kinodynamic motion planning with moving obstacles, Algorithmics and Computational Robotics, vol. 4, pp. 247–264, 2000.

[11] O. Brock and O. Khatib, Real time replanning in high-dimensional configuration spaces using sets of homotopic paths, in Proceedings of the IEEE International Conference on Robotics and Automation, pp. 550–555, 2000.

[12] N. S. J. Minguez L. Montano and R. Alami, Global nearest diagram navigation, in Proceedings of the IEEE International Conference on Robotics and Automation, pp. 33–39, 2001.

[13] M.D. Feron and E. Frazzoli, Real time motion planning for agile autonomous vehicles, AIAA Journal of Guidance Control and Dynamics, vol. 25, pp. 116–129, 2002.

[14] W. Fox, E. Burgard, and S. Thrun, The dynamic window approach to collision avoidance, IEEE Robotics and Automation Magazine, vol. 4, pp. 23–33, 1997.

[15] T. Wikman and W. N. M.S. Branicky, Reflexive collision avoidance: a generalized approach, in Proceedings of the IEEE International Conference on Robotics and Automation, pp. 31–36, 1993.

[16] S. Lavalle. J. Kuffner, Randomized kinodynamic planning, International Journal of Robotics Research, vol. 20, pp. 378–400, 2001.

[17] T. Fraichard, A short paper about safety, in Proceedings of the IEEE International Conference on Robotics and Automation, pp. 1140–1145, 2007

[18] S. P. T. Fraichard, Safe motion planning in dynamic environment, in International Conference on Intelligence Robots and Systems, pp. 885–897, 2005.

[19] T. Fraichard and H. Asama, Inevitable collision state-a step towards safer robots? Advanced Robotics, vol. 18, pp. 1001–1024, 2004.

[20] N. Chan and M. Z. J. Kuffner, Improved motion planning speed and safety using region of in- evitable collision, in ROMANSY, pp. 103–114, July 2008.

[21] O. Gal, Z. Shiller, and E. Rimon, Efficient and safe on-line motion planning in dynamic environment, in Proceedings of the IEEE International Conference on Robotics and Automation, pp. 88–93, 2009.

[22] Z. Shiller. F. Large and S. Sekhavat, Motion planning in dynamic environments: Obstacle moving along arbitrary trajectories, in Proceedings of the IEEE International Conference on Robotics and Automation, pp. 3716–3721, 2001.

[23] H. Plantinga, and R. Dyer, Visibility, Occlusion, and Aspect Graph, The International Journal of Computer Vision, vol. 5, pp. 137-160, 1990.

[24] Y. Doytsher, and B. Shmutter, Digital Elevation Model of Dead Ground, Symposium on Mapping and Geographic Information Systems (Commission IV of the International Society for Photogrammetry and Remote Sensing), Athens, Georgia, USA, 1994.

[25] F. Durand, 3D Visibility: Analytical Study and Applications, PhD thesis, Universite Joseph Fourier, Grenoble, France, 1999.

[26] W.R. Franklin, Siting Observers on Terrain, in Proc. of 10th International Symposium on Spatial Data Handling. Springer-Verlag, pp. 109–120, 2002.

[27] J. Wang, G.J. Robinson, and K. White, A Fast Solution to Local Viewshed Computation Using Grid-based Digital Elevation Models, Photogrammetric Engineering & Remote Sensing, vol. 62, pp. 1157-1164, 1996.

[28] J. Wang, G.J. Robinson, and K. White, Generating Viewsheds without Using Sightlines, Photogrammetric Engineering & Remote Sensing, vol. 66, pp. 87-90, 2000.

[29] C. Ratti, The Lineage of Line: Space Syntax Parameters from the Analysis of Urban DEMs', Environment and Planning B: Planning and Design, vol. 32, pp. 547-566, 2005.

[30] L. De Floriani, and P. Magillo, Visibility Algorithms on Triangulated Terrain Models, International Journal of Geographic Information Systems, vol. 8, pp.13-41, 1994.

[31] B. Nadler, G. Fibich, S. Lev-Yehudi, and D. Cohen-Or, A Qualitative and Quantitative Visibility Analysis in Urban Scenes, Computers & Graphics, vol. 5, pp. 655-666, 1999.

[32] B. Mederos, N. Amenta, L. Velho, L.H. Figueiredo, Surface reconstruction from noisy point clouds. In: Euro- graphics Symposium on Geometry Processing, pp. 53-62, 2005.

[33] J.P. Grossman, Point sample rendering. In: Rendering Techniques, pp. 181-192, 1998.

[34] G. Vosselman, B. Gorte, G. Sithole, and T. Rabbani. Recognizing structure in laser scanner point clouds. The International Archives of the Photogrammetry Remote Sensing and Spatial Information Sciences (IAPRS), vol. 36, pp. 33–38, 2004.

[35] R. Schnabel, R. Wahl, R. Klein, Efficient RANSAC for Point-Cloud Shape Detection, Computer Graphics Forum, vol. 26, no.2, pp. 214-226, 2007.

[36] R. Kalman. A new approach to linear filtering and prediction problems. Transactions of the ASME-Journal of Basic Engineering, vol. 82, no. 1, pp. 35–45, 1960.

[37] J. Lee, M. Kim, and I. Kweon. A kalman filter based visual tracking algorithm for an object moving, In IEEE/RSJ Intelligent Robots and Systems, pp. 342–347, 1995.

[38] O. Gal, and Y. Doytsher, Fast Visibility Analysis in 3D Procedural Modeling Environments, in Proc. of the, 3rd International Conference on Computing for Geospatial Research and Applications, Washington DC, USA, 2012.

[39] H. Boulaassal, T. Landes, P. Grussenmeyer, and F. Tarsha-Kurdi. Automatic segmentation of building facades using terrestrial laser data. The International Archives of the Photogrammetry Remote Sensing and Spatial Information Sciences (IAPRS), vol. 36, no. 3, 2007.

[40] Velodyne 2007: Velodyne HDL-64E: A high definition LIDAR sensor for 3D applications. Available at: http://www.velodyne.com/lidar/products/white paper.

Emulating a Sensor for the Measurements of the Hydraulic Resistances of Nozzles in Agricultural Sprayers Based on the Use of the Point-Wise Thévenin's Theorem

Rafael F. Q. Magossi[1,2], Elmer A. G. Peñaloza[1,2], Shankar P. Battachharya[3],
Vilma A. Oliveira[2], Paulo E. Cruvinel[1]

[1]Embrapa Instrumentation
Brazilian Agricultural Research Corporation, São Carlos, SP, Brazil
Email: paulo.cruvinel@embrapa.br

[2] Department of Electrical and Computer Engineering
University of São Paulo, São Carlos, SP, Brazil
Email: rafael.magossi, egamboa, voliveira@usp.br

[3]Department of Electrical and Computer Engineering
Texas A&M University, College Station, Texas, USA
Email: bhatt@ece.tamu.edu

Abstract—**In agriculture, the chemicals should be applied evenly and at a prescribed rate. An accurately calibrated boom will ensure that this is achieved. In addition, the correct use of pesticides can deliver significant environmental and socio-economic benefits in the form of safe, healthy, and affordable food, as well as to decrease the impact in natural resources such as soil, water and overall land use. The quality of pesticides application is dependent on the hydraulic fluidic resistance present in the nozzles of the sprayers. This paper presents a method to evaluate the hydraulic pressure drop in bars of agricultural sprayer systems using the fluid hydraulic resistance as a part of a sensor element associated with point-wise Thévenin's equivalents. This method makes it possible to control and measure the pressure drop at lower cost and greater accuracy. In this context, taking into account a measurement-based approach, a parameterized relationship among operating conditions and the fluidic resistance was defined. Therefore, it was possible to obtain the hydraulic equivalents of a sprayer system with direct injection based only on the hydraulic flow and pressure measurements. The results have shown that it is possible to obtain the hydraulic equivalent resistances with a relative error equal to 2.15%. Furthermore, the relationship among the orifice nozzle diameter, pressure and flow was also found.**

Keywords–Measurement theory; Parameterized model; Point-wise Thévenin's equivalent; Electrical-hydraulic analogy; Agricultural quality sensor; Food safety; Risk analysis.

I. INTRODUCTION

Nowadays, hydraulic systems can be found in a wide variety of applications, including agriculture. For such systems it is important to determine the internal losses occurring not only for the set up of upstream and downstream pressure valves, but also to calculate the flow rates through piping systems. In this context, the fluid hydraulic resistance from the nozzles used in the agricultural sprayers plays an important role. A previous discussion related to such content was presented in [1]. In addition, such information can assist in establishing the flow rate range associated with pumps, compressors, turbines, and relief headers to ensure that back pressure on the relief devices does not prevent them from functioning properly [2].

Pesticide application is a vital component for food security, and production is directly connected to pest control. Agricultural sprayers are used to apply liquid chemicals on plants to control pests and diseases. In addition, it can be used to apply herbicides to control weeds and to apply fertilizers to enhance plants growth. There are many types of sprayers commercially available to producers designed for their own specific functions and use. One may find backpack sprayers, hand compression sprayers, self-propelled sprayers, aerial sprayers, and pull-behind sprayers, among others.

The manual application method was the first to be used in agriculture, but it has the disadvantage that it presents a higher risk to humans. On the other hand, turning off sprayers when there is no target, or adjusting application rates based on canopy size and density became essential for production with sustainability, that is, in such matters the automated sprayers play an important role. Close to the 90's, manufacturers introduced precision spraying technology in boom sprayers [3]. Despite being still an open field for research and innovation, the variable rate methods, using the Global Position System (GPS) and the Geographic Information System (GIS) technologies were integrated into boom sprayers and became already commercially available.

The adoption of precision agriculture (PA) for localized application of agrochemicals can reduce pesticide wastage and environmental aggression, providing a more efficient production of large-scale food and increasing agricultural productivity. With localized application of agrochemicals, herbicide savings is in the order of 30 to 80% compared to the uniform application in the total area. Automatic sprayers designed and developed for localized application are currently available, allowing the use of large volume of syrup, covering large agricultural areas [4]–[7].

In this field of knowledge, there are the use of conventional and direct injection sprayer systems. The first type of direct injection system was developed between the 70's and 80's. However, in that time such a system presented high cost, complexity of operation and low performance. According to

Baio and Antuniassi [6], the main characteristic of direct injection systems is related to the storage of the diluent (water) and pesticide in separate containers.

The mixing of pesticides and water is carried out only at the time of application, by injection of the pesticide into the piping, which carries the syrup to the nozzles of the sprayer. The amount of injected pesticide can be accomplished, among other ways, by controlling the rotation of the piston or peristaltic injection pumps. The main advantages of the injection system are the reduction of risks involved during the application process [8].

Other aspects one should take into account, in relation to this matter, is the benefit/cost rate in terms of the use of energy in the agricultural machinery. Most fluid energy systems are configured with a positive flow displacement pump that is large enough to meet the flow requirements of many circuits. Different work functions require a variety of flow and pressure values to provide the desired operation. Branches of the system therefore must include specific flow and pressure regulating valves.

This paper presents a method based on a measurement approach to evaluate the hydraulic pressure drop in booms of agricultural sprayer systems using the fluid hydraulic resistance as part of a sensor element associated with a point-wise Thévenin's equivalent measurement method.

The next sections of the paper are organized as follows. In Section II the concepts of spraying quality and fluidic resistance are given. In Section III, the theoretical background for the understanding of the parameterized input-output model and the theoretical development of the measurement based approach for unknown systems and the analog models between the electrical and hydraulic circuits to obtain point-wise hydraulic Thévenin's equivalent are studied. Subsequently, in Section IV, the method used to obtain the internal loss, pressure equivalents and the function relating the nozzle orifice diameter and pressure with the flow in a full cone nozzle is given. In Section V, the experimental validation of both the nozzle flow in terms of operating conditions and the point-wise Thévenin's equivalents using a laboratory sprayer setup are performed. Finally, some concluding remarks are presented in Section VI.

II. AGRICULTURAL SPRAYING QUALITY

As the fluid moves inside a pipe occur a turbulence of the fluid with itself and a fluid friction with the inner walls of this pipe. This causes the pressure inside the pipe to gradually decrease as the fluid moves. The pressure decrease is known as the pressure drop. In this way, the load loss would be related to a resistance to the passage of the flow of the fluid inside the pipe. This resistance is known as fluidic resistance and directly affects the volumetric flow [9], [10]. Moreover, the fluid hydraulic resistance is subject to temporal variations requiring a considerable effort to be determined. In Figure 1 it can be observed the functioning of a full cone nozzle and the characterization of a fluidic resistance.

In the process of agricultural spraying, it is of great importance to know the value of the fluidic resistance of the spray boom since variations in this resistance can affect the quality of the application, that is, size and volume of drops, distribution of drops on the crop and the drift of the drops produced by the wind [11].

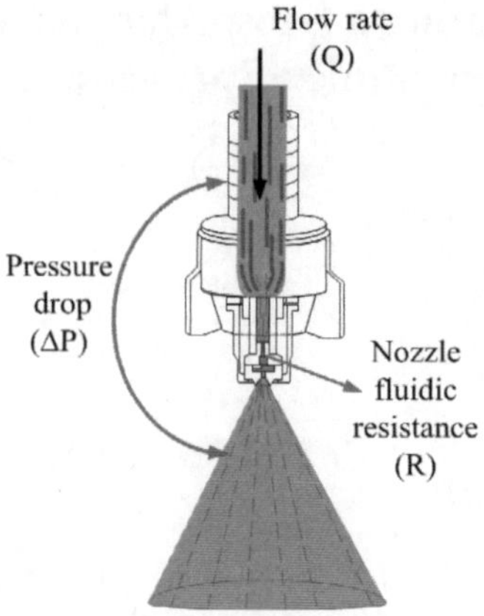

Figure 1. Representation of a hydraulic full cone nozzle where for a given flow rate there is a pressure drop caused by the fluidic resistance, which is related to the internal mechanical characteristics of this nozzle.

Therefore, the value of the fluidic resistance as well as its behavior as a function of the operating conditions yield relevant information to infer the quality of the pesticides application. Droplet size and its distribution are critical factors in such processes because can affect the penetration, coverage and drift of the application on the crop [12].

The design of a hydraulic system can be improved with the use of mathematical simulation. Numerous approaches to energy systems modeling fluids and components can be found in the literature. Analysis of a fluid feed system can cover the flow distribution, the functioning of components, or a combination of both. Most of the useful equations for fluid analysis are derived from the law of conservation of energy, the principle of continuity, and Newton's second law [13].

Equations used to calculate flow in circuits involve the use of empirical expressions or laboratory-derived flow coefficients. Therefore, when two or more circuits are used simultaneously, the principle of continuity may not be obeyed exactly, because of the use of such empirical coefficients.

To determine the desired pressure and flow values, a set of equations can be solved via an iterative method. Iterative methods work well under steady state flow conditions. However, they are difficult to apply under non-steady state operations. In relation to this subject Akers and collaborators proposed a method based on electrical-hydraulic analogy [9]. In such method, the fluid pressure, the flow, and the fluidic resistance are analogous to voltage, current, and electrical resistance, respectively. The method uses the basic principle of Ohm's law, also referred to as the hydraulic Ohm.

In this scenario, a sensor that can measure the internal losses of the hydraulic boom in sprayers is very much required. The boom pressure drop denoted ΔP can be related to the volumetric flow rate denoted Q by:

$$\Delta P = f_a \frac{L\rho}{2DA^2} Q^2 \tag{1}$$

for a rough pipe with turbulent flow or:

$$\Delta P = \frac{8\pi L\mu}{A^2} Q^2 \tag{2}$$

for a flat tube with laminar flow, where f_a is the coefficient of friction [dimensionless], ρ is the specific mass of the fluid $[kg/m^3]$, L is the equivalent pipe length $[m]$, D is the internal diameter of the pipe $[m]$, A is the inner area of the straight section of the pipe $[m^2]$ and μ is the absolute viscosity of the fluid $[P_a \cdot s]$.

The coefficient of friction f_a, sometimes known as a Moody friction factor or also as a distributed load loss coefficient determined by mathematical equations, is a function of the Reynolds number and relative roughness. Experimental identification of f_a is more common due to the non linear characteristics involved. For pipes that undergo changes in pipe diameters, in general, flow type or over-curves, the fluidic resistance denoted R may be related to the pressure drop as:

$$\sqrt{\Delta P} = RQ. \quad (3)$$

For a tube, the fluidic resistance is given by:

$$R = \sqrt{f_a \frac{L\rho}{2DA^2}}. \quad (4)$$

For a nozzle (Fig 1), the fluidic resistance is given by:

$$R = \sqrt{\frac{\rho}{2}} \frac{1}{C_d A} \quad (5)$$

where the unitless C_d is the discharge coefficient. The discharge coefficient of an orifice atomizer is governed in part by the pressure losses undergoing at the flow passages of the nozzle and also by the extent to which the liquid flows through the final discharge orifice diameter denoted d $[mm]$ [14].

In addition, the pressure drop and the outlet orifice diameter affects the size of the droplets in the spray [15]. In Figure 2, it can be observed the volume median diameter of the drops denoted VMD $[\mu m]$ influenced by the diameter of the discharge orifice d.

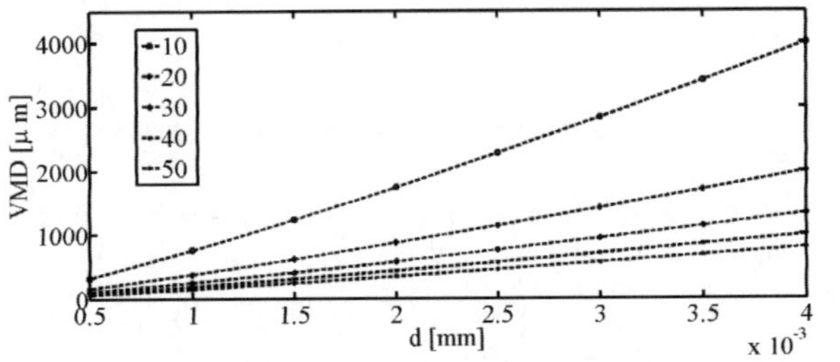

Figure 2. Relationship between the diameter of the nozzle orifice d and the mean diameter of the drops, which where simulated for different values of exit velocity V_l in $[m/s]$ for a full cone nozzle (figure extracted from [15]).

The output velocity of the mixture V_l $[m/s]$ is also shown in Fig. 2. This velocity depends on the pressure and flow of the liquid in the nozzle.

III. Theoretical Background

In this section the theoretical background of the parameterized input-output model and the point-wise Thévenin's equivalent are presented.

A. A Parameterized Input-Output Model

In many design problems there is a set of parameters denoted by a vector $\mathbf{p}$, whose influence on the output is important to know. The parameters of interest in this work are the orifice diameter, drop pressure, and the Thévenin's equivalent fluidic resistance.

For easy reference, in this section it is describe the main results used in this work following [16]. Consider a linear, parameterized, input-output in matrix form:

$$\begin{aligned} A(\mathbf{p})\mathbf{x} &= B\mathbf{u} \\ \mathbf{y} &= C(\mathbf{p})\mathbf{x} + D\mathbf{u} \end{aligned} \quad (6)$$

where A, B, C, D are matrices of size $n \times n, n \times r, n \times m$ and $m \times r$, respectively and, $\mathbf{y}$, $\mathbf{u}$, $\mathbf{x}$ and $\mathbf{p}$ denotes the m-output vector, r-input vector, n-state vector and ℓ-parameter vector, respectively. With $\mathbf{z} \triangleq (\mathbf{x}\ \mathbf{y})'$, (6) can be written as:

$$T(\mathbf{p})\ \mathbf{z} = \begin{pmatrix} B \\ -D \end{pmatrix} \mathbf{u} \text{ where } T(\mathbf{p}) \triangleq \begin{pmatrix} A(\mathbf{p}) & 0 \\ C(\mathbf{p}) & -I \end{pmatrix}.$$

Let

$$T_{ij}(\mathbf{p}) \triangleq \begin{pmatrix} A(\mathbf{p}) & b_j \\ c_i(\mathbf{p}) & -d_{ij} \end{pmatrix}, i = 1, \cdots, m,\ j = 1, \cdots, r \quad (7)$$

with $c_i(\mathbf{p})$, $i = 1, \cdots, m$ being the i-th row of $C(\mathbf{p})$, $b_j, j = 1, \cdots, r$ the j-th column of B, d_{ij} the ij-th element of D, and

$$\beta_{ij}(\mathbf{p}) \triangleq |T_{ij}(\mathbf{p})|,\ \alpha(\mathbf{p}) \triangleq |T(\mathbf{p})|. \quad (8)$$

For the model (6), the outputs can be determined in terms of inputs and parameters. This is established below using the results given in [17] and [18]. The following assumptions are needed to establish the results.

Assumption 1: The parameter $\mathbf{p}$ appears affinely in $A(\mathbf{p})$ and $C(\mathbf{p})$:

$$\begin{aligned} A(\mathbf{p}) &= A_0 + p_1 A_1 + \cdots + p_\ell A_\ell \\ C(\mathbf{p}) &= C_0 + p_1 C_1 + \cdots + p_\ell C_\ell. \end{aligned} \quad (9)$$

Assumption 2:

$$|T(\mathbf{p})| \neq 0, \mathbf{p} \in \mathcal{P}. \quad (10)$$

Theorem 1: For system (6), the output is given by

$$y_i = \sum_{j=1}^{r} \frac{\beta_{ij}(\mathbf{p})}{\alpha(\mathbf{p})} u_j,\ i = 1, 2, \cdots, m \quad (11)$$

with $\beta_{ij}(\mathbf{p})$ and $\alpha(\mathbf{p})$ as already defined.

To describe the solution $\mathbf{y}$ from (6), one can use a form for the functions $\alpha(\mathbf{p})$ and $\beta_{ij}(\mathbf{p})$.

Lemma 1: Let $A(\mathbf{p}) = A_0 + p_1 A_1 + \cdots + p_\ell A_\ell$ with rank $(A_i) = r_i, i = 1, 2, \cdots, \ell$. Then $\alpha(\mathbf{p}) = |A(\mathbf{p})|$ is a multivariate polynomial in $\mathbf{p}$, of degree at most r_i in $p_i, i = 1, 2, \cdots, \ell$.

Now consider (7) written in polynomial form:

$$T_{ij}(\mathbf{p}) = T_{ij0} + p_1 T_{ij1} + \cdots + p_\ell T_{ij\ell}. \quad (12)$$

Applying Lemma 1, one can see that

$$|T_{ij}| = \beta_{ij}(\mathbf{p}) \quad (13)$$

is a multivariate polynomial in $\mathbf{p}$ of degree at most r_{ijk} in p_k where

$$r_{ijk} = \text{rank}(T_{ijk}), \quad (14)$$

with $i = 1, 2, \cdots, m, j = 1, 2, \cdots, r, k = 1, 2, \cdots, \ell$.

Then, it can be shown that the determinants of multivariate polynomials in $\mathbf{p}$ can be written as:

$$|A(\mathbf{p})| = \sum_{i_\ell=0}^{r_\ell} \cdots \sum_{i_1=0}^{r_1} \alpha_{i_1 \cdots i_\ell} p_1^{i_1} \cdots p_\ell^{i_\ell} \quad (15)$$

with rank $(A_i) = r_i, i = 1, 2, \cdots, \ell$. In the form of (15), the number of coefficients in $|A(\mathbf{p})|$ is $\mu \triangleq \sum_{i=1}^{\ell}(r_i + 1)$. The following example shows the use of the rank of the matrices A_i, $i = 1, 2, \cdots, m$ to obtain the determinant of a multivariate polynomial in $\mathbf{p}$.

Example 1: Let

$$A(\mathbf{p}) = \begin{bmatrix} 1 & 2p_1 & 0 \\ p_1 & p_2 & p_1 \\ 3 & p_1 & 3p_2 \end{bmatrix}. \quad (16)$$

As the parameter $\mathbf{p}$ appears affinely in $A(\mathbf{p})$, following (1), one can write

$$A(\mathbf{p}) = \begin{bmatrix} 1 & 0 & 0 \\ 0 & 0 & 0 \\ 3 & 0 & 0 \end{bmatrix} + \begin{bmatrix} 0 & 2 & 0 \\ 1 & 0 & 1 \\ 0 & 1 & 0 \end{bmatrix} p_1 + \begin{bmatrix} 0 & 0 & 0 \\ 0 & 1 & 0 \\ 0 & 0 & 3 \end{bmatrix} p_2.$$

In this example, $\text{rank}(A_1) = 2$, $\text{rank}(A_2) = 2$. Matrix $A(\mathbf{p})$ is said to be rank 2 with respect to p_1 and p_2, which yields $r_1 = 2$ and $r_2 = 2$. Thus,

$$|A(\mathbf{p})| = \sum_{i_2=0}^{2} \sum_{i_1=0}^{2} \alpha_{i_1 i_2} p_1^{i_1} p_2^{i_2}$$

is a polynomial of degree at most 2 in both p_1 and p_2. Calculating the determinant, it yields

$$|A(\mathbf{p})| = -6p_1^2 p_2 + 5p_1^2 + 3p_2^2.$$

Now consider (7) written in polynomial form:

$$T_{ij}(\mathbf{p}) = T_{ij0} + p_1 T_{ij1} + \cdots + p_\ell T_{ij\ell}.$$

Applying Lemma 1, one can see that

$$|T_{ij}| = \beta_{ij}(\mathbf{p})$$

is a multivariate polynomial in $\mathbf{p}$ of degree at most r_{ijk} in p_k where

$$r_{ijk} = \text{rank}(T_{ijk}), i = 1, 2, \cdots, m$$
$$j = 1, 2, \cdots, r, k = 1, 2, \cdots, \ell$$

and its determinant can be described in a similar manner as in (15).

B. A Measurement Based Approach To Unknown Systems

The solution (11) suggests that knowledge of the functions $\alpha(\mathbf{p})$ and $\beta_{ij}(\mathbf{p})$ are sufficient to determine the behavior of the outputs y_i as a function of $\mathbf{p}$ and $\mathbf{u}$ [18], [19]. The knowledge of $\alpha(\mathbf{p})$ and $\beta_{ij}(\mathbf{p})$ reduces to the knowledge of the coefficients of these polynomial functions. In an unknown system (black box, for instance) these coefficients are unknown a priori. However, if one can conduct tests on the system by setting the design parameter $\mathbf{p}$ and input $\mathbf{u}$ to various values and measuring the corresponding y_i, the polynomial functions coefficients can be determined. It is possible illustrate this concept for the special case of a single output y_i with inputs u_1, u_2 and parameters $\mathbf{p} = p_1$ for a rank one model from Lemma 1. Here,

$$y_i = \frac{\beta_{i1}(\mathbf{p})}{\alpha(\mathbf{p})} u_1 + \frac{\beta_{i2}(\mathbf{p})}{\alpha(\mathbf{p})} u_2 \quad (17)$$

with

$$\begin{aligned} \beta_{ij}(\mathbf{p}) &= \beta_{ij0} + \beta_{ij1} p_1, j = 1, 2 \\ \alpha(\mathbf{p}) &= \alpha_0 + \alpha_1 p_1. \end{aligned} \quad (18)$$

Assuming $\alpha_1 \neq 0$, one may divide both the numerator and denominator of the right hand side of (17) and write a linear algebraic equation to find the unknown coefficients of $\alpha(\mathbf{p})$ and $\beta_{ij}(\mathbf{p})$ from measurements as follows.

Set $u_2 = 0, u_1 = u_1^*$ and measure y_i for three different sets of values ($p_1 \triangleq p$) to determine the coefficients of $\alpha(\mathbf{p})$ and $\beta_{ij}(\mathbf{p}), j = 1, 2$ from the following measurement equation with $y_i(k)$ denoting the three measurement values and $p(k)$ the three sets of parameters with $k = 1, 2, 3$:

$$\begin{pmatrix} y_i(1) & -u_j(1) & -u_j(1)p(1) \\ y_i(2) & -u_j(2) & -u_j(2)p(2) \\ y_i(3) & -u_j(3) & -u_j(3)p(3) \end{pmatrix} \begin{pmatrix} \alpha_0 \\ \beta_{ij0} \\ \beta_{ij1} \end{pmatrix} = \begin{pmatrix} -y_i(1)p(1) \\ -y_i(2)p(2) \\ -y_i(3)p(3) \end{pmatrix} \quad (19)$$

with $j = 1, 2$.

C. Thévenin's Equivalent From The Input-Output Parameterized Model

Consider a nonlinear source, connected to a linear load named R as shown in Fig. 3.

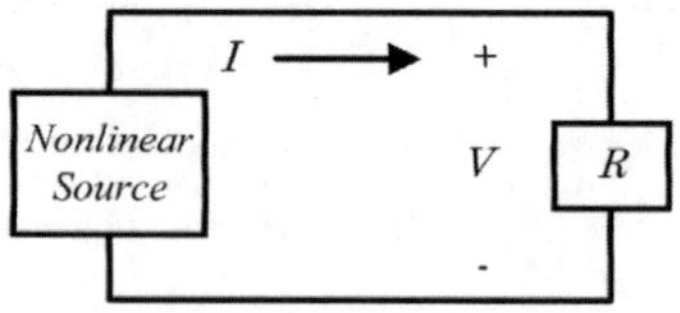

Figure 3. Nonlinear source.

The V-I characteristic of the source is described by:

$$I = f(V) \quad (20)$$

where $f(V)$ is assumed to be a continuous and differentiable function. The operating point (V_o, I_o) of the circuit in Fig. 3 can be obtained graphically as shown in Fig. 4.

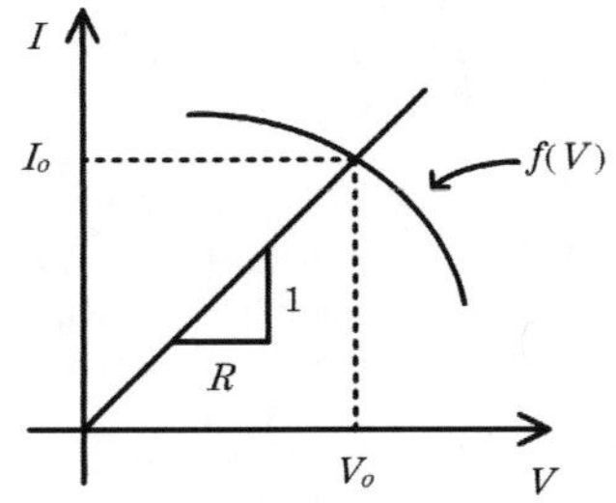

Figure 4. Operating point of a nonlinear circuit.

D. Point-wise Thévenin's Equivalents

Now consider a Thévenin's equivalent of the nonlinear circuit described by the V-I characteristic at the operating point (V_o, I_o), which yields the characteristic line L illustrated in Fig. 5.

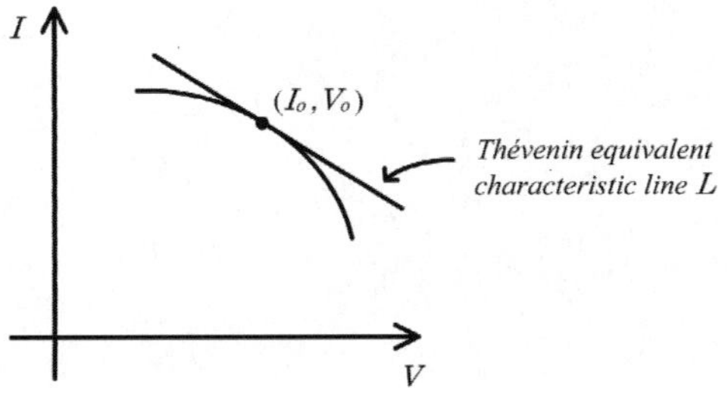

Figure 5. Point-wise Thévenin's equivalent.

The Thévenin's equivalent circuit is represented by the resistance denoted R_{th} and the voltage denoted V_{th} connected as shown in Fig. 6. Thus

$$V = V_{th} - IR_{th} \tag{21}$$

and

$$I = -\frac{1}{R_{th}}V + \frac{V_{th}}{R_{th}}. \tag{22}$$

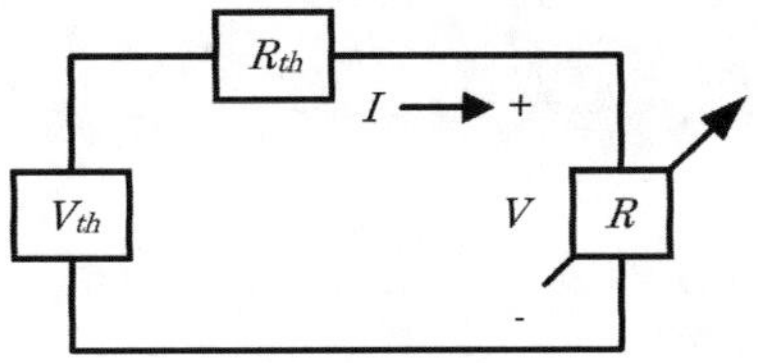

Figure 6. Equivalent circuit.

If (22) is to represent the line shown in Fig. 5, which is tangent to $f(V)$ at (V_o, I_o), one must have:

$$I = MV + C \tag{23}$$

with

$$\begin{aligned} M &= \frac{\partial I}{\partial V}\Big|_{(V_o, I_o)} \triangleq M_o \\ C &= I_o - M_o V_o \triangleq C_o. \end{aligned}$$

Comparing (22) and (23) it follows that:

$$-\frac{1}{R_{th}} = M_o \tag{24}$$

$$\frac{V_{th}}{R_{th}} = C_o. \tag{25}$$

Thus, the Thévenin's equivalent of the nonlinear circuit of Fig. 3 at (V_o, I_o) is given by:

$$R_{th} = -\frac{1}{M_o} \tag{26}$$

$$V_{th} = -\frac{C_o}{M_o}. \tag{27}$$

Note that the above parameters can be determined, if the nonlinear characteristic is known, at any point (V_o, I_o) and thus a family of point-wise Thévenin's equivalents may be constructed. If the $I = f(V)$ characteristic is not known, the Thévenin's equivalents may be determined by estimating the parameters of the tangent line L using a fixed number of measurements.

IV. Method

It is known that the flow in a nozzle is a function of the orifice diameter, drop pressure and other hydraulic parameters, which may change with different types of nozzle. Then, it is possible to find a function that relates the orifice diameter and pressure with the flow in a nozzle.

It is assumed that the rank of the matrices appearing in the description of the flow Q in relation to parameter d and boom pressure ΔP is unity. According to Bhattacharyya and collaborators [18], it is possible to find the rational function:

$$Q = \frac{\beta_0 + \beta_1 d + \beta_2 \Delta P + \beta_3 d \Delta P}{\alpha_0 + \alpha_1 d + \alpha_2 \Delta P + d \Delta P} \tag{28}$$

where $\beta_0, \beta_1, \beta_2, \beta_3, \alpha_0, \alpha_1$ and α_2 are constants and $(\alpha_0 + \alpha_1 d + \alpha_2 \Delta P + d\Delta P) \neq 0$. To obtain these constants, one should take just 7 measurements with different values of d and ΔP and solve the following linear system:

$$\begin{bmatrix} 1 & d(1) & \Delta P(1) & d(1)\Delta P(1) & -Q(1) & -Q(1)d(1) & -Q(1)\Delta P(1) \\ 1 & d(2) & \Delta P(2) & d(2)\Delta P(2) & -Q(2) & -Q(2)d(2) & -Q(2)\Delta P(2) \\ 1 & d(3) & \Delta P(3) & d(3)\Delta P(3) & -Q(3) & -Q(3)d(3) & -Q(3)\Delta P(3) \\ 1 & d(4) & \Delta P(4) & d(4)\Delta P(4) & -Q(4) & -Q(4)d(4) & -Q(4)\Delta P(4) \\ 1 & d(5) & \Delta P(5) & d(5)\Delta P(5) & -Q(5) & -Q(5)d(5) & -Q(5)\Delta P(5) \\ 1 & d(6) & \Delta P(6) & d(6)\Delta P(6) & -Q(6) & -Q(6)d(6) & -Q(6)\Delta P(6) \\ 1 & d(7) & \Delta P(7) & d(7)\Delta P(7) & -Q(7) & -Q(7)d(7) & -Q(7)\Delta P(7) \end{bmatrix} \begin{bmatrix} \beta_0 \\ \beta_1 \\ \beta_2 \\ \beta_3 \\ \alpha_0 \\ \alpha_1 \\ \alpha_2 \end{bmatrix} = \begin{bmatrix} Q(1)d(1)\Delta P(1) \\ Q(2)d(2)\Delta P(2) \\ Q(3)d(3)\Delta P(3) \\ Q(4)d(4)\Delta P(4) \\ Q(5)d(5)\Delta P(5) \\ Q(6)d(6)\Delta P(6) \\ Q(7)d(7)\Delta P(7) \end{bmatrix}. \tag{29}$$

The well known Thévenin's equivalent circuit of a linear circuit is composed of an equivalent impedance and voltage, which for some cases are represented as a resistor and a source of continuous voltage. This equivalent circuit is obtained through Thévenin's Theorem.

Theorem 1 (Thévenin's Theorem): The voltage and resistance equivalent of a circuit is given by:

$$V_{th} = V_{oc} \quad (30)$$

$$R_{th} = \frac{V_{oc}}{I_{sc}} \quad (31)$$

where I_{sc} is the short-circuit current and V_{oc} the open circuit voltage [20]–[23].

The Thévenin's equivalent circuit can be represented by Fig 6. In Fig. 6, the voltage and current are described by:

$$I = \frac{V_{th}}{R_{th} + R} \quad (32)$$

$$V = RI = -R_{th}I + V_{th}. \quad (33)$$

Let $y(1)$ and $y(2)$ denote current measurements taken with the values of the load R denoted $R(1)$ and $R(2)$, respectively. According to Bhattacharyya and collaborators [18] and Mohsenizadeh and collaborators [19], the Thévenin's equivalent can also be obtained by solving the linear equation system, in terms of α_0 and β_0:

$$\begin{pmatrix} y(1) & -1 \\ y(2) & -1 \end{pmatrix} \begin{pmatrix} \alpha_0 \\ \beta_0 \end{pmatrix} = \begin{pmatrix} -y(1)R(1) \\ -y(2)R(2) \end{pmatrix} \quad (34)$$

where α_0 and β_0 are given by:

$$\alpha_0 = R_{th} \quad (35)$$

$$\beta_0 = V_{th}. \quad (36)$$

If one is considering a linear characteristic then is possible to write:

$$V_{oc} = V_{th} \quad (37)$$

$$I_{sc} = \frac{V_{th}}{R_{th}}. \quad (38)$$

One can consider, as a further step, the electric analog already described in Section I, then $V = \sqrt{\Delta P}$ e $V_{th} = \sqrt{\Delta P_{th}}$. Now, let $y(1)$ e $y(2)$ be measures of flow in the boom with the nozzles of interest, and let $R(1)$ and $R(2)$ correspond to the equivalent fluidic resistance of the nozzles of the boom of interest, thus:

$$\begin{pmatrix} Q(1) & -1 \\ Q(2) & -1 \end{pmatrix} \begin{pmatrix} \alpha_0 \\ \beta_0 \end{pmatrix} = \begin{pmatrix} -\sqrt{\Delta P}(1) \\ -\sqrt{\Delta P}(2) \end{pmatrix} \quad (39)$$

where α_0 e β_0 are given by:

$$\alpha_0 = R_{th} \quad (40)$$

$$\beta_0 = \Delta P_{th}. \quad (41)$$

where R_{th} and ΔP_{th} are the internal loss and pressure equivalent, respectively. As the behavior of pressure and flow is nonlinear, then there will be more than one possible representation of the Thévenin's equivalent. If the measurements are taken as close as possible to each other, it is then said that a point-wise Thévenin's equivalent is obtained.

V. EXPERIMENTAL VALIDATION

The Agricultural Sprayer Development System (SDPA) used to obtain experimental results is located at the Laboratory for Precision Agricultural inputs Applications of the Embrapa Instrumentation (Figs. 7 and 8) in São Carlos, SP, Brazil [24]–[28]. The goal is to describe the flow in function of the orifice d and pressure drop ΔP and to obtain the linear pressure and fluidic resistance equivalent by selecting a boom with nozzles of interest using regular measurements.

(a)

(b)

Figure 7. Detail in photos of the SDPA containing: a) spray booms of agricultural pesticides and monitoring platform, b) control panel and data acquisition devices.

The results were separated into two different experiments. The first experiment was performed to find the coefficients of (28), which are related to the orifice diameter and pressure in the nozzle. The second experiment was carried out to obtain the Thévenin's equivalent, where the goal was to obtain the linear pressure and the fluidic resistance equivalent by selecting a boom with nozzles of interest and using regular measurements, which is possible by solving (34).

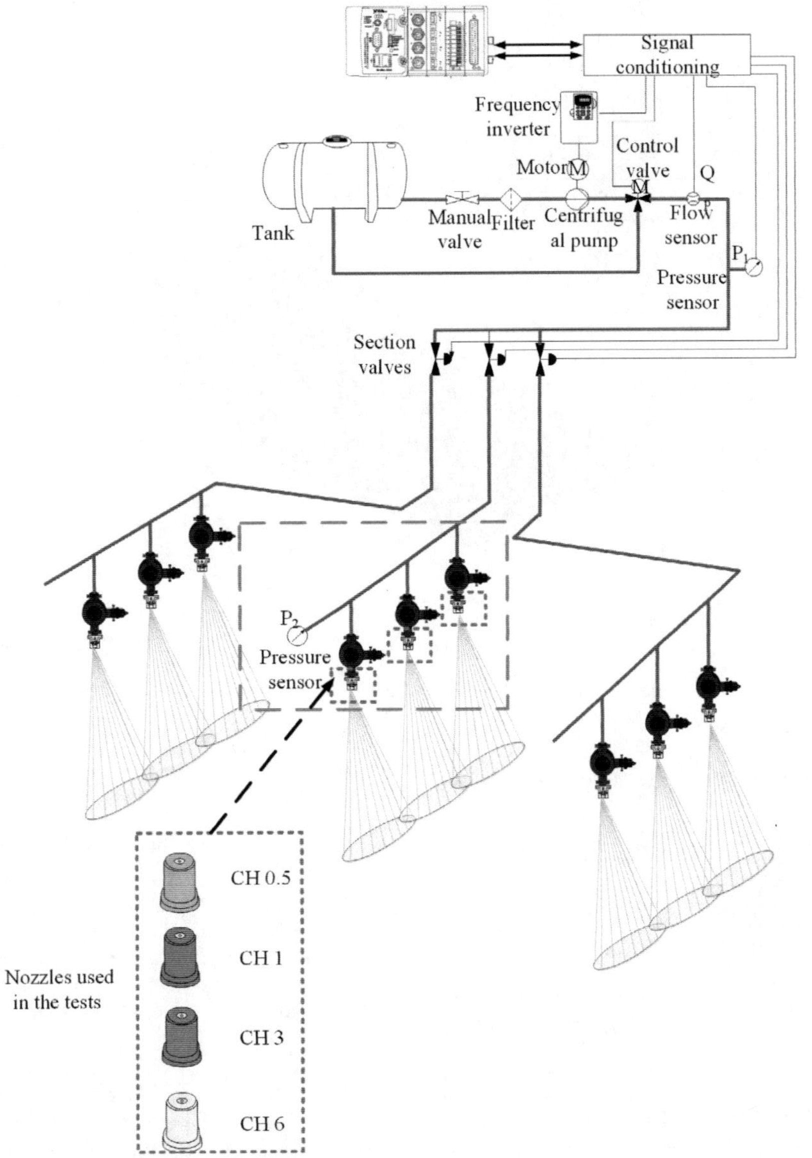

Figure 8. Hydraulic and electrical configuration of the SDPA for testing and estimation of the fluidic resistance of the nozzles.

A. Nozzle Flow Validation

To validate (28), which relates the flow to the orifices diameters, the nozzles were used. The datasheet of a nozzle MAG CH, produced by MAGNOJET®, was used. Then it was possible to find the values of pressure and flow for each nozzle. The orifices diameters were measured using a pachymeter. The 7 points shown in Table I were selected, which cover the entire producer table, and were used to solve the linear system (29). The evaluated matrix is shown in (42) and the coefficients solution are shown in Table II. With the solution of (29), it was possible to generate the surface shown in Fig. 9.

$$\begin{bmatrix} 1.00 & 0.50 & 3.40 & 1.70 & -0.56 & -0.28 & -1.90 \\ 1.00 & 1.50 & 3.40 & 5.10 & -1.50 & -2.25 & -5.10 \\ 1.00 & 2.00 & 3.40 & 6.80 & -2.40 & -4.80 & -8.16 \\ 1.00 & 0.50 & 10.40 & 5.20 & -0.94 & -0.47 & -9.78 \\ 1.00 & 1.50 & 10.40 & 15.60 & -2.55 & -3.83 & -26.50 \\ 1.00 & 2.00 & 10.40 & 20.80 & -4.08 & -8.16 & -42.40 \\ 1.00 & 1.50 & 7.60 & 11.40 & -2.20 & -3.30 & -16.70 \end{bmatrix} \begin{bmatrix} \beta_0 \\ \beta_1 \\ \beta_2 \\ \beta_3 \\ \alpha_0 \\ \alpha_1 \\ \alpha_2 \end{bmatrix} = \begin{bmatrix} 0.95 \\ 7.65 \\ 16.30 \\ 4.89 \\ 39.80 \\ 84.90 \\ 25.10 \end{bmatrix}. \quad (42)$$

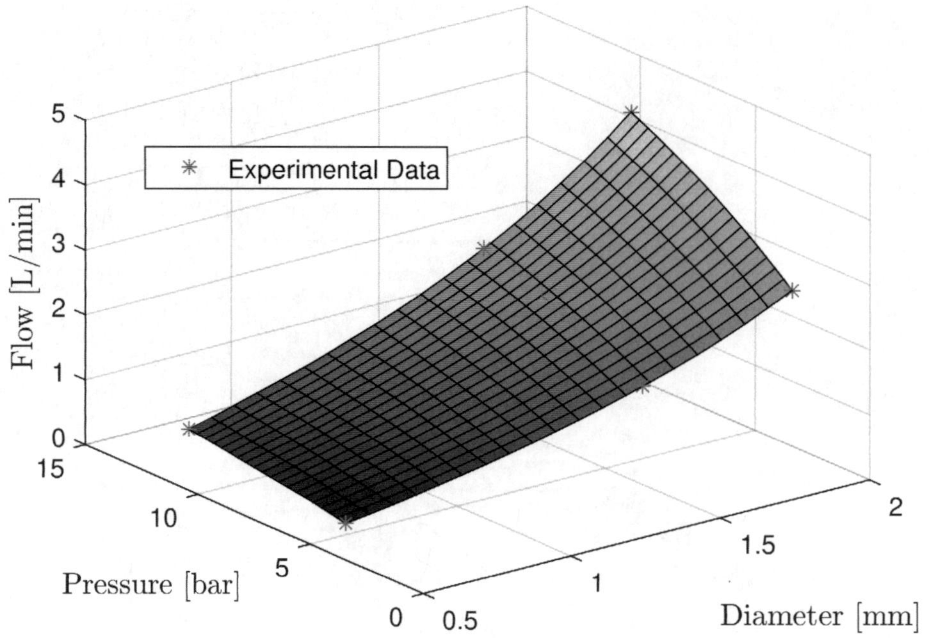

Figure 9. Surface relating the orifice diameter d and the pressure with the output flow for the full cone nozzle.

TABLE I. SELECTED MEASUREMENTS FROM THE MAGNOJET PRODUCER DATASHEET.

Nozzle	Pressure [bar]	Q [L/min]	d [mm]
CH05	3.40	0.56	0.50
CH3	3.40	1.50	1.50
CH6	3.40	2.40	2.00
CH05	10.40	0.94	0.50
CH3	10.40	2.55	1.50
CH6	10.40	4.08	2.00
CH3	7.60	2.20	1.50

TABLE II. COEFFICIENTS of (29) obtained.

β_0	β_1	β_2	β_3
-9.81	-11.61	-3.81	-5.99
α_0	α_1	α_2	
-67.54	18.65	-3.74	

TABLE III. PREDICTED FLOW AND THE CATALOG FLOW TO CH1 NOZZLE USING THE SURFACE

Pressure [bar]	d [mm]	Predicted flow [L/min]	Catalog Flow [L/min]	Relative error [%]
3.40	1.00	0.94	1.00	5.90
4.80	1.00	1.10	1.20	8.00
6.20	1.00	1.25	1.33	6.17
7.60	1.00	1.38	1.47	6.39
9.00	1.00	1.49	1.63	8.54
10.40	1.00	1.60	1.74	8.39

Using Fig. 9 it is possible now to predict the flow of the nozzle given the diameter of the orifice and the pressure in the nozzle, what can help in the design of the nozzle. In Table III, the results of the prediction using the nozzle CH1 are shown.

B. Thévenin's Equivalent Validation

To obtain the hydraulic Thévenin equivalent, according to the proposed methodology, only two different fluidic resistances are required. However, it is necessary that when the fluidic resistance changes, a significant variation of pressure and flow occurs at the point of interest. Otherwise, if any of these measures are kept constant, a solution does not exist.

A pressure variation, in relation to the pump pressure, of approximately 0.1 bar at the point of interest was considered significant because of the inherent noise of the spray sensors. The objective is to extract the Thévenin's equivalent of the central sprayer boom, which is also shown in Fig. 8. All nozzles of the central sprayer boom are of type CH05.

1) Measurements set-up: Firstly, the central sprayer boom had 3 spray nozzles type CH05. The pump pressure was set to 3.5 bar and the corresponding pressure at the center boom spray nozzles was found to be about 3.48 bar. Then, only one of the 3 nozzles was changed to type CH3. The pressure in the spray nozzles rose to 3.47 bar and was therefore again considered as noise. Another attempt was made by replacing the same nozzle by a nozzle type CH6 (which allowed the largest flow in this line). The pressure at the nozzles rose to 3.46 and was again considered as noise. Two nozzle were then replaced by CH3 type nozzles and the pressure at the spray nozzles was found to be 3.44 bar, again considered to be noise. In this way, all the nozzles of the central bar were changed to type CH3 and the pressure was equal to 3.39 bar. This pressure drop was then considered as significant and thus concluding that it was necessary to change all the nozzles of the boom to take the measurements.

To extract the Thévenin's equivalent, only two different nozzles were required. To validate the Thévenin's equivalent obtained, a third different nozzle with a intermediate fluidic resistance between the other two nozzles were used to extract the equivalent. The resulting data are shown in Table IV.

TABLE IV. DATA OBTAINED FOR DIFFERENT FULL CONE NOZZLES

Nozzles	Pressure [bar]	Flow [L/min]
CH05	3.40	0.53
CH3	3.35	1.42
CH6	3.29	2.23

Using (39), the following equivalent was obtained:

$$\Delta P_{th} = 1.85\ [bar]$$
$$R_{th} = 0.02\ [bar \cdot min \cdot L^{-1}].$$

Thus, this equivalent was used to estimate the flow of arbitrary pressure values. The result is shown in Fig. 10. The error of estimated flow was around 2.15%.

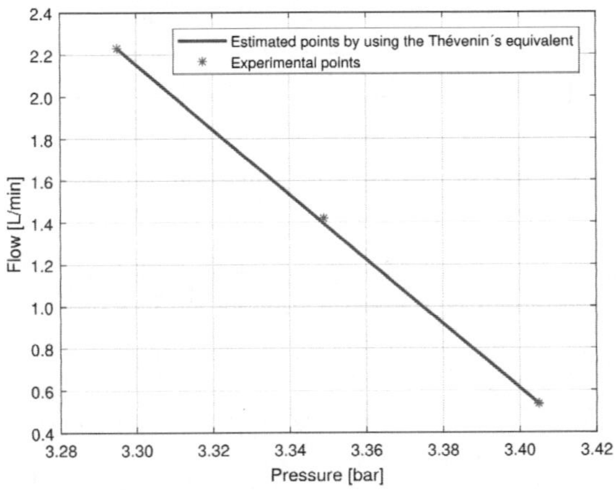

Figure 10. Thévenin's equivalent for full cone nozzles.

VI. CONCLUSION

In this paper, a measurement-based approach was used to emulate the behavior of a sensor to allow the control quality analyses of direct injection sprayers. With few measurement, a flow function of a full cone nozzle relating the nozzle internal diameter and pressure were estimated. In addiction, the fluidic resistance equivalent of a piping system was obtained.

The results presented showed that using the proposed method, one can be able to find the relationship among the orifice diameter of the nozzles, pressure and the flow for an adjusted operation using a graphical surface inspection. In addiction, from the point-wise fluidic resistance the conditions necessary for the correct operation of each nozzle can be defined.

The experimental results obtained were satisfactory and the extension of this work includes the hardware implementation of the sensor and the application of the measurement-based approach to analyze the control quality of spray droplets in agriculture.

ACKNOWLEDGMENT

This work was supported by the Brazilian Agricultural Research Corporation - Embrapa (grant numbers MP2 - 02.11.07.025.00.00, MP1 - 01.14.09.001.05.05); the National Counsel of Technological and Scientific Development - CNPq (grant number 306.477/2013-0). The authors also thank the MAGNOJET® by the availability of the nozzles for validation of the developed method.

REFERENCES

[1] R. F. Q. Magossi, E. A. G. Peñaloza, S. P. Battachharya, V. A. Oliveira, and P. E. Cruvinel, "Using the measurement-based approach to emulate the behavior of a sensor for internal hydraulic pressure drop measurements of sprayers in the agricultural industry," in *ALLSENSORS 2017: The Second International Conference on Advances in Sensors, Actuators, Metering and Sensing*. IARIA, Mar. 2017, pp. 10–15.

[2] R. Mulley, *Flow of industrial fluids: theory and equations*. CRC Press, 2004.

[3] L. E. Bode and S. M. Bretthauer, "Agricultural chemical application technology: a remarkable past and an amazing future," *Transactions of the ASAE*, vol. 51, no. 2, p. 391, 2008.

[4] P. Chueca, C. Garcera, E. Molto, and A. Gutierrez, "Development of a sensor-controlled sprayer for applying low-volume bait treatments," *Crop Protection*, vol. 27, no. 10, pp. 1373–1379, 2008.

[5] S. Han, L. L. Hendrickson, B. Ni, and Q. Zhang, "Modification and testing of a comercial sprayer with pwm solenoids for precision spraying," *Applied Engineering in Agriculture*, vol. 5, no. 17, pp. 591–594, 2001.

[6] F. H. R. Baio and U. R. Antuniassi, "Sistemas de controle eletrônico e navegação para pulverizadores (electronic control and navigation systems for sprayers)," in *Tecnologia de Aplicação para Culturas Anuais (Application Technology for Annual Crops)*, U. R. Antuniassi and W. Boller, Eds. Passo Fundo: Aldeia Norte, 2011.

[7] P. E. Cruvinel, D. Karam, and M. G. Beraldo, "Method for the precision application of herbicides in the controlling of weed species into a culture of maize," in *VII Simpósio Internacional de Tecnologia de Aplicação (International Symposium on Application Technology)*. Uberlândia, MG: SINTAG, 2015.

[8] B. L. Steward and D. S. Humburg, "Modeling the raven scs-700 chemical injection system with carrier control with sprayer simulation," *Transactions of the ASAE*, vol. 43, no. 2, pp. 231–245, 2000.

[9] A. Akers, M. Gassman, and R. Smith, *Hydraulic Power System Analysis*. Broken Sound Parkway: CRC Press, 2006.

[10] J. Zhang, Y. Ju, S. Zhou, and C. Zhou, "Air-pasty propellant pressure drop and heat transfer through round pipe," in *2008 Asia Simulation Conference - 7th International Conference on System Simulation and Scientific Computing*, Oct. 2008, pp. 1282–1285.

[11] Y. Suzumura and P. E. Cruvinel, "Análise de qualidade da eficiência da pulverização agrícola com processamento de imagem e rede neural (quality analysis of crop spray efficiency with image processing and neural network)," *Sinergia*, vol. 6, no. 2, pp. 129–137, 2005.

[12] R. A. Kohl, "Drop size distribution from medium-sized agricultural sprinklers," *Transaction of the ASAE*, vol. 17, no. 4, pp. 690 – 693, 1974.

[13] P. A. Tipler and G. Mosca, *Physics for Scientists and Engineers*, 6th ed. New York: W. H. Freeman, 2007.

[14] A. Lefebvre, *Atomization and Sprays*, ser. Combustion, Hemisphere Publishing Corporation. Boca Raton, FL, USA: Taylor & Francis, 1988.

[15] E. A. G. Peñaloza, H. V. Mercaldi, V. A. Oliveira, and P. E. Cruvinel, "An advanced model based on analytical and computational procedures for the evaluation of spraying processes in agriculture," in *2016 IEEE Tenth International Conference on Semantic Computing (ICSC)*. IEEE, Feb. 2016, pp. 432–436.

[16] D. N. Mohsenizadeh, V. A. Oliveira, L. H. Keel, and S. P. Bhattacharyya, "Extremal results for algebraic linear interval systems," in *Optimization and Its Applications in Control and Data Sciences*, B. Goldengorin, Ed. Switzerland: Springer International Publishing, 2016, pp. 341–351.

[17] V. A. Oliveira, K. R. Felizardo, and S. P. Bhattacharyya, "A model-free measurement based approach to circuit analysis and synthesis based on linear interval systems," in *IEEE International Symposium on Industrial Electronics (ISIE)*, June 2015, pp. 1–6.

[18] S. P. Bhattacharyya, L. H. Keel, and D. Mohsenizadeh, *Linear Systems: A Measurement Based Approach*, ser. Springer Briefs in Applied Sciences and Technology. Springer, 2013.

[19] N. Mohsenizadeh, H. Nounou, M. Nounou, A. Datta, and S. P. Bhattacharyya, "Linear circuits: a measurement-based approach," *International Journal of Circuit Theory and Applications*, vol. 43, no. 2, pp. 205–232, 2015.

[20] L. Thévenin, "Extension de la loi d'ohm aux circuits électromoteurs complexes (Extension of Ohm's law to complex electromotive circuits)," *Annales Télegraphiques*, vol. 10, no. 222-224, 1883.

[21] L. Thévenin, "Sur un nouveau théorème d'électricité dynamique (On a new theorem of dynamic electricity)," *C. R. des Séances de l'Academie des Sciences*, vol. 97, no. 159-161, 1883.

[22] J. Brittain, "Thevenin's theorem," *Spectrum, IEEE*, vol. 27, no. 3, pp. 42–, 1990.

[23] D. Johnson, "Origins of the equivalent circuit concept: the current-source equivalent," *Proceedings of the IEEE*, vol. 91, no. 5, pp. 817–821, 2003.

[24] P. E. Cruvinel, V. A. Oliveira, H. V. Mercaldi, E. A. G. Peñaloza, and K. R. Felizardo, "An advanced sensors-based platform for the development of agricultural sprayers," in *Sensors and Applications in Measuring and Automation Control Systems*. IFSA, Dec. 2016, pp. 181–204.

[25] P. E. Cruvinel, V. A. Oliveira, K. R. Felizardo, and H. V. Mercaldi, "Bancada automatizada para ensaios e desenvolvimento de pulverizadores de agrotóxicos, aplicadores de fertilizantes líquidos e maturadores em culturas agrícolas sob manejo baseado em agricultura de precisão (Automated bench for testing and development of pesticide sprays, liquid fertilizer applicators and ripeners in agricultural crops under precision agriculture based management)," in *Agricultura de Precisão: um Novo Olhar*. São Carlos, SP: Embrapa Instrumentação, 2011, pp. 96–100.

[26] H. V. Mercaldi, C. H. Fujiwara, E. A. G. Peñaloza, V. A. Oliveira, , and P. E. Cruvinel, "An intelligent and customized electrical conductivity sensor to evaluate the response time of a direct injection system," in *SENSORDEVICES 2015 The Sixth International Conference on Sensor Device Technologies and Applications*. IARIA, 2015, pp. 19 – 24.

[27] K. R. Felizardo, H. V. Mercaldi, P. E. Cruvinel, V. A. Oliveira, and B. L. Steward, "Modeling and model validation of a chemical injection sprayer system," *Applied Engineering in Agriculture*, vol. 32, no. 3, pp. 285–297, 2016.

[28] E. A. G. Peñaloza, P. E. Cruvinel, V. A. Oliveira, and A. G. F. Costa, "A model approach to infer the quality in agricultural sprayers supported by knowledge bases and experimental measurements," *International Journal of Semantic Computing*, vol. 11, no. 03, pp. 279–292, 2017.

International Journal on Advances in Systems and Measurements, vol 10 no 3 & 4, year 2017, http://www.iariajournals.org/systems_and_measurements/

A Practical Forensic Method for Enhancing Speech Signals Drowned in Loud Music

Robert Alexandru Dobre, Radu-Mihnea Udrea, Cristian Negrescu, Dumitru Stanomir
Telecommunications Department
Politehnica University of Bucharest
Bucharest, Romania
e-mail: rdobre@elcom.pub.ro, mihnea@comm.pub.ro, negrescu@elcom.pub.ro, dumitru.stanomir@elcom.pub.ro

Abstract—**Recording audio or video is nowadays easier than ever. Almost every phone can do this task with high quality. This has some serious implications in forensic: almost every dialogue or event can be recorded and used as evidence in trials. The problem is that editing multimedia content has also become a very accessible operation. The advances of editing software make it possible with very convincing results for the untrained audience. Forged recordings could be used in trials. The need for multimedia forensic is imminent. There are two main directions of this field: probe authentication and noise reduction. This paper presents the research activities conducted to extract speech signal masked by loud music. The developed system is based on an adaptive system identification configuration. Various scenarios are studied showing the advantages and disadvantages of the adaptive algorithms that were tested. The influence of the acoustic environment over the performances of the proposed system is also studied and the results can help to determine if placing a microphone in a specific room could be used to intercept a speech.**

Keywords-adaptive algorithms; system identification; noise reduction; multimedia forensic.

I. INTRODUCTION

The technological advances made the recording of high quality multimedia content available to almost everyone. Phones have rapidly turned into small pocket computers and they are more affordable as time passes. Since phones are mainly used for speech communication, it is self-understood why audio recording is an easy task, but most of them are also fitted with at least one video camera allowing the user to capture full HD video for a decent period, like tens of minutes. On high end terminals, even state of the art 4K video can be recorded.

From the security point of view, there are two sides of this situation, explained onwards. The first implication is: if anyone can store a clear multimedia recording of an event, it means that many trials should end very quickly. With clear evidence of the events, very little is, apparently, remaining to be evaluated. It is necessary to mention that along the evolution of the recording devices, the industry of multimedia editing software also grew, allowing one can edit the recordings before presenting them as evidence. This brings to light the second implication: the multimedia content can be edited and the verdict may not reflect the consequence of the real events. Special training to use these editing software is not needed, and some of them are available for free, so the malicious editing can be considered as easy as the recording. To the untrained audience, the forgeries could be very convincing. These two implications show the necessity of some authorities and technologies to counteract these illegal actions. This paper concentrates on the latter part.

Before allowing some multimedia content as evidence into a trial, it must be determined if it is the original, unaltered version. This process is called content authentication and it represents one large field of multimedia forensics. There are other situations in which the material is not forged, but greatly affected by noise in such way that the key element (some specific spoken phrase or a zone of an image) is heavily masked. This is another research direction called noise reduction. The work presented in this paper is part of this topic and it extends the results shown in [1].

In [2], power spectral subtraction based methods for speech enhancement are presented. These methods could give very good results if the noise is slowly varying in time and the speech signal is not drowned into it. Other methods based on Wiener filtering or which use singular values decomposition (SVD) are presented in [3][4]. The method presented in this paper has the advantages of simplicity and good performances in harsh signal-to-noise ratio conditions, but, unlike the other methods, it is specifically designed for one particular situation.

Besides this introduction, the rest of this paper is organized as follows. Section II describes a speech recovery method, Section III thoroughly describes the suitable adaptive algorithms [5][6], Section IV presents and discusses the results, and Section V concludes the paper.

II. THE DESCRIPTION OF THE SPEECH RECOVERY APPROACH

The studied situation is the following: if a group of people would like to speak about something confidential, it is obvious that they will take some measures to avoid being intercepted. If they suspect that there is a high chance for a microphone to be placed in the room, the easiest way to avoid being recorded when talking is to turn very loud any nearby music player. This will make the speech signal (i.e., the secret discussion) to be heavily masked (or "drowned") by the loud music. The captured audio signal will be dominated by the music and could be considered useless. It is a very high chance that the source for the musical signal is a radio station or a labeled CD and so the melody has some notoriety. Music identification software (like Shazam or SoundHound) very rarely fail to recognize even the most exotic tunes nowadays and they could be used to determine the masking melody. The original, studio quality, full length melody can be bought (or simply downloaded in many cases since an important part of artists give their music for free) and made available to the forensic engineer. The problem restates as: if the recorded signal is a mixture of the sought speech signal and a masking melody and if the melody is identified and available in studio quality, can the latter be processed in a way that could make it match the recorded melody so by subtracting these two signals, the speech would be recovered? This is a typical adaptive system identification situation.

The real situation has some specific elements like the acoustic properties of the room that were not discussed in the short description above. All the audio signals that propagate in a room will be affected by the acoustic impulse response of the room. The microphone will record the direct wave, but also all the waves that are reflected by the various objects present in the room. Since the recorded signal will be composed of multiple delayed replicas of the direct wave, the propagation of the sound waves between two points in a room can be modelled using a finite impulse response (FIR) filter. Taking this added element into consideration, a more accurate situation is illustrated in Figure 1. The properties of the impulse response (length, sparsity, etc.) have great impact on determining the solution that could be used to extract the speech from the masking music, as it is shown in the following sections.

Let us denote with $s_{speech}(n)$ the speech signal unaffected by the acoustic environment (i.e., that speech signal that would be recorded if the microphone and the speaker are in open space conditions) and with $n_{music}(n)$ the studio quality masking musical signal. The signal recorded using the microphone that is placed in the room [$r(n)$] is modelled as a mixture of the two aforementioned signals filtered with the acoustic impulse response, denoted with $h(n)$. Keeping in mind the speakers' intention to conceal their dialogue, the musical signal dominates the mixture. The recorded signal is analyzed using a music identification software, and the masking song is found and acquired. Furthermore, the louder the masking music is turned, the easier becomes the job of the music identification software. This means that in their try to conceal their secret, the speakers could unintentionally help the extraction of the masked dialogue. There are high chances that the music being played in the room is in the same format as the music that is acquired in studio quality, since radio stations use the commercially available version also. If the music is played from a CD, a CD can also be made available. In the event that the music is transcoded, the problem gets tougher because the CD version must be encoded using various codecs, various encoding settings, then decoded and processed by the forensic software. This scenario involving the estimation of the encoder is not considered in this paper. The final element that is required to recover the speech is a good estimate for the room's acoustic impulse response denoted with $h_{est}(n)$, which could be determined using an adaptive filter connected in the system identification configuration. The result of filtering the acquired studio quality melody with $h_{est}(n)$ and then subtracting it from the recorded mixture will be called the error signal [$e(n)$] and it will represent a good estimate for the secret speech signal. In fact, in the ideal situation of perfect extraction (no trace of music can be identified in the extracted signal), the recovered speech will be the ideal speech (the direct sound wave) filtered with the room's acoustic impulse response. This is not a problem since this kind of signals are heard every day when speaking with somebody in a room. The presented method is practical in the considered scenarios.

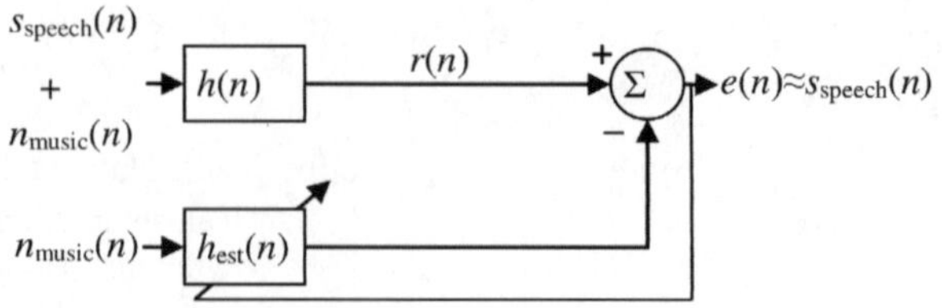

Figure 1. The adaptive noise reduction configuration in the proposed approach.

III. ADAPTIVE ALGORITHMS

The operation that is at the foundation of eliminating the masking music is the identification of the system that models the acoustic properties of the room. An adaptive filter will evolve in such way to match the filter that models the sound waves' propagation in the room. Generally, an adaptive algorithm's task is to minimize a cost function. Updating the impulse response of the adaptive filter can be done in multiple ways, using various adaptive algorithms.

Typically, an adaptive algorithm has two input signals denoted with $x(n)$ and $d(n)$. Usually $x(n)$ is called the input signal and $d(n)$ is known as the desired signal. In the described system identification problem, the signal $d(n)$ is the output of the unknown filter (i.e., the acoustic impulse response of the room). The vector containing the coefficients of the unknown filter is denoted onward with $\mathbf{w}_o$ and the one containing the coefficients of the adaptive filter is denoted with $\mathbf{w}$ because these are the common notations used in literature. The quantity that gives and characterizes the quality of the estimation is known as the misalignment and is evaluated as:

$$m(n) = \left\|\mathbf{w}(n) - \mathbf{w}_o(n)\right\|. \tag{1}$$

where $\|\cdot\|$ is the l_2 norm of a vector.

Another variant to evaluate the performance of the algorithm is the normalized misalignment, computed as:

$$m_{normalized}(n) = \frac{\left\|\mathbf{w}(n) - \mathbf{w}_o(n)\right\|}{\left\|\mathbf{w}_o(n)\right\|}. \quad (2)$$

A cost function based on the error signal [the difference between $d(n)$ and the output of the adaptive filter, denoted with $y(n)$] is considered and its minimization represents an optimization problem. Various approaches are used by different algorithms to give the solution. Only real signals are considered in this paper (the signal samples and filter coefficients are real numbers).

A. The least-mean-squares and the normalized least-mean-squares algorithms

The cost function used in the case of the least-mean-squares (LMS) algorithm is the square error, hence the name of the algorithm. It is defined as:

$$C(n) = e^2(n) \quad (3)$$

where $e(n)$ denotes the aforementioned error signal.

The minimization of the cost function is done with respect to the $\mathbf{w}$ vector. The solution gives the impulse response of the adaptive filter at the n sample time:

$$\mathbf{w}(n) = \mathbf{w}(n-1) + \mu\mathbf{x}(n)\left[d(n) - \mathbf{w}^{\mathrm{T}}(n-1)\mathbf{x}(n)\right], \quad (4)$$

where μ is a parameter known as step-size and $\{\cdot\}^{\mathrm{T}}$ is the transposition operator. If the length of the adaptive filter is considered equal to L, the structure of the input data vector involved in (4) is:

$$\mathbf{x}(n) = \left[x(n), x(n-1), \ldots, x(n-L+1)\right]^{\mathrm{T}}, \quad (5)$$

The step-size will be chosen by making a compromise between a better estimation quality (given by a smaller step-size) and a faster, but coarser estimation. The μ parameter cannot take any value. For assuring the convergence of the algorithm, μ must respect the following relation:

$$0 < \mu < \frac{2}{\mathrm{tr}\{\mathbf{R}\}}, \quad (6)$$

Where $\mathrm{tr}\{\cdot\}$ is the trace of a matrix and $\mathbf{R}$ is the autocorrelation matrix of the input signal computed as:

$$\mathbf{R} = \mathrm{E}\left\{\mathbf{x}(n)\mathbf{x}^{\mathrm{T}}(n)\right\}, \quad (7)$$

where $\mathrm{E}\{\cdot\}$ is the statistical expectation.

A great disadvantage of the LMS algorithm arises from equations (6) and (7): in practice, choosing a step-size that will guarantee convergence is a difficult task since the LMS depends on the scaling of the input signal. This important problem is solved in the normalized LMS (NLMS) algorithm by scaling the step-size with the power of the input signal. Equation (4) becomes:

$$\mathbf{w}(n) = \mathbf{w}(n-1) + \frac{\mu\mathbf{x}(n)\left[d(n) - \mathbf{w}^{\mathrm{T}}(n-1)\mathbf{x}(n)\right]}{\mathbf{x}^{\mathrm{T}}(n)\mathbf{x}(n)}, \quad (8)$$

where μ must now respect only $0 < \mu < 2$. The greatest convergence speed is obtained when $\mu = 1$. Since the behavior of the algorithm on the $0 < \mu \leq 1$ interval is similar with the behavior on the $1 \leq \mu < 2$ interval, the first one is preferred in practice because it greatly reduces the risk of the algorithm going out of convergence.

Since in (8) a division to the power of the input signal is computed, this could generate problems if $\mathbf{x}(n)$ is almost zero. To avoid the situation, a small positive number named the regularization parameter (usually denoted with δ) is introduced, and the final update equation for the NLMS algorithm becomes:

$$\mathbf{w}(n) = \mathbf{w}(n-1) + \frac{\mu\mathbf{x}(n)\left[d(n) - \mathbf{w}^{\mathrm{T}}(n-1)\mathbf{x}(n)\right]}{\mathbf{x}^{\mathrm{T}}(n)\mathbf{x}(n) + \delta}. \quad (9)$$

The main advantages of the NLMS algorithm are its simplicity and reduced computational cost. One disadvantage could be considered the limited performance tweaking parameters (in this form, only the step-size can be adjusted by the user).

B. The affine projection algorithm

One cause of the performance limitation in the case of the NLMS algorithm is the fact that it uses only one input signal vector [$\mathbf{x}(n)$]. The performance worsens for correlated input data. The affine projection algorithm (APA) increases the performance in the mentioned situation by using more than one input signal vector. The number of the input signal vectors used by the algorithm is controlled by a specific parameter named "projection order", denoted with M. The existence of this new tweakable parameter increases the flexibility of the algorithm in terms of the convergence speed/misalignment compromise. The obvious consequence of this operation is an increase in the computational complexity. The $M \times L$ matrix containing the M input signal vectors, denoted with $\mathbf{A}$, is constructed as:

$$\mathbf{A}^{\mathrm{T}}(n) = \left[\mathbf{x}(n), \mathbf{x}(n-1), \ldots, \mathbf{x}(n-M+1)\right]. \quad (10)$$

Using this new matrix approach, it can be shown that equation (9) becomes:

$$\mathbf{w}(n) = \mathbf{w}(n-1) + \mu\mathbf{A}^{\mathrm{T}}(n)\left[\mathbf{A}(n)\mathbf{A}^{\mathrm{T}}(n) + \delta\mathbf{I}_M\right]^{-1}\mathbf{e}(n), \quad (11)$$

where $\mathbf{I}_M$ is the M order identity matrix and now

$$\mathbf{e}(n)=\mathbf{d}(n)-\mathbf{y}(n), \tag{12}$$

$$\mathbf{d}(n)=\left[d(n),d(n-1),...,d(n-M+1)\right]^{\mathrm{T}}, \tag{13}$$

$$\mathbf{y}(n)=\mathbf{A}(n)\mathbf{w}(n-1). \tag{14}$$

A major computational load represented by the inverse of a matrix can be observed in (11). Larger projection orders lead to an increase in the convergence speed, but also to a worse system identification. Another observation is that the NLMS algorithm is a particular case of APA, obtained when $M=1$. An actual topic of interest is the convergence of the APA. If the evolution of the misalignment can be computed in some sufficiently general situations, M and μ can be chosen to obtain the desired performances. The quality of the estimation can be evaluated by:

$$\mathrm{E}\left\{\left\|\mathbf{c}(n)\right\|^2\right\}=\mathrm{E}\left\{\left\|\mathbf{w}_{\mathrm{o}}(n)-\mathbf{w}(n)\right\|^2\right\}, \tag{15}$$

In a more realistic situation, a zero mean white noise (named system noise) denoted with $v(n)$, having a variance equal to where σ_v^2 is intervening at the output of the unknown system, transforming the desired signal in:

$$\mathbf{d}(n)=\mathbf{A}(n)\mathbf{w}_{\mathrm{o}}+\mathbf{v}(n), \tag{16}$$

with $\mathbf{v}(n)$ respecting the structure in (13). In these conditions, by denoting:

$$\mathbf{C}(n)\triangleq\mathbf{A}^{\mathrm{T}}(n)\left[\mathbf{A}(n)\mathbf{A}^{\mathrm{T}}(n)+\delta\mathbf{I}_M\right]^{-1}, \tag{17}$$

equation (15) becomes:

$$\begin{aligned}&\mathrm{E}\left\{\left\|\mathbf{c}(n)\right\|^2\right\}=\\&\mathrm{tr}\left\{\mathrm{E}\left\{\mathbf{c}(n-1)\mathbf{c}^{\mathrm{T}}(n-1)\left[\mathbf{I}_L-\mu\mathbf{C}(n)\mathbf{A}(n)\right]^2\right\}\right\}\\&+\mu^2\mathrm{tr}\left\{\mathrm{E}\left\{\mathbf{v}(n)\mathbf{v}^{\mathrm{T}}(n)\mathrm{E}\left\{\mathbf{C}^{\mathrm{T}}(n)\mathbf{C}(n)\right\}\right\}\right\}+T_M,\end{aligned} \tag{18}$$

where

$$\begin{aligned}&T_M=\\&-2\mu\mathrm{tr}\left\{\mathrm{E}\left\{\mathbf{v}(n)\mathbf{c}^{\mathrm{T}}(n-1)\left[\mathbf{I}_L-\mu\mathbf{C}(n)\mathbf{A}(n)\right]\mathbf{C}(n)\right\}\right\}.\end{aligned} \tag{19}$$

The general solution in the case of a first level of approximation [7] shows that:

$$\begin{aligned}\mathrm{E}\left\{\left\|\mathbf{c}(n)\right\|^2\right\}&=\mathrm{E}\left\{\left\|\mathbf{c}(0)\right\|^2\right\}a^n\left(\beta,\sigma_x^2,M,L\right)\\&+\frac{b\left(\beta,M,L,\sigma_x^2,\sigma_v^2\right)\left(1\text{-}a^n\left(\beta,\sigma_x^2,M,L\right)\right)}{1\text{-}a\left(\beta,\sigma_x^2,M,L\right)},\end{aligned} \tag{20}$$

where σ_x^2 is the variance of the input signal and

$$a\left(\beta,\sigma_x^2,M,L\right)=1-2\beta M\sigma_x^2+\beta^2LM\sigma_x^4, \tag{21}$$

$$b\left(\beta,M,L,\sigma_x^2,\sigma_v^2\right)=\beta^2\sigma_x^2\sigma_v^2LM+T_M, \tag{22}$$

$$\beta\triangleq\frac{\mu}{L\sigma_x^2+\delta}, \tag{23}$$

Equation (21) gives the convergence speed, while the residual misalignment can be computed using (22). Under the convergence condition, in this first level of approximation the residual misalignment is found as:

$$\lim_{n\to\infty}\mathrm{E}\left\{\left\|\mathbf{c}(n)^2\right\|\right\}=\frac{\beta L\sigma_v^2}{\left(2-\beta L\sigma_x^2\right)}+\frac{T_M}{1-a\left(\beta,\sigma_x^2,M,L\right)}, \tag{24}$$

with $T_M=0$, which would mean that the residual misalignment is independent of M. Experimental results contradict this statement.

The analysis done using a second order approximation shows that:

$$T_M\cong2\beta^2\left(1-\beta L\sigma_x^2\right)L\sigma_x^2\sigma_v^2\sum_{m=1}^{M-1}(M-m)\left(1-\beta L\sigma_x^2\right)^{m-1}. \tag{25}$$

This analysis can be used to decide on choosing the APA working parameters to satisfy the necessities of a specific situation. Further details based on less restrictive conditions are given in [8].

C. *Proportionate variants of APA*

The aforementioned adaptive algorithms do not make use of any information about the filter to be estimated. In particular situations, some properties of the unknown filter can be known *a priori*. In the context of the application presented in this paper, the unknown system is represented by acoustic impulse responses, which are usually sparse (a small part of coefficients is significant and the rest are almost equal to zero). The residual misalignment in a situation when only the significant coefficients are estimated (and the others are considered equal to zero) will be almost equal with the residual misalignment when the filter evolves to estimate the whole impulse response. It would clearly be an advantage to prioritize the estimation of the significant coefficients because it would lead to increase the convergence speed. The proportionate variants of adaptive algorithms exploit these properties. The update equation of APA in this case becomes:

$$\mathbf{w}(n)=\mathbf{w}(n-1)+\mu\mathbf{G}(n-1)\mathbf{A}^{\mathrm{T}}(n)\mathbf{Z}^{-1}\mathbf{e}(n), \qquad (26)$$

$$\mathbf{Z}=\mathbf{A}(n)\mathbf{G}(n-1)\mathbf{A}^{\mathrm{T}}(n)+\delta\mathbf{I}_M, \qquad (27)$$

where $\mathbf{G}(n-1)$ is a $L\times L$ diagonal matrix of gains representing the way of exploiting the properties of sparse impulse responses. Each element of the $\mathbf{G}(n-1)$ matrix is computed using [9]:

$$g_l(n-1)=\frac{1-\alpha}{2L}+(1+\alpha)\frac{|w_l(n-1)|}{2\sum_{k=0}^{L-1}|w_k(n-1)|+\varepsilon}, \qquad (28)$$

with $l=\overline{0,L-1}$, $-1\le\alpha<1$ and w_l representing the elements of the **w** vector. Typically, the **w** vector is initially filled with zeros, which would lead to similar problems as the ones discussed about equation (8). The problem is solved in a similar manner, by introducing a small positive constant denoted with ε. This version of APA is named improved proportionate APA (IPAPA). In the particular case of $M=1$, a proportionate NLMS algorithm is obtained.

The operations presented in (26) can be simplified by exploiting the structure of the **A** matrix. A more efficient version of IPAPA was proposed in [10]. The update equation for this algorithm is:

$$\mathbf{w}(n)=\mathbf{w}(n-1)+\mu\mathbf{P}(n)\left[\mathbf{A}(n)\mathbf{P}(n)+\delta\mathbf{I}\right]^{-1}\mathbf{e}(n), \qquad (29)$$

where the structure of **P** matrix is

$$\mathbf{P}(n)=\left[\mathbf{p}_1(n),\mathbf{p}_2(n),\dots,\mathbf{p}_M(n)\right]. \qquad (30)$$

The elements of **P** can be computed recursively as:

$$\mathbf{P}(n)=\left[\mathbf{g}(n-1)\odot\mathbf{x}(n)\ \ \mathbf{P}_{2\cdots M}(n-1)\right], \qquad (31)$$

where $\mathbf{P}_{2\cdots M}(n-1)$ is a $L\times M-1$ matrix containing the last $M-1$ columns of $\mathbf{P}(n-1)$:

$$\mathbf{P}_{2\cdots M}(n-1)=\left[\mathbf{p}_2(n-1),\mathbf{p}_3(n-1),\dots,\mathbf{p}_M(n-1)\right], \qquad (32)$$

and $\odot$ is the Hadamard product. The structure of $\mathbf{g}(n-1)$ can be found by knowing:

$$\mathbf{g}(n-1)\odot\mathbf{x}(n)=\mathbf{G}(n-1)\mathbf{x}(n). \qquad (33)$$

This variant of IPAPA is called memory IPAPA (MIPAPA).

D. The recursive least-squares algorithm

The algorithms presented above have difficulties in situations in which the input signals are highly correlated. The recursive least-squares (RLS) algorithm offers a higher convergence rate in such situations, but its drawback is its high computational complexity. This algorithm is part of the Kalman filters family. Unlike the LMS and the NLMS algorithms, the RLS uses more than one sample of the error signal in its coefficients update equation. The cost function that is used by the RLS is:

$$C_L(\mathbf{w}(n))=\sum_{l=1}^{n}\lambda^{n-l}|e(l,n)|^2, \qquad (34)$$

where λ is the RLS specific parameter called "forgetting factor". For real signals:

$$e(l,n)=d(l)-\mathbf{w}^{\mathrm{T}}(n)\mathbf{x}(l), \qquad (35)$$

The coefficients of the adaptive filter are found by minimizing the cost function with respect to the **w** vector. The solution is found as:

$$\mathbf{R}_L(n)\mathbf{w}(n)=\mathbf{D}_L(n), \qquad (36)$$

where $\mathbf{R}_L$ is the correlation matrix and $\mathbf{D}_L$ is the cross-correlation vector. These two quantities are computed as:

$$\mathbf{R}_L(n)=\sum_{l=1}^{n}\lambda^{n-l}\mathbf{x}(l)\mathbf{x}^{\mathrm{T}}(l), \qquad (37)$$

$$\mathbf{D}_L(n)=\sum_{l=1}^{n}\lambda^{n-l}\mathbf{x}(l)d(l), \qquad (38)$$

Keeping in mind that **x** is a vector with the length equal to *L*, solving the above equations would require more and more memory as the time index *n* grows. Fortunately, as the name implies, the **w** vector can be computed recursively.

The relations that define the RLS algorithm are:

$$e(n)=d(n)-\mathbf{w}^{\mathrm{T}}(n-1)\mathbf{x}(n), \qquad (39)$$

$$\mathbf{k}(n)=\frac{\mathbf{R}_L^{-1}(n-1)\mathbf{x}(n)}{\lambda+\mathbf{x}^{\mathrm{T}}(n)\mathbf{R}_L^{-1}(n-1)\mathbf{x}(n)}, \quad (40)$$

$$\mathbf{w}(n)=\mathbf{w}(n-1)+\mathbf{k}(n)e(n), \quad (41)$$

$$\mathbf{R}_L^{-1}(n)=\frac{1}{\lambda}\left[\mathbf{R}_L^{-1}(n-1)-\mathbf{k}(n)\mathbf{x}^{\mathrm{T}}(n)\mathbf{R}_L^{-1}(n-1)\right], \quad (42)$$

where $\mathbf{k}(n)$ is called the Kalman gain vector.

The forgetting factor, in the classical approach, is a positive constant ($0<\lambda\leq 1$) that affects the convergence speed, the residual misalignment, the stability and, very important in the stated problem, the tracking capabilities in the case in which the unknown system changes over time. Unfortunately, a compromise must be made between the previous performance elements [11]. A forgetting factor very close to 1 will make the RLS algorithm to function with good stability and low residual misalignment, but the tracking capabilities are affected.

Typically, in a system identification configuration, the output of the unknown filter is summed with another signal called system noise, as shown in (16). In the context of extracting a speech signal from loud music, the speech signal plays the role of the system noise. The main objective is to make the error signal equal to the speech signal, not to make it equal to zero. It is shown in [12] that a low forgetting factor would determine $y(n)\cong\mathbf{x}^{\mathrm{T}}(n)\mathbf{w}_{\mathrm{o}}(n)+v(n)$ which means $y(n)\cong d(n)$ and $e(n)\cong 0$, while in the case of $\lambda\cong 1$ the output of the adaptive filter would be $y(n)\cong\mathbf{x}^{\mathrm{T}}(n)\mathbf{w}_{\mathrm{o}}(n)$ and consequently $e(n)\cong v(n)$. It can be concluded that in the system identification configuration, the RLS algorithm should work with a forgetting factor very close to 1. While the initial convergence speed would be satisfactory, the algorithm would lack tracking capabilities. A smaller λ would improve the tracking, but will determine $e(n)\cong 0$, so a compromise must be made, which led to the development of the variable forgetting factor RLS (VFF-RLS) algorithms.

E. The variable forgetting factor recursive least-squares algorithm

The $e(n)$ signal in (39) uses $\mathbf{w}^{\mathrm{T}}(n-1)$, hence its name could be considered *a priori* error, with its power being $\mathrm{E}\{e^2(n)\}=\sigma_e^2(n)$. Starting from it, an *a posteriori* error can also be defined as:

$$\varepsilon(n)=d(n)-\mathbf{w}^{\mathrm{T}}(n)\mathbf{x}(n)=e(n)\left[1-\mathbf{x}^{\mathrm{T}}(n)\mathbf{k}(n)\right]. \quad (43)$$

In the stated problem, the aim is to recover the speech signal which is, at this stage, modeled by the system noise leading to imposing $\mathrm{E}\{\varepsilon^2(n)\}=\sigma_v^2$. Using this new condition in (43), if the input signal is not correlated with the error signal, the result is:

$$\mathrm{E}\left\{\left[1-\frac{p(n)}{\lambda(n)+p(n)}\right]^2\right\}=\frac{\sigma_v^2(n)}{\sigma_e^2(n)}, \quad (44)$$

where $p(n)=\mathbf{x}^{\mathrm{T}}(n)\mathbf{R}_L^{-1}(n-1)\mathbf{x}(n)$. Another assumption is that the forgetting factor is time dependent and deterministic. The quadratic equation (44) has the following solution:

$$\lambda(n)=\frac{\sigma_p(n)\sigma_v}{\sigma_e(n)-\sigma_v}, \quad (45)$$

where $\mathrm{E}\{p^2(n)\}=\sigma_p^2(n)$. Statistical expectation is avoided in practice, so another method is used to estimate the power of the $e(n)$, $p(n)$ and $v(n)$ signals. By using exponential windows:

$$\hat{\sigma}_e^2(n)=\psi\hat{\sigma}_e^2(n-1)+(1-\psi)e^2(n), \quad (46)$$

$$\hat{\sigma}_p^2(n)=\psi\hat{\sigma}_p^2(n-1)+(1-\psi)p^2(n), \quad (47)$$

where the weighting factor is $\psi=1-1/(K_\psi\cdot L)$, with $K_\psi\geq 2$. The initial values of the two power estimates are $\hat{\sigma}_e^2(0)=\hat{\sigma}_p^2(0)=0$. If a longer exponential window is used, the power of $v(n)$ can be estimated from $e(n)$, from practical reasons, resulting:

$$\hat{\sigma}_v^2(n)=\theta\hat{\sigma}_v^2(n-1)+(1-\theta)e^2(n), \quad (48)$$

with $\theta=1-1/(K_\theta\cdot L)$, $K_\theta>K_\psi$.

Care must be taken in practice when evaluating (45) because it is constructed using power estimates. A solution is to impose $\lambda(n)=\lambda_{\max}$ in the case of:

$$\hat{\sigma}_e(n)\leq\varphi\hat{\sigma}_v(n),\ \text{with}\ 1<\varphi\leq 2. \quad (49)$$

The forgetting factor can now be evaluated using [13]:

$$\lambda(n)=\begin{cases}\lambda_{computed}(n), & \hat{\sigma}_e(n)\leq\varphi\hat{\sigma}_v(n)\\ \lambda_{\max}, & \hat{\sigma}_e(n)>\varphi\hat{\sigma}_v(n)\end{cases}, \quad (50)$$

$$\lambda_{computed}(n) = \min\left(\frac{\hat{\sigma}_p(n)\hat{\sigma}_v(n)}{\xi + \left|\hat{\sigma}_e(n) - \hat{\sigma}_v(n)\right|}, \lambda_{\max}\right), \quad (51)$$

where ξ is a small positive constant to prevent problems that could occur when $\hat{\sigma}_e(n) \cong \hat{\sigma}_v(n)$. Before the algorithm converges (i.e., the adaptive filter is not yet a very good estimation of the unknown system), $\hat{\sigma}_e(n)$ is larger than $\hat{\sigma}_v(n)$ and the forgetting factor will have lower values, determining fast convergence. This situation occurs when there is a change in the unknown system. The lower value of $\lambda(n)$ will offer also good tracking capabilities. In the other case, when the algorithm reaches the steady-state, $\hat{\sigma}_e(n) \cong \hat{\sigma}_v(n)$ and $\lambda(n) = \lambda_{\max}$, which assures low residual misalignment.

IV. Results

A. *The forensic speech recovery software based on the recursive least-squares algorithm*

A forensic application for recovering speech signals drowned in loud music, based on the principles described in Section II and which uses the RLS algorithm for identifying was initially implemented using Simulink. Its interface is presented in Figure 2. All the parameters can be controlled very ergonomically by turning knobs. Its functioning is detailed onwards.

Before using this software, the user must have at his disposal the two input signals, the mixture recorded in the room and the studio quality masking melody, identified with a music identification software. The studio quality melody is recommended to be processed before loading it into the system from two points of view. First, its sample rate must match the sample rate of the recorded mixture, which is typically 8 kHz since the targeted signal is a speech and speech signals, thanks to their spectral properties, are sampled with 8 kHz in most general-purpose applications. Second, the masking signal in the recorded mixture, in most of the situations, is not temporarily aligned with the studio quality masking melody (i.e., the recorded mixture does not start at the very beginning of the masking melody) and the two input signals should be pre-aligned. This aspect can be handled by the adaptive filter if its length is sufficiently large, but the length of the filter increases the computational complexity. A very important aspect is the fact that the adaptive filter can only delay the input signal to align it with the studio quality melody. The user must take into account this very important necessity. The pre-alignment operation can be done in multiple ways [14] and itself it represents an independent field of research.

After these operations are done, the two signals are ready to be processed by the forensic software. The signals must be available in PCM (Pulse Code Modulation) Wave format. The multimedia file reading blocks, named "From Multimedia File" load the input signals. The next block in the way of the signals is a splitter with the structure presented in Figure 3, which will determine if the signals are routed directly into the adaptive algorithm or each of them will pass through a band pass filter. The splitter is controlled by the rocking switch labeled "Band-pass filtering". If it is set to "On", the signals are routed through the band-pass filter. In the other case, the signals are fed straight into the adaptive algorithm. The parameters of the band-pass filter (i.e., the central frequency and the bandwidth) can be set using two knobs: "Central frequency knob" and "Bandwidth knob". The role of the band-pass filters is to pre-select the spectral band of interest (the band in which the speech signal

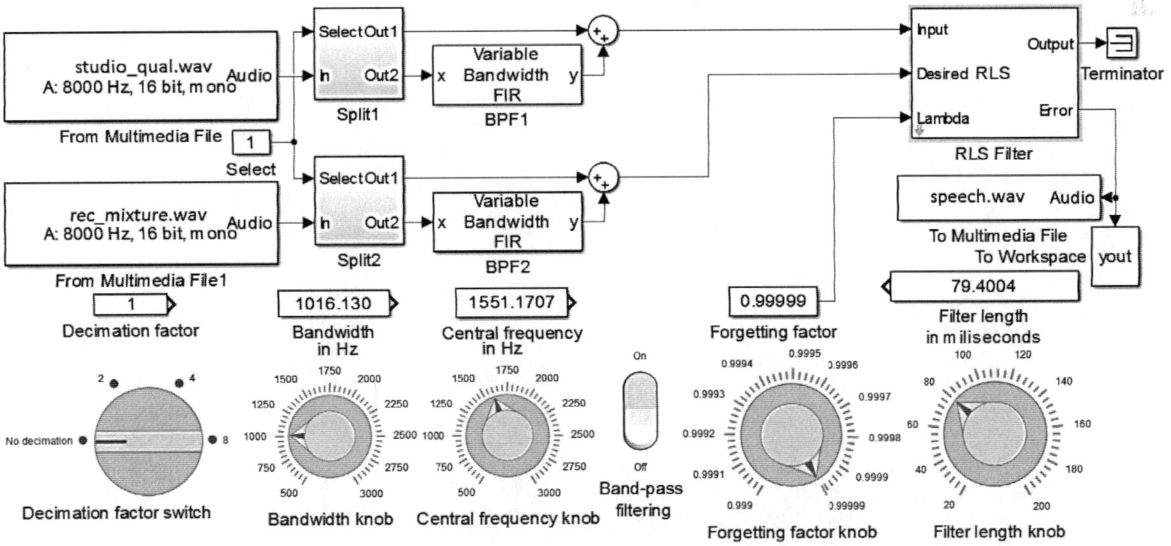

Figure 2. The forensic software for speech recovering based on the RLS algorithm.

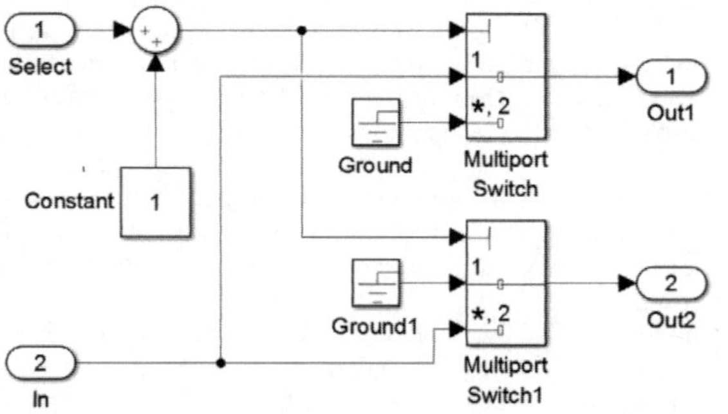

Figure 3. The contents of the Split block that was created to permit the selection of the signals to be fed in the adaptive filter (original signals or band-pass filtered signals).

is concentrated). This way some efforts of the adaptive filter are removed, increasing the efficiency. It is obvious that the two band-pass filters must be identical, or else the effect of an unbalance must be countered by the adaptive filter, increasing the computational effort.

The "RLS Filter" block implements the RLS algorithm described in the previous section. The forgetting factor of the algorithm can be tuned in real time using the "Forgetting factor knob". The recorded mixture will represent the desired signal and the studio quality melody (after pre-processing) will represent the input signal. The speech signal will be recovered as the error signal.

The last very important parameter is the length of the adaptive filter, which can be set using the "Filter length knob". The theory states that the adaptive algorithm will work if its length is equal or greater that the length of the unknown system. It is also intuitively true: if a filter with a length equal to L_1 is estimated using an adaptive filter with a length equal to $L_2>L_1$, in the ideal case, the first L_1 coefficients of the adaptive filter will be equal to the coefficients of the filter that is estimated and the remaining L_2-L_1 coefficients of the adaptive filter will be equal to zero. If $L_2<L_1$, then only L_2 coefficients of the unknown filter can be estimated. Depending on the difference of the two lengths and the properties of the unknown filter, a good enough estimation can be obtained, but clearly it cannot be guaranteed. Because the system can work using various sample rates, the length of the adaptive filter is set in milliseconds, to simplify the user's task to compute it in samples for each sampling frequency that is used. The length of the adaptive filter greatly affects the computational complexity. If information about the physical properties of the room (volume, furniture etc.) is known, the length of the filter which will represent the acoustic impulse response of the room can be roughly determined *a priori* using acoustic notions like reverberation time.

The software features a decimation knob named "Decimation factor switch" which, as the name suggests, will decimate both input signals before processing. It is useful when the recorded mixture has a higher sample rate or when a quick test run is desired, to reduce the computational complexity and the processing time consequently.

For testing the software, a speech signal was mixed with a musical signal (which played the role of the masking noise) in –40 dB signal-to-noise ratio. Afterwards, this mixture was filtered using an acoustic impulse response illustrated in Figure 4. The filtered mixture and the original musical signal were used as input signals in the presented software. The RLS algorithm provide very fast convergence rate and good misalignment, visible in Figure 5, which can be observed in the very accurate recovery of the speech signal in Figure 6. In this case changes in the unknown system were not considered.

B. The forensic speech recovery software based on the variable forgetting factor recursive least-squares algorithm

In a real situation, the people that are having the confidential conversation that they try to conceal will not remain perfectly still. Instead, naturally, they can move around affecting the acoustic impulse response of the room. The impulse response of interest is the one that characterizes the propagation of the masking signal. To subtract the musical signal, this impulse response must be accurately

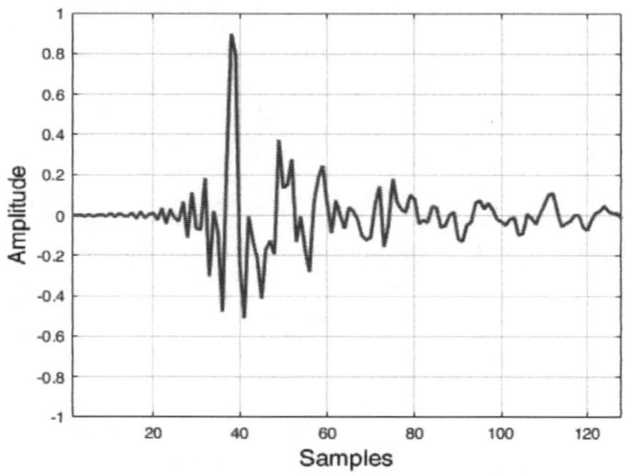

Figure 4. The impulse response used to model the acoustic environment.

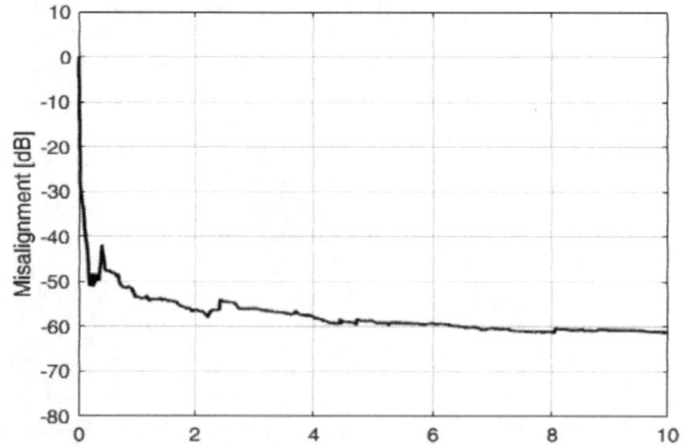

Figure 5. The variation of the misalignment for the RLS algorithm.

estimated. Other events could happen, which also will lead to the modification of the discussed impulse response like the opening or closing of a door, the entrance or exit of a person in/from the room, the opening of a window, etc. In conclusion, a real-world unknown system has a high chance of changing over time.

Testing the RLS based software in such situations confirmed the poor tracking capabilities of the algorithm when the forgetting factor is close to 1, as it can be observed in Figure 7. After 5 seconds, the unknown system changes (the impulse response was shifted with 8 samples). The absolute error means the absolute values of the signal obtained by subtracting the recovered signal from the original (reference) signal. In practice, the reference signal would not be available. It is used here to highlight the performances of the proposed software. The RLS algorithm

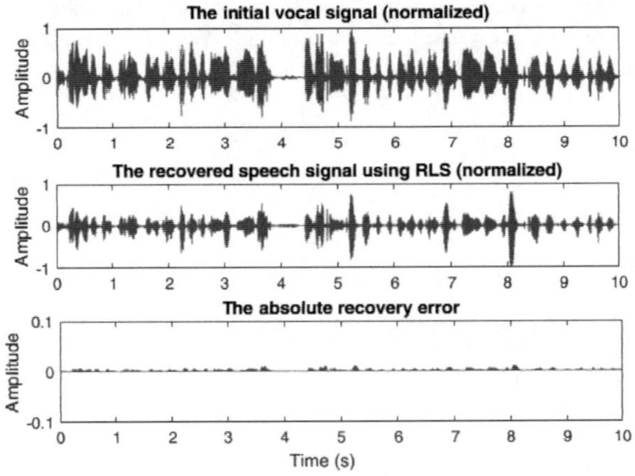

Figure 6. The performances of the RLS algorithm in the given situation.

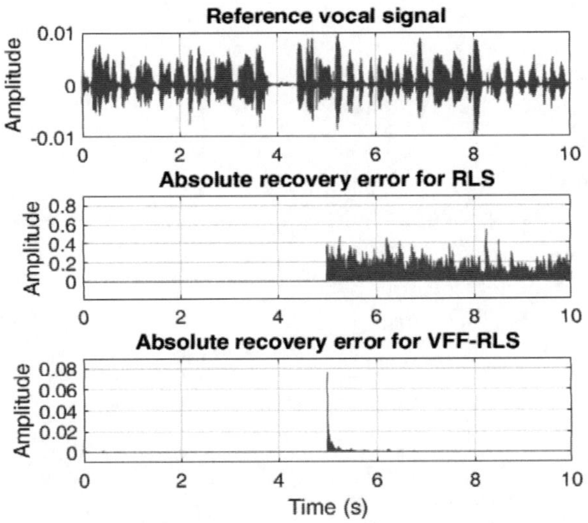

Figure 7. The performances of the RLS and VFF-RLS algorithms in the case in which a change in the acoustic parameters occurs.

gives a very high recovery error after the change, which decreases very slowly. The VFF-RLS algorithm tracks the system change very quickly [15]. The largest absolute value of the recovery error for the VFF-RLS is still much smaller than the error given by the classical RLS algorithm. The

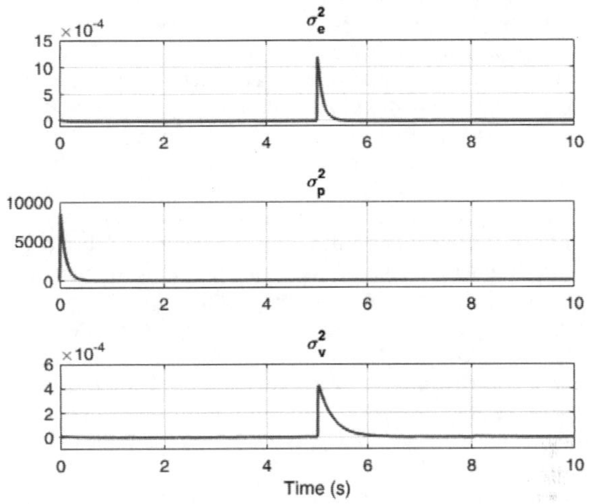

Figure 8. The variation of the VFF-RLS parameters (see the title of each graph for identifying the parameters).

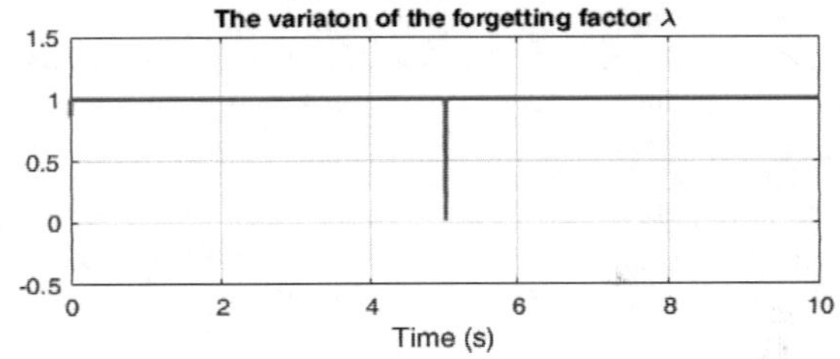

Figure 9. The variation of the forgetting factor.

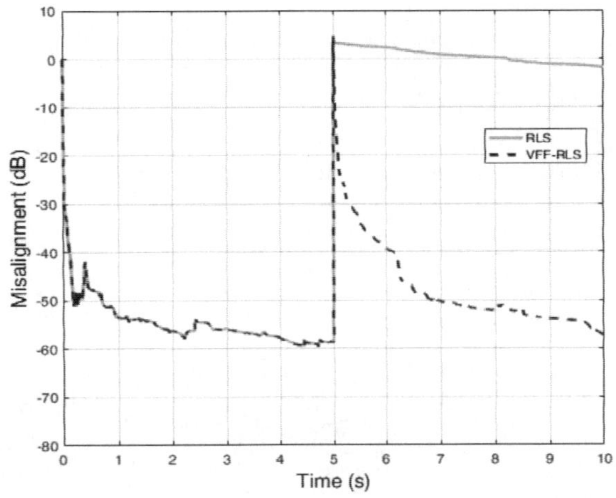

Figure 10. The variation of the misalignment for the two adaptive algorithms.

variation of the VFF-RLS specific parameters and of the forgetting factor can be observed in Figure 8 and Figure 9, respectively. The variation of the misalignment is presented in Figure 10.

C. *The impact of the acoustic environment on the proposed forensic software*

The acoustic impulse response greatly affects the performances of the proposed system. One key parameter is its length. Since the unknown system can be considered that it changes frequently, it becomes of importance to determine the length of the unknown system for which the performances are acceptable.

For these experiments, a longer impulse response was used (512 samples long), depicted in Figure 11. The length of the impulse response used in the experiments was progressively increased, starting with 128 samples and incrementing it with 64 samples. It was determined that acceptable quality of the recovered speech signal is achieved when the misalignment reaches –20 dB. The results are illustrated in Figure 12.

The RLS algorithm failed to track the change even in the shortest case and it was not tested for longer impulse responses. In the case of 512 samples, the VFF-RLS would take around one second to achieve the desired misalignment, meaning that the same duration of the recovered signal would be unintelligible. The results in this section could help in taking the decision if placing a microphone in a specific room is worth it or not. The length of the impulse response of the room can be coarsely determined by a trained person if he/she enters the room, by studying the volume of the room and the materials that are placed there. After the inspection, knowledge about acoustics can be used, like Sabine's reverberation time formula detailed in (52), for determining the approximate length of the impulse response:

$$RT_{60} \cong 0.161\frac{V}{S\cdot a}, \qquad (52)$$

where V is the volume of the room, S is the total surface area of the room and a is the average absorption coefficient of the surfaces present in the room.

D. *The performances of the affine projection algorithm in the given situation*

The RLS gives very good results in recovering the speech signal if the unknown system does not change in time. It was shown that the VFF-RLS can handle the situations in which there are changes in the system to be estimated if its length is reasonably short. It is very important to remember that RLS and VFF-RLS have a great computational complexity and consequently the processing times can be very long. The affine projection algorithm is a good candidate for decreasing the computational complexity. The software was implemented with this algorithm and similar tests were

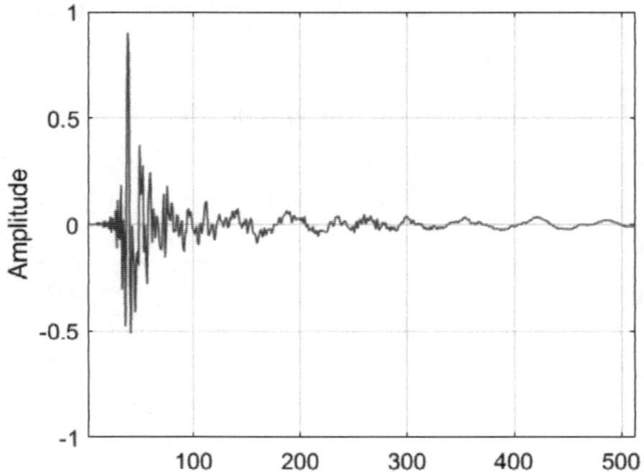

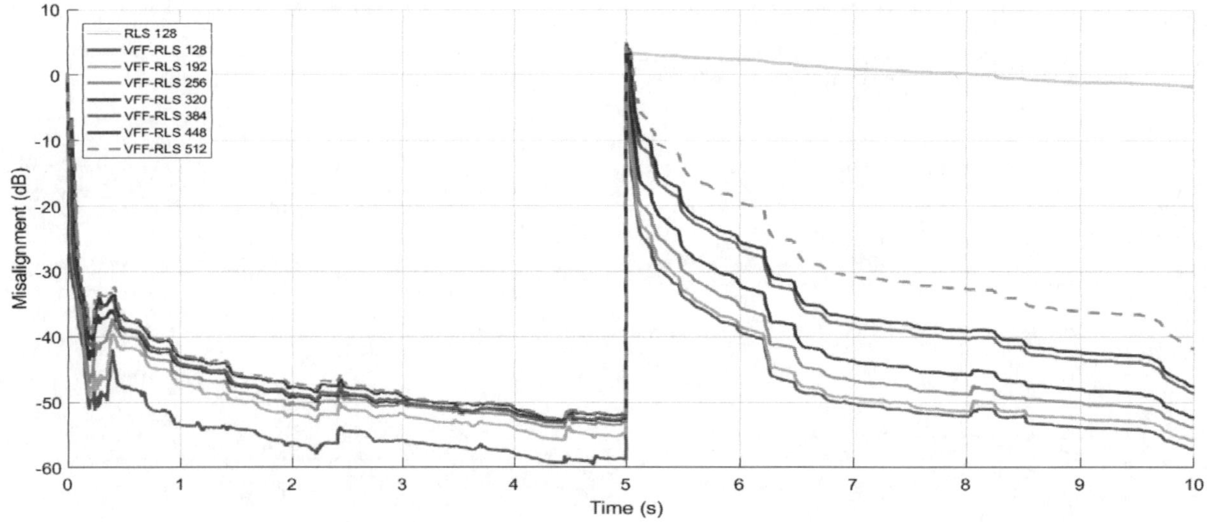

Figure 12. The variation of the misalignment for the two adaptive algorithms with respect to the length of the impulse response.

performed. For the 512 samples long impulse response, the results are illustrated in Figure 13 and Figure 14.

The performances that were obtained qualify APA for solving the investigated situation, but they are lower than in the case of VFF-RLS. It is very important to observe the initial convergence in the case of the two algorithms. The RLS based solutions have a very fast initial convergence, while the convergence of APA is almost the same in the beginning as it is after a system change.

Since the acoustic impulse responses are usually sparse, a proportionate version of APA could show better performances that the classical APA. The MIPAPA was tested and it achieved a better convergence speed than the classical APA, as it can be observed in Figure 15. For comparison, the NLMS algorithm and its proportionate version IPNLMS obtained by using a projection order equal to 1 in MIPAPA, were also tested and their misalignment

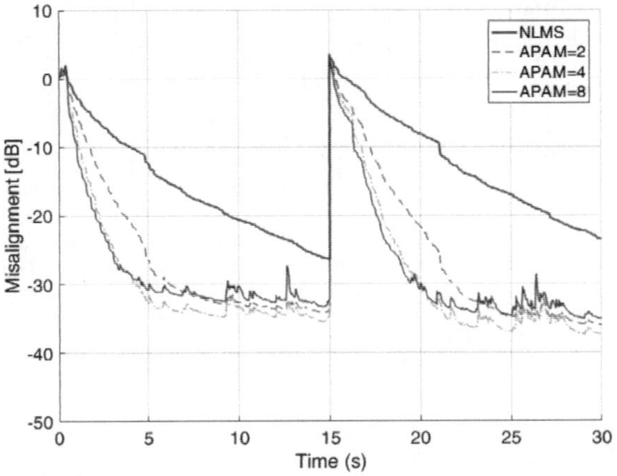

Figure 13. The variation of the misalignment for the estimation of an impulse response with $L = 512$, $\mu = 0.5$ and various projection orders M, from 1 to 8.

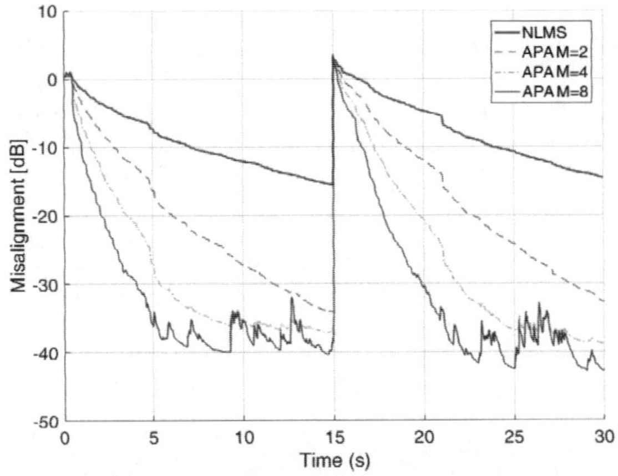

Figure 14. The variation of the misalignment for the estimation of an impulse response with $L = 512$, $\mu = 0.2$ and various projection orders M, from 1 to 8.

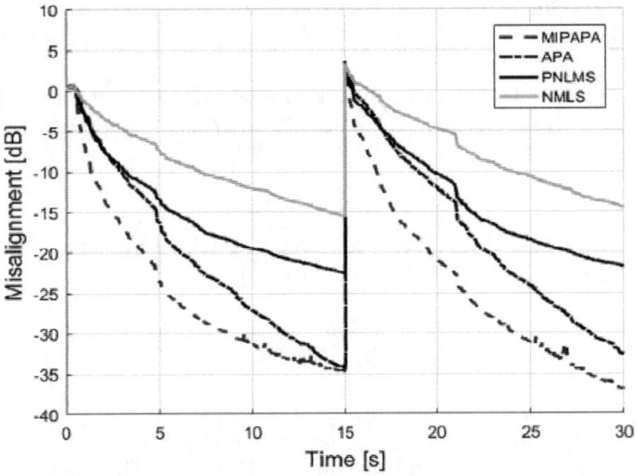

Figure 15. The variation of the misalignment of various adaptive algorithms when estimating the impulse response illustrated in Figure11 with change after 15 seconds (M=2, L=512, μ=0.2).

was illustrated in the same figure.

V. CONCLUSION AND FUTURE WORK

This paper describes the importance of multimedia forensic field and presents a practical method for extracting a speech signal drowned in loud music. The core of a forensic software capable of succeeding at such task is a system identification problem, which is a typical adaptive systems application.

Various adaptive algorithms were presented in detail to clearly observe their behavior and understand their suitability to be used in developing the desired forensic software. The unknown system in the stated problem is an acoustic impulse response which is usually sparse. A proportionate variant of the affine projection algorithm (MIPAPA) was also presented because this class could perform very well in such conditions. The importance of system tracking was highlighted and a variable forgetting factor recursive least-squares algorithm was described. It combines the great performances of the RLS algorithm with a good capacity of tracking, without drastically increasing the computational complexity.

A forensic software based on the RLS algorithm was implemented in Simulink to make its interface very easy to use. All the details about the implementation were given and the obtained performances were presented and discussed. The second variant was implemented based on the VFF-RLS algorithm and noticeable performance improvements were observed.

The impact of the acoustic environment on the software's performance was studied. Using the results in this paper, it can be determined if a microphone is worth to be placed in a certain room based on its acoustic properties.

To decrease the computational complexity, the RLS based algorithms were replaced by APA, with an expected (but not dramatic) decrease in performance. Since most acoustic impulse responses are sparse, the MIPAPA was investigated and it was shown that it behaves better than

APA. Since the computational complexity of the two algorithms is similar, the MIPAPA is preferred for solving this problem.

Future work will include the investigation of the method when other types of impulse response changes are considered.

ACKNOWLEDGMENT

This work was supported by UEFISCDI Romania under Grant PN-II-RU-TE-2014-4-1880.

REFERENCES

[1] R. A. Dobre, R. M. Udrea, C. Negrescu, and D. Stanomir, "The impact of the acoustic environment on recovering speech signals drowned in loud music," The Sixteenth International Conference on Networks (ICN), Venice, pp. 92-97, April 2017.

[2] A. Ghule and P. Benakop, “A review of LPC methods for enhancement of speech signals,” International Journal of Innovations in Engineering Research and Technology, vol. 2, pp. 1–6, 2015.

[3] P. C. Loizou, Speech Enhancement: Theory and Practice. Second Edition, Boca Raton, CRC Press, 2013.

[4] J. Benesty, S. Makino, and J. Chen, Speech Enhancement. First Edition, Berlin, Springer-Verlag, 2005.

[5] S. Haykin, Adaptive Filter Theory. Fourth Edition, Upper Saddle River, NJ:Prentice-Hall, 2002.

[6] A. H. Sayed, Adaptive Filters. New York, NY: Wiley, 2008.

[7] R. A. Dobre, V. A. Niţă, S. Ciochină, and C. Paleologu, "New insights on the convergence analysis of the affine projection algorithm for system identification," 2015 International Symposium on Signals, Circuits and Systems (ISSCS), Iaşi, pp. 1-4, July 2015.

[8] V. A. Niţă, R. A. Dobre, S. Ciochină, and C. Paleologu, "Improved convergence model of the affine projection algorithm for system identification," 2017 International Symposium on Signals, Circuits and Systems (ISSCS), Iaşi, pp. 1-4, July 2017.

[9] J. Benesty and S. L. Gay, “An improved PNLMS algorithm,” in Proc. IEEE ICASSP, 2002, pp. II-1881–II-1884.

[10] C. Paleologu, S. Ciochină, and J. Benesty, “An efficient proportionate affine projection algorithm for echo cancellation,” IEEE Signal Processing Letters, vol. 17, pp. 165–168, 2010.

[11] S. Ciochina, C. Paleologu, J. Benesty, and A. A. Enescu, “On the influence of the forgetting factor of the RLS adaptive filter in system identification,” in Proc. IEEE ISSCS, 2009, pp. 205–208.

[12] C. Paleologu, J. Benesty, and S. Ciochină, “A robust variable forgetting factor recursive least-squares algorithm for system identification,” IEEE Signal Processing Letters, vol. 15, pp. 597–600, 2008.

[13] C. Paleologu, J. Benesty, and S. Ciochină, “A practical variable forgetting factor recursive least-squares algorithm,” in Proc. ISETC, 2014, pp. 1–4.

[14] R. A. Dobre, C. Negrescu, and D. Stanomir, “Development and testing of an audio forensic software for enhancing speech signals masked by loud music,” Advanced Topics in Optoelectronics, Microelectronics, and Nanotechnologies 2016, pp. 100103A-100103A-7, 2016.

[15] R. A. Dobre, C. Elisei-Iliescu, C. Paleologu, C. Negrescu, and D. Stanomir, "Robust audio forensic software for recovering speech signals drowned in loud music," 22nd IEEE International Symposium for Design and Technology in Electronic Packaging (SIITME), Oradea, pp. 232-235, October 2016.

Aluminum-doped Zinc Oxide Nanoparticles Sensing Properties Enhanced by Ultraviolet Light

Short paper

Sandrine Bernardini[1], Tomas Fiorido[1], Khalifa Aguir[1]
[1] Aix Marseille Univ, Univ Toulon, CNRS, IM2NP, Marseille, France
e-mail: sandrine.bernardini@im2np.fr
e-mail: tomas.fiorido@im2np.fr
e-mail: khalifa.aguir@im2np.fr

Meriem Gaceur[2], Olivier Margeat[2], Jörg Ackermann[2], Christine Videlot-Ackermann[2]
[2] Aix Marseille Univ, CNRS, CINaM, Marseille, France
e-mail: gaceur@cinam.univ-mrs.fr
e-mail: margeat@cinam.univ-mrs.fr
e-mail: ackermann@cinam.univ-mrs.fr
e-mail: videlot@cinam.univ-mrs.fr

***Abstract* — The development of room-temperature gas sensors for nitrogen dioxide gases is of great importance for air quality monitoring due to unhealthy impact on human life and environment. In this work, we focus on Aluminum-doped Zinc Oxide sensing properties. We compare nitrogen dioxide detection at room temperature in dark and under ultraviolet or blue illuminations. Working temperature from 25°C up to 100°C have been also performed in dark and under UV and blue Light Emitted Diodes. Aluminum-doped Zinc Oxide nanoparticles have been deposited by drop coating from colloidal solution as sensitive layer for air quality monitoring on Si/SiO$_2$ substrate. Herein, a brief description of the process steps will be provided. We demonstrate that UV light and temperature enhance gas-sensing properties with good reversibility and repeatability.**

Keywords-Gas sensor; NO$_2$ sensor; light excitation; Al-ZnO nanoparticules; Ultraviolet illumination; blue illumination.

I. INTRODUCTION

Nitrogen dioxide (NO$_2$) comes from vehicles, power plants, industrial emissions and off-road sources, such as construction, lawn and gardening equipment. It is one of the most dangerous air pollutants. It plays a major role in the formation of ozone and acid rain. Continued or frequent exposure to NO$_2$ concentrations higher than 0.15 ppm may cause incidence of acute respiratory. To detect NO$_2$, resistive gas sensors are the most attractive due to easy fabrication, simple operation, low production cost and miniaturization. Zinc oxide (ZnO) is a wide band gap (about 3.37 eV at room temperature) II–IV n-type semiconductor that has many applications. It is one of the best candidates for air quality monitoring having large accessibility for the targeted gases. Moreover, doping is one possible way to improve the sensibility of the ZnO nanoparticles (NPs). ZnO is usually doped with small amounts of metal ions, such as Al, Ga, etc. We have recently reported our preliminary work on room temperature NO$_2$ detection achieved by Aluminum-doped Zinc Oxide (Al-ZnO) sensitive layer on Si/SiO$_2$ substrate enhanced by UltraViolet (UV) light [1]. Al-ZnO can be produced as nanoparticles and keep the same advantages as ZnO NPs in terms of layer processing. However, its conductivity can be three orders of magnitudes higher [2]. Operating at room temperature is interesting for working in explosive environment and also with flexible substrate to fit any shape needed on smart objects. In literature, several technics have been described to decrease the operating temperature and improve the sensitivity and stability of metal oxide (MOX) gas sensors, such as noble metal doping [3], transition metal oxide incorporation [4-5], light activation [6-8]. Among them, adding UV light at ZnO surface is the most studied to achieve room temperature sensitivity [9-12].

Recently, Prof. Zhang's team has reported that visible light illumination can greatly enhance the NO$_2$ sensing performance of sensors performed with solution precursor plasma spray (SPPS) of n-n heterojunctions formed between $SnO_{1-\alpha}$, $ZnO_{1-\beta}$ and $SnO_{2-\gamma}$ [13]. However, SPPS is a process with ultra-high heating temperatures. In this work, we used low temperature process and we achieved NO$_2$ detection at temperatures not higher than 100°C to be compatible with most of flexible substrate aging. These detections have been made under UV activation by Al-ZnO NPs deposited on interdigitated electrodes fabricated on Si/SiO$_2$ substrate using photolithography. In Section II, the Al-ZnO solution process will be described and the results will be discussed in Section III.

II. DESCRIPTION OF APPROACH AND TECHNIQUES

This description is composed of two parts, one is the sensing film fabrication; the other is the measurement system set-up.

A. Al-ZnO solution

In order to maintain a cost efficient integration process, solution based materials are used as they show an outstanding tradeoff between cost and system complexity. The use of a nanoparticle dispersion of the ZnO semiconducting material doped by aluminum avoids most of the issues related to temperature. It is an attractive method for the following reasons: good homogeneity, ease of composition control, and large area coatings with cost effective processes. Al-ZnO (or AZO) NPs were prepared following procedures described previously [14,15]. In a typical experiment, Al-ZnO NPs were produced by adding zinc acetate, aluminum isopropylate and distilled water into a flask containing anhydrous ethanol. After heating at 80°C, potassium hydroxide dispersed in ethanol was added dropwise to the flask, and heating was kept at 80°C during 16h. The as-synthesized Al-ZnO NPs were washed by centrifugation. By controlling the initial ratio of the aluminum to zinc precursor during synthesis while keeping constant all the other parameters, a precise control of Al doping content (atomic percentage, at.%) can be obtained. In the present study, Al-ZnO NPs with 0.8 at.% Al doping level have been synthesized. Size distribution of the NPs within the solutions was determined with Dynamic Light Scattering methods (DLS) using a NanoZetaSizer from Malvern. The solution-processable dispersions were prepared by transferring the synthesized Al-ZnO NPs from alcohol solutions to isopropanol at constant concentrations of 30 $mg.mL^{-1}$. Additionally, cluster-free dispersion of Al-ZnO NPs was obtained in isopropanol by using 0.2 vol.% of ethanol amine (EA) as surfactant [14]. EA is a small organic molecule giving high dispersions in alcohols and avoiding the need of bulky or long surfactants.

Morphological study of Al-ZnO NPs was carried out by the high-resolution transmission electron microscope (HR-TEM) JEOL 3010, where samples were prepared by drop casting of diluted solution on a mesh-coated carbon film. Fig. 1 shows the EA-modified Al-ZnO NPs disperse in solution, which is not a complete translucent solution due to the Al doping. A typical Transmission Electron Microscopy (TEM) image of this Al-ZnO nanocrystals is shown on the right side of the Fig. 1, evidencing their size (diameter about 10 nm) and homogeneous size and shape dispersions.

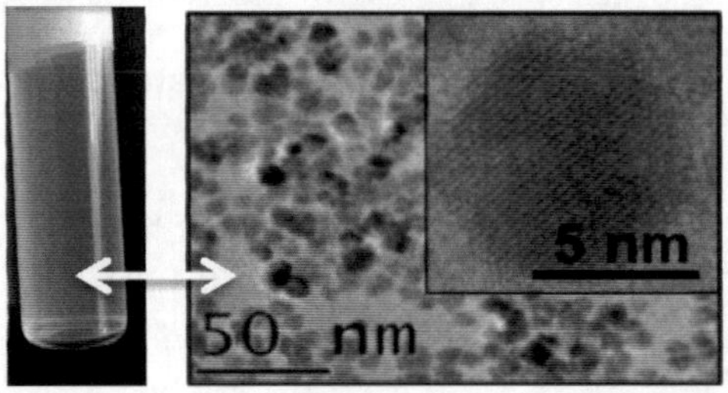

Figure 1. Optical image of solution based on Al-ZnO NPs in isopropanol (Al-ZnO NPs with 0.8 at.% of Al et 0.2 vol.% of EA) and TEM image of Al-ZnO nanocrystals drop-casted on a TEM grid [1].

Microstructure of thin films has been investigated using high-resolution scanning electron microscope (JEOL JSM 6320F). SEM micrographs were made on top sections on NPs-based thin films deposited on silicon substrates covered with 300 nm thick SiO_2 dielectric layers. In order to get details in microstructure of thin films, solutions containing NPs in isopropanol were deposited by spin-coating on SiO_2 substrates following by a thermal post-treatment at 150°C for 30 min. With a boiling point (Tbp) of 82.6°C for isopropanol, solvent molecules were completely evaporated for annealing temperature reaching 150°C, but the EA surfactant molecules stayed adsorbed on the surface of NPs (Tbp = 170°C for EA) [16]. Previous analyses have shown that the Al-ZnO nanocrystals are monocrystalline with a classical wurtzite structure [14]. Starting from a dispersion state (i.e., the ink), the resulting solid states will depend not only on the chemical parameters of the materials but also on physical parameters such as deposition technique, substrate, drying process, thermal post-annealing, etc. The implementation and characterization of solution-processed gas sensors by drop casting or spin-coating require the thin film characterization. The morphological properties of the AZO thin films grown on SiO_2 substrates were examined by Scanning Electron Microscopy (SEM).

Fig. 2 shows SEM images of Al-ZnO thin films deposited by spin coating with a speed of 2000 rpm/min during 30 s.

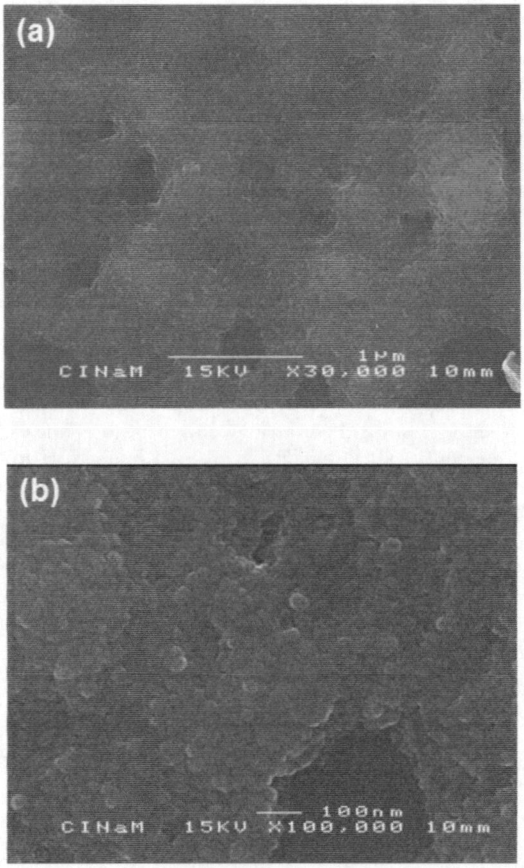

Figure. 2. SEM images of Al-ZnO nanoparticles deposited on Si/SiO_2 substrates and heated at 150°C.

After the solution deposition, the coated substrates were annealed onto a preheated hotplate at 150°C for 30 min as a post-treatment in a nitrogen-filled glove box.

Fig. 2 shows the surface uniformity of Al-ZnO thin films on a large scale and a smaller scale. Small agglomerates, with a diameter of 15-25 nm, uniformly and densely dispersed on the surface were formed. By drop coating, Al-ZnO NPs entirely cover the substrate surface but with a less uniform morphology where the presence of tightly packed grains is observed. In both case, the free-spaces between NPs offer a high surface-area-to-volume-ratio to the thin film. Such surface structure gives a porous property to the thin films where gas molecules can diffuse in the volume structure.

B. *Gas sensors and set up*

The gas sensing properties of Al-ZnO films were investigated in a sealed stainless test cell to control the substrate temperature and NO_2 concentrations. Our gas sensor consists of Ti/Pt interdigitated electrodes for gas detection. Temperature can be controlled underneath to improve the gas detection. The metal electrodes Ti/Pt were deposited on Si/SiO_2 by magnetron sputtering with thicknesses of 5 and 100 nm, respectively. In this work, Al-ZnO nanoparticles were deposited by drop coating. They were used as sensitive material with thickness of 200±10 nm measured by a Dektak 6M stylus profiler. The Al-ZnO films obtained were annealed for 30 min at 150°C for removing solvents and improving their quality and stability. The aim was to study the possible use, in a future work, on flexible substrates, which do not allow high temperature process. In order to find the best operating conditions, the gas sensing properties of Al-ZnO films were investigated in a sealed stainless test cell to control the substrate temperature and NO_2 concentrations. The measurements were made keeping in mind that the maximum NO_2 concentration is 100 ppb for 1h exposure and 75 ppb per day [17]. Dry air was used as both the reference and the carrier gas maintaining a constant total flow of 500 standard cubic centimeters per minute (SCCM) via mass flow controllers. The sensor was exposed to dry air (i.e. 0% relative humidity) with different concentrations of NO_2 (0.2, 0.5, 1, and 2 ppm) during 30 s and finally exposed to a clean dry airflow for recovery. The dry air and NO_2 gas were blown directly onto the sample placed on a heated holder. The applied DC voltage was 0.1 V. The electrical resistance was measured using a Keithley (model 2450) source-meter connected to a computer with a homemade program. Gas response of the sensor is defined by (1) as the ratio of the resistance change on the surface of the gas sensor before and after being exposed to NO_2:

$$R = R_{NO2} / R_{dry\ air} \quad (1)$$

where R_{NO2} is the sensor resistance in presence of NO_2 and $R_{dry\ air}$ is the sensor resistance through dry air flow.

The time exposure was fixed to 30s. Even if this time not allows reaching the sensor saturation, sufficient changes in resistance can be observed to extract information about the gas detection. The sensor response time is defined as the time required for a change in the sample's electrical resistance to reach 90% of the initial value when exposed to ozone gas. In the same way, the recovery time is defined as the time required for the electrical resistance of the sensor to return 90% of the initial value after turning off the NO_2 gas. Several preliminary tests on conductivity change have been made using blue, red, UV, and green Light Emitted Diode (LED) under dry airflow without gas. The highest conductivity improvements have been obtained with UV LED. Gas sensing measurements under UV-light irradiation were performed using a UV-LED (Ref. UV5TZ-390-30 peak wavelength of 390 nm). Respectively, the blue LED (Ref. 247-1690, peak wavelength of 430 nm) was used with the same power than the UV one fixed at 60 mW. The distance between one LED and the sensing material is an important parameter. In our homemade test cell, this distance can be adjusted to obtain the higher conductivity under dry airflow than kept it constant during the gas detection. Measurement system pictures for testing gas sensors under UV light are given in Fig. 3.

Figure 3. Experimental setup for gas sensors with Light Emitted Diode.

Before measurements, the sample was illuminated for 60 min with the chosen LED under dry air 500 SCCM, to stabilize the electrical resistance.

III. Results and Discussion

The gas sensor fabricated with Al-ZnO nanoparticles as sensitive material and deposited by drop coating on Si/SiO_2 substrate is presented in Fig. 4.

Figure 4. Sensor fabricated on Si/SiO_2 substrate.

The sample studied here was initially exposed to NO_2 at room temperature (at 25°C) without any illumination. As can be seen in Fig. 5, low resistance increases were observed without recovery. In the presence of gases, the electrical conductivity of semiconductor film sensor changes due to two main reactions occurring on the surface. The gas response is related to the number of oxygen ions adsorbed on the film surface. In n-type semiconductors, the majority charge carriers are electrons. When they are exposed to an oxidizing gas a decrease of conductivity occurs. After the gas is absorbed on the ZnO surface, the O atoms of oxidative gas molecules extract the electrons from the ZnO nanostructure; consequently, the depletion layer becomes thicker due to the decreasing of the carrier concentration [18].

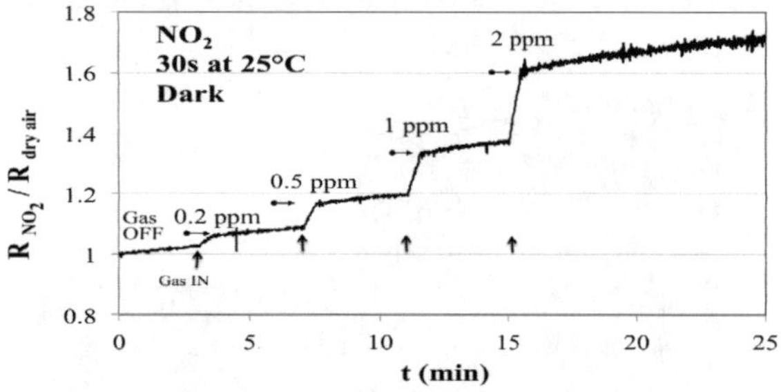

Figure 5. Sensor responses at 25°C in dark for 0.2 ppm to 2 ppm NO_2.

At temperatures less than 150°C, the ionic species O_2 are dominant. These O_2 species contribute to form a high-resistance depletion layer in the NPs surfaces, increasing electrical resistance in the nanoparticles. Moreover, more oxygen vacancy related defects are introduced by Al doping, which increase the surface depletion thickness and the potential barrier height at the contact [19]. First, when the Al-ZnO NPs are exposed to an air atmosphere, oxygen molecules are adsorbed on the different surfaces. These oxygen molecules capture free electrons from the ZnO conduction band, forming ionized oxygen anions. Then, when Al-ZnO NPs gets exposed to NO_2 (a typical oxidizing gas), the NO_2 gas molecules adsorb on the Al-ZnO NPs surface, implying the formation of an electron-depletion layer due to adsorption of ions, which increases the potential barrier and diminishes Al-ZnO NPs conductivity. However, this last reaction needs enough energy to occur and the gas desorption is not possible at room temperature due to a lack of energy. When the NPs are exposed to UV irradiation (3.3 eV), electron–hole pairs are photogenerated ((e-) + (h+)) in the Al-ZnO NPs surface. The photogenerated holes (h+) could migrate to the Al-ZnO NPs surface, and O_2 species photodesorbed. As consequence, the depletion layer is diminished and the remaining unpaired electrons contribute to an increase in the electrical conductivity. Upon exposure to NO_2 gas, NO_2 molecules adsorb on the Al-ZnO NPs surfaces. This reaction widens the depletion-layer in the Al-ZnO NPs surface, and consequently, the electrical resistance is increased when the sensing material is exposed to NO_2 gas, as shown in Fig. 5 at room temperature without humidity. Fig. 6 presents a comparison between the sensor responses without and with light illumination at room temperature for the NO_2 concentrations used in this work.

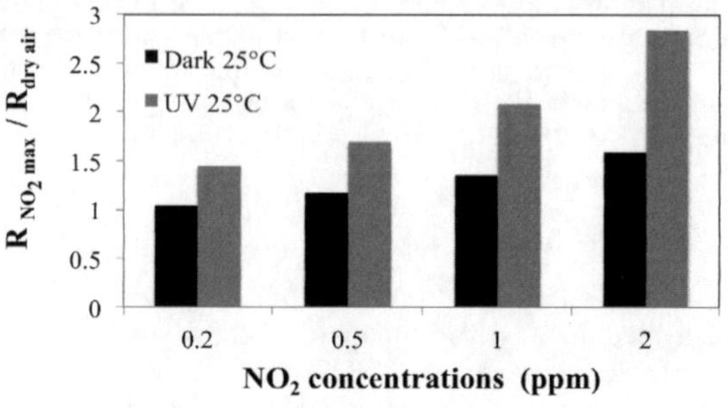

Figure 6. Comparison of sensor responses at 25°C in dark and under UV light at room temperature.

Under continuous UV illumination, the interaction between NO_2 and Al-ZnO NPs is enhanced over than without UV light due to the abundant photo generated free electrons.

The responses plotted in Fig. 7a at 25°C under UV light, demonstrate the total reversibility and good stability of the base line. However, about 45 minutes are needed to return to the baseline. The responses plotted in Fig. 7b at 25°C under a blue LED show great amplitude improvements but the return times were three times longer compare to the return times obtained under a UV LED.

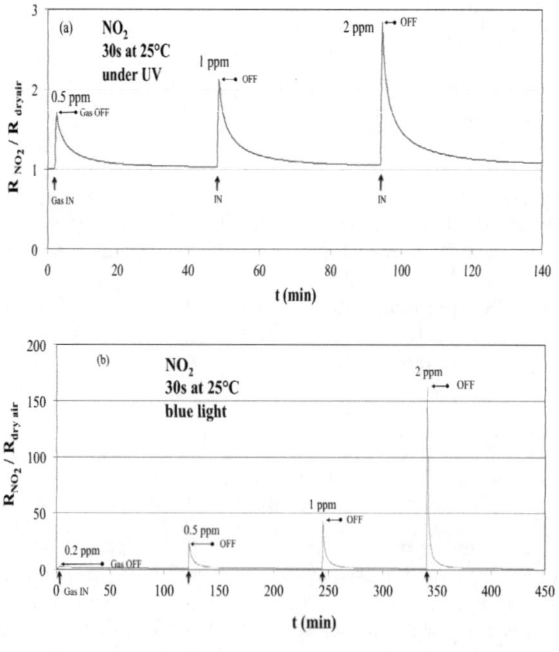

Figure 7. Sensor responses at 25°C for 0.5 ppm to 2 ppm NO_2 a) under a UV LED and b) under a blue LED.

Heating excitations were also tested up to 100°C in dark and under UV and blue illuminations. In dark, at 25°C and 50°C the resistance increases were observed without recovery. From 75°C in dark, the resistance returns to its reference value obtained through dry airflow for 1 and 2 ppm. At an operating temperature equals to 100°C the response is slightly higher than at 75°C, however, the recovery was observed for all concentrations. Fig. 8 shows responses in dark for 0.2 ppm to 2 ppm of NO_2 at 100°C. The response and the recovery time were improved by the heating excitation.

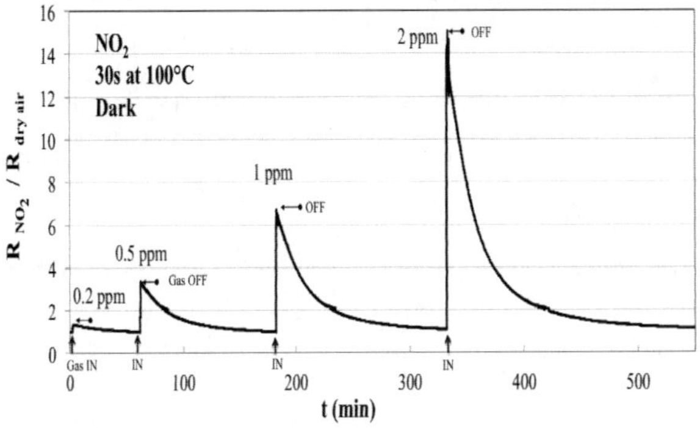

Figure 8. Sensor responses at 100°C in dark for 0.2 ppm to 2 ppm NO_2.

To decrease the recovery time under light illuminations, temperature excitation is required. Indeed, the heating temperatures improve the chemical reactions at the sensitive surface layer. The response amplitudes were therefore enhanced for the four tested concentrations under UV light. Fig. 9a presents the best response in terms of amplitudes and recovery times obtained at 100°C under UV illumination for 0.2 ppm to 2 ppm of NO_2. Fig. 9b highlights that the amplitude responses were greatly improved at 100°C by the blue light compare to the measurements performed in dark or under UV LED at this temperature. Nevertheless, the return times were around five times longer than the return times obtained under UV illumination.

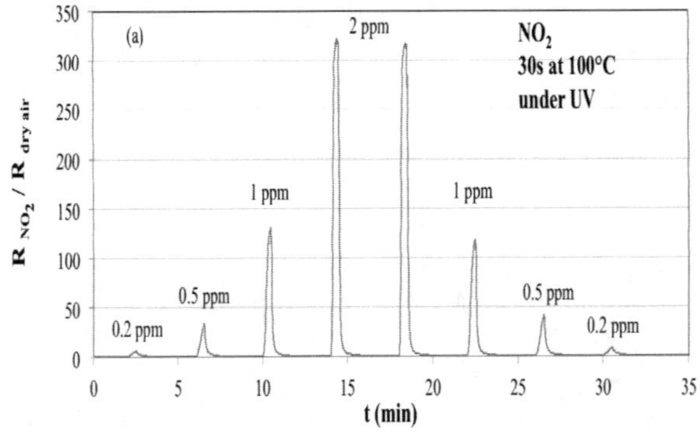

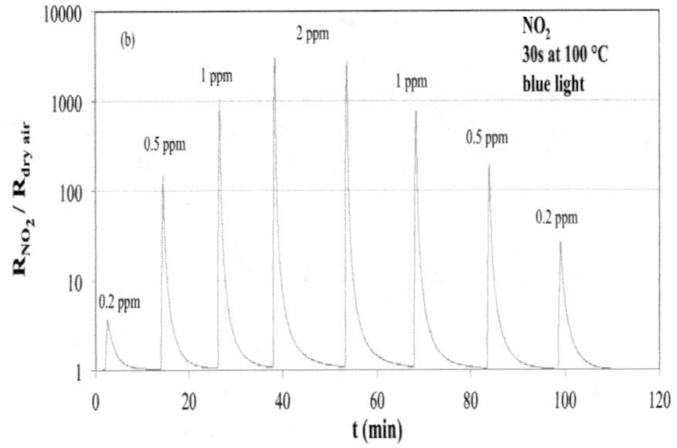

Figure 9. Sensor responses at 100°C for 0.2 to 2 ppm NO_2 : a) under a UV LED and b) under a blue LED.

Under UV illumination, the results obtained show fast response at low level of NO_2 concentration and good reversibility without sensor saturation. By increasing the temperature up to 100°C, the response amplitude for 2 ppm under the UV LEDt was multiplied by 200 at least and the time to return to the baseline was divided by 10.

Fig. 10 illustrates the good sensor response repeatability at 100°C under UV light illumination for 0.2 ppm of NO_2.

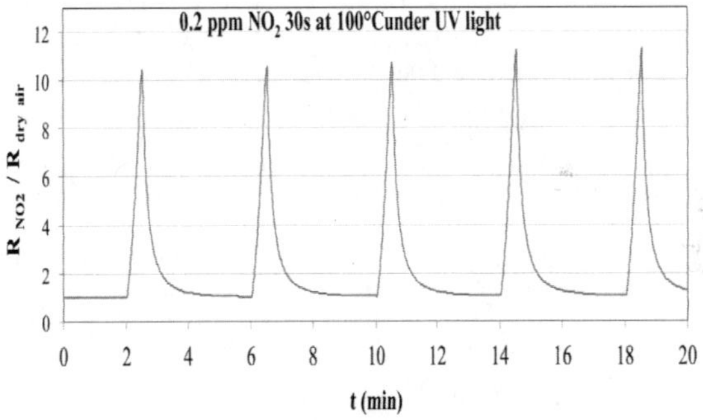

Figure 10. Response repeatability at 100°C under a UV LED for 0.2 ppm NO_2.

IV. CONCLUSION

This paper reports nitrogen dioxide (NO_2) detection at temperature up to 100°C. Room temperature NO_2 detection have been achieved by sensors on rigid substrate and improved with one UV Light Emitted Diode illumination. The gas measurements in our experiments under UV showed good responses with fast response and return times towards NO_2 even at 0.2 ppm. The photogenerated charge carriers (electrons and holes) present important benefits for working at low temperatures. UV light illumination results in an increase in the response signal, enhanced sensing reversibility, and an enhanced recovery rate at 100°C with good repeatability. It is open a new way to use Al-ZnO nanoparticles as sensitive layer for gas sensor devices on flexible substrates.

ACKNOWLEDGMENT

The authors would like to thank A. Combes from IM2NP (UMR 7334) for his technical support in this work. The authors are grateful to D. Chaudansson from CINaM (UMR 7325) for assistance in TEM and SEM measurements.

REFERENCES

[1] S . Bernardini, B. Lawson, K. Aguir, O. Margeat, C. Videlot-Ackermann, and J. Ackermann, "Aluminum-doped zinc oxide nanocrystals for NO_2 detection at low temperature", Allsensors 2017, The Second International Conference on Advances in Sensors, Actuators, Metering and Sensing, pp. 56–57, March. 2017, ISBN: 978-1-61208-543-2

[2] T. Stubhan, I. Litzov, N. Li, M. Salinas,; M. Steidl, G. Sauer, et al., "Overcoming interface losses in organic solar cells by applying low temperature", Solution Processed Aluminum-doped zinc oxide electron extraction layers", Journal of Materials Chemistry A 2013, vol. 1, pp. 6004–6009, April 2013, doi:10.1039/c3ta10987a

[3] M. Othman, D. Lollman, K. Aguir, P. Ménini, W. Belkacem, and N. Mliki, "Response enhancement of WO_3 gas sensors by metallic nanograins", IEEE Sensors conference, Baltimore, SENSORS, 2013 IEEE, ISSN: 1930-0395, December 2013, doi: 10.1109/icsens.2013.6688193

[4] G.N. Chaudhari, A.M. Bende, A.B. Bodade, S.S. Patil, and V.S. Sapkal, "Structural and gas sensing properties of nanocrystalline TiO_2 :WO_3 -based hydrogen sensors", Sensors and Actuators B: Chemical, vol. 115, pp. 297–302, May 2006, doi: 10.1016/j.snb.2005.09.014

[5] M. Ivanovskaya, D. Kotsikau, G. Faglia, P. Nelli, and S. Irkaev, "Gas sensitive properties of thin film heterojunction structures based on Fe_2O_3–In_2O_3 nanocomposites", Sensors and Actuators B: Chemical, vol. 93, August 2003, pp. 422–430, doi:10.1016/S0925-4005(03)00175-8

[6] E. Comini, A. Cristalli, G. Faglia, and G. Sberveglieri, "Light enhanced gas sensing properties of indium oxide and tin dioxide sensors", Sensors and Actuators B: Chemical, vol.65, pp. 260–263, June 2000, doi: 10.1016/S0925-4005(99)00350-0

[7] E. Comini, G. Faglia, and G. Sberveglieri, "UV light activation of tin oxide thin films for NO_2 sensing at low temperatures", Sensors and Actuators B: Chemical, vol. 78, pp.73–77, August 2001, doi: 10.1016/S0925-4005(01)00796-1

[8] L.B. Deng, X.H. Ding, D.W. Zeng, S.Q. Tian, H.Y. Li, and C.S. Xie, "Visible-light activate mesoporous WO_3 sensors with enhanced formaldehyde-sensing property at room temperature", Sensors and Actuators B: Chemical, vol. 163, pp. 260–266, March 2012, doi: 10.1016/j.snb.2012.01.049

[9] B.P.J. de Lacy Costello, R.J. Ewen, N.M. Ratcliffe, and M. Richards, "Highly sensitive room temperature sensors on the UV-LED activation of zinc oxide nanoparticles", Sensors and Actuators B: Chemical, vol. 134, pp. 945–952, September 2008, doi: 10.1016/j.snb.2008.06.055

[10] S.W. Fan, A.K. Srivastava, and V.P. Dravid, "UV-activated room-temperature gas sensing mechanism of polycrystalline ZnO", Applied Physics Letters, vol. 95, pp. 142106–142108, October 2009, doi: 10.1063/1.3243458

[11] J.D.Prades, R. Jimenez-Diaz, F. Hernandez-Raminez, S. Barth, A. Ciera, A. Romano-Rodriguez, et. al., "Equivalence between thermal and room temperature UV light-modulated responses of gas sensors based on individual SnO_2 Nanowires", Sensors and Actuators B: Chemical, vol. 140, pp. 337–341, July 2009, doi:10.1016/j.snb.2009.04.070

[12] L. da Silva, J.C. M'Peko, A. C. Catto, S. Bernardini, V.R. Mastelaro, K. Aguir, et al., "UV-enhanced ozone gas sensing response of ZnO-SnO_2 heterojunctions at room temperature", Sensors and Actuators B: Chemical, vol. 240, pp. 573–579, March 2017, doi: 10.1016/j.snb.2016.08.158

[13] Xin Geng, Chao Zhang, Yifan Luoa, Hanlin Liaod, Marc Debliquyc "Light assisted room-temperature NO_2 sensors with enhanced performance based on black $SnO_{1-\alpha}$@$ZnO_{1-\beta}$@$SnO_{2-\gamma}$ nanocomposite coatings deposited by solution precursor plasma spray", Ceramics International, vol. 43 pp. 5990–5998, January 2017, doi: 10.1016/j.ceramint.2017.01.136

[14] M. Gaceur, S. Ben Dkhil, D. Duché, F. Bencheikh, JJ. Simon, L. Escoubas, et al. , "Ligand-free synthesis of aluminium-doped zinc oxide nanocrystals and their use as optical spacers in color-tuned highly efficient organic solar cells", Advanced Functional Materials, vol. 26, pp. 243–253, January 2016, doi:10.1002/adfm.201502929

[15] A.K. Diallo, M. Gaceur, S. Fall, Y. Didane, S. Ben Dkhil, O. Margeat, et al. , "Insight about electrical properties of low-temperature solution-processed Al-doped ZnO nanoparticle based layers for TFT applications". Materials Science and Engineering: B, vol. 214, pp. 11–18, July 2016, doi: 10.1016/j.mseb.2016.07.015

[16] A.K. Diallo, M. Gaceur, S. Ben Dkhil, Y. Didane, O. Margeat, J. Ackermann, et al. , "Impact of surfactants covering ZnO nanoparticles on solution-processed field-effect transistors: from dispersion state to solid state". Colloids and Surfaces A, vol. 500, pp. 214–221, April 2016, doi: 10.1016/j.colsurfa.2016.04.036

[17] WHO guidelines for NO_2, http://www.who.int/mediacentre/factsheets/fs313/en/

[18] M. Acuautla, S. Bernardini, L. Gallais, T. Fiorido, L. Pattout, and M. Bendahan, "Ozone flexible sensors fabricated by photolithography and laser ablation processes based on ZnO nanoparticles", Sensors and Actuators B: Chemical vol. 203, pp: 602–611, November 2014, doi: 10.1016/j.snb.2014.07.010

[19] T.A. Moore, I.M. Miron, G. Gaudin, G. Serret, S. Auffret, B. Rodmacq, et al. , "High domain wall velocities induced by current in ultrathin Pt/Co/AlOx wires with perpendicular magnetic anisotropy", Applied Physics Letters, vol. 93, pp. 263103–263103-3, January 2009, doi: 10.1063/1.3062855.

Automated Driving – Testing at the Functional Limits

Steffen Wittel*, Daniel Ulmer* and Oliver Bühler*
*Steinbeis Interagierende Systeme GmbH, Esslingen, Germany
Email: {steffen.wittel,daniel.ulmer,oliver.buehler}@interagierende-systeme.de

***Abstract*—As vehicles move toward a high degree of automation, the control of the vehicles is taken over from the human drivers for increasing periods of time. This will allow the human drivers to turn their attention away from the vehicles and to focus on non-driving activities instead. With the takeover of the vehicle control, the automobile manufacturers also take over the responsibility for the driving maneuvers automatically performed by the vehicles. As a result, they can no longer rely on immediate interventions of the human drivers in case of critical situations, where the vehicles cannot cope with the road traffic or if the vehicles behave in an unexpected way. Intensive testing activities are necessary to ensure the safety of the vehicles in any situation. Even when the vehicles do not work as expected, a safe state must be achieved without endangering the passengers or other road users. To test automated driving, the established software testing techniques, which have been in use so far in the automotive development, seems no longer sufficient due to the temporary unavailability of the human driver as an immediate fallback level. Revised test approaches that do not require immediate human interventions to ensure the safety of the vehicles are therefore needed. This paper depicts the characteristics of automated driving from a functional point of view and presents an approach based on those characteristics to test the system at its functional limits. Therefore, it makes no difference whether the system reaches its limits by itself or by the individual behavior of other road users on the street.**

Keywords–Automated Driving; Automotive Testing; Functional Limits; Individual Behavior.

I. Introduction

This paper extends our previous approach to test automated driving [1], which distinguishes between the functional and temporal behavior of the system, as well as demands the use of automation for the test case generation and the test execution. The approach presented here in addition incorporates the functional system limits [2] of the vehicle for increased testing activities in areas, where fallback strategies are necessary to ensure the safety of the vehicle. Each function of the vehicle which is looked at is pushed to its limits to evaluate the vehicle behavior in situations that exhibit behaviors different from the original functionality while exceeding limits. Moreover, the approach also takes the individual behavior of the road users who surround the vehicle into account as they can also take the vehicle beyond its functional limits. Therefore, the evaluation of the vehicle behavior is done at the system level as introduced in [3].

With technological progress, human activities are being shifted to technical systems. Automation can help to execute actions that are difficult for humans to perform or go beyond human abilities. But it also changes the role of humans working with systems. The use of automation transforms the human participation in the execution of tasks from the execution of activities through the supervising of activities to the complete replacement by the automated systems. Thereby, the level of automation differs in the way of human interaction. As the level of automation rises, the systems are increasingly independent in executing actions. At a low automation level, the systems only support the humans while an action is executed autonomously without human confirmation at a high degree of automation. The automation levels can be categorized like it is in [4]:

a) There is no automation.
b) The system proposes different possibilities of action and highlights its favorite action.
c) The system proposes a single possibility of action, but it does not execute the action.
d) The system executes the action after a confirmation by a human.
e) The system executes the action, when it is not contradicted by a human within a certain time.
f) The system executes the action and informs the humans in retrospect.
g) The system executes the action and informs the humans on demand.
h) The system executes the action without any interaction with a human.

It is assumed that automation can contribute to the traffic safety by taking over the vehicle control and thus remove the human driver out of the loop in as many situations as possible. Incorrect performing of driving maneuvers, carelessness or wrong decisions lead to road accidents, which are caused by the human drivers. The human driver is therefore one of the causes for road accidents and thus offers the potential to improve the traffic safety.

The term "automated driving" or "autonomous driving" is used in many different meanings. Several institutions, e.g., the German Federal Highway Research Institute (BASt), the US National Highway Traffic Safety Administration (NHTSA), the Society of Automotive Engineers (SAE) and the German Association of the Automotive Industry (VDA), have classified the different levels of driving automation. In this paper, the driving automation levels are used according to the definition specified in SAE J3016 [5]:

No Automation: The system does not take over the vehicle control with the exception of short-term interventions of emergency functions in critical traffic situations. The human driver is fully responsible for the vehicle.

Driver Assistance: The vehicle is controlled either in the lateral or longitudinal direction by the system. The human driver controls the remaining direction, while she or he has to monitor the behavior of the vehicle and has to intervene immediately in case of a critical situation.

Partial Automation: The system controls the longitudinal and lateral direction. The human driver has to monitor the behavior of the vehicle and has to intervene immediately in case of a critical situation.

Conditional Automation: The vehicle is controlled in the longitudinal and lateral direction by the system. The human driver has to react within a reasonable time after a warning by the system.

High Automation: The system controls the longitudinal and lateral direction. It has to handle all traffic situations, even if the human driver does not react appropriately.

Full Automation: The system has to handle all traffic situations on its own.

With the increasing automation of the driving tasks, the automobile manufacturers are taking over more and more responsibility from the human drivers for the driving maneuvers automatically performed by the vehicles as shown in Table I. While the first safety assistance systems, like the Electronic Stability Control (ESC) [6] or the Antilock Braking System (ABS) [6], only supported the driver to cope with critical situations, nowadays the Advanced Driver Assistance Systems (ADAS) [7] provide comfort functions for specific driving scenarios. But until now, the automobile manufacturers were able to use the human driver as an immediate fallback level in case the system could not handle the situation or if the vehicle behaved in an unexpected way.

It is not sufficient for automated driving that the vehicles are working as expected in known environments, but also in unknown traffic situations. Each drive is different from the previous one, e.g., with respect to the encountered environmental conditions like traffic or weather. With each step in the direction towards automated driving, the operating hours of the vehicle functions, as well as the time required for a handover of the vehicle control to the human driver, is increased. In consequence, this means that the period of time for which the automobile manufacturers are responsible for the vehicle also increases. A technical solution to keep this time as short as possible would be an early and safe handover to the human driver. But in the premium market especially the customers do not tolerate vehicle functions, which have been degraded by the safety concept of the vehicle and are therefore not available in a large number of situations. Hence, the automobile manufactures have to find a balance between the safety of the vehicle and the availability of the vehicle functions.

According to [8], current software testing techniques do not adequately take into account the temporary unavailability of the human driver as an immediate fallback level for automated driving. Most of them are based on the assumption that the human driver continuously monitors the vehicle and its surroundings, and is able to intervene immediately in case of a critical situation that cannot be handled by the vehicle itself. The software testing techniques that have been used so far in the automotive development expect certain abilities from human drivers, which they prove by passing the driving test necessary to legally control vehicles in most countries. With the driving license, a person can show that she or he meets the necessary physical and mental requirements to be responsible for the vehicle behavior at any time. The complete takeover of responsibility by the human driver at present still allows the automobile manufactures to reduce the number of test cases required for ensuring the safety of the vehicles. Due to the temporary unavailability of the human driver as an immediate fallback level, the software testing techniques have to deal with the large number of different environmental conditions and timing behaviors, which occur in the road traffic. Without revised or new software testing techniques, representative driving scenarios can no longer be used for the testing to show that the vehicle reaches its destination without endangering occupants or other road users in the automated driving mode.

The following section shows the related work. Section III evaluates the road accident statistic of Germany to give an idea about the current accident situation and how the number of accidents has changed in recent years due to automation. In Section IV, the human factor in the road traffic is investigated as a cause for road accidents, whereas Section V shows how driving automation can play a part in contributing to a higher level of traffic safety and how otherwise it can affect the human driver in a negative way. Section VI addresses the challenges in the field of automated driving with the view of functional testing. Finally, Section VII presents the extended approach for increased testing activities at the functional limits of the system.

II. Related Work

While so far the complexity and performance of the vehicle were limited by the hardware, the embedded software, as well as the development and test process, which now seem to be the limiting factors as elaborated in [9]. The report predicts that the distribution of the functionality over several components leads to a level of testing beyond the economical and temporal feasible possibilities. Thus, the authors see the testing of such systems, which have to work in any traffic situation, as one of the highest technical hurdles for automated driving.

The national research project with the name "PEGASUS" [10], founded by the Federal Ministry for Economic Affairs and Energy (BMWi) in conjunction with automobile companies, suppliers, small and medium-sized companies and research institutes from Germany, should provide standards

TABLE I. Overview about the driving automation levels based on SAE J3016 [5].

Level	*Name*	*Functions*	*Monitoring*	*Controlling*	*Fallback*	*Responsibility*
0	No Automation	None	Human Driver	Human Driver	Human Driver	Human Driver
1	Driver Assistance	Some	Human Driver	System / Human Driver	Human Driver	Human Driver
2	Partial Automation	Some	Human Driver	System	Human Driver	Human Driver
3	Conditional Automation	Some	System	System	Human Driver	Automobile Manufacturer / Human Driver
4	High Automation	Some	System	System	System	Automobile Manufacturer
5	Full Automation	All	System	System	System	Automobile Manufacturer

for the automated driving to close essential gaps in the field of testing and the release of vehicles. Among others, the research project should answer the questions about the requirements that must be met by self-driving vehicles, how the safety and reliability of these systems can be demonstrated and the role the human factor plays in the future. As published by the project, new and uniform quality standards and methods are necessary for the accreditation of automated driving functions. The project goal is to establish generally accepted quality criteria, tools and methods. Moreover, scenarios and situations shall be provided for the release of automated driving functions, as well as procedures for the testing. The main project objectives are:

a) Definition of a common approach for the testing of automated vehicle systems in the simulation, at test benches and in real-world environments
b) Development of a continuous and flexible tool chain for the testing of automated driving
c) Integration of the tests in the development process at an early stage
d) Creation of a test method for automated driving features among manufactures

According to [11], the formal verification is currently the only known way to ensure that a system works as specified. This means that the implementation strictly follows the specification and thus it is possible to determine its behavior in any situation. To perform a formal verification, the specification must meet some preconditions. Among others, the specification must be complete and correct. This precondition can be a big challenge, especially in large projects with many dependencies to external components from different suppliers.

Driving automation can bypass current risks as described in [12], but can also lead to new risks, which have not existed before. The paper shows that "demonstrating safety of automated driving in advance of introduction is nearly impossible". Thereby, they illustrate that the necessary number of kilometers to demonstrate the safety of a system cannot be provided economically by real test vehicles due to the complexity of the possible traffic situations. The statement is based, among others, on the assumptions that it is not possible to drive the required number of kilometers in the available time for testing and that the testing must be at least partially repeated after changes in the software or hardware.

III. Road Accidents Statistic

Over the years, the number of road accidents rose with the increasing number of road users in Germany as shown in Figure 1. But this did not lead to an increase in the number of injured or dead people. The technical progress in passive and active safety systems of the vehicles significantly contributed to the mitigation of the road accidents and personal injuries. Safety systems, which already belong to the standard equipment of almost all new vehicles on the market, prevent road accidents or reduce their impact. Thereby, driving automation helps to eliminate weaknesses of human drivers by finding appropriate reactions in critical situations.

As explained in Section I, the human driver is one of the cause of road accidents. The road accidents statistic [13] shows mistakes of human drivers in Germany, which led to road accidents that were reported to the police. These are mainly the accidents with serious consequences. Minor road accidents with only material damages or minor injuries are not covered by the statistic, because they are usually not reported to the police. A list of common areas in which mistakes made by improper human driving can be categorized as presented in the following to show the complexity of today's road traffic as provided by the Federal Statistical Office of Germany in the road accidents statistic:

a) Use of the road
b) Speed
c) Distance
d) Overtaking
e) Driving past
f) Driving side by side
g) Priority, precedence
h) Turning, U-turn, reversing, entering the flow of traffic, starting off the edge of the road
i) Improper behavior towards pedestrians
j) Stationary vehicles, safety measures
k) Failure to observe lighting regulations

When looking at the road accident statistic of Germany as visualized in Figure 2, it is noticeable that the risk potential varies accordingly with the street location. Within villages or towns, road accidents occur due to the accumulation of road users or confusing traffic situations. There are a lot of different reasons for road accidents in urban environments (66.8 %) that could not be assigned to a single major cause, which can be seen in Figure 2a. In non-urban environments, there are first major causes of accidents that are the result of the increased velocity in comparison with urban environments. With more than 30 percent of all road accidents in non-urban

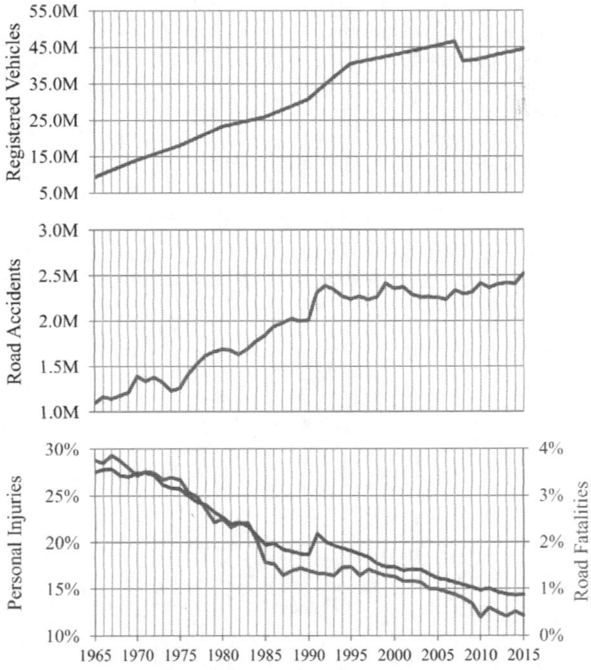

Figure 1. Statistic about road accidents in Germany over a period of 50 years [13].

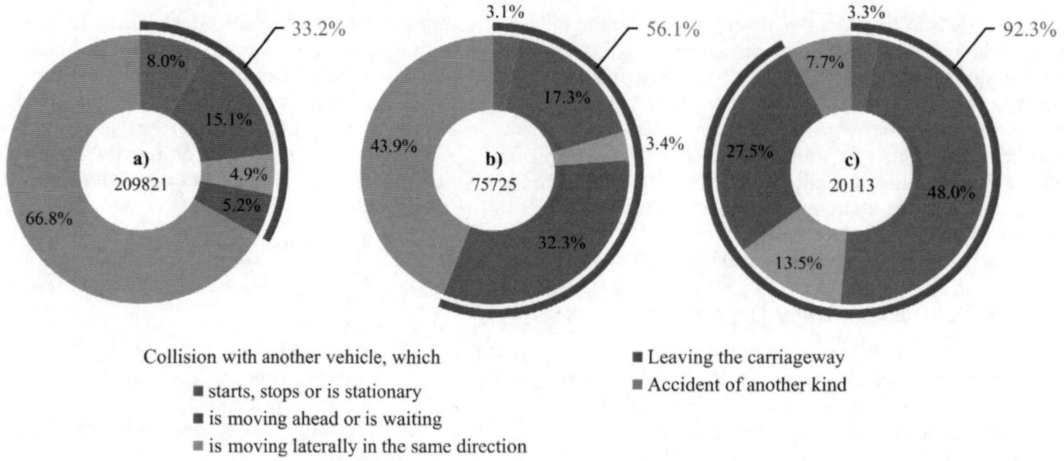

Figure 2. Summary about road accidents in Germany in 2015 [13] separated by the street location: a) urban environments b) non-urban environments c) freeways.

environments, leaving the carriageway is the most common reason. On freeways, the human driver is confronted with a simpler road course, which limits the number of causes for road accidents. Almost half of all road accidents on the freeway are rear-end collisions.

The number of road fatalities and seriously injured people in urban environments (14.5 %) represent in total a lower percentage than in non-urban environments (25.7 %) or on freeways (19.1 %) as illustrated in Figure 3. But in absolute numbers, most of the people are seriously injured or even killed in accidents within towns and villages. A majority of them are pedestrians or cyclists, who hardly have any protection to mitigate the consequences of the road accidents. On freeways, which represent only a small percent of the entire road network of Germany, road accidents with injured people occur relatively more often in relation to urban and non-urban environments. This can, however, be explained by the high usage of freeways, which is about one third of all kilometers driven for Germany.

IV. THE HUMAN FACTOR

According to [14], about 94 % of the road accidents are caused by the human drivers. The human driver is therefore the main cause of the majority of all road accidents. There is not only a single human driver on the road, but also many other road users, whose misbehavior must be taken into account as well. Driving in a dynamic environment is subject to a variety of cognitive demands [15] of the human driver. The human driver has to correctly perceive relevant objects and events, interpret them, and derive his or her actions from them. It is also necessary to recognize new circumstances and make appropriate adjustments well in advance to have time to react.

Research activities on the driving behavior have shown that the personality of a human driver has an impact on the driving style and thus on the involvement in critical traffic situations and road accidents. In the course of life, the personality of a human changes only insignificantly despite external influences. The five-factor model [17], which can be used to describe individual behavior, suggests that the characteristics of personality vary in their intensity for each human. As defined in [18], the five characteristics that lead to the individual behavior of humans are:

Openness (inventive/curious vs. consistent/cautious): Appreciation for art, emotion, adventure, unusual ideas, curiosity, and variety of experience.

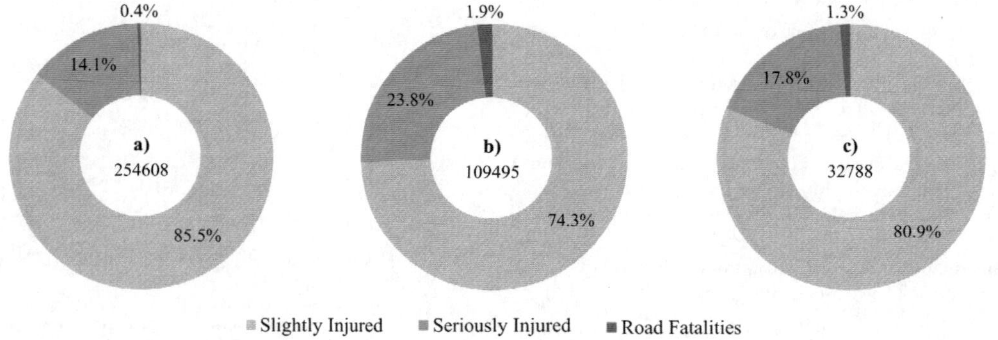

Figure 3. Summary about personal injuries caused by road accidents in Germany in 2015 [13] separated by the street location: a) urban environments b) non-urban environments c) freeways.

Conscientiousness (efficient/organized vs. easy-going/ careless): A tendency to show self-discipline, act dutifully, and aim for achievement; planned rather than spontaneous behavior.

Extroversion (outgoing/energetic vs. solitary/reserved): Energy, positive emotions, urgency, and the tendency to seek stimulation in the company of others.

Agreeableness (friendly/compassionate vs. cold/unkind): A tendency to be compassionate and cooperative rather than suspicious and antagonistic towards others.

Neuroticism (sensitive/nervous vs. secure/confident): A tendency to experience unpleasant emotions easily, such as anger, anxiety, depression, or vulnerability.

Various studies [19][20][21][22][23][24][25][26] have revealed that traffic violations and road accidents are related to risky driving, which is motivated by the personalities of the human drivers. Particularly vulnerable to risky driving are humans who score low on conscientiousness, have a high level of openness, extroversion and neuroticism, as well as indicate a lack of agreeableness as illustrated in Figure 4. A human that score low on conscientiousness is described as impulsive and careless, while somebody with a high level of openness, extroversion and neuroticism is keen to experiment, willing to improvise, distracted and prone to react to stress. This mix of personal traits in combination with a lack of agreeableness, which leads to aggression in terms of emotions as well as behavior, makes the involvement in road accidents more likely.

In the road traffic, people with different personalities meet each other. There is an interaction between the road users in a specific area and their behavior. The road users influence each other through different behaviors they show in certain traffic situations. The behavior of a road user is not only influenced by the current traffic situation, but can also vary based on situations experienced previously. A human driver has to cope with her or his personality and with the personalities of the other road users in the road traffic.

V. AUTOMATED DRIVING

Current vehicle generations already have the necessary technical equipment, i.e., sensors and actuators, to automatically cover a distance in the road traffic independent from the human driver, if certain conditions are fulfilled. On the freeway, it is already customary for premium vehicles that the human driver can preset a time interval to the vehicle ahead, which is automatically maintained by the vehicle. If the traffic situation requires, the vehicle can decelerate to a standstill and then continue to drive as soon as the traffic flow allows it. In addition, the vehicle is able to keep the lane by steering interventions, if a wheel of the vehicle is close to the left or right lane mark when a lane change is not indicated.

It is hardly surprising that the automobile manufacturers will provide their first automated vehicle functions for the use on freeways [27], because 92.3 % of all road accidents on freeways can be avoided or significantly reduced in their consequences by automation as shown in Figure 2. Road accidents in non-urban environments (56.1 %) and urban environments (33.2 %) are much less suitable for introducing automated driving due to the high number of different accident causes. Simplified, it can be said that the freeways offer a manageable complexity, both in the driving tasks and the road characteristics, and thus the vehicle control is limited to approaching and overtaking. From the view point of automation, it would make more sense to introduce automated driving in urban environments, since human drivers there fail most often and thus the greatest impact can be had through the driving automation.

Currently it is accepted in the literature that automated driving contributes to increasing traffic safety. Automated driving can usually achieve a better performance than human drivers in situations which lead to a high degree of criticality or even traffic accidents due to the misconduct of the human driver. However, the vision of accident-free driving still seems far away. Automation can not only contribute to the traffic safety, but also leads to a contrary effect. The use of automation can lead to new critical situations and road accidents that were not present before when the vehicle was controlled only by the human driver. It is also assumed that the number of serious accidents will be reduced by automated driving. However, the number of minor accidents will increase as it is not possible to completely avoid all accidents and only a mitigation of the consequences of the accidents is achieved. Moreover, the use of automated driving can lead to a reduction of the awareness of the situation, which means that the driver is overwhelmed

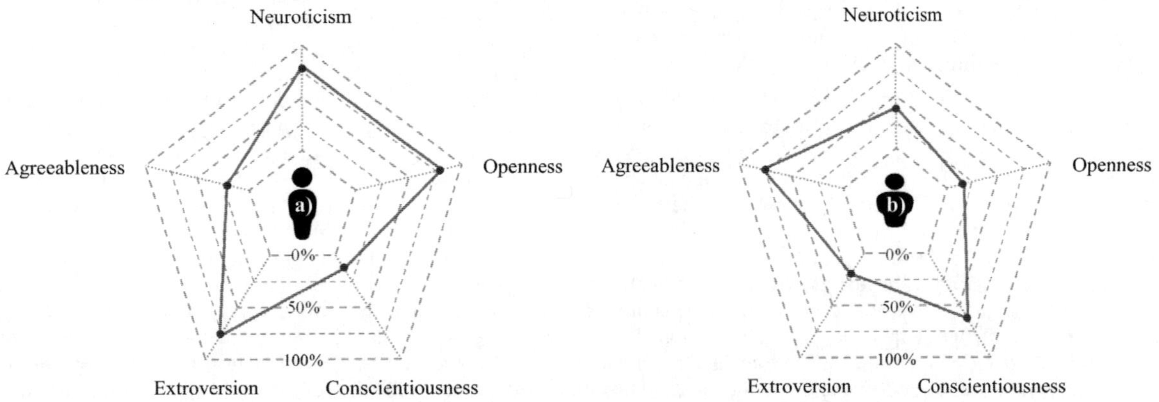

Figure 4. Characterization of two human drivers with different personalities and therefore with individual driving styles illustrated according to [16]: a) higher risk of road accident b) lower risk of road accident.

by the takeover of the vehicle control and misjudges the traffic situation. The cognitive demands described in Section IV, which a human driver must satisfy in order to participate in the road traffic, are lost without an adequate training and thus are either not available, or only to an insufficient degree. Studies [28][29] have already shown that the use of a low degree of automation can lead to a deteriorated lane-keeping and to delayed reactions in critical situations. In addition, the speed is underestimated and it is driven too fast.

VI. Challenges for Automated Driving

With automated driving, the automobile manufacturers are responsible for the driving maneuvers to be performed automatically by the vehicles as soon as they allow the human drivers to divert attention from the environmental conditions and the vehicle. Until now, it was not necessary for the automobile manufacturers to take full responsibility as the human driver was an immediate fallback level in the case of an unintended vehicle behavior. This applies not only to ADAS, but also to emergency functions like the Collision Mitigation System (CMS) [30], which usually intervene only in critical situations. The automated interventions of the emergency functions are additionally limited in time and thus their effects on the moving vehicle. The human driver has to monitor the vehicle all the time and immediately take over the control of the vehicle to perform an intervention. In the event of damage, the human drivers have the sole responsibility and not the automobile manufactures. Extensive test activities are nevertheless performed at test benches and with test vehicles, particularly in the premium segment, to make sure that the human driver rarely has to intervene. Especially for automated driving, the period of time, until the human driver has taken over the vehicle control, needs a closer look. Within this period of time, automated driving has to be maintained by the vehicle. This means, e.g., that a takeover just before a collision, in which the human driver has no possibility to avoid the collision, is not a suitable measure for handing over the vehicle control. Depending on the degree of distraction and the complexity of the current traffic situation, the necessary time until the takeover differs. In addition, characteristics of the human driver, e.g., the age and the mental state, play an essential role for the time required for the takeover of the vehicle control. The automobile manufacturers must assume that an appropriate time, which is expected to be in the double-digit seconds range [31], will be required by the human driver after the takeover notification from the vehicle.

Automation takes the human driver out of the loop from the driving task as often as possible to contribute, among other things, to an increase in the road safety. However, driving automation cannot avoid all accidents, which happen on the road. On the one hand, it is to be assumed that due to the complexity of automated driving, faultlessness cannot be guaranteed. On the other hand, unpredictable actions by other road users can also result in accidents, which can sometimes only be mitigated and not avoided. Individual behavior of road users is a challenge. Especially in the transition, where there is a mixed operation between conventional and automated vehicles in the road traffic, individual behavior must be taken into account. Individual behavior occurs not only with human drivers, but also with different implementations of automated vehicles. There are already initial efforts to develop global standards, e.g., World Forum for Harmonization of Vehicle Regulations [32], which define conditions and limits with the goal of harmonization across manufacturers. Even in the case of harmonization, individual behavior can still occur as long as the human driver can intervene at any time by taking over the vehicle control.

The degradation of the vehicle's functionality, which is part of the safety concept for automated driving, is based on the assumption that the vehicle knows its state and its operating limits at all times. On the basis of the current vehicle state and the exact characteristics of its functional limits [33], the vehicle can decide when and how it comes into a safe state in the event of a fault. A certain tolerance between the operating limits and the limits used for the degradation thereby ensures the robustness of the automated driving, even if there are deviations due to tolerances of individual components. But in practice, it is difficult to determine the limits in advance for all situations and to specify fallback strategies to reach a safe vehicle state, which do not endanger the passengers or other road users. Moreover, the vehicle has to predict its state so as to have enough time to react appropriately to changes in the environmental conditions.

While the emergency functions are active for only a few seconds, comfort functions are often activated for several hours at a time. Over this long period of time, the testing for automated driving must ensure that the vehicle can cope with all situations that occur. The diversity of environmental conditions can no longer be tested only with real vehicles. Simulation allows the execution of the tests on the computer by representing the reality, which is reproduced as a model with some precision. If a comparison between the real vehicle and the simulation shows deviations, which affect the test result, an improvement of the model is necessary in order to get closer to the real world. The closer to reality, the greater the effort involved for the modeling. A perfect representation of reality would be desirable, but for many test scenarios a less precise representation is sufficient, if it does not affect the test result. However, it is not possible to dispense with real vehicles, since they are required to demonstrate the significance of the simulated test result.

As described in [8], current test activities for vehicles primarily focus on the controllability of the vehicles by the human drivers. Even emergency functions of the vehicle, which should only become active in the event of a loss of control by the human driver, can be overruled. The responsibility for the behavior of the vehicles stays with the human drivers for the entire time and does not pass over to the automobile manufacturers. Technical solutions, e.g., the hands-free detection, explicitly point out the driver's responsibility for the vehicle through acoustic and haptic signals. The human driver thereby constitutes a mainstay for the vehicle testing. The safety of the vehicle is built on the combination of the vehicle and the human driver, implicitly assuming that each human driver has the ability to drive the vehicle. Usually, the human driver learns this ability, if not already present, in the driving school and proves them by passing the driving test. Due to the fact that the human driver is at least temporarily distracted from the driving activity during the automated driving, the mainstay is increasingly moving away from the human driver as the degree of automation increases. As a result of this, the vehicle must assume the tasks of the human driver for this period. The responsibility for the driving maneuvers performed independently by the vehicle is handed over to the automobile manufacturer, while the human driver is allowed to be distracted from the vehicle and its surroundings. In the case of a handover, it is no longer possible to refer to the human driver until the vehicle control has been taken over again. This changes the perspective on the vehicle testing, which means that the safety must now only be ensured by the vehicle and no longer by the combination of the vehicle and the human driver. With the increasing automation level, the human drivers can take over the vehicle control after the notification from the vehicle, but they do not have to until the end of the takeover period. The testing will still have to ensure the controllability of the vehicle by the human driver, but it does not play such a decisive role as before. Until the vehicle is taken over by the human driver, the vehicle is placed on its own and has to cope with the environmental conditions encountered during this time.

State of the art test methods [34][35] are based on the approach that a certain selection of the system input represents the complete input range. Examples of such test methods are the Boundary Value Analysis, the Equivalence Class Analysis and the Classification Tree Analysis. These approaches to the system input can reduce the number of tests tremendously. To apply such an approach, it is necessary that the test method divides the system input into classes in which the test object is expected to show the same response independently of the value taken out of the class. However, the classes are usually derived from the system requirements. Both, the requirement process and the derivation of the classes are human tasks and are therefore error-prone. In complex implementations with a large number of parameters, there might be branches implemented, which cannot be seen in the requirements. Even with systematic testing, it is sure that not every input pattern is tested, which can result in a misbehavior of the system. As a worst case scenario, this misbehavior can lead to a road accident, if it is either not compensated by the system itself or recognized and corrected by the human driver. Since the human driver is assumed to be distracted, the system either has to avoid such traffic situations or has to be able to cope with them, if they are in the period of time before the vehicle control is taken over. As a result of the possible distraction of the human driver during the automated driving, the human driver can no longer be used as an immediate fallback level. Thus, a limitation of the input space on the basis of the human fallback level can no longer be performed according to [8]. During the testing, the additional tasks of the vehicle must now be taken into account that are otherwise assumed by the human driver. The test methods must be adapted in such a way that human errors are largely excluded and that they can be used with an economically justifiable effort for the testing of automated driving.

VII. The Approach

According to [36], the test aim is transformed into an optimization problem in which the input of the test object creates the so called search space. The search space is a numeric representation for the possible stimulations that can be applied to the test object to obtain a response. For obtaining a specific system response, it is necessary to stimulate the system with the corresponding input pattern from the search space. The other way round, a specific input pattern from the search space causes a specific response of the system. Since automated driving algorithms are time variant [3], it is not sufficient to test only static input patterns, but also variations of the test scenarios that differ over time. Changes in the timing of the input sequence can affect the system, e.g., feedback control loops. The same input values with a different timing might lead to a different response of the system. For this reason, it is proposed that the search space shall be divided into the following two parts:

a) Functional behavior
b) Temporal behavior

The consideration of the temporal behavior adds another dimension to the system input many times over. However, the proposed separation between the functional and the temporal behavior allows a prioritization during the test execution. Thus, it is possible to test the functional behavior of the system at first, followed by the testing of the temporal behavior. The temporal behavior is especially important for systems that have memories as explained in [3]. For this kind of systems, the points of time, e.g., at which a vehicle performs a specific action, are crucial factors.

Given the expected number of test cases derived from the system input, a manual creation of the test cases is infeasible. Common sense is that test case generators must be used for the test creation. The usage of test case generators multiplies the number of test cases, but not necessarily increases the quality of the tests or the covered system input. Generated test cases, which are redundant or outside the operating limit of the system, do not contribute to the improvement of the system. Hence, test case generators shall be optimized to focus on the relevant parts of the test object. Having said that, from a coverage point of view, many test cases are needed to ensure the safety of the vehicle. It is to be stated that an execution of these test cases is only feasible, if the test execution is fully automated. This requirement is valid to both test generation and test execution. In contrast to today's available test case generators, which mostly leave the specification of the expected system response to the testers, they must be able to provide the system response based on the generated stimulation even for complex systems. But the handling of the test execution also takes a lot of time, if the allocation of the test cases to the test resources is not automated. A huge number of generated test cases require the corresponding amount of test resources, which can be optimized without human interaction. In summary, it can be said that the usage of test case generators leads to the following requirements:

a) Effective test case generators for the automated driving domain
b) Test resources that are fully automated to increase the throughput
c) Scalable test resources to cope with the number of generated test cases
d) Test case generators that also provide the expected system behavior for the evaluation

Particularly critical in automated driving is the unexpected exceeding of a system limit, where the provided functionality of the vehicle is no longer available. With the approach of a functional limit, the vehicle behavior changes increasingly until it has deteriorated to such an extent that the functionality of the vehicle can no longer be provided within an acceptable manner as shown in Figure 5. Even before such a functional limit is crossed, the vehicle must have a strategy, which ensures that the vehicle retains its control. In order to prevent the vehicle from exceeding the limit, taking a safe state is considered to be an effective means. According to [37], a safe vehicle state is achieved, when the current and future risk is below a threshold accepted by the society and therefore no unreasonable risk exists. The threshold represents the value up to which the risk is still accepted from an ethical, moral, and social point of view. Depending on the situation and its criticality, a safe state can be achieved in different ways. The higher the criticality of a situation, the more drastic measures are used in order to achieve a safe state for the vehicle. The range varies from changing the lane to stop the vehicle at the edge of the road to the immediate stop of the vehicle at the current position as described in [38]. In order to test the vehicle behavior shortly before the loss of functionality, the approach suggests that the test activities are intensified at the transition area around the functional limits. However, since the functional limits of a system are situation-dependent and only partially known in advance, the used method must be systematic and with the greatest possible variation of the test scenarios as is possible to push the vehicle functions to their limits. The variation, which is necessary to take the different environmental conditions and the individual behavior of the road users into account, results in a large number of test cases that must not only be executed, but also evaluated. For the evaluation, the approach proposes an evaluation at the system level from the viewpoint of an external observer as described in [3].

VIII. Conclusion and Future Work

Automation plays an important role in the technical progress. Technical systems are increasingly taking on human tasks. Some of the technical systems overcome human beings at present. Currently, automation facilitates driving and helps to reduce or even eliminate risks caused by human drivers. However, the human driver has to monitor the vehicle and its surroundings for the whole drive to be immediately available as a fallback level in case that the vehicle cannot cope with a situation or a malfunction occurs. The responsibility for the vehicle and possible damages lies with the human driver. In contrast to emergency functions, which only intervene in critical traffic situations for a short period of time, the latest comfort functions temporarily take over the lateral and longitudinal control of the vehicle for longer time. With further steps in the direction of automated driving, the automobile manufacturers will have to take over the responsibility for the driving maneuvers automatically performed by the vehicles until the human driver takes over the vehicle control from the vehicle.

The safety of current vehicle generations is built on the combination of the vehicle and the human driver. If the vehicle has a malfunction or cannot handle the situation, the human driver should be ready to take over the vehicle control immediately. This means that the test activities for vehicles primarily focus on the controllability of the vehicle by the human driver. With the transition in the direction of automated driving, the human driver is less and less often available for a takeover of the vehicle control and if the human driver is up to it, it will take longer due to the possible distraction from the driving task. The temporary unavailability of the human driver as an immediate fallback level requires new or revised test concepts and test methods, which take these changes into account for the testing of the vehicle's functionality.

Driving automation can contribute to the traffic safety by removing the human driver out of the loop in as many situations as possible. But driving automation, which does not endanger the passengers or other road users, can only be achieved, if a correct operation of the vehicle is ensured at all times and in any situation. The presented approach proposes that the search space of the system shall be divided into the functional behavior and the temporal behavior, which allows a prioritization during the test execution. It demands in addition the full automation of the test generation and test execution to increase efficiency. The approach assumes that the number of test cases required for a release of a vehicle will increase considerably in order to meet the variety of different environmental conditions. The expected number of test cases will

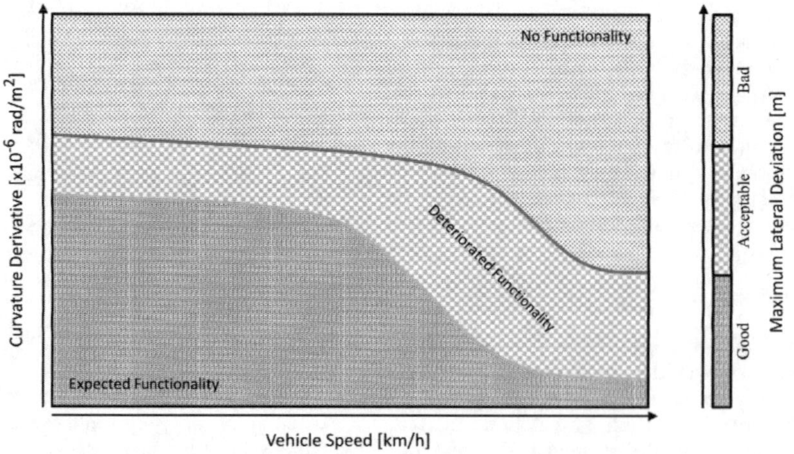

Figure 5. Schematic representation of a functional limit (marked with a red line) on the example of lane keeping assistant.

result in mostly a manual test process with low throughput and poor scalability infeasible for automated driving. An increased test activity is intended by the approach to find situations, where functional limits are crossed unexpectedly and neither the provided vehicle's functionality is no longer available nor the time remaining to reach a safe state is sufficient. It proposes therefore a systematic method, which considers the environmental conditions and the individual behavior of the road users to bring the generated test scenarios iteratively closer to the functional limits of the system by evaluating the vehicle behavior on the system level.

It is left for future work to implement the presented approach and to apply it to a real vehicle function in a case study. Furthermore, efficient techniques are needed to push the function which is looked at specifically to its limits. Metrics must be determined to evaluate the vehicle behavior. From the vehicle behavior, the distance to the functional limits can be estimated. It is assumed that the vehicle behavior does not change abruptly, but continuously deteriorates if the safety strategies are not active.

REFERENCES

[1] S. Wittel, D. Ulmer, and O. Bühler, "Challenges in Functional Testing on the Way to Automated Driving," in The Twelfth International Conference on Systems, 2017, pp. 16–21. [Online]. Available: https://www.thinkmind.org/download.php?articleid=icons_2017_1_30_40051

[2] S. Wittel, D. Ulmer, and O. Bühler, "The Testing Aspects of Automated Driving," 2017, [Online]. Available: http://www.steinbeis.de/fileadmin/content/Publikationen/transfermagazin/191523-2017-02.pdf [retrieved: December, 2017].

[3] S. Wittel, D. Ulmer, and O. Bühler, "Automatic Test Evaluation for Driving Scenarios Using Abstraction Level Constraints," in The Eighth International Conference on Advances in System Testing and Validation Lifecycle, 2016, pp. 14–19. [Online]. Available: https://www.thinkmind.org/index.php?view=article&articleid=valid_2016_2_20_40023

[4] S. Eschen, Personality as predictor for performance in highly automated man-machine teams in aviation (Persönlichkeit als Prädiktor für Leistung in hoch automatisierten Mensch-Maschine-Teams der Luftfahrt). Shaker Verlag, 2014. [Online]. Available: http://elib.dlr.de/89149/

[5] SAE International, "Automated Driving - Levels of Driving Automation are Defined in New SAE International Standard J3016," 2014, [Online]. Available: https://www.smmt.co.uk/wp-content/uploads/sites/2/automated_driving.pdf [retrieved: December, 2017].

[6] A. Zanten and F. Kost, Handbook of Driver Assistance Systems: Basic Information, Components and Systems for Active Safety and Comfort. Cham: Springer International Publishing, 2016, ch. Brake-Based Assistance Functions, pp. 919–967. [Online]. Available: http://dx.doi.org/10.1007/978-3-319-12352-3_40

[7] A. Paul, R. Chauhan, R. Srivastava, and M. Baruah, "Advanced driver assistance systems," in SAE Technical Paper. SAE International, 02 2016. [Online]. Available: https://doi.org/10.4271/2016-28-0223

[8] W. Wachenfeld and H. Winner, The Release of Autonomous Vehicles. Berlin, Heidelberg: Springer Berlin Heidelberg, 2016, pp. 425–449. [Online]. Available: https://doi.org/10.1007/978-3-662-48847-8_21

[9] Fraunhofer Institute for Industrial Engineering IAO, "Highly Automated Driving on Freeways - Industrial Policy Conclusions ("Hochautomatisiertes Fahren auf Autobahnen Industriepolitische Schlussfolgerungen")," 2015, [Online]. Available: http://www.bmwi.de/Redaktion/DE/Downloads/H/hochautomatisiertes-fahren-auf-autobahnen.html [retrieved: December, 2017].

[10] German Aerospace Center, "Research Project PEGASUS," URL: http://www.pegasus-projekt.info [retrieved: December, 2017].

[11] G. Klein, J. Andronick, K. Elphinstone, T. Murray, T. Sewell, R. Kolanski, and G. Heiser, "Comprehensive formal verification of an os microkernel," ACM Trans. Comput. Syst., vol. 32, no. 1, pp. 2:1–2:70, Feb. 2014. [Online]. Available: http://doi.acm.org/10.1145/2560537

[12] H. Winner, W. Wachenfeld, and P. Junietz, "(How) Can Safety of Automated Driving be Validated?" 2016, [Online]. Available: http://www.fzd.tu-darmstadt.de/media/fachgebiet_fzd/publikationen_3/2016_5/2016_Wi_Wf_Ju_ViV-Symposium_Graz.pdf [retrieved: December, 2017].

[13] Federal Statistical Office of Germany, "Road Traffic Accidents - 2015 ("Verkehrsunfälle - 2015")," 2016, [Online]. Available: https://www.destatis.de/DE/Publikationen/Thematisch/TransportVerkehr/Verkehrsunfaelle/VerkehrsunfaelleJ2080700157004.html [retrieved: December, 2017].

[14] NHTSA's National Center for Statistics and Analysis, "Critical Reasons for Crashes Investigated in the National Motor Vehicle Crash Causation Survey," 2015, [Online]. Available: https://crashstats.nhtsa.dot.gov/Api/Public/ViewPublication/812115 [retrieved: December, 2017].

[15] D. Rösler, "The relevance of traffic elements in driving situations definition, measurement, and application," Ph.D. dissertation, Chemnitz University of Technology, 2010. [Online]. Available: http://nbn-resolving.de/urn:nbn:de:bsz:ch1-201000403

[16] F. Lorig and I. Timm, "How to model the "human factor" for agent-based simulation in social media analysis? work in progress paper," vol. 46, pp. 89–94, 01 2014.

[17] J. M. Digman, "Brake-based assistance functions," in Annual Review of Psychology, vol. 41, 11 2003, pp. 417–440.

[18] Crowe Associates, "The "BIG 5" PERSONALITY TRAITS," URL: http://www.crowe-associates.co.uk/coaching-and-mentoring-skills/the-big-5-personality-traits/ [retrieved: December, 2017].

[19] W. Arthur and W. G. Graziano, "The five-factor model, conscientiousness, and driving accident involvement," Journal of Personality, vol. 64, no. 3, pp. 593–618, 1996. [Online]. Available: http://dx.doi.org/10.1111/j.1467-6494.1996.tb00523.x

[20] B. A. Jonah, "Sensation seeking and risky driving: a review and synthesis of the literature," Accident Analysis & Prevention, vol. 29, no. 5, pp. 651–665, 1997.

[21] D. F. Cellar, Z. C. Nelson, and C. M. Yorke, "The five-factor model and driving behavior: Personality and involvement in vehicular accidents," Psychological Reports, vol. 86, no. 2, pp. 454–456, 2000. [Online]. Available: http://dx.doi.org/10.2466/pr0.2000.86.2.454

[22] R. Lancaster and R. Ward, The contribution of individual factors to driving behaviour: Implications for managing work-related road safety . HSE Books, 2002. [Online]. Available: http://www.hse.gov.uk/research/rrpdf/rr020.pdf

[23] N. Sümer, T. Lajunen, and T. Özkan, "Big five personality traits as the distal predictors of road accident involvement," pp. 215–227, 01 2005.

[24] E. Constantinou, G. Panayiotou, N. Konstantinou, A. Loutsiou-Ladd, and A. Kapardis, "Risky and aggressive driving in young adults: Personality matters," vol. 43, pp. 1323–31, 07 2011.

[25] J. Vazquez, "Personality factors, age, and aggressive driving: A validation using a driving simulator," 2013.

[26] A. af Whlberg, P. Barraclough, and J. Freeman, "Personality versus traffic accidents; meta-analysis of real and method effects," Transportation Research Part F: Traffic Psychology and Behaviour, vol. 44, pp. 90 – 104, 2017. [Online]. Available: http://www.sciencedirect.com/science/article/pii/S1369847816304156

[27] Verband der Automobilindustrie e.V., "Automation - From Driver Assistance Systems to Automated Driving," 2015, [Online]. Available: https://www.vda.de/dam/vda/publications/2015/automation.pdf [retrieved: December, 2017].

[28] N. J. Ward, "Task automation and skill development in a simplified driving task," Proceedings of the Human Factors and Ergonomics Society Annual Meeting, vol. 44, no. 20, pp. 3–302–3–305, 2000. [Online]. Available: http://dx.doi.org/10.1177/154193120004402020

[29] N. Merat, A. H. Jamson, F. C. H. Lai, and O. Carsten, "Highly automated driving, secondary task performance, and driver state," Human Factors, vol. 54, no. 5, pp. 762–771, 2012, pMID: 23156621. [Online]. Available: http://dx.doi.org/10.1177/0018720812442087

[30] B. Danner, T. Dohmke, J. Hillenbrand, V. Schmid, and A. Spieker, "Method and apparatus for avoiding or mitigating vehicle collisions," Apr. 3 2012, US Patent 8,150,583.

[31] Gesamtverband der Deutschen Versicherungswirtschaft e.V., "Takeover times in highly automated driving - Compact accident research," 2016, [Online]. Available: https://udv.de/en/publications/compact-accident-research/takeover-times-highly-automated-driving [retrieved: December, 2017].

[32] United Nations Economic Commission for Europe (UNECE), "World Forum for Harmonization of Vehicle Regulations (WP 29)," URL: http://www.unece.org/trans/main/wp29/meeting_docs_wp29.html [retrieved: December, 2017].

[33] A. T. Kleen, "Controllability of partially automated interventions in vehicle guidance ("Beherrschbarkeit von teilautomatisierten Eingriffen in die Fahrzeugführung")," Ph.D. dissertation, 2014. [Online]. Available: http://publikationsserver.tu-braunschweig.de/receive/dbbs_mods_00056694

[34] O. Bühler, "Evolutionary functional testing of embedded systems for distance-based automotive driver assistance functions ("Evolutionärer Funktionstest von eingebetteten Systemen für abstandsbasierte Fahrerassistenzfunktionen im Automobil")," Ph.D. dissertation, University of Tübingen, 2007.

[35] I. Jovanovic, "Software Testing Methods and Techniques," in The IPSI BgD Transactions on Internet Research, 2009, pp. 30–41. [Online]. Available: http://tir.ipsitransactions.org/2009/January/Full%20Journal.pdf

[36] F. Rothlauf, Optimization Problems. Berlin, Heidelberg: Springer Berlin Heidelberg, 2011, pp. 7–44. [Online]. Available: http://dx.doi.org/10.1007/978-3-540-72962-4_2

[37] A. Reschka, Safety Concept for Autonomous Vehicles. Berlin, Heidelberg: Springer Berlin Heidelberg, 2016, pp. 473–496. [Online]. Available: https://doi.org/10.1007/978-3-662-48847-8_23

[38] M. Binfet-Kull and P. Heitmann, "System safety for an autonomous driving vehicle," 1998.

Dynamic Fuzzy Cognitive Maps Embedded and Intelligent Controllers Applied in Industrial Mixer Process

Lucas Botoni de Souza
Patrick Prieto Soares
Ruan Victor Pelloso Duarte Barros
Márcio Mendonça
DAELE (Electric Academic Department)
UTFPR-CP
Cornélio Procópio, Brazil
{lucasbotoni; p.prietosoares}@hotmail.com
ruan_pelloso@yahoo.com.br
mendonca@utfpr.edu.br

Elpiniki I. Papageorgiou
Department of Computer Engineering
Technological Education Institute/ University of Applied Sciences of Central Greece
Lamia, Greece
epapageorgiou@teiste.gr

Abstract— **This paper presents the application of certain intelligent techniques to control an industrial mixer. The controller design is based on a Hebbian modification of the Fuzzy Cognitive Maps learning mechanism. This research develops a Dynamic Fuzzy Cognitive Map (DFCM) based on Hebbian Learning algorithms. Fuzzy Classic Controller was used to help validate simulation results of an industrial mixer controlled by DFCM. Experimental analysis of simulations in this control problem was conducted. Additionally, the results were embedded using efficient algorithms into the Arduino platform to acknowledge the performance of the codes reported in this paper.**

Keywords-Fuzzy Cognitive Maps; Hebbian Learning; Arduino Microcontroller; Process Control; Fuzzy Logic; Artificial Neural Network.

I. INTRODUCTION

This work is an evolution of the article shown in [1]. In general, some of the difficulties found in acquiring knowledge in different areas of engineering (such as robotics, control or process control) are: how to recognize the processes /systems; how to identify important variables and parameters; to classify the type of physical problem; o identify the family of mathematical models that can be associated; to select the method and / or tool for the search and analysis of the model.

Indeed, the final output of modern processes is significantly influenced by the selection of the set points of the process variables, as they fundamentally impact the product quality characteristics and the process performance metrics [2]. In this context, it is possible to define the main goal of this research, to develop techniques based on knowledge for the process control of a classic problem of Fuzzy Cognitive Maps area, an industrial mixer; this work is an evolution of the previous work [3].

The article proposal is to use a different setup, in special the initial state and a comparison with a new controller using Fuzzy-Logic with ANN (artificial neural network). The motivation of this research is: developments in optimal control theory, robust control and adaptive control, expanding significantly the automation concept and, also studying the feasibility of an autonomous control in practice.

On the other hand, intelligent control techniques take control actions without depending on a complete or partial mathematical model. Otherwise, the ability of a human to find solutions to a particular problem is known as human intelligence. In short, human beings can deal with complicated processes based on inaccurate and/or approximate information. The strategy adopted by them is also of imprecise nature and usually capable of being expressed in linguistic terms. Thus, by means of Fuzzy Logic concepts, it is possible to model this type of information [4].

Some previous works that used Fuzzy techniques can be cited, such as [5], which applies a Fuzzy-Neuro predictive control tuned by Genetic Algorithms (GA) on a fermentation process. A Proportional Derivative Fuzzy Logic Controller (Fuzzy-PD) was initially used to control the process, a non-linear system with non-minimal phase, and a large accommodation time.

More recently, [6] presented a FCM used to tune PI controllers' parameters used on a non-linear system. These controllers cannot achieve satisfactory results in this type of system, by the difference of their static and dynamic properties.

There is also [7], where new types of concept and relation, not restricted to cause-effect ones, are added to the model resulting in a dynamic fuzzy cognitive map (DFCM). In this sense, a supervisory system is developed in order to control the fermentation process.

II. FUZZY COGNITIVE MAPS – BACKGROUND

Fuzzy Cognitive Maps (FCM) was introduced by Kosko's work, which added Fuzzy values to the causal relationships of Axelrod's Cognitive Maps paper. In fact, FCMs are system models represented in a graph-form, the nodes are the concepts related to the problem and the lines connecting them are the causal relationships. A FCM is a 4-tuple, as described in works as [8] and [9]. It is commonly used to study system's dynamics because of its mathematically simplicity. The relationship's influence is calculated using normalized states and matrix multiplications.

The inference of the system's dynamics might reach a steady state, a limit cycle of states or even a chaotic state [10-11]. Every concept's activation level is based on its own previous iteration and the propagated weighted values of all the concepts connected to it (it means all concepts that have influence over it).

In the literature, there are many examples of FCMs that use monotonic and symmetric weight cause-effect relationships between the concepts that might work on controlled environments but cannot be applied on the real world considering its dynamic aspects. In order to bring FCMs to a more realistic environments, there are a few techniques that can be used such as using Fuzzy rules and feedback mechanisms [12-13] or algebraic equations to define the causal relationships when the real system have been modeled by crisp relations [14].

In general, a Fuzzy Cognitive Map (FCM) is a tool for modeling the human knowledge. It can be obtained through linguistic terms, inherent to Fuzzy Systems, but with a structure like the Artificial Neural Networks (ANN), which facilitates data processing, and has capabilities for training and adaptation. FCM is a technique based on the knowledge that inherits characteristics of Cognitive Maps and Artificial Neural Networks [10-15], with applications in different areas of knowledge [16-17].

Besides the advantages and characteristics inherited from these primary techniques, FCM was originally proposed as a tool to build models or cognitive maps in various fields of knowledge. It makes the tool easier to abstract the information necessary for modeling complex systems, which are similar in the construction to the human reasoning.

Dynamic Fuzzy Cognitive Maps (DFCM) needs to be developed to a model that can manage behaviors of non-linear time-dependent systems and sometimes in real time. Examples of different variation of the classic FCMs can be found in the recent literature, e.g., [18-19].

This paper has two objectives. The first objective is the development of two controllers using an acyclic DFCM with same knowledge of a Fuzzy and Fuzzy Neural controller, and with similar heuristic, thus producing comparable simulated results. The second goal is to show an embedded DFCM in the low-cost processing microcontroller Arduino with more noise and disturbances (valve locking) to test the adaptability of the DFCM.

To succeed the goals, we initially use the similar DFCM proposed initially in [20] to control an industrial mixing tank. In contrary to [20], it is used the Hebbian algorithm to dynamically adapt the DFCM weights. In order to validate the DFCM controller, its performance was compared with a Fuzzy Logic controller. This comparison is carried out with simulated data.

III. Development

To demonstrate the evolution of the proposed technique (DFCM) we will use a case study well known in the literature as seen in [3-21] and others. This case was selected to illustrate the need for refinement of a model based on FCM built exclusively with knowledge.

The process shown in Fig. 1 consists of a tank with two inlet valves for different liquids, a mixer, an outlet valve for removal of the final product and a specific gravity meter that measures the specific gravity of the produced liquid. In this research, to illustrate and exemplify the operation of the industrial mixer, the liquids are water with specific gravity 1 and soybean oil with a specific gravity of about 0.9.

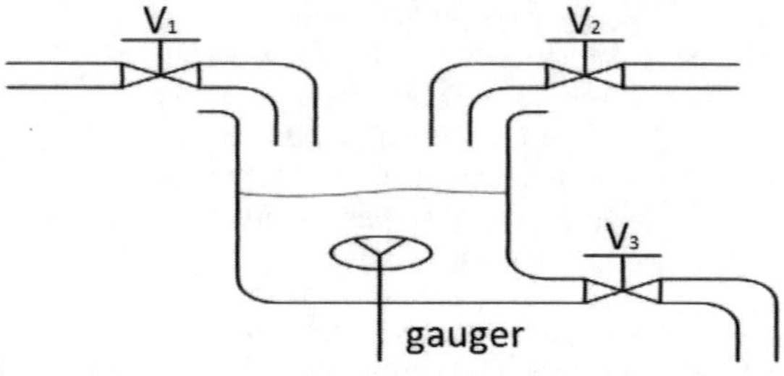

Figure 1. Mixer tank (Source: adapted from [21]).

Valves (V1) and (V2) insert two different liquids (specific gravities) in the tank. During the reaction of the two liquids, a new liquid characterized by its new specific gravity value is produced. At this time, the valve (V3) empties the tank in accordance with a campaign output flow, but the liquid mixture should match the specified levels of the volume and specific gravity.

Although being relatively simple, this process is a TITO (Two Inputs and Two Outputs) type with coupled variables. To establish the quality of the control system of the produced fluid, a weighting machine placed in the tank measures the specific gravity of the liquid produced.

When the value of the measured variable G, liquid mass, reaches the range of values between the maximum and minimum [Gmin, Gmax] specified, the desired mixed liquid is ready. The removal of liquid is only possible when the volume (V) is in a specified range between the values [Vmin and Vmax]. The control consists to keep these two variables in their operating ranges, as:

$$V_{min} < V < V_{max} \quad (1)$$

$$G_{min} < G < G_{max} \quad (2)$$

In this study, it was tried to limit these values from approximately the range of 810 to 850 [mg] for the mass and approximately the range of 840 to 880 [ml] for the volume. The initial values for mass and volume are 800mg and 850ml, respectively. According to Papageorgiou and collaborators [23], through the observation and analysis of the process, it is possible for experts to define a list of key concepts related to physical quantities involved. The concepts and cognitive model are:

- Concept 1 - State of the valve 1 (closed, open or partially open);
- Concept 2 - State of the valve 2 (closed, open or partially open);

- Concept 3 - State of the valve 3 (closed, open or partially open);
- Concept 4 - quantity of mixture (volume) in the tank, which depends on the operational state of the valves V1, V2 and V3.
- Concept 5 - value measured by the G sensor for the specific gravity of the liquid.

Considering the initial proposed evolution for FCM, it is used a DFCM to control the mixer, which should maintain levels of volume and mass within specified limits.

The process model uses the mass conservation principle in incompressible fluid to derive a set of differential equations representing the process used to test the DFCM controller. As a result, the tank volume is the volume over the initial input flow of the inlet valves V1 and V2 minus the outflow valve V3, this valve V3 and the output campaign was introduced in this work to increase the original process' complexity [22].

Similarly, the mass of the tank follows the same principle as shown below. The values used for m_{e1} and m_{e2} were 1.0 and 0.9, respectively.

$$V_{tank} = V_i + V_1 + V_2 - V_3 \tag{3}$$

$$Weight_{tank} = M_i + (V_1 . m_{e1}) + (V_2 . m_{e2}) - M_{out} \tag{4}$$

IV. Fuzzy Controller Development

To establish a correlation and a future comparison between techniques, a Fuzzy controller was also developed. The Fuzzy rules base uses the same heuristic control strategy and conditions.

Fuzzy logic has proved being able to provide satisfactory non-linear controllers even when only the nominal plant model is available, or when plant parameters are not known with precision [24-25]. Fuzzy Control is a technique used for decades, especially in process controlling [21].

It is a motivation to validate DFCM, so in this study it was used the same approach for two controllers, with two different formalisms. It is not in the scope to discuss the development of the Fuzzy controller, but some details of the structure are pertinent: functions are triangles and trapezoidal and 6 rules are considered in its base. The Fuzzy controller surfaces are shown in Fig. 2. Moreover, the rules are symmetric and similar by two output valves; in this specific case, the surface of valve 1 is the same as in valve 2. The base rules and its respective weights are:

1. If (Level is low) then (V1 is medium) (V2 is medium)(1);
2. If (Level is medium) then (V1 is low) (V2 is low) (1);
3. If (Level is high) then (V1 is low) (V2 is low) (1);
4. If (Weight is low) then (V1 is high) (V2 is high) (1);
5. If (Weight is medium) then (V1 is low) (V2 is low) (0.5);
6. If (Weight is high) then (V1 is low) (V2 is low) (1);
7. If (ValveOut is high) then (V1 is high) (V2 is high) (0.5);
8. If (ValveOut is medium) then (V1 is medium) (V2 is medium) (0.5);
9. If (ValveOut is low) then (V1 is low) (V2 is low) (0.5).

The rules and structure of the Fuzzy Controller used on its development was based on the DFCM heuristic.

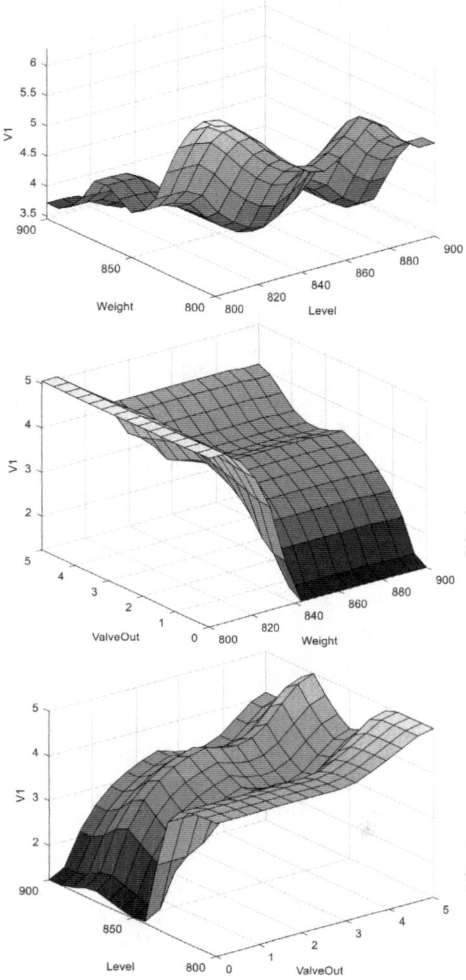

Figure 2. Fuzzy Controller Surfaces for V1 and V2

Fig. 3 shows the Fuzzy structure with same variables input and output like DFCM.

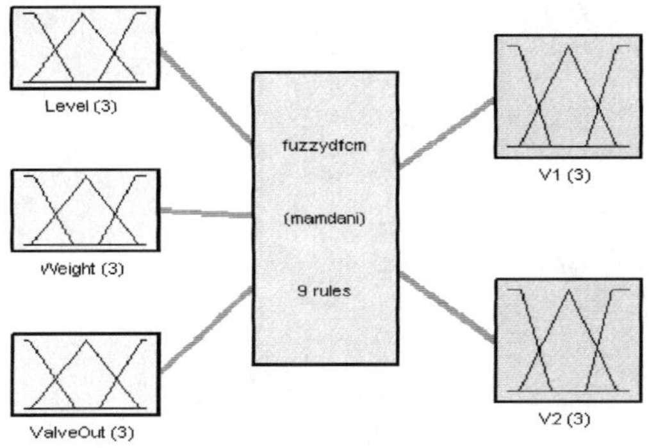

Figure 3. Fuzzy Structure

This model represents the weakest degree of possible integration between two techniques and the consistency of two subsystems connected in series. As an example, we can cite a neuro-Fuzzy model which a Fuzzy system admits inputs to a neural network as shown in Fig. 4.

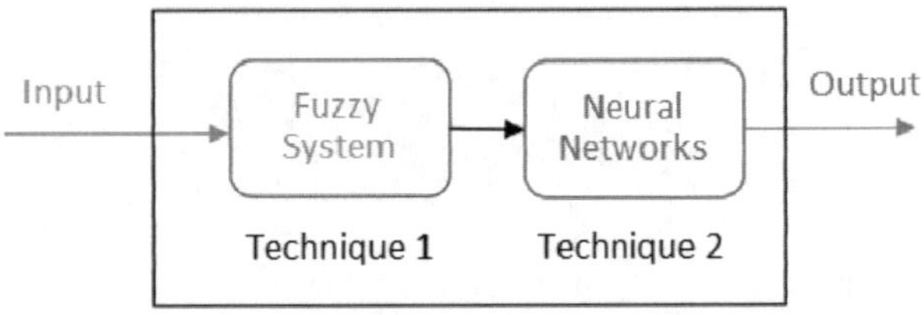

Figure 4. Sequential hybrid model

A Fuzzy-ANN cascade controller had its ANN (multilayer perceptron) trained with the output data of the Fuzzy controller. The topology was empirically chosen by observing the learning time and output error. Therefore, 200 neurons were used on its hidden layer. Moreover, there were used 6000 points from inside the control region. The results of the Fuzzy-ANN controller are shown in Figs. 21-24.

V. DFCM DEVELOPMENT

The structure of the DFCM controller is similar to the developed Fuzzy controller, using same heuristics, e.g., if the output valve (V3, in accordance to Fig. 1) increases its flow, the inlet valves (V1 and V2) increase too. On the other hand, in case volume and weight of the mixture increase, the inlet valves decrease. For example, the relationships W54 and W53, in the DFCM, are similar in effects or control actions of the Fuzzy controller's base rules.

The development of the DFCM is made through three distinct stages. First, the DFCM is developed as structure, concepts and causal relationships, similar to a classic FCM, where concepts and causal relationships are identified through sensors and actuators of the process. The concepts can be variables and/or control actions, as already mentioned.

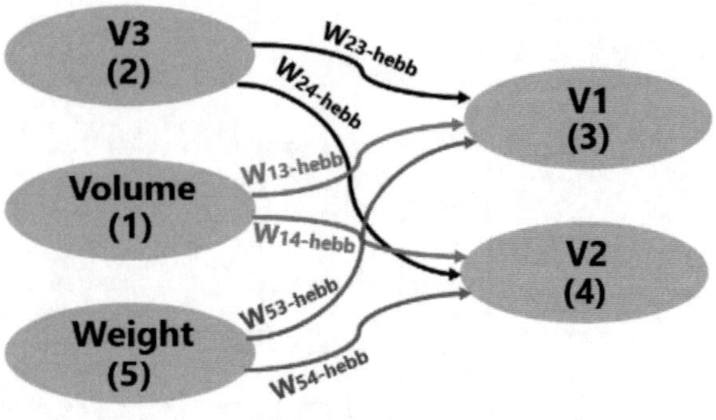

Figure 5. DFCM Controller

The output valve is defined by a positive relationship, i.e., when the campaign increases, the output flow (V3) also increases, similarly, the input valves increase too; moreover, when the mixture volume and weight increase, V1 and V2 decrease. In both cases, the flow of the valves increases or decreases proportionally. The second development stage is the well-known GA [26]. Fig. 5 shows the schematic graph of a DFCM controller.

In this research, the initial values of causal relationships are determined through offline Genetic Algorithms. The GA used is a conventional one, with a population of 30 individuals, simple crossing and approximately 1% of mutation. The chromosomes were generated by real numbers with all the DFCM weights, individuals were random and the initial method of classification was the tournament method with 3 individuals.

Finally, the fitness function, for simplicity, considers the overall error of the two desired outputs with 15 generations of the proposed GA. It stabilizes and reaches the initial solution for the opening of the valves, approximately 44% (V1) and 42% (V2), as shown in Fig. 6. In short, some of the GA parameters used in this work are:

- Recombination method: single-point crossover;
- Mutation method: randomly chosen;
- Selection method: tournament;
- Initial causal relationships: randomly chosen nearby expected values;
- Fitness function $E(i)$, given by (5):

$$Ei=\{0.44-A3k+12+0.42-A4k+12\}0.5 \quad (5)$$

- Probability of recombination: 1;
- Initial population size: 30 chromosomes.

Table I shows the initial values of the DFCM weights. Different proposals and variations of this method applied in tuning FCM can be found [26]. Fig. 6 shows the initial causal relationships' evolution by GA optimizing valve locking.

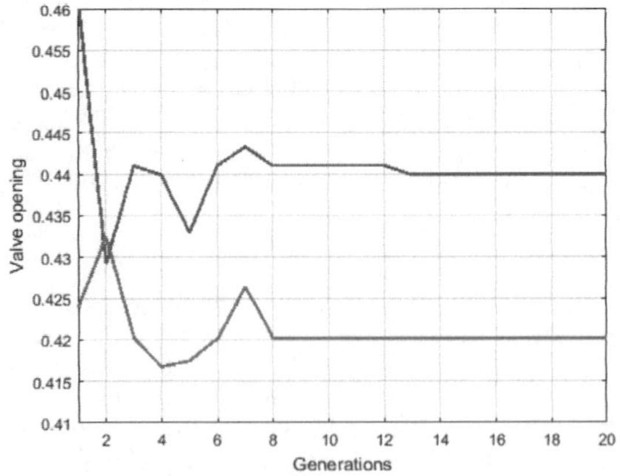

Figure 6. Initial weight's evolution by GA

TABLE I. INITIAL CAUSAL RELATIONSHIP WEIGHTS

W13	*W14*	*W23*	*W24*	*W53*	*W54*
-0.2647	-0.324	-0.2831	-0.3339	0.2648	0.2754

The third stage of the DFCM development concerns the tuning or refinement of the model for dynamic response of the controller. In this case, when a change of output set point in the campaign occurs, the weights of the causal relationships are dynamically tuned. To perform this function, a new kind of concept and relation was included in the cognitive model.

To dynamically adapt the DFCM weights it was used the Hebbian learning algorithm for FCM, which is an adaptation of the classic Hebbian method [10]. Different proposals and variations of this method applied in tuning or in learning for FCM are known in the literature, for example, [28]. In this paper, the method is used to update the intensity of causal relationships in a deterministic way according to the variation or error in the intensity of the concept or input process variable; equations (5) and (6) show this.

Specifically, the application of the Hebbian learning algorithm provides online control actions as follows: if the weight or volume of the liquid mixture increases, the inlet valves have a causal relationship negatively intensified and tend to close quicker. On the other hand, if the volume or weight mixture decreases, the inlet valves have a causal relationship positively intensified. The mathematical equation is presented in (6).

$$W_i(k) = W_{ij}(k-1) \pm \gamma \Delta A_i \quad (6)$$

Where: ΔAi is the concept variation resulting from causal relationship, and it is given by $\Delta Ai = Ai(k) - Ai(k-1)$, γ is the learning rate at iteration k.

This version of the Hebbian algorithm is an evolution of the two proposals of Matsumoto and collaborators [28].

Causal relationships with negative causality have negative sign and similarly to positive causal relationships. The equations applied in this work are adapted of the original version (7).

$$W_i(k) = k_p \,.\, (W_{ij}(k-1) - \gamma \,.\, \Delta A_i) \quad (7)$$

Where: $\gamma=1$ for all, and **kp** is different for every weight pairs. It has their assigned values empirically by observing the dynamics of process performance, recursive method, **kp**=40 for (W14; W23), **kp**=18 for (W13; W24) and kp=2.35 for (W53; W54), with normalized values.

The DFCM inference is like Classic FCM [10], and the inference equations are shown below (equations (8) and (9)).

$$A_i = \int \left(\sum_{\substack{j=1 \\ j \neq i}}^{n} (A_j . W_{ji}) \right) \quad (8)$$

$$f(x) = \frac{1}{1+e^{-\lambda x}} \quad (9)$$

Fig. 7 and Fig. 10 show the results of Hebbian Learning algorithm for DFCM considering the variations ΔAi of the concepts concerning volume, weight, outlet valve state, and the weights of the causal relationships in the process, considering two campaigns. These figures also show the evolution of the weights of the causal relationships during the process within a range of [-1, 1].

These equations combined suggest stability similarly to the work [30], which shows that threshold sigmoid functions have interval previous defined and are continuous differentiable. This observation is attributed to the use of the sigmoid function, which lures the calculated values and causes their convergence to the same specific value [31].

The stability initials analyses and results have been presented by the same authors in [32], this study was done by using an appropriately defined contraction mapping theorem and the non-expansive mapping theorem. In other way, Kosko examined Associative Memories stability by identifying a Lyapunov or energy function with associative memory states [33-34]. The DFCM uses the same equations of FCM, with dynamic tune, thus experimental results show stability.

VI. SIMULATED EXPERIMENTAL RESULTS

The results of DFCM are shown in Figs. 8, 9, 11, and 12, which show the behavior of the controlled variables within the predetermined range of the volume and weight of the mixture.

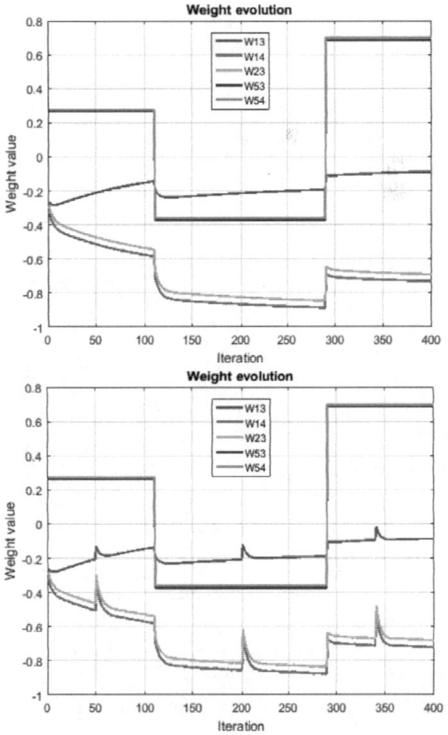

Figure 7. Weight evolution in the Hebbian Learning, 1st campaign without and with disturbances

It is noteworthy that the controller keeps the variables in the control range and pursues a trajectory according to a campaign, where the output flow is also predetermined. In this initial experiment, a campaign with a sequence of values ranging from 7.5 and 11 ml/min can be a set point output flow (outlet valve).

Similarly, the results for the first and second campaigns of the Fuzzy controller are shown in Figs. 13-16. It is observed that: the behaviors of DFCM and Fuzzy controllers were similar when the tank is empty, with a slightly advantage for the Fuzzy controller, which reached the desired result after 230 steps, while the DFCM needed 250 steps with the adaptation off.

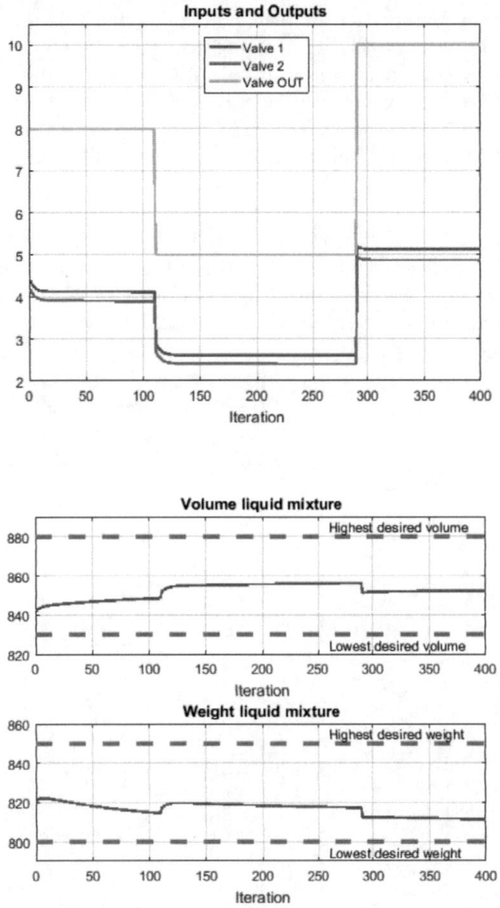

Figure 8. Valves and Results of the DFCM Controller, 1st campaign without disturbances

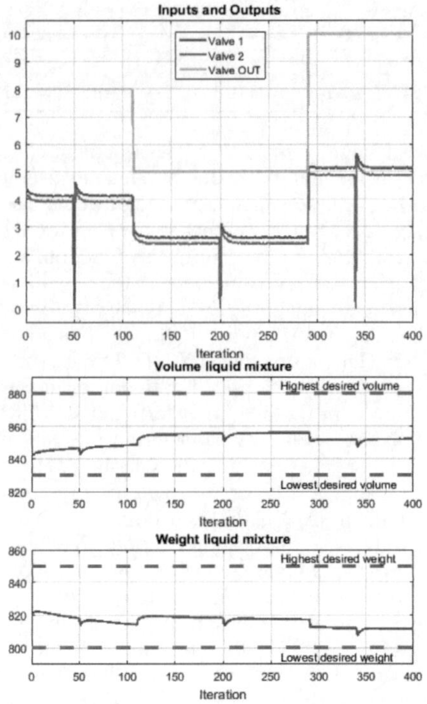

Figure 9. Valves and Results of the DFCM Controller, 1st campaign with disturbances

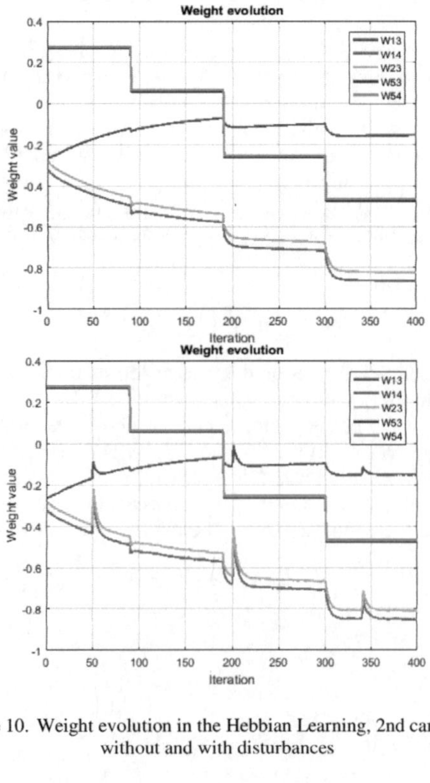

Figure 10. Weight evolution in the Hebbian Learning, 2nd campaign without and with disturbances

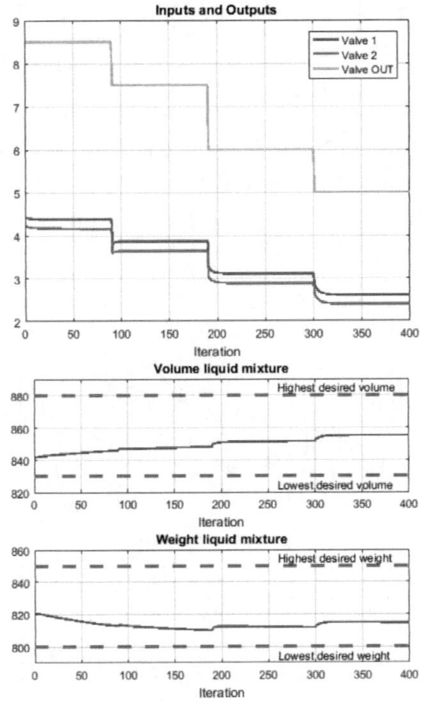

Figure 11. Valves and Results of the DFCM Controller, 2nd campaign without disturbances

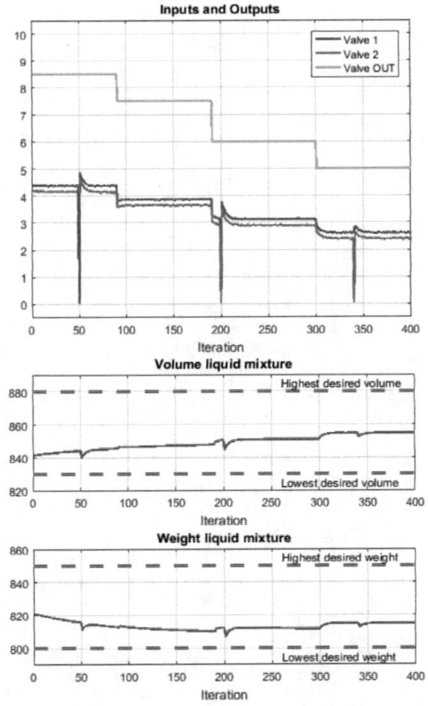

Figure 12. Valves and Results of the DFCM Controller, 2nd campaign with disturbances

Tables II and III show that the simulated numeric results of the DFCM controller had a similar performance compared to the conventional Fuzzy Logic controller, and DFCM embedded in Arduino with small difference under same conditions, with simulated noise and valve locking.

TABLE II. QUANTITATIVE RESULTS WITHOUT DISTURBANCES

	DFCM		*Fuzzy Logic*		*DFCM-Arduino*		*Fuzzy-ANN*	
	Max-min		**Max-min**		**Max-min**		**Max-min**	
Campaign	**1**	**2**	**1**	**2**	**1**	**2**	**1**	**2**
Volume mix (mL)	14.07	13.52	35.55	38.20	24.74	26.11	36.69	38.11
Weight mix (mg)	10.74	10.68	22.87	16.65	9.23	8.66	25.31	25.28

TABLE III. QUANTITATIVE RESULTS WITH DISTURBANCES

	DFCM		*Fuzzy Logic*		*DFCM-Arduino*		*Fuzzy-ANN*	
	Max-min		**Max-min**		**Max-min**		**Max-min**	
Campaign	**1**	**2**	**1**	**2**	**1**	**2**	**1**	**2**
Volume mix (mL)	13.82	14.79	35.51	38.12	24.79	26.05	36.69	38.10
Weight mix (mg)	14.69	14.31	28.02	20.64	13.05	11.49	25.28	25.29

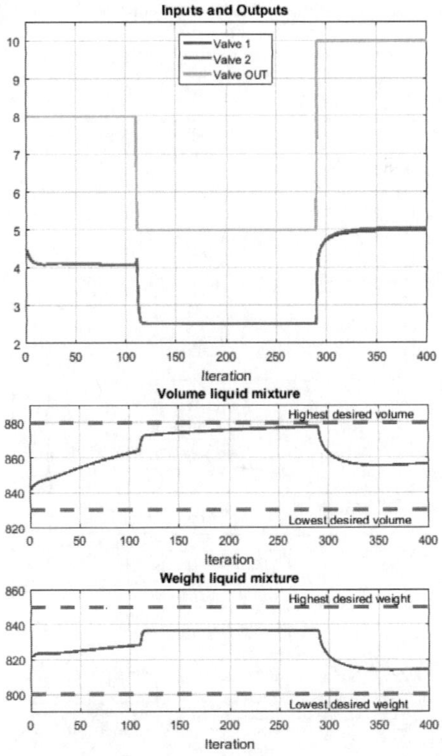

Figure 13. Valves and Results of the Fuzzy Controller, 1st campaign without disturbances

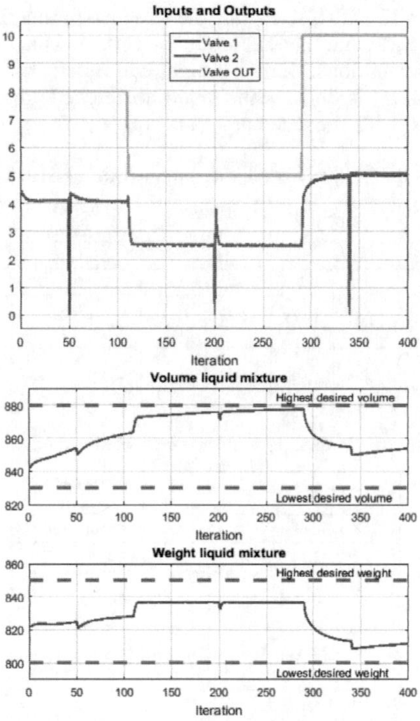

Figure 14. Valves and Results of the Fuzzy Controller, 1st campaign with disturbances

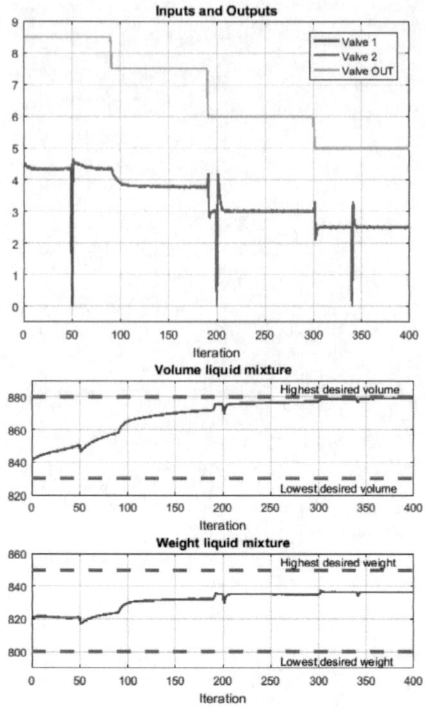

Figure 16. Valves and Results of the Fuzzy Controller, 2nd campaign with disturbances

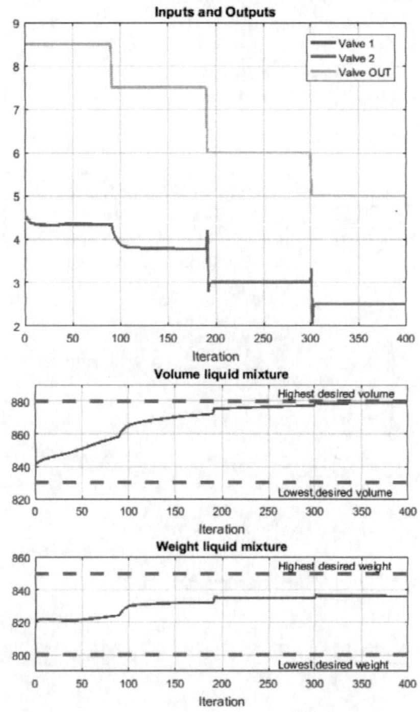

Figure 15. Valves and Results of the Fuzzy Controller, 2nd campaign without disturbances

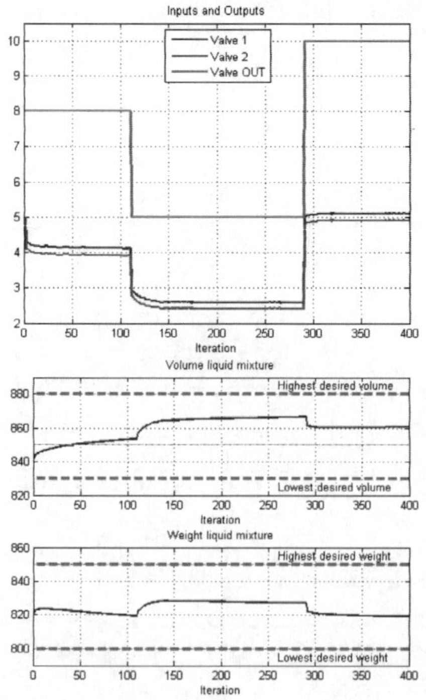

Figure 17. Valves and Results of the Arduino embedded DFCM Controller, 1st campaign without disturbances

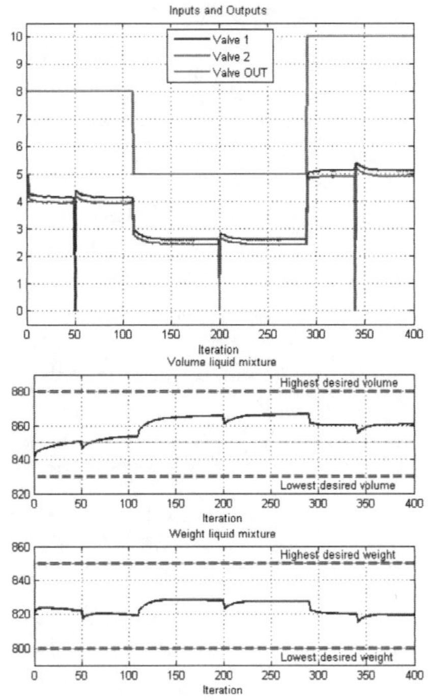

Figure 18. Valves and Results of the Arduino embedded DFCM Controller, 1st campaign with disturbances

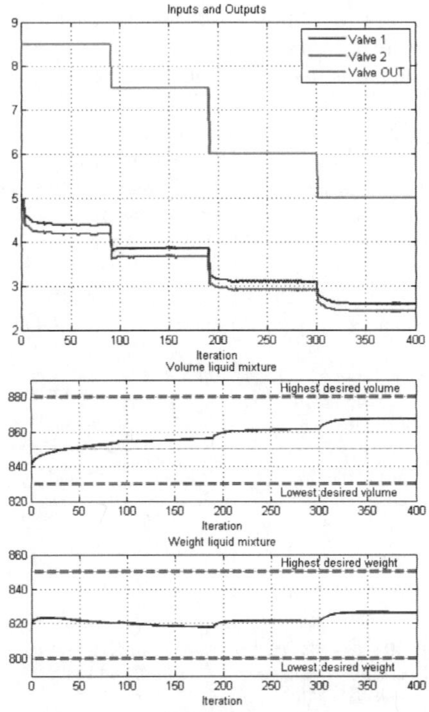

Figure 19. Valves and Results of the Arduino embedded DFCM Controller, 2nd campaign without disturbances

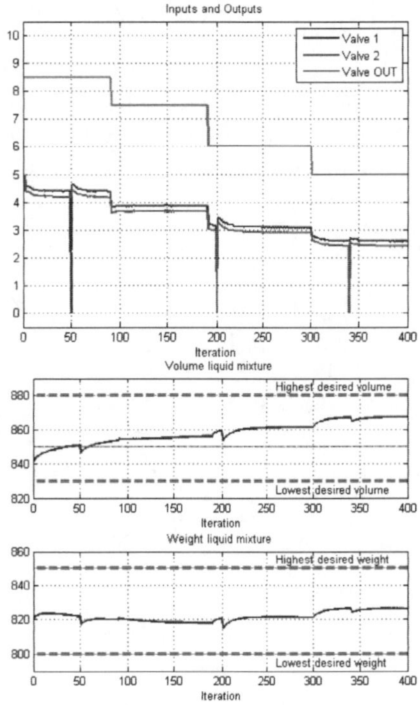

Figure 20. Valves and Results of the Arduino embedded DFCM Controller, 2nd campaign with disturbances

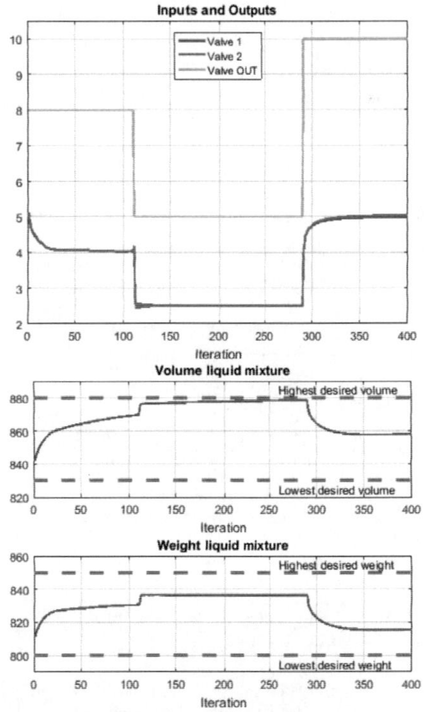

Figure 21. Valves and Results of the Fuzzy-ANN Controller, 1st campaign without disturbances

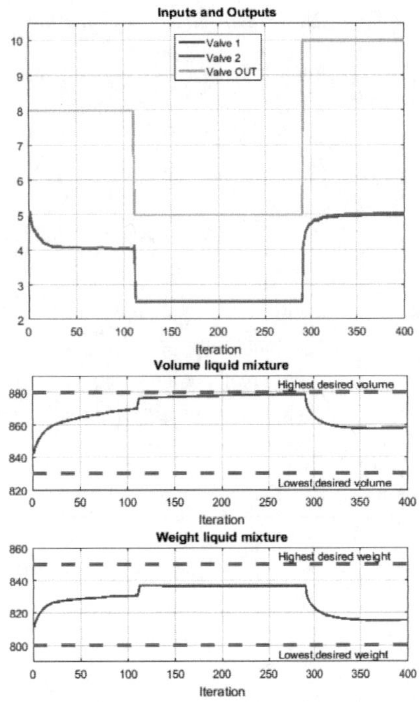

Figure 22. Valves and Results of the Fuzzy-ANN Controller, 1st campaign with disturbances

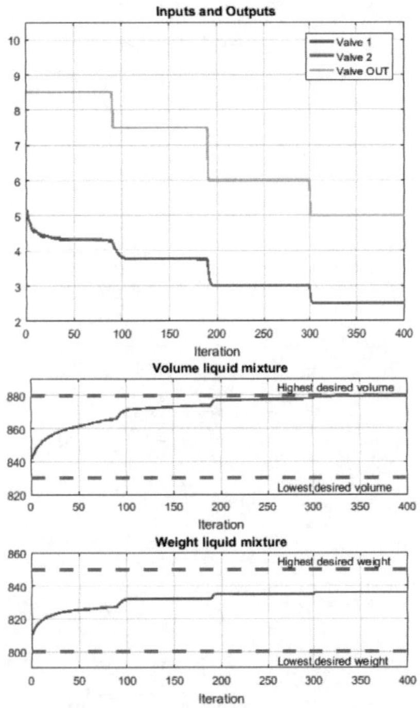

Figure 23. Valves and Results of the Fuzzy-ANN Controller, 2nd campaign without disturbances

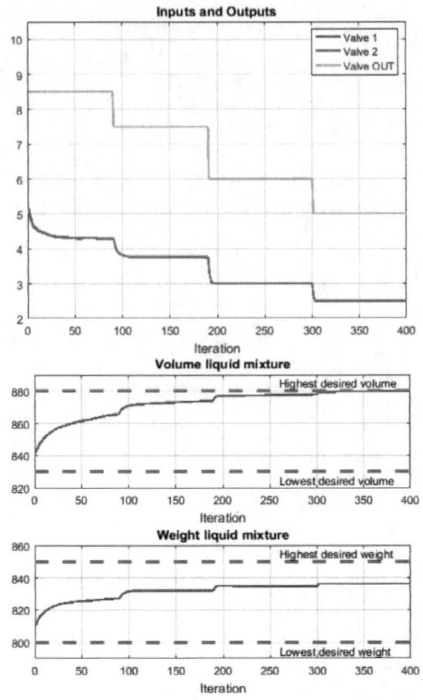

Figure 24. Valves and Results of the Fuzzy-ANN Controller, 2nd campaign with disturbances

In order to extend the applicability of this work, the developed DFCM controller is embedded into an Arduino platform, which ensures the portability of the FCM generated code. Arduino is an open-source electronic prototyping platform. Arduino was chosen because it is a cheap controller, and mainly because of its low processing capacity, to emphasize the low computational complexity of FCM [27].

Matlab, simulating the process, calculates the equations for volume and weight. Through a serial communication established with Arduino, Matlab sends the current values of volume, weight and output valve to Arduino that receives these data, calculates the values of the concept 3 (Valve 1) and concept 4 (Valve 2) and then returns these data to Matlab.

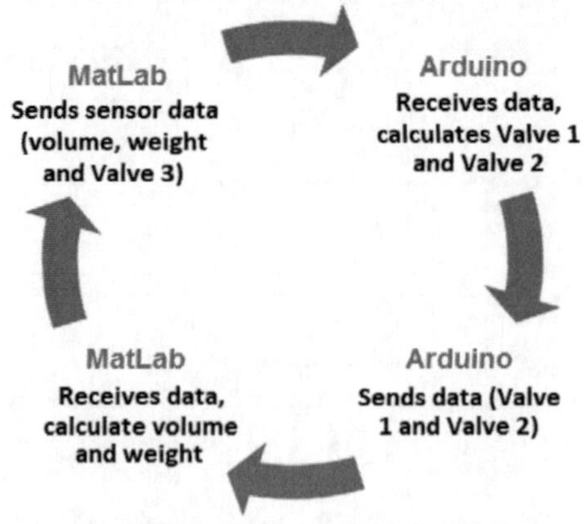

Figure 25. Matlab-Arduino comunication cycle [29]

After that, new values of volume and weight are recalculated. Details on how this technique can be used are presented in Matlab Tutorial, Matlab and Arduino codes, by accessing the link [35]. The cycle of communication between Arduino to Matlab can be checked in Fig. 25.

Figs. 17-20 show the results obtained with the Arduino platform providing data of the actuators, Valve 1 and Valve 2, with Matlab performing data acquisition. The algorithm switches the sets of causal relations that operate similarly to a DFCM simulated with noise and disturb in the Valve 1.

The noise in Figs. 18 and 20 is the sum of the real noise, observed in data transference between Arduino and Matlab, and a simulated white noise. Equation (10) shows the composition of the experiment noise. The Arduino script updates the causal relationships weights every iteration, according to (7). While the MatLab emulates the studied process and plot the results.

$$Noise_{Experiment} = Noise_{Simulated} + Noise_{Arduino-Matlab} \quad (10)$$

Some metrics aspects of the controllers were observed, such as the processing time of the simulations ran on a Intel Core I5™, 6 GB RAM computational base. The results of the Fuzzy logic and DFCM were quite the same, with a small advantage for the DFCM, due to its low computational complexity, as shown in Figs. 17 and 18.

Profile Summary
Generated 12-Sep-2017 20:38:23 using performance time.

Function Name	Calls	Total Time	Self Time*	Total Time Plot (dark band = self time)
dfcm_tanque_revista_icas_c1_comruido	1	4.911 s	1.556 s	
close	1	1.438 s	0.002 s	
close>request_close	1	1.298 s	0.028 s	
legend	2	1.252 s	0.012 s	
legend>make_legend	2	1.238 s	0.032 s	
closereq	3	1.225 s	0.850 s	

Figure 26. DFCM controller performance, 1st campaign with disturbances

Profile Summary
Generated 12-Sep-2017 20:41:09 using performance time.

Function Name	Calls	Total Time	Self Time*	Total Time Plot (dark band = self time)
fuzzy_tanque_revista_icas_c1_comruido	1	5.387 s	1.597 s	
close	1	1.307 s	0.002 s	
close>request_close	1	1.146 s	0.014 s	
closereq	3	1.099 s	0.717 s	

Figure 27. Fuzzy controller performance, 1st campaign with disturbances

In this paper, the DFCM controller is not recursive (that can be seen on equations (7) and (8)), but is compact with just 6 lines of code, as shown in Fig. 28.

The microcontroller chosen for this work was the most basic version of the Arduino software, Arduino UNO R2, with the lowest processing power; it suggests the algorithm has low computational complexity. Future works addresses the quantitative definition of the computational complexity of the algorithm.

```
arduino_final_12_09 §
  W24old=W24;
  W53old=W53;
  W54old=W54;

//*********** DFCM CONTROLLER ***********
        xx = (C1*W13)+(C2*W23)+(C5*W53);
        termo_exp = (1+exp(-xx));
        C3 = 1.0/termo_exp;

        xx = (W14*C1)+(W24*C2)+(C5*W54);
        termo_exp2 = (1+exp(-xx));
        C4 =(1.0/termo_exp2);
//**************************************
  Ve1=C3*10.0; //normalize
  Ve2=C4*10.0;
```

Figure 28. DFCM controller in Arduino IDE

VI. CONCLUSION

The contribution of this study focuses of Fuzzy Cognitive Maps in the embedded control area. In simulated data, the results are similar for the three controllers, with advantage for DFCM with or without Arduino, observed that DFCM controller is adaptive.

Two different campaigns (two different set-point, with and without disturbances) were used to test the algorithms, which, the results obtained from both controllers were quite the same. However, the Fuzzy-ANN did not have any significant improvement, there was a slightly reduction of the noise which can be a major factor on industrial plants.

Thus, one can emphasize the portability and the possibility of developing DFCM controllers on low cost platforms. From the data obtained from Arduino microcontroller, based on the variations of the DFCM embedded in the platform, it is observed that the controlled variables were in well-behaved ranges, which suggests that the DFCM codes have low computational complexity due to the simplicity of its inference mathematical processing. The low computational complexity can be seen through the metrics aspects observed.

Future studies will quantify the computational complexity of the DFCM, for a more general conclusion, and results with a real prototype.

REFERENCES

[1] E. I. Papageorgiou, M. Mendonça, R. V. P. D. Barros, P. P. Soares, L. B. de Souza, "Dynamic Fuzzy Cognitive Maps Embedded and Classical Fuzzy Controllers Applied in Industrial Process," ICAS 2017: The Thirteenth International Conference on Autonomic and Autonomous Systems, vol. 1, pp. 54-59, May 2017.

[2] P. C. Marchal, J. G. García, J. G. Ortega, "Application of Fuzzy Cognitive Maps and Run-to-Run Control to a Decision Support System for Global Set-Point Determination," IEEE Transactions on Systems, Man, and Cybernetics: Systems, vol. PP, no. 99, pp. 1-12, 2017.

[3] M. Mendonça, F. Neves Jr, L. V. R. Arruda, E. I. Papageorgiou, I. R. Chrun, "Embedded Dynamic Fuzzy Cognitive Maps for Controller in Industrial Mixer," 8th International KES Conference on Intelligent Decision Technologies KES-IDT-16, Tenerife. KES-IDT-16, pp. 1-10, 2016.

[4] L. A. Zadeh, "An introduction to Fuzzy logic applications in intelligent systems," Boston: Kluwer Academic Publisher, 1992.

[5] J. A. Fabro, L. V. R Arruda, "Fuzzy-neuro predictive control, tuned by genetic algorithms, applied to a fermentation process," Proceedings of the 2003 IEEE International Symposium on Intelligent Control, Houston, TX, USA, pp. 194-199, 2003.

[6] E. Yesil, T. Kumbasar, O. Karasakal, "Selftuning interval type-2 fuzzy PID controllers based on online rule weighting," 2013 IEEE In-ternational Conference on Fuzzy Systems (FUZZ-IEEE), Hyderabad, pp. 1-6, 2013.

[7] M. Mendonça, B. Angelico, L. V. R. Arruda, F. Neves Jr, "A dynamic fuzzy cognitive map applied to chemical process supervision," Engineering Applications of Artificial Intelligence – Journal – Elsevier, 2012.

[8] W. Stach, L. Kurgan, W. Pedrycz M. Reformat, "Evolutionary Development of Fuzzy Cognitive Maps, The 14th IEEE International Conference on Fuzzy Systems, 2005. FUZZ '05., Reno, NV, pp. 619-624, 2005.

[9] L. V. R. Arruda, M. Mendonca, F. Neves-Jr, I. R. Chrun, E. I. Papageorgiou, "Artificial Life Environment Modeled by Dynamic Fuzzy Cognitive Maps," IEEE Transactions on Cognitive and Developmental Systems, vol. PP, no. 99, pp. 1-1, 2016.

[10] B. Kosko, "Fuzzy cognitive maps," International Journal Man-Machine Studies, vol. 24, no. 1, pp. 65-75, 1986.

[11] R. Taber, " Fuzzy cognitive maps model social systems," AI Expert, 1994.

[12] J. P. Carvalho, J. A. Tome, "Rule based Fuzzy cognitive maps-qualitative systems dynamics," Proceedings 19th International Conference of the North America. Fuzzy Information Fuzzy Processing Society, 2000.

[13] J. P. Carvalho, J. A. Tome, "Rule Based Fuzzy Cognitive Maps in Socio-Economic Systems," European Society for Fuzzy Logic and Technology Conference, 2009.

[14] J. Aguilar, "Dynamic random Fuzzy cognitive maps," Computación y Sistemas, vol. 7, no. 4, 2004.

[15] B. Kosko, "Neural networks and fuzzy systems: a dynamical systems approach to machine intelligence," New York: Prentice Hall, 1992.

[16] K. C. Lee, S. Lee, S., "A cognitive map simulation approach to adjusting the design factors of the electronic commerce web sites," Expert Systems with Applications, vol. 24, no. 1, pp. 1-11, 2003.

[17] M. Mendonça, I. R. Chrun, F. Neves- Jr; L. V. R. Arruda, "A cooperative architecture for swarm robotic based on dynamic fuzzy cognitive maps," Engineering Applications of Artificial Intelligence. vol. 59. pp. 122-132, 2017.

[18] E. I. Papageorgiou, "Fuzzy Cognitive Maps for Applied Sciences and Engineering from Fundamentals to Extensions and Learning Algorithms," Springer, 2013.

[19] Y. Miao, Z. Q. Liu, C. K. Siew, C. Y. Miao, "Dynamical cognitive network - an Extension of fuzzy cognitive," IEEE Trans. on Fuzzy Systems, vol. 9, no. 5, pp. 760-770, 2001.

[20] M. Mendonça, B. Angélico, L. V. R. Arruda, F. Neves-Jr, "A dynamic fuzzy cognitive map applied to chemical process supervision," Engineering Applications of Artificial Intelligence, vol. 26, pp. 1199-1210, 2013.

[21] M. Glykas, "Fuzzy Cognitive Maps: Advances in Theory, Methodologies, Tools and Applications," Springer-Velarg Berlin Heidelberg, 2010.

[22] C. D. Stylios, P. P. Groumpos, V. C. Georgopoulos, "An Fuzzy Cognitive Maps Approach to Process Control Systems," J. Advanced Computational Intelligence, no. 5, pp. 1-9, 1999.

[23] E. I. Papageorgiou, K. E. Parsopoulos, C. S. Stylios, P. P. Groumpos, M. N. Vrahatis, "Fuzzy cognitive maps learning using Particle Swarm Optimization," Journal of Intelligent Information Systems, vol. 25, pp. 95–121, 2005.

[24] T. J. Ross, "Fuzzy logic, with Engineering Aplications," 2nd Ed., England, John Whiley & Sons, 2004.

[25] S. S. Farinwata, D. Filev, R. Langari(editors), "Fuzzy Control, Synthesis and Analysis," West Sussex, England, John Wiley & Sons, 2000.

[26] D. E. Goldberg, "Genetic algorithms in search optimization and machine learning," Mass: Addison-Wesley, 1989.

[27] E. I. Papageorgiou, "Learning Algorithms for Fuzzy Cognitive Maps," IEEE Transactions on Systems and Cybernetics. Part C: Applications and Reviews, vol. 42, pp. 150-163, 2012.

[28] Y. Miao, Z. Q. Liu, C. K. Siew, C. Y. Miao, "Transformation of cognitive maps," IEEE Transactions on Fuzzy Systems, vol. 18, no. 1, pp. 114-124, 2010.

[29] D. E. Matsumoto, M. Mendonça, L. V. R. Arruda, E. I. Papageorgiou, "Embedded Dynamic fuzzy cognitive maps applied to the control of industrial mixer," Brazilian Symposium on Intelligent Automation – XI SBAI. 2013.

[30] Y. Boutalis, T. L. Kottas, M. Christodoulou, "Adaptive Estimation of Fuzzy Cognitive Maps With Proven Stability and Parameter Convergence," IEEE Transactions on Fuzzy Systems, vol. 17, no. 4, pp. 874-889, Aug. 2009.

[31] V. Eleni, G. Petros, "New concerns on fuzzy cognitive maps equation and sigmoid function," 2017 25th Mediterranean Conference on Control and Automation (MED), Valletta, pp. 1113-1118, 2017.

[32] Y. Boutalis, T. L. Kottas, M. Christodoulou, "On the existence and uniqueness of solutions for the concept values in Fuzzy Cognitive Maps," 2008 47th IEEE Conference on Decision and Control, Cancun, pp. 98-104, 2008.

[33] B. Kosko, "Bidirectional associative memories," IEEE Transactions on Systems, Man, and Cybernetics, vol. 18, no. 1, pp. 49-60, Jan./Feb. 1988.

[34] A. S. Martchenko, I. L. Ermolov, P. P. Groumpos, J. V. Poduraev, C. D. Stylios, "Investigating Stability Analysis Issues for Fuzzy Cognitive Maps," 11th Mediterranean Conference on Control and Automation - MED'03, 2003.

[35] <https://www.dropbox.com/s/2sn76n64n48qgp3/Tutorial%20Arduino%20Matlab%20in%20English.pdf?dl=0> Last access date: 17/12/2017.

Improved Distribution of Locally Sourced Energy in Smart Grids During Brownouts and in Times of Energy Scarcity

Rolf Egert, Florian Volk, Jörg Daubert, Max Mühlhäuser,
Telecooperation Lab
Technische Universität Darmstadt,
Email: {egert,volk,daubert,max}@tk.tu-darmstadt.de

Abstract—**Brown-out situations are cases of electricity distribution in which demand exceeds production and transportation capabilities. In contrast to black-outs, energy is available to some extent, but not enough to meet the demand of all consumers. Traditionally, centrally organized power grids with large production capabilities on the one end of the distribution grid and only consumers on the other end are struggling to cope with brown-out situations. In order to achieve a somewhat fair distribution of the available energy, street busses are supplied in a round-robin-like distribution scheme. For that, some streets busses are supplied with energy, while others encounter local black-outs. Due to the round-robin-like scheme, all consumers receive some energy eventually. Modern, ICT-enhanced "smart grids", which also include small and local production capabilities (often-times renewable energy sources like photovoltaic) provide new means of addressing brown-outs. In this paper, we evolve the current round-robin-like scheme further to take the properties of smart grids into account. This affects the fairness of energy distribution, but—in total—increases the amount of supplied consumers. Extensive simulations that are based on real-world street busses of the German electrical grid are conducted. These simulations are conducted with our smart grid simulation tool HOLEG and they indicate improved supply rates during brown-outs, even in the presence of volatile local energy production. We extend our model to a hierarchical scheme, spanning from the distribution grid down to household items, for which we imagine fine-grained control capabilities in the future smart grid.**

Keywords–Smart Grid;Micro Gird; Demand and Response; Fairness; Electrical Grid; Optimization.

I. Introduction

This work is an extension of the authors previous work, *Mitigating Brown-Outs: Fair Distribution of Locally Sourced Energy in Smart Grids* [1].

The current electrical grid is already undergoing a change, which will accelerate even more in the future. Nowadays, the production architecture is based on large nuclear- and fossil-fuelled producers, which are located centrally in the grid. This concept will turn into an architecture that uses *local and distributed* energy resources (DER) in addition to a reduced number of central producers. DERs are based on renewable energy sources, amongst those, the most established ones are solar- and wind-energy. However, this increasing amount of DERs in the electricity production introduces several new problems for the electrical grid. For instance, the flow of electricity can become bidirectional, if the production of the DERs is high [2], which can cause problems in the network infrastructure. Furthermore, in contrast to the fossil-fuelled producers, the production of DERs is dependent on environmental circumstances like the wind and weather conditions. This connection renders the electricity production of the DERs highly fluctuating and thus, difficult to plan for [3]. This unpredictable behaviour in combination with the increased number of producers and consumers that take part in the network, makes it impossible for human operators to control the future grid. Therefore, the establishment of an information and communication infrastructure (ICT) that provides monitoring and control capabilities becomes mandatory. If such a system is integrated into the electrical grid, the concept of a smart grid (SG) emerges.

A big step into the direction of increasing the share of renewable resources in the production of electricity was conducted recently in Germany. There, the *Renewable Energy Sources Act* (EEG) [4] was passed. This act states that, until the year 2025, Germany must generate 40%-45% of the electricity demand by renewable energy sources like solar panels, wind turbines and biomass power plants.

These changes, which the electrical grid is facing in terms of infrastructure, do not fit to the rules and network policies for maintaining controlled operation that are currently in use. A response to these changes, by adapting and establishing new policies and rules according to the new situation, is necessary.

A subproblem concerning the outdated rules and policies, and the main focus of this work, is the demand and response (D&R) behaviour of the electrical grid in brown-out scenarios. An energy grid enters a brown-out state if the production capabilities do not suffice to supply the demand of all consumers in the network. This also holds for the black-out scenario; however, the complete absence of electricity introduces additional difficulties, like frequency synchronization. The black-out state is a problem that needs to be addressed separately and is not part of this work.

The German state of the art procedure to cope with the problem of D&R in a brown-out scenario works as follows: If a brown-out state has been entered and cannot be solved by backup power plants or other emergency electricity sources, the network is logically divided into (preferred equally consuming) subnets. Each of these subnets has to be separable and reconnectible to the grid, such that these are allowed to either consume electricity or not. Subsequently, one after another of these subnets is separated from the grid in a round-robin like manner. After each separation of a subnet, the current network stability is measured. If the network has stabilized, the currently active consumers will be supplied for a certain amount of time and a plan is generated that schedules the connected and disconnected time intervals for all subnets in the network. In case the network does not stabilize, additional subnets are disconnected until a demand and supply equilibrium is reached. The round-robin approach guarantees fairness in the brown-out-scenario. This is done by only allowing to disconnect the same subnet for a second time, after all other subnets have been disconnected at least once. In the very end, this method guarantees that each subnet is supplied, as well as disconnected for the same amount of time. Note that the very last round of the disconnection process (which is the round directly before the brown-out situation is resolved) might change the equality of supplied time for the latest supplied groups. However, this will be taken into account in case of further brown-out cases, such that consumers with lower supplied time during the last incident will be preferred next time.

However, the procedure has one major flaw that renders it not suitable for the future changes in the electrical grid. The currently used method does not take the production capabilities of the subnets into account, but enforces equal supplied times for each consumer by deactivating the subnets in a round-robin based manner. However, this also means that the production capabilities, in terms of DERs, which are located in these subnets are deactivated and can therefore not contribute to mitigate problems in the brown-out state. Therefore, this attempt might even promote further destabilization of the network if the prosumers are capable of producing high amounts of electricity, but are simply dismissed by disconnecting them from the grid. To face these challenges of the future energy grid it is important to develop new rules and policies that adapt to the necessities of these future changes. Additionally, with the introduction of ICT and DERs, novel algorithms need to be developed for controlling the new electrical infrastructure and providing fair electricity distribution.

This work is an extension of our previous work [1]. We extend this work in Section III, where a formal model for representing grid levels in an undersupplied state is introduced and a novel fairness metric is described. This model is extended to recursively represent all abstraction levels from micro grids down to individual components in each single house. However, there is no general definition of fairness. As of this, our fairness definition focuses on the following two optimization goals: on the one hand, to provide equal supplied times for all consumers and, on the other hand, to maximize the number of supplied subnets in the grid. Additionally, a time-discrete simulation environment for modelling and testing simplified smart grids (HOLEG) is introduced in Section V. Moreover, HOLEG is used in Section VI to conduct the simulation of an exemplary electrical test network and to evaluate the modelled network. As a use case, a recursively defined model of an low-voltage electrical distribution network is implemented in the HOLEG simulation environment. To be more precise, without loss of generality, each modelled abstraction level encompasses five prosumers from the next lower recursive level. In this work, all four introduced levels are modelled using real measurement data for the consumption and production behaviour of the prosumers. Additionally, the network is only provided with a limited amount of electricity to represent a brown-out scenario.

The remainder of this work is organized as follows. In Section II, an overview over scenarios in the domain of the electrical grid is provided, where fairness is an important goal. In Section IV, fair electricity distribution algorithms are presented. Followed by the paper conclusion of this work in Section VII.

II. Related Work

Fairness is a term discussed in many fields, most prominently in economics [5] and psychology [6]. However, fairness also became an important criterion in application of information technology [7] and especially in the area of scheduling algorithms [8] and resource allocation [9]. In this Section, a selection of work is presented that is concerned with the definitions and fields of application in the SG scenario. One of the most popular fields for applying fairness in the domain of SGs is the area of dynamic demand and response, where demand is dynamically adapted according to different strategies or algorithms to reach certain optimization goals. The approach of [10] uses a daily consumption schedule for the consumers in the network. The loads in this schedule are divided into two categories, namely fixed- and flexible-loads, where the latter can be moved within the schedule. In this work, consumers try to reduce their electricity bill by scheduling their flexible loads in such a way that the overall production cost for energy in the network is reduced. Hereby, fairness is achieved by charging users for electricity based on their contribution to minimize the production costs in the network. In [11], dynamic demand and response management is discussed in the environment of smart objects that can be activated and deactivated dynamically. In this scenario, fairness is introduced by using different scheduling approaches like round-robin or by assigning priorities for scheduling algorithms. The authors of [12] discuss fairness in the sense of a trade-off between the maximization of a consumers utility function (level of satisfaction dependant on the electricity consumption) and the minimization of production costs imposed to the energy provider. Another approach that defines the fairness of an algorithm as a matter of consumer satisfaction is presented in [13]. Hereby, the difference in starting time of so-called *soft loads* is used as a metric. A slightly different fairness notion is used by the authors of [14]; they present a day-ahead energy resource scheduling algorithm using DERs and Vehicle-to-Grid (V2G). To prevent unnecessary battery deterioration of the vehicles, the authors establish pricing levels, which are dependent on the power level of the batteries, to establish a fair remuneration scheme.

Another field of application is the planning of SG communication networks. The authors of [15] use equal quality of service as a fairness metric in their approach of planning wireless mesh neighbourhood area networks (NANs). They discuss fair placement of gateways to ensure an equal number of participants to be covered by each gateway.

Although there is a lot of ongoing work that uses fairness metrics in the SG scenario, the considered scenarios are mainly based on cases of normal operation. In contrast, this work considers the state of the art fairness metric and presents its drawbacks in the SG domain. Moreover, the presented algorithm aims to maximize the use of DERs, while simultaneously maintaining fairness of electricity distribution among consumers.

III. Recursive System Model Definition

In this section, the extended model that is used for the conducted simulations is described in detail. First, the four different recursive levels, *Micro-Grid, Street, House* and *In-House* are introduced. Recursive in this sense means that starting from the *Micro-Grid* level, each lower level is part of the previous one (e.g., each micro grid can contain an arbitrary number of streets). Figure 1 shows an overview of the general recursive structure of the system model. For all levels, a general description is provided. Second, a formal definition of the model constraints and assumptions is given. Finally, the section concludes with the presentation of the fairness notion used in this work.

A. Micro-Grid Level

The first level is the *Micro-Grid level*, which is concerned with individual micro grids that are inter-connected via the transmission grid. In this work, the micro grids are considered to encompass residential areas. Those can be, for instance, larger residential areas in cities that have a connection via an adjustable transformer to the transmission grid. This transformer is responsible for managing the incoming electricity from the transmission grid as well as the outgoing electricity provided by the micro grids. Moreover, the transformer has the ability to connect or separate each individual micro grid from the transmission grid, and thus, control consumption and production behaviour by allowing or declining participation in the electricity distribution. More formally, the micro grid level can be defined as a set of micro grids $MG = \{mg_0, \ldots, mg_n\}, n \in \mathbb{N}$

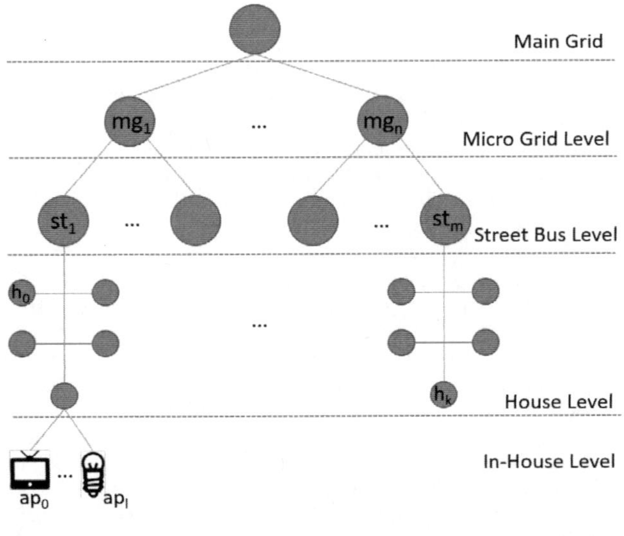

Figure 1. General structure of the model and the individual recursive levels

Each micro grid mg_i has an overall consumption and production. Those values are measured at the transformer that connects the micro grids to the transmission grid. The overall consumption is, in general, the overall sum of all the loads provided by the consumers located in the micro grids and similarly the overall production represents the sum of the production of all producers in the micro grid. Note that all elements in this model are prosumers, which can switch between being a consumer or a producer at different points in time. A producer or a consumer at this abstraction level is represented as a street bus and is explained in the following in more detail.

B. Street Bus Level

The street bus level represents the second abstraction level in our model and can be represented as a set of street busses $ST = \{st_0, \ldots, st_m\}, m \in \mathbb{N}$. The set ST represents the street busses that are connected via an adjustable transformer to form a micro grid mg. Each individual street bus again has an overall consumption and production that is defined as the sum of all loads or production capabilities of the houses that are located in the street busses. The adjustable transformer allows to measure the ingoing and outgoing electricity of the individual busses and, additionally, can disconnect and connect busses to control their participation in electricity distribution.

C. House Level

The third abstraction level is described as the house level. On this level, it is assumed that novel technology like Smart Meter Gateways introduce the capabilities to control individual houses, which are connected to the distribution grid. Let H be a set of houses $H = \{h_0, \ldots, h_k\}, k \in \mathbb{N}$ that are contained in a single street bus st. The overall load and production of a house h is the sum of all loads and producers that are located in the house. For instance, loads can be devices like fridges and TVs and producers can be locally installed solar panels. Each individual house, again, can be connected and disconnected to control it's participation in the electrical grid.

D. In-House Level

The last abstraction level is concerned with the distribution of electricity to prosumers that are encompassed in a house level prosumer. For instance, this can be all prosumers in a normal house in a city or all the prosumers contained in a building of a factory. Let AP be a set of *atomic* prosumers $AP = \{ap_0, \ldots, ap_l\}, l \in \mathbb{N}$, where *atomic* indicates that these producers can not be further divided into lower level prosumers. It is assumed that the Smart Meter Gateway allows a user to connect and disconnect prosumers to supply them with electricity. Note that this domain is currently significantly different from the previous abstraction levels, because the responsibility of the domain belongs to the house owner and not to the electricity provider. A user would have to adapt to the changes that happen on previous abstraction levels to contribute in the mitigation of system problems. The reason for this is that the energy providers are not allowed, or can not influence what a user is doing in his environment and they are not permitted to control the consumption or production behaviour of any components in the house from the outside.

E. Model Constraints and Assumptions

In this section, the constraints and assumptions that are required to define the recursive model used in this work are presented in more detail. First, information about the modelled prosumers as well as load and production calculation over time is provided. Second, the a formal definition of a brown-out state is presented. Finally, the novel fairness notion is introduced.

Let $cons(\cdot, \cdot)$ and $prod(\cdot, \cdot)$ be functions that take as an input a prosumer $x \in Y$ and a timestep t, where $Y \in \{MG, ST, H, AP\}$ and t is taken from the interval $[0, \ldots, T-1]$. The output of $cons(x, t)$ returns the overall load of the prosumer x at the point in time t and the output of $prod(x, t)$ is the overall production. As long as the prosumer is not an *atomic* prosumer, the functions recursively sum up the production or consumption of the next lower recursive level. Without loss of generality it will be assumed for the remainder of the paper that the granularity of the time interval is based on the hours of the day, such that $T = 24$. Any other time interval would be suitable too; especially smaller ones, when taking into account the volatile nature of SGs that include renewable energy sources like photovoltaic and wind power. More formally, those functions are described as follows:

$$prod(x,t) := \begin{cases} \sum_{j=0}^{n} \int_{t}^{t+1} prod(y,t)\mathrm{d}t & if x \notin AP \\ \int_{t}^{t+1} prod(x,t)\mathrm{d}t & else \end{cases} \quad (1)$$

$$cons(x,t) := \begin{cases} \sum_{j=0}^{n} \int_{t}^{t+1} cons(y,t)\mathrm{d}t & if x \notin AP \\ \int_{t}^{t+1} cons(x,t)\mathrm{d}t & else \end{cases} \quad (2)$$

Where n is the number of prosumers y of the next recursive level that are contained in x. Note that these functions are recursively defined to calculate their output based on the result of the next recursive level. The recursive process stops at the in-house level, where the prosumers are *atomic* and the production or consumption of an prosumer can not be based on another recursive sum, but is directly represented as the measured amount of produced or consumed electricity in this timestep.

At every point in time t in a day, a prosumer can be either a consumer or a producer. Let all consumers be represented as a set C and the producers likewise as a set P. A prosumer x is a consumer $x \in C$, if its consumption of electricity is higher than the production provided by its next recursive level prosumers. Whereas, a prosumer is a producer $x \in P$ if the electricity provided by its next recursive level prosumers exceeds the local consumption. A more formal representation of these relations can be expressed as follows:

$$\forall x \in Y \ \{x \in C \mid cons(x,t) > prod(x,t)\} \quad (3)$$

$$\forall x \in Y \ \{x \in P \mid cons(x,t) \leq prod(x,t) \quad (4)$$

Where $Y \in \{MG, ST, H, AP\}$ defines the recursive level for the calculation of production and consumption. Note that this assignment to a set of producers and consumers is used later in the fairness notion used for the conducted simulations.

In the following, a formal definition for an undersupplied state (brown-out) is provided. At each point in time, a prosumer can either be a consumer or a producer. In case it is part of the set of consumers, it requires more energy than it produces itself; and thus, it needs additional electricity delivered by the previous recursive level. Note that in this work the recursive model starts with micro grids as the first level that is connected to the transmission grid via an adjustable transformer. For the micro grid level the preceding level is simply referred to as the *main grid*. In the case that a prosumer is part of the producer set, the prosumer provides energy to its preceding level.

The general electrical supply situation is considered to represent a brown-out scenario. In this scenario it is assumed that the grid is not able to provide enough electricity to fully supply all prosumers that are connected to the transmission grid simultaneously. Moreover, the electrical grid is in a brown-out state, if a single point in time during the day exists, where the electricity provided by the grid is not sufficient to cover the overall demand of the grid at the same time.

The formal definition of a brown-out state is as follows:

$$\exists t \, 0 \leq t < T \, prod_{Main}(t) < \sum_{i=0}^{n} cons(x,t) \quad (5)$$

Where $prod_{Main}(t)$ represents the amount of electricity the main grid can provide for supplying the prosumers located in the microgrids. Additionally, it is necessary to distinguish the brown-out scenario from the black-out scenario. In contrast to the brown-out state, where the grid is partially supplied, none of the elements of the grid is supplied in a black-out scenario. Without loss of generality, this work focuses on an undersupplied state that is critical (brown-out), but not fatal (black-out) for the grid. In particular, this means that the amount of energy provided by the main grid should at least cover the demand of some of the prosumers located in grid. The assumption for the minimal amount of supply provided by the main grid is that the amount needs to be sufficient to cover the demand of the largest prosumer in the network. A formal definition can be as follows:

$$\forall t \, 0 \leq t < T \ prod_{Main}(t) \geq \max\{cons(x,t) | x \in C\} \quad (6)$$

This definition guarantees that, for each point in time, the main grid provides enough energy to supply a single prosumer in the grid. Without this assumption we may have situations where the electricity is not enough to supply a single prosumer. However, this represents a black-out-state in our model, and is not part of the current work. In addition to the electricity that is provided by the main grid to supply the micro grids, the prosumers in the model may be producers and provide additional electricity for the grid. Note that a prosumer is a producer, if it generates more electricity than it consumes. This can happen if, for instance, a part of the grid contains a high number of DERs like solar panels, wind turbines and similar, as well as batteries and alike. Thereby, solar panels and wind turbines are inherently volatile in availability and power output, while the availability of batteries and other energy storage systems is much easier to plan. In this paper, without loss of generality, we simulate local energy production with solar panels. If a prosumer at any of the recursive levels of the model is supplied, it's DERs are active and contribute to the amount of electricity in the grid. However, if a prosumer is not supplied, the corresponding DERs are deactivated and neither produce nor consume electricity. To successfully supply a prosumer x at time t it is sufficient to provide the amount of electricity, such that the sum of the production of the local DERs in addition to the electricity provided by the main grid equals the consumption of the prosumer. A more formal definition can be as follows:

$$cons(x,t) \leq prod_{Main}(t) + prod(x,t) \quad (7)$$

The function $prod_{Main}(t)$ hereby represents the amount of energy that is centrally provided by the main grid. Changes of state, like from being supplied to being unsupplied or changing from being a consumer to being a producer, can be performed instantly in the digital representation of a system. However, the physical system consists of electrical and mechanical components that have time constraints for changing their state (e.g., electrical switches). To consider these constraints in the discrete simulation model, it is assumed that after a change of status has happened, this new status is kept for one timestep.

To evaluate the fairness in the described model, in the following a new fairness notion is proposed. The currently used metric, which is based on equal supplied time, is not optimal anymore in the presence of future technological changes in the domain of the electricity grid. The transition from centralized to distributed production changes the way how the presence of prosumers influences the performance of the network. However, DERs can only contribute to the system if the corresponding prosumer (e.g., the street where solar panels are connected to the grid), where they are located, is connected to the network. One part of the novel fairness notion is based on the assumption that strategies, which maximize the use of DERs, are able to supply more prosumers than other strategies. To represent this in the fairness notion, the average number of supplied prosumers is used as a parameter. This also includes those prosumers that act as producers at specific points in time due to high electricity production by DERs. In particular, prosumers that are able to sustain themselves are considered to be supplied, even if they supplied themselves and are not depending on external electricity. Furthermore, to include the fairness of handling the consumers, the sum of differences between the supplied time of all consumers is calculated. Therefore, the fairness assumption extended in this metric is again based on the equality of overall supplied time of all consumers. If an algorithm can supply a large number of prosumers, while minimizing the differences in the number of timesteps, in which consumers are supplied, the fairness metric is maximized. To achieve maximum performance of the DERs, prosumers that are producers are not taken into account in the supplied time difference calculation. This is due to the benefit the network gets in terms of produced surplus electricity; and thus, producers are allowed to stay connected. A more formal description of the fairness metric is as follows:

$$\forall i,j \in C \;\; f = \max \frac{\mathit{avg\#ofsuppliedprosumers}}{1 + \sum_{i,j \in C} |t_{sup,i} - t_{sup,j}|} \tag{8}$$

where $t_{sup,i}$ represents the number of supplied timesteps for consumer $i \in C$.

IV. Description of (Fair) Algorithms

In this section, several algorithms that aim to solve the resource allocation problem for the undersupplied state scenario, are presented. First, a slightly adapted version of the round-robin based approach, which is used in the German electrical grid, is introduced. Second, an iterative algorithm, which does not aim to provide equal supplied times for the prosumers, but indirectly prefers small consumers, is described. Finally, an algorithm that aims to maximize the use of DERs and, additionally, equalises the number of supplied time for each prosumer, is presented.

A. TRR - Traditional Round-Robin

This algorithm is a slightly extended version of the mechanism currently used in the German electrical grid. The Traditional Round-Robin algorithm, which is shown in Figure 2

```
procedure TRR(production, timestep, prosumers)
    for i ← prosumers.length() do
        prosumer ← getLowestUptime(prosumers);
        if prosumer == null then
            break;
        else
            if isSupplyable(prosumer) then
                markAsActive(prosumer);
            end if
        end if
    end for
     return activeProsumers;
end procedure
```

Figure 2. TRR - Traditional Round-Robin.

works in a round-robin based manner and solves the problem of fair supply distribution as follows. The algorithm uses a list of prosumers and the information about the amount of production that is centrally provided by the main grid or the previous recursive level, to determine a subset of supplyable prosumers for the current timestep. Since the algorithm uses a round-robin approach, it is not allowed to activate a specific prosumers for a second time before all other prosumers have been activated at least once. With this design it is ensured that each prosumer stays active and inactive for an equal amount of time. An additional important remark is that this algorithm does not take the surplus electricity, which is provided by local DERs, and its influence on the network into account. To make this approach comparable with the other algorithms presented in this work, the round-robin approach was extended such that surplus electricity production provided by prosumers can be leveraged to supply additional prosumers in the network. Note that the in the currently deployed electrical grid the applicability of the traditional round-robin approach is limited to the second abstraction level (street bus level) using a adjustable transformer. However, it is assumed that with further technical progress this approach will be applicable to the lower abstraction levels as well.

B. IIA - Improved Iterative Approach

The Improved Iterative Approach (IAA), which is shown in Figure 3, iteratively selects prosumers from its list and tries to supply them. In contrast to the original version of TRR (Figure 2) it takes the production of the DERs located in the prosumers and uses it for current production calculations. The algorithm provides a very rudimentary kind of fairness by indirectly favouring producers and consumers with a very low demand. The algorithm works as follows: first, if there still remains unused capacity, iteratively choose a prosumer from the list of prosumers and check if the required demand can be met. If this is the case, then activate the prosumer and add the resulting production capabilities of its DERs to the overall production. If the selected prosumer cannot be supplied in this timestep mark it as unfit. After the algorithm terminates, it returns a list of all prosumers that will stay active in this timestep and all remaining prosumers will be deactivated.

C. UEA - Uptime Equalizing Algorithm

The Uptime Equalizing Algorithm (UEA), which is shown in Figure 4 aims to maximize the use of DERs while maintain-

```
procedure IIA(production, timestep, prosumers)
    while consumption < production do
        prosumer ← getNextProsumer(prosumers);
        if supplyable(prosumer) then
            markAsActive(prosumer);
            production += prosumer.getProduction();
        else
            markUnfit(prosumer);
            if AllProsumersProcessed then
                return activeProsumers;
            end if
        end if
    end while
end procedure
```

Figure 3. IIA - Improved Iterative Algorithm.

```
procedure UEA(production, timestep, prosumers)
    while consumption < production do
        for all prosumer ∈ prosumers do
            if isSelfSustaining(prosumer) then
                markAsActive(prosumer);
                production += prosumer.getProduction();
            end if
        end for
        prosumer ← getMinUptimeProsumer(prosumers);
        if supplyable(prosumer) then
            markAsActive(prosumer);
        else
            markUnfit(prosumer);
        end if
        if AllProsumersProcessed then
            return activeProsumers
        end if
    end while
end procedure
```

Figure 4. UEA - Uptime Equalizing Algorithm.

ing equal supplied times for the prosumers. To achieve this, the algorithm distinguishes in a first step between consumers and producers. To make this distinction the algorithm uses the definition provided in Section III-E. Second, all producers are activated and their local production capabilities are added to the overall electricity provided by the previous level or the main grid. This is possible, since the definition of the brown-out-scenario states that there is enough centrally produced electricity to supply least a single individual prosumer. After the activation of the prosumer, the local DERs are providing enough energy to fully cover the local demand and thus make the prosumer self-sustaining. After all the producers are activated, the algorithm chooses a prosumer that is currently inactive and has a minimal amount of supplied time. In the next step, the algorithm checks if the selected prosumer can be supplied using the currently available production. If this is the case, the prosumer is activated, otherwise it is marked as unfit. After all prosumers are supplied or marked as unfit, the algorithm returns a list of prosumers that will stay active during this timestep and all remaining ones will be deactivated.

V. Simulation Environment for Algorithm Development and Evaluation

Testing of novel algorithms is a mandatory task to ensure correct functionality; however, it is also task not easily done in the domain of electricity distribution. Due to the necessity of continuous operation, testing can not be done on the currently deployed electrical grid. Another possibility for conducting tests is the construction of physical testbeds that represent a part of the grid. However, those testbeds can become expensive quite fast and, additionally, only cover a part of the overall grid, which may neglect cascading effects. A more suitable strategy for testing novel approaches is modelling and simulating the environment in a digital manner.

In this section, a simulation environment for energy grids based on a holar structure is introduced. This simulation environment, called HOLEG [16], is a previous work of the authors and allows to model and simulate the behaviour of a simplified electrical grid. In particular, HOLEG makes the following contributions:

- Simplified representation of an electrical distribution grid based on a holar approach.
- Detailed modelling capabilities for network components. It allows to model all types of components ranging from large producers, to connection lines and houses, up to individual components like small solar panels, TVs and alike.
- It provides an API that allows to develop novel optimization algorithms using the Java programming language. Those algorithms can then be run in a time-discrete fashion in the HOLEG environment.
- Many plotting capabilities for a diverse set of metrics for the evaluation of the simulation (see Figure 7)

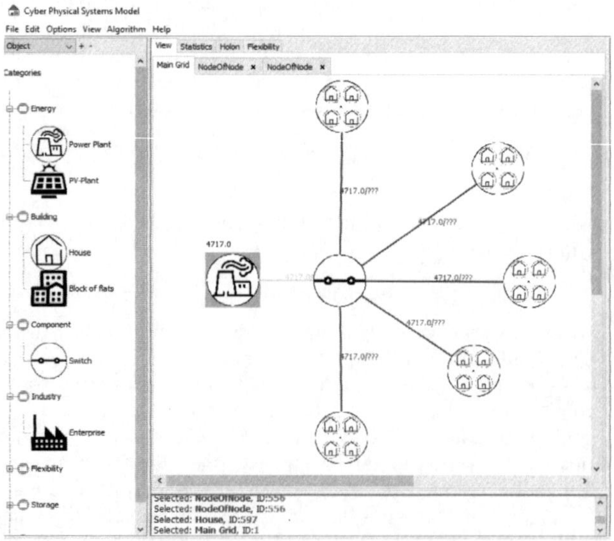

Figure 5. View of the Micro-Grid level modelled in HOLEG. The power plant represents the main grid which is connected to a switching node that connects or disconnects the individual micro grids

In this work the HOLEG simulation tools purpose is twofold. One of the purposes is the generation of a simplified environment that allows to model typical components of an electrical grid in a detailed manner, which can be seen in Figure 5. Moreover, the individual components of the network needed to be fully customizable. Figure 6 shows the the in-house level with the different prosumers displayed in the table at the top right corner. The graph below allows the user do define the consumption or production behaviour of the component over the total simulation time.

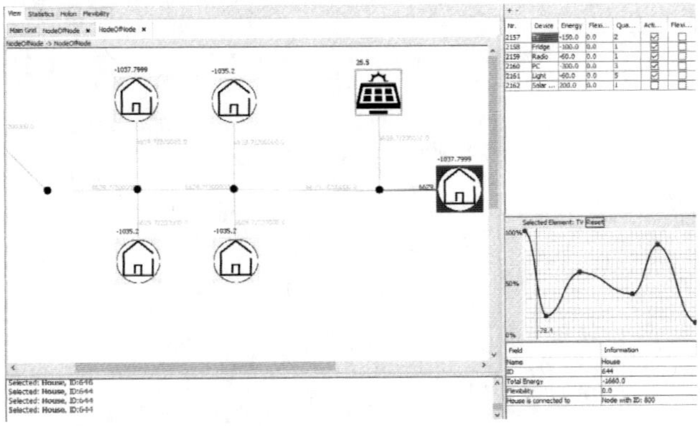

Figure 6. View of the house level modelled in HOLEG. On the right side the in-house level is displayed as a table of elements contained in the highlighted house. On the bottom right side, the consumption and production behaviour can be manipulated by modifying the graph

The more important feature provided by HOLEG is it's capability of running optimization algorithms in a time-discrete fashion during the simulation of the network. In particular, in each step of the simulation, the algorithm is executed while being able to access and manipulate all individual components in the network. The impact of the algorithms decisions can then be observed in real-time and, additionally, be represented in metric plots. In this work HOLEG is used to run the different fair algorithms on an example network and to observe the effects on the network. The detailed setup for the simulation is described in the next section.

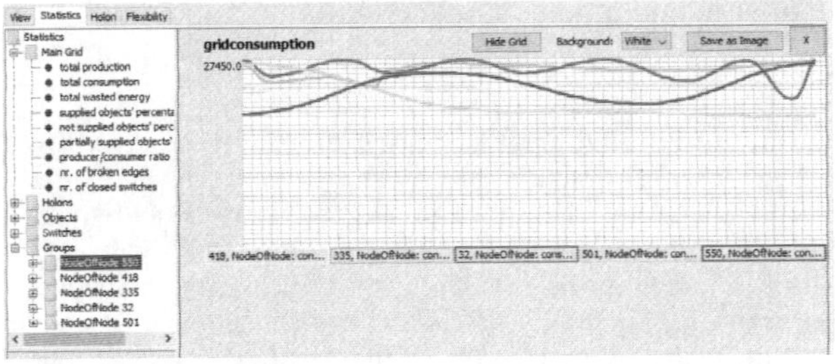

Figure 7. The statistics view of HOLEG allows a user to track and plot diverse data about the different prosumers or groups in the network. In this picture the consumption behaviour of the five micro grids is presented as the coloured graphs

VI. Simulation of the Algorithms

In this section, the conducted simulation is explained. The goal of this simulation is to evaluate the performance of the presented algorithms in a realistic scenario. Moreover, the simulation aims to evaluate the performance in the presence of our presented fairness metric. First, the general simulation setup is introduced. Second, the datasets that are used for demand and supply are described. Third, the simulation execution and corresponding results are presented. Finally, the results of the simulation are discussed.

A. Simulation Setup

The complete simulation was conducted using the capabilities provided by the simulation environment HOLEG [16]. HOLEG allows to build large hierarchically structured networks. The individual recursive levels can be modelled by using HOLEGs grouping capabilities to form subnets that hide the representation details of the underlying subnet. Each of those subnets then represents a lower hierarchical level in the model. The complete model, which is explained in Section III is modelled using HOLEG. More precisely, all four abstraction levels were implemented and each level encompasses five prosumers from the next lower abstraction level (e.g., the first abstraction level contains five micro grids and each microgrid contains five streets). Note that HOLEG is not limited to this amount of abstraction levels or prosumer numbers, but can model arbitrary topologies. To generate a more realistic scenario the values for consumption and production are loaded from external datasets. For this setup, two different load profiles for streets and one production curve of a solar panel are used. The lower level consumption configuration was modelled to align with the real data for the street. This means that the consumption of the devices located in the houses were adapted to fit the consumption data from the real measurements. Figure 8 shows HOLEGs capabilities to model individual load curves for the different devices located in the houses. For simulating a brown-out scenario, the central production is derived using (6). This allows that in each step of the simulation there is enough energy provided by the previous level to supply at least one prosumer.

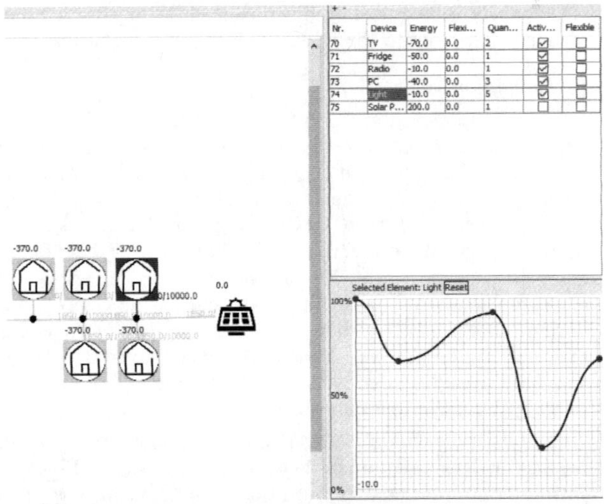

Figure 8. HOLEG allows to model arbitrary components located in the house and configure their consumption and production behaviour using individual load/production curves.

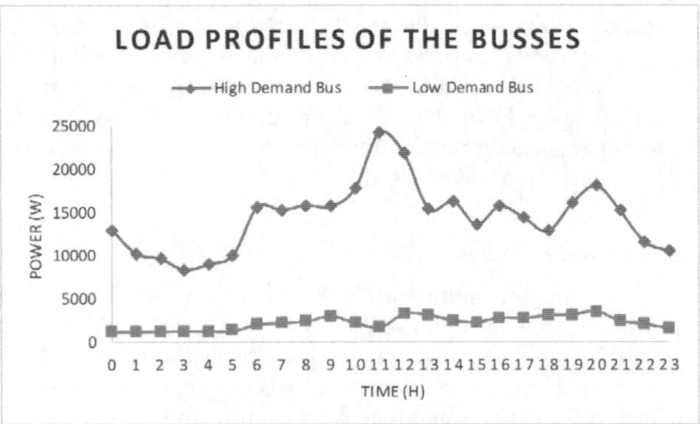

Figure 9. Load curves of the high/low demand busses connected to the adjustable transformer in Saarland (Germany).

1) Load Set: For realistic load data of prosumers in residential areas, real recordings of an adjustable transformer are used. The consumption for the lower recursive level was modelled in such a way that it fit to the overall consumption of the streets. This transformer is located in Saarland in Germany and it is connected to several streets containing housing areas. The real time data was monitored every second and the hourly average of the data is used for the simulation process. Two different load sets are used for simulation. One of the sets was generated by monitoring a larger street and represents a prosumer with a very high electricity demand, whereas the second set represents the consumption of a smaller street. Figure 9 shows the load curves of the street busses for a day.

2) DER Production Set: For modelling realistic production behaviour, real-world solar panel production data is taken from Kronberg, Germany. Figure 11 shows the production curve of the solar panel over a day. The solar panel has a capacity of 4.51 kWp and the recordings are provided in an hourly resolution. For the simulation, one of the previously mentioned solar panels is assigned to the prosumer in the low demand scenario and three to the in the high demand scenario.

B. Simulation and Results

The simulation consists of 1,000 iterations, where in each iteration, a new scenario is generated. In each iteration, the production and consumption values are allowed to randomly deviate by $\pm 10\%$ from the data set values to induce additional variation between the busses. During the simulation, each of the algorithms presented in Section IV is executed and compared in each run. The active prosumers in each run, are prosumers that stay online in the current timestep, either, because they are self-sustaining, or are supplied by the energy provided by the previous abstraction level. Moreover, the full simulation process is conducted for both, the high demand set as well as for the low demand set.

1) Low Demand Bus Results: This section presents the results for the simulation of the low demand dataset. Figure 12 shows the average results for 1,000 simulation runs with the data set of the low demand bus. From this set, the consumption data for the five street-level prosumers is derived and used for evaluation. The setup for the street level scenario is displayed in Figure 10, where exemplary two busses are displayed in more detail. The green bus is currently connected to the grid and is fully supplied by the electricity provided by the the higher abstraction level. The second bus, coloured in red, is disconnected through an open switch and thus, not supplied. Note that the current consumption (negative value) or production (positive value) is displayed above the individual prosumers. Figure 12 shows the average number of supplied components during the corresponding time of the day for each of the algorithms.

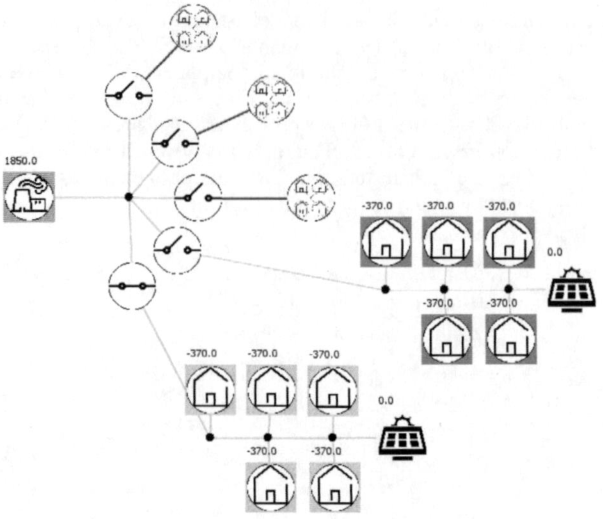

Figure 10. Representation of the street bus abstraction level in the low demand scenario modelled in HOLEG. The bottom two street busses are displayed with extended details to show what lower level prosumers are located in the streets.

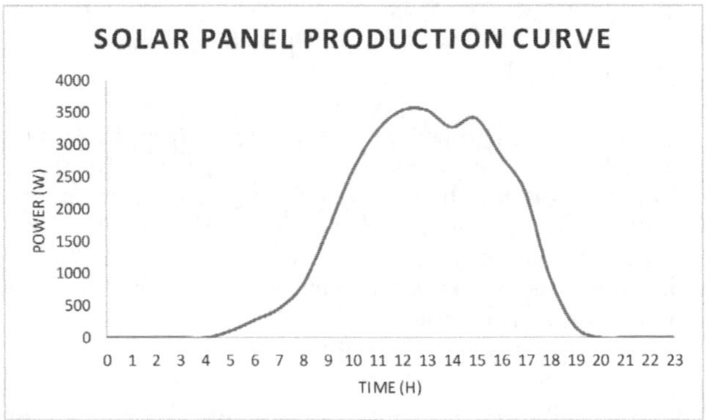

Figure 11. Production profile of a 4.51 kWp solar panel located in Kronberg Germany.

The graph shows a significant performance drop of all algorithms starting from 5am in the morning. While the TRR algorithm can not really cope with this situation, IAA and UEA perform better. This is due to the consumption behaviour of the busses. While the overall production stays the same for TRR, the demand of the busses increases during the morning until about 12pm. As this gap grows with each timestep, busses must be deactivated to keep the consumption below the production provided by the MG. Most of the time, TRR is only able to

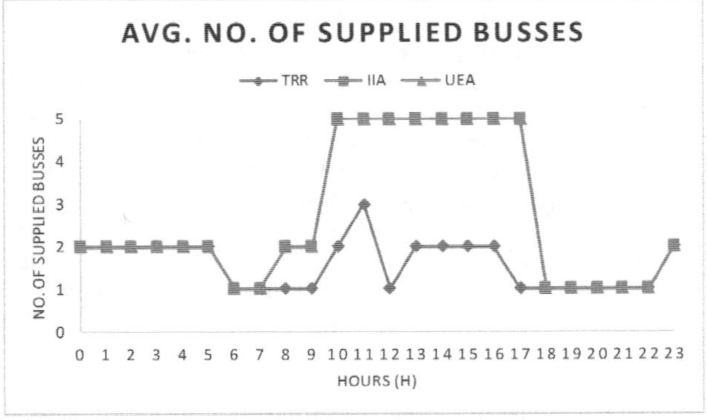

Figure 12. Average number of active low demand street busses during a time interval of 24 hours.

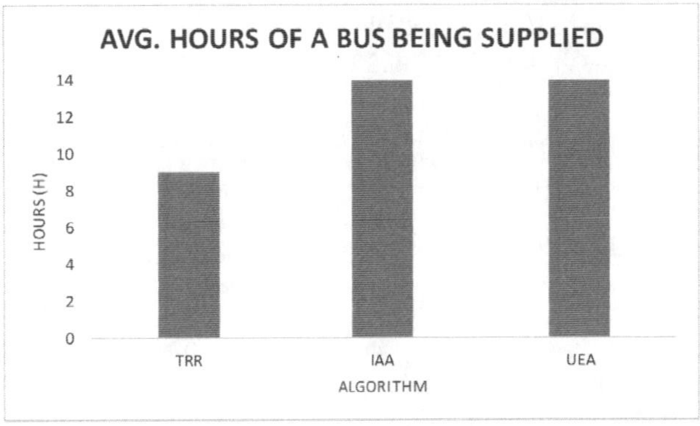

Figure 13. Total average number of how long busses were active during a day using the different algorithms in the low demand scenario.

supply between one and two busses while the rest remains deactivated.

IIA (Figure 3) and UEA (Figure 4) perform equally in this scenario as shown in Figure 12. Since both algorithms use the electricity provided by the solar panel located in the busses, the main difference is the way they choose the next candidate that should be supplied. IIA iteratively chooses the next element in its list of busses and its performance thus depends on the ordering of the busses, whereas UEA performs two steps: first, it activates all prosumers that are real producers in the current time step to uses their production for supplying additional busses. Second, it chooses the least supplied element out of the set of real consumers as a next candidate. The equality in performance of UEA and IIA, is due to the ratio between the required supply of the low demand busses and the provided electricity of the solar panels. The supply for the low demand bus deviates between 1,000Wh and 2,500Wh. In contrast, the solar panel is capable of producing 1,500Wh - 3,000Wh of electricity between 9am and 1pm. With this, the production of the solar panels highly likely exceeds the consumption of their individual busses during peak hours and the busses change from being consumers to being producers. Therefore, most of the prosumers in the low demand scenario become producers, and thus, the ordering of the busses for IIA does not influence the outcome anymore. Moreover, with the assumption provided in (6), each individual bus can be supplied and since most of them are producers, they are self sustaining. If every consumer becomes a producer, the iterative selection of elements equals the first activation step of UEA. This can be seen in Figure 12 at around 9am where IIA and UEA significantly increase the number of supplied components, as well as in the average uptime of busses shown in Figure 13. At about 6pm, the production of the solar panels can be omitted and, therefore, all algorithms perform equally.

The main difference between the algorithms becomes apparent if they are evaluated using the introduced fairness metric presented in (8). As mentioned before, a simple equality approach, like the one provided by the round-robin algorithm, is not suitable anymore for future distributed electricity production. Figure 14 shows the performance of the algorithms with regard to the fairness metric.

As mentioned in Section III, this metric is based on the average performance of the algorithms while treating all consumers

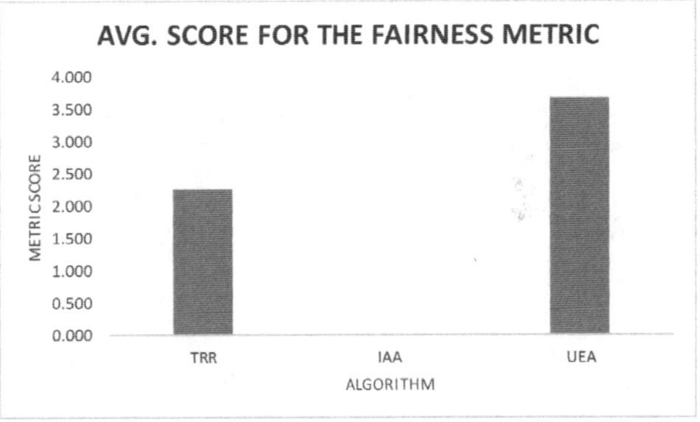

Figure 14. Average metric score of the algorithms in the low demand scenario.

equally. TRR performs quite well, because it is purely based on a round-robin approach. This minimizes the denominator of the fraction in the metric. IIA scores a rounded value of 0. In spite of outperforming TRR with regard to the average supplied time of busses, IIA does not use any techniques to equalize the supplied times of busses. However, this drastically increases the sum of differences in the metrics denominator and thus decreases the metric score. UEA on the one hand maximizes the use of real producers and, on the other hand, favours the bus with lowest supplied time. This leads to small differences between the supplied times, as well as it leads to a good performance with regard to average hours of supplied busses.

2) High Demand Bus Result: Figure 15 shows the average results of 1,000 simulation runs. For providing equal starting positions for both scenarios, again five different busses are derived from the dataset and their values are allowed to deviate from the original data by $\pm 10\%$. However, since the demand of the bus is around ten times as high as the demand of the low demand scenario, the number of solar panels in each bus is set to three. If only one solar panel is located in each bus, they would not be able to influence the outcome of the simulation because the maximum production of the solar panel is significantly lower than the demand of a single bus. Therefore, it is assumed that, in a larger bus in a residential area with a high demand, the number of installed solar panels is higher than in a low demand area.

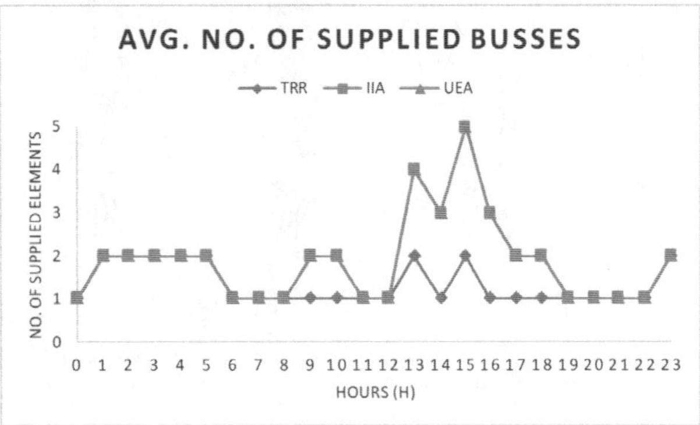

Figure 15. Average number of active high demand street busses during a time interval of 24 hours.

Most of the time TRR (Figure 2) is only able to supply between one and two busses. This is possible due to our assumption about the centrally provided energy and, additionally, due to the missing use of the surplus production of the DERs. The two algorithms that use the production of the DERs again perform equal in the simulation with regard to the average of supplied busses. The rapid changes in the performance of algorithms IIA (Figure 3) and UEA (Figure 4) at 12pm is due to the demand spike that can be seen in Figure 9 at the same time. This is a moment, in which the electricity provided by the DERs simply did not suffice and additional busses had to be deactivated.

The application of the fairness metric in the high demand scenario shows similar results as in the low demand scenario. IIA and UEA perform equal with regard to the average uptime of the busses, whereas TRR performs worse due to the missing use of DERs. With regard to the fairness metric, the overall value decreased due to the smaller number of supplied busses, but still TRR and UEA perform better than IIA.

VII. Conclusion

The results of this work indicate that, with the introduction of a widespread monitoring infrastructure and the increasing installation of DERs in the electricity grid, traditional algorithms and their corresponding definition of fair electricity distribution are outdated. Traditional load shedding based on round-robin selection used in Germany, in case of brown-out phases, is compared to novel algorithms that use the electricity provided by local DERs to improve the quality of service. Therefore, a simulation of an electrical grid in a low-voltage residential area is conducted.

The presented method, however, is not limited to the low-voltage scenarios. The current work showed that a recursive approach that encompasses all different levels of an electrical grid, ranging from the micro grid level down to the house level, is feasible. Moreover, further development of smart meter technologies will even allow to apply the presented method to in-house appliances and, therefore, provide detailed regulation capabilities for distributing electricity. This in-house area however, is a fundamentally different from the other levels in the electrical grid, since energy providers are not allowed to connect or disconnect individual components in peoples homes. Novel ideas and solutions that encourage a user to actively take part in the development of the future energy grid are necessary to make the whole potential of this recursive level accessible for demand and response handling.

As long as real testing of novel applications is restricted by outdated policies, laws and regulations, novel simulation techniques can help to understand the behaviour and impact of novel algorithms and methods in the electrical domain. The model used in this work was implemented in HOLEG, a simulation environment that allows to model simplified electrical grids.

While this paper had the German regulations in focus, future work will encompass and compare international laws and regulations. Our results indicate a lot of optimization potential in brown-out scenarios when local energy producers can be leveraged. In future, we intend to further explore this potential, especially with regards to volatile energy producers and local balancing of production and consumption, in order to reduce the influence of constantly changing energy levels on the transmission grid.

Acknowledgment

The work in this paper was partially performed in the context of the PolyEnergyNet (PEN) research project and partially funded by the Germany Federal Ministry for Economic Affairs and Energy (BMWi) under grant no. "0325737E".

References

[1] R. Egert, F. Volk, J. Daubert, and M. Mühlhäuser, "Mitigating brown-outs: Fair distribution of locally sourced energy in smart grids," in *The Seventh International Conference on Smart Grids, Green Communications and IT Energy-aware Technologies - ENERGY 2017*, IARIA. IARIA, 2017, pp. 33–39.

[2] G. Pepermans, J. Driesen, D. Haeseldonckx, R. Belmans, and W. Dhaeseleer, "Distributed generation: definition, benefits and issues," *Energy policy*, vol. 33, no. 6, pp. 787–798, 2005.

[3] N. D. Hatziargyriou and A. S. Meliopoulos, "Distributed energy sources: Technical challenges," in *Power Engineering Society Winter Meeting, 2002. IEEE*, vol. 2. IEEE, 2002, pp. 1017–1022.

[4] "Renewable energy sources act," https://www.gesetze-im-internet.de/bundesrecht/eeg_2014/gesamt.pdf, accessed: 2017-02-02.

[5] A. Falk, E. Fehr, and U. Fischbacher, "Testing theories of fairnessintentions matter," *Games and Economic Behavior*, vol. 62, no. 1, pp. 287–303, 2008.

[6] E. A. Lind, L. Kray, and L. Thompson, "The social construction of injustice: Fairness judgments in response to own and others' unfair treatment by authorities," *Organizational behavior and human decision processes*, vol. 75, no. 1, pp. 1–22, 1998.

[7] A. Wierzbicki, *Trust and Fairness in Open, Distributed Systems*, ser. Studies in Computational Intelligence. Springer Berlin Heidelberg, 2010.

[8] M. Zaharia *et al.*, "Delay scheduling: a simple technique for achieving locality and fairness in cluster scheduling," in *Proceedings of the 5th European conference on Computer systems*. ACM, 2010, pp. 265–278.

[9] S. K. Baruah, N. K. Cohen, C. G. Plaxton, and D. A. Varvel, "Proportionate progress: A notion of fairness in resource allocation," *Algorithmica*, vol. 15, no. 6, pp. 600–625, 1996.

[10] Z. Baharlouei, M. Hashemi, H. Narimani, and H. Mohsenian-Rad, "Achieving optimality and fairness in autonomous demand response: Benchmarks and billing mechanisms," *IEEE Transactions on Smart Grid*, vol. 4, no. 2, pp. 968–975, 2013.

[11] G. Koutitas, "Control of flexible smart devices in the smart grid," *IEEE Transactions on Smart Grid*, vol. 3, no. 3, pp. 1333–1343, 2012.

[12] P. Samadi, A.-H. Mohsenian-Rad, R. Schober, V. W. Wong, and J. Jatskevich, "Optimal real-time pricing algorithm based on utility maximization for smart grid," in *Smart Grid Communications (SmartGridComm), 2010 First IEEE International Conference on.* IEEE, 2010, pp. 415–420.

[13] M. Shinwari, A. Youssef, and W. Hamouda, "A water-filling based scheduling algorithm for the smart grid," *IEEE Transactions on Smart Grid*, vol. 3, no. 2, pp. 710–719, 2012.

[14] T. Sousa, H. Morais, J. Soares, and Z. Vale, "Day-ahead resource scheduling in smart grids considering vehicle-to-grid and network constraints," *Applied Energy*, vol. 96, pp. 183–193, 2012.

[15] F. Ye, Y. Qian, and R. Q. Hu, "Energy efficient self-sustaining wireless neighborhood area network design for smart grid," *IEEE Transactions on Smart Grid*, vol. 6, no. 1, pp. 220–229, 2015.

[16] R. Egert, C. G. Cordero, A. Tundis, and M. Mühlhäuser, "Holeg: a simulator for evaluating resilient energy networks based on the holon analogy," in *21st IEEE/ACM International Symposium on Distributed Simulation and Real Time Applications*, ACM/IEEE. IEEE, 2017.

Introducing Load Management Analysis and Measures in Manufacturing Companies

Steffen Nienke, Jan Hicking, Günther Schuh
Institute for Industrial Management
at RWTH Aachen University (FIR)
Aachen, Germany
E-mail: {Steffen.Nienke, Jan.Hicking, Guenther.Schuh@fir.rwth-aachen.de}

***Abstract*—In order to introduce load management in the manufacturing industry, some obstacles need to be pointed out. This paper presents a feasible approach on how to implement load management measures in companies. To this end, load management and energy management are explained and distinguished in a first step. Subsequently, the implementation method is introduced. Therefore, by means of this paper, companies will be enabled to use load management measures and significantly reduce their energy costs. In the second part of the paper, the introduced approach will be applied. Hence, a use case of a manufacturing company is described. Alongside energy analyses with consumption data, specific measures are presented.**

Keywords - Load management; Energy management; Energy Monitoring; Manufacturing industry; Renewable energies.

I. Introduction

This paper ist an extended version of [1]. For the majority of companies in a continuously changing production environment, the ability to stay competitive depends on the production price of a product [2–4]. The ability to produce a product at lower costs can lead to a significant market advantage. Therefore, the ideal adjustments of essential target values like occupancy, timelines, or process costs are crucial for a company's success [3]. However, the costs for resource, energy and production utility have been raised dramatically in the last decades [5].

In particular, the price for electrical energy in Germany has risen severely over recent years. This development is connected to the increasing expansion of renewable energy [2]. Due to the implementation of the priority access of renewable energy, the prices for electrical energy rose [6]. This development refers to the fact, that the EEG-allocation (EEG: German Renewable Energy Sources Act, legislation to foster the use and invest in renewable energies) increases in the amount of expanding renewable energies in Germany [7]. As a result of the expansion of renewable energy generation capacities, the grid stability is endangered [8]. The priority access of volatile renewable energy leads to a decrease in energy supply reliability, which is one of the most important location factors for the German manufacturing industry [9].

Rising energy prices, as shown for Germany in Figure 1, promote a significant competitive disadvantage for the manufacturing industry [6]. Moreover, a growing scarcity of resources pushes energy prices [2]. Especially the scarcity of resources has increased environmental awareness in society and industry in the past [3, 10].

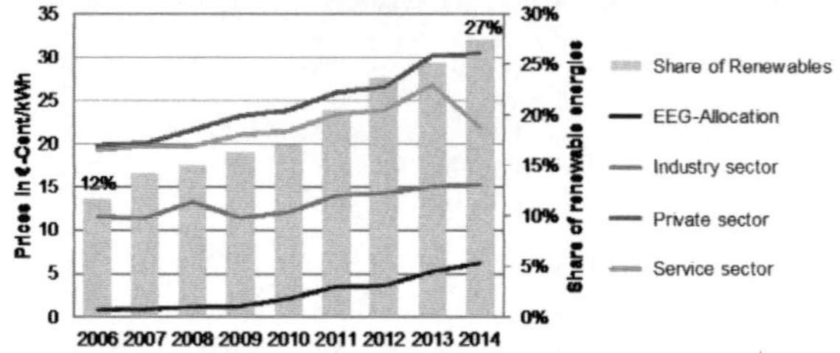

Figure 1. Development of energy prices [11]

In order to guarantee the grid security and create a greater environmental compatibility, Germany set a target to develop the most energy efficient and environmentally friendly economy in the world [12]. The focus of this program is the expansion of renewable energy. To compensate the incoming side effects like increasing energy prices, flexibility mechanisms are even more relevant. To stabilize the electrical grid, load management can be realized by using flexibility potentials in manufacturing industry. The identification of those potentials is very important. Hence, the survey of process-specific energy data in the manufacturing industry is necessary to point out any potential [13–15]. In this context, the gathering of information can be done by continuous energy monitoring of manufacturing companies [3]. Many companies are struggling to identify information relevant for load management as well as possible collection strategies. Apparently, a structured approach on how to create the information base to achive energy transparency as a first step to load management is missing. The presented approach focusses on the manufacturing industry, as literature research confirms that this area has the greatest potential for load management. However, the concept can easily be adopted to other application areas (e.g., office buildings).

In Section II, this paper describes fundamentals of load management concepts. In Section III it then focusses on the implemention of load management in the manufacturing industry. Considering, among other things, organisational requirements as well as the necessary transparency of the energy system, this paper develops a general approach to introduce load management in manufacturing companies. Finally, in the last section, the approach is applied to a specific use case that evaluates the described method.

II. Definitions and Fundamentals

Describing basic concepts and distinguishing several terms within the field of energy management, load management, and energy efficiency is essential in order to understand work at hand. In contrast to conventional base load power plants like lignite-fired power plants or nuclear power plants, the sustainable generation in renewable energy plants usually cannot be controlled. These circumstances lead to a discrepancy between feed-in time and amount of fed-in power of renewable energy technologies like wind and solar systems [8, 16, 17]. To gain a more profound understanding of this, Figure 2 visualizes a comparison of installed and generated power of renewable energy technologies. The Figure displays the discrepancy of installed and generated power of renewable energy technologies in January, May and June. Biomass and hydropower are not volatile. Therefore, the loads are nearly constant or were reduced by demand side management. The behaviours of Solar and Wind plants are quite different. The strong volatility of solar can be seen in the difference between January and May. Wind, on the other hand, covers 70% of the installed load in January, but drops the production close to zero in June.

German electricity transmission system operators compensate the incoming volatility by using control energy. Within this concept, controllable power plants like gas turbine plants or pumped-storage power plants are usually used [18]. The control energy concept leads to dealing with peak loads or loss of loads properly [19]. In summary it can be said that through expanding renewable energy in the electrical grids the supply reliability cannot be guaranteed. So secure the network, control energy uses load flexibilities. This is necessary to maintain the critical success factor of low energy prices for a society with a manufacturing industry as leading edge. However, energy prices are rising. Therefore, load management is one possible opportunity to compensate increasing energy prices.

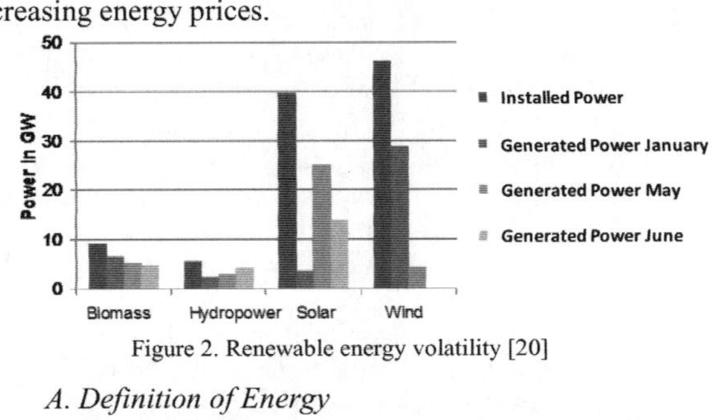

Figure 2. Renewable energy volatility [20]

A. Definition of Energy

Energy is a fundamental factor. Several types of energy can be transformed into each other, but neither be created nor exterminated [8, 15, 21]. Energy is used to heat buildings or to warm up process fluids to a high temperature (space or process heat). Apart from that, energy is used to drive engines within machines or vehicles. In this context, energy is called mechanical energy or electrical energy.

B. Definition of Energy efficiency

The term "efficiency" follows its Latin origin "efficientia", which means efficacy [22]. Energy efficiency is the relation between benefit and initial energy input [23]. Energy efficiency also describes an intelligent usage of the initial input aiming to use the available energy as efficient as possible [14]. Following this definition, energy efficiency is increased by reducing energy consumption while (simultaneously) keeping the energy benefit constant [24].

C. Definition of energy management

The introduction of energy management in the manufacturing industry will have an impact on increasing sustainability and lowering energy costs [10, 25–27]. Energy management is defined as an instrument of coordination aiming at an ecological and economical satisfaction of energy requirements in companies. This goal is realized by a predictive, organized and systematic approach of energy production, procurement, storage, distribution and usage [28, 29].

Energy management can be considered from two perspectives. There is a technical perspective dealing with energy monitoring, analysing the energy data and deriving plans of action to achieve defined goals. Furthermore, there is an organisational perspective, which follows a holistic view of energy consumption and usage in processes, proceedings and procedures in the manufacturing industry [10]. To achieve goals, such as raising energy efficiency or reducing energy costs, energy management uses approaches like investing in new technologies, changing behaviours and identifying energy saving opportunities [30]. Referring to the identified approaches and goals of energy management, load management describes one aspect of energy management.

D. Definition of load management

First, load management must be distinguished from demand side management (DSM), since both terms are easily mixed up. Demand Side Management is a generic term for different approaches of systematically switching loads. It contains load management, energy saving approaches, fuel substitution and load optimisation [31–33]. Load management, however, describes the way to achieve the goal of changing the point of time and amount of load that is required [32]. Hence, load management describes the temporal relocation of energy consumption [13]. In addition to that definition load management is defined as switching loads on and off [14]. Therefore, load management focuses on internal processes, to reduce load peaks and thus reduce energy costs [34]. Examples of load management are described in the following section.

E. Measures of load management

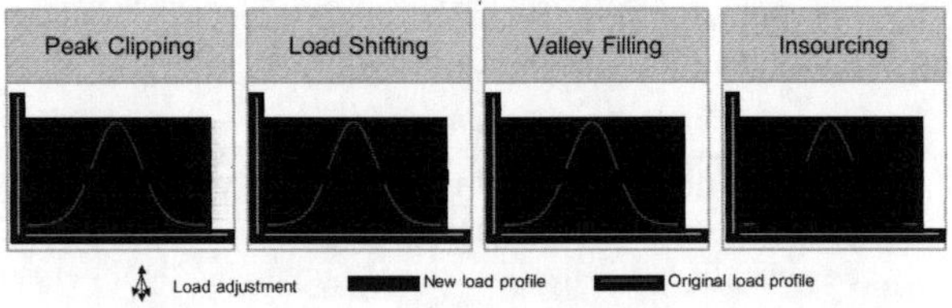

Figure 3. Load management measures

To avoid energy costs due to load peaks, load management focuses four different types of measures as shown in Figure 3 [31–33, 35]. In the following, the different types are explained. "Peak Clipping" describes the immediate handling of peak loads. Thereby peak loads are reduced by a specific amount, which reduces the energy costs significantly [31–33]. It is achieved by ejecting loads to prevent a significant peak load [36, 37]. Using energy storage technologies are another opportunity to prevent peak loads by feeding-in energy at the point a peak load would occur [38].

"Load Shifting" also describes the immediate handling of peak loads. However, in this case, technologies are introduced to reduce peak loads. Energy storage technologies enable companies to temporarily switch production processes. The change of organisational or production processes can lead to a reduction of peak loads. Although energy is not saved, energy costs are significantly reduced. The energy consumption of several production procedures is not saved but switched to a point in time when there is no risk of a peak load [31–33].

"Valley Filling" describes a load management measure, which lifts the base load of a company to cut the average electricity price. This measure goes with a change of energy contract of the energy supplier. Because the total energy consumption is increased, the load profile is polished. Any energy supplier prefers a polished load profile and will remunerate those profiles. Another use case is a loading of electric cars in the night. The raised load in off-peak times polishes the whole load profile.

The last measure of load management is named "Insourcing". It describes the reduction of energy purchase. Unlike "peak clipping", "insourcing" reduces the load profile holistically. There is no need for a specific peak load analysis. Companies reduce the energy purchase by producing a specific energy amount themselves. Achieving this goal, companies need new energy production technologies like cogeneration units or PV-plants in combination with an energy storage.

In order to summarize and classify these findings, the following Figure 4 explains in several layers how terms like energy and load management relate. The top layer represents the concept layer. As described earlier, operational energy management is the primary term. Energy management comprises several goals and measures.

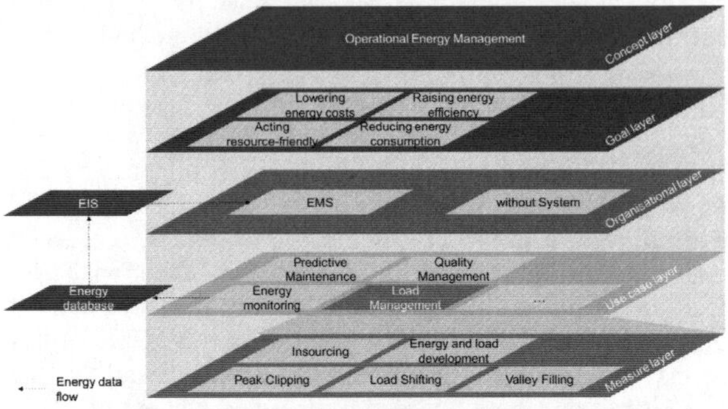

Figure 4. Content of operational energy management

Hereafter follows the goal layer. In this layer, all goals of energy management are summed up. It starts with lowering energy costs, raising energy efficiency, acting resource-friendly and finishes with reducing energy consumption. These goals, which have their origin in the operational energy management, can be achieved by various actions. The organisational layer describes two typical types of how energy management topics can be addressed. On the one hand, companies can implement a holistic energy management system (EMS) that is standardized by a German, European or international institutions. On the other hand, a not standardized solution to achieve the formulated goals can be realized without using such a system. In this case, the organisation of the individual solution falls in the responsibility of the company. For the appropriate application of an energy management system, the information flow must be organized properly. Therefore, an energy database for continuous memorizing energy data would be crucial. Thus, the measured data is always ready for a delivery on demand. For a company, it is important to receive data and information to the exact right point of time, spot and quality. To achieve this, the introduction of an energy information system (EIS) is necessary. The combination of an energy management system, energy information system and energy database is the best way to deliver information and data in the desired quality as explained above. The use caser layer describes different applications within the energy management context. The focus of this paper is on the field of load management, but it is worth mentioning, that use cases like predictive maintenance, quality management and energy monitoring can also achieve energy management goals. All aspects have in common that they collect data, which must be memorized for later use.

The last layer is the measure layer. This layer contains all load management approaches. In principle, all terms of the layer above have their own measures on the layer below.

III. Implementation of Load Management in the Manufacturing Industry

The following approach should support companies to introduce load management. It should give answers to questions such as: how can load management be implemented holistically? What are the benefits?

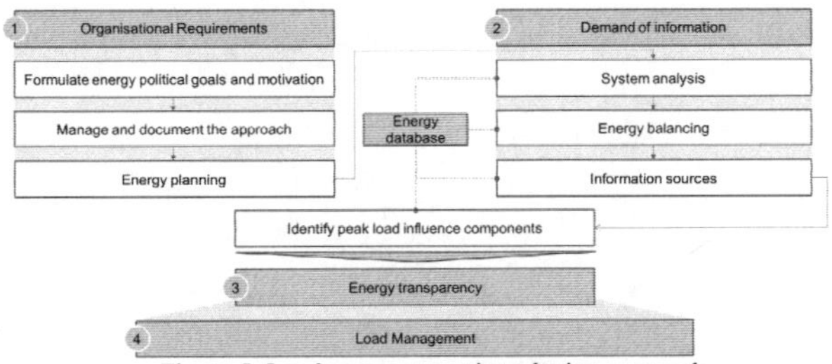

Figure 5. Load management introducing approach

The approach in Figure 5 contains four essential steps. First, companies must meet the organisational requirements. Second, companies must fulfil the demand of information. Third, when the demand of information is accomplished, the required energy generation/consumption transparency can be achieved. Fourth, once all required foundations are provided, load management can be introduced by implementing load management measures.

A. Organisational requirements

The reduction of energy consumption is a long term process. Therefore, it is recommended that the introduction of load management must be well organized and controlled. The organisational requirements are basically described by the DIN EN ISO 50001:2011. But not all requirements to introduce load management are addressed in this standard. First, it is important that companies create an energy policy. A policy in this context must contain energy long-term goals. Furthermore, it must contain a motivation that is communicated within the company, because the employees shall live and realise those policies. The policy must be formulated close to reality, comprehensible and goal-orientated. Moreover, a company must implement a process of documentation. Besides that, a company has to develop an energy plan to summarize all goals, approaches and review processes. Within an energy plan, a company determines, which energy data must be collected, how data can be collected, how a data working process looks like and how a company would work with the flows of information. Those steps are important to lay the foundations for the introduction of load management.

B. Demand of information

Every measure within the context of load management works with real time data. Collecting those data is therefore a necessary requirement. To acquire the required information in a continuously changing environment, data must be collected in various dimensions of the company, e.g., company's location, buildings, rooms, production processes and energy sources. This kind of consideration is called system analysis. The objective is to create a holistic flow sheet of all forms of energy and its use locations. Assuming an overall system, to achieve a holistic flow sheet, it has to be broken down to its source elements.

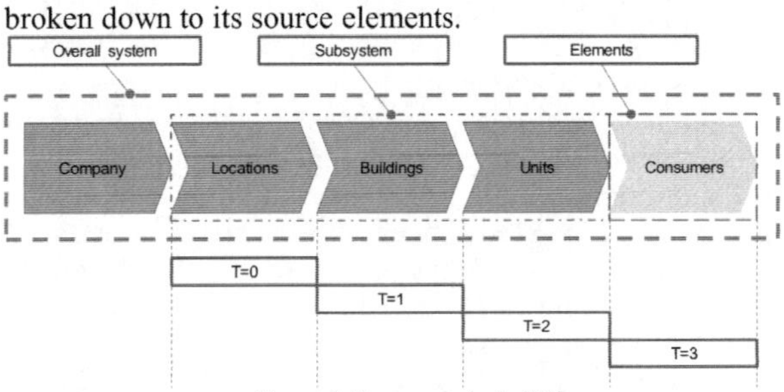

Figure 6. System analysis [23]

Figure 6 represents a typical construct of a company in the manufacturing industry. Dividing this construct in three types of system elements, it is shown that there are different degrees of depth. Starting with the overall system, which contains all given components, a company has its locations (T=0). The location level is the first layer. Diving in the subsystem, a location contains at least one building (T=1). The building level is the second layer. Each building contains at least one unit of its company, for example production, supply, quality management or services (T=2). The unit level is the third layer. The deepest layer represents the energy consumers (T=3). For example, there are machine tools, cooling energy generation or printers. The consumer level is the last layer. In order to achieve energy transparency in a company, a system analysis is fundamental. The concept of balancing is close to a system analysis. The goal of both concepts is to disperse the areal boundaries of energy consumers in a company for transparent visible consumer structure.

Once all energy consumers in a company have been identified, the next step would be to determine where they are located, what form of energy they are using and when they are consuming how much energy. Consequently, an energy monitoring system must be implemented to collect the real-time consumption data. The collected real-time data must be memorized in a database. But there are circumstances, for example, financial barriers, which inhibit a company to implement an energy monitoring system. In this case, there are different options to collect data. Literature has shown that there are just few energy consumers in the manufacturing industry with high impact on peak loads. By comparing the main energy consumers and the main energy conservation potentials in the manufacturing industry, a measurement priority listing can be determined:

1. Compressed air generation
2. Energy generation for cooling purposes
3. Ventilation system
4. Machine tools
5. Electrical system

6. Pumps

Influences to peak loads due to illumination or information and communication technologies are usually neither significant nor manageable. The list above shows which consumers in the manufacturing industry must be prioritised when collecting real-time data.

C. Energy transparency

Collecting real-time data is a fundamental component to achieve energy transparency in a company. Real-time data is required to implement an autonomous load management in the future. The needed data acquisition is a separate challenge, which is discussed in other publications. In addition, the issue of IT security must be considered. The acquired data is now used to identify specific components of the maximum load peak of a company's load profile. Figure 7 presents an activity diagram, which contains an approach to identify specifics peak load components.

Deriving essential elements of the diagram, it is noted that load profiles of energy consumers and the main load profile of a company are required. Furthermore, the specific consumer load profiles must be inspected for load peaks to the point of time when the main peak load occurs. After this step, all specific loads are summarized and compared with the amount of the main peak load. If there is a difference (<<if(n)>>) it must be ensured, that the data set is complete as possible. If there is no difference (<<if(y)>>) a visualisation of the result should be created. The next question to be asked is whether the result is detailed enough or not. To answer this question, a company's layer must be determined. As explained before, a company has several layers. Load management requires information about the peak load components in sufficiently detailed depth. The ideal case would be at plant level (T=3). When including these last steps, energy transparency is guaranteed. The described steps enable companies to get a detailed view over their energy consumption and which kind of consumer has the highest impact on the total consumption. Another advantage of implementing the whole energy monitoring process is that the result can be used to identify energy wastage.

This procedure was validated at a company. The energy transparency was established and it was shown that the energy generation for cooling purposes had a peak load share of 20%. This transparency allowed counter-measures to be implemented.

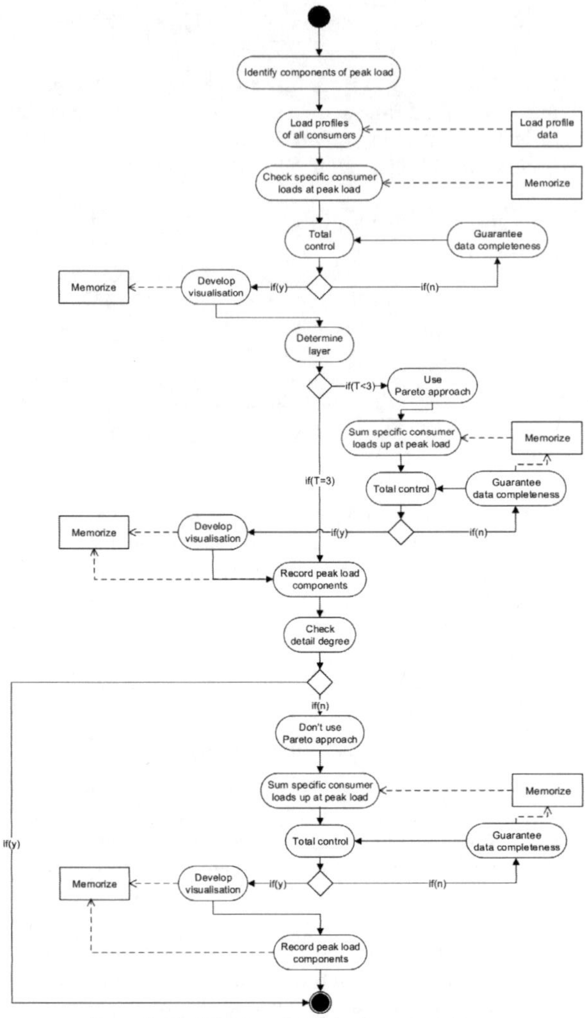

Figure 7. Identification of peak load components

IV. Applying the Approach

To validate the proposed model, it has been applied within use cases in companies. One example is described in the following section. First, the setting and circumstances of the considered company are described. Subsequently, the measurements are visualised and described. Finally, the possible measures to implement load management are introduced.

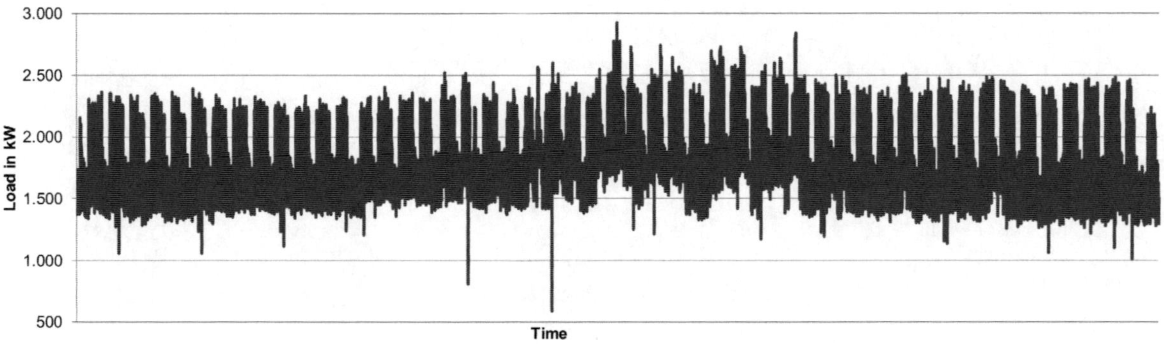

Figure 8. Anual Load Curve of the whole company

A. Setting

The considered measurements could correspond to a classic manufacturing company in Germany with more than 500 employees. Such a company is considered to be a large company according to EU definitions and is due to German regulations consequently obliged to carry out energy audits according to DIN EN 16247-1. The production usually runs in two shifts. The two shifts run from 8 am to 10 pm. Furthermore, a seven-day workweek is also considered. The load curve is characteristic for a company is in the metal sector, e.g., a company producing body parts for the automotive industry.

B. Measurements

This section displays and analyzes the measured data. Various statistical and non-statistical methods are used for the analysis. Figure 8 shows the overall consumption of the company. The resolution of the measured data is 15 minutes and thus contains 34050 measurement points. There is an increase of the minimum and maximum load during summer between the beginning of June and the middle of September. During winter and early spring, the loads are at a constant level of 2350 kW. The load profile suggests that the increase in power consumption in the summer is attributable, for example, to cooling. However, this cannot be confirmed by only considering the consumption of the whole company. The minimum loads are within a range of 1300 to 1700 kW, with few exceptions. The peak load was 2930.48 kW and occurred on July 2, 2015 at 12 am.

Figure 9 shows the annual load duration curve of the measured values. This shows that the load demand decreases rarely below 1300 kW over the entire year. There are a few points in time at which the load is less than 1000 kW. As seen in the earlier figure, there is a night reduction as well as a weekend lowering of the load.

If the median over 24 hours is considered, it is noticeable that between 8 am and 4 pm the load reference is constant. Between 4 pm and 10 pm, it decreases. From 0 am to 5 am in the morning, the load is almost constant 1500 kW. Thus, during 5 hours a day the load has decreased to 1500 kW. As a result, a high load reference is recorded for 19 hours over 365 days a year. The basic load can therefore be seen at 6935 hours (365 days * 5 hours / day). It has to be noted that the basic load is more than 50% of the peak load.

Figure 8 also shows the weekly load cycle at the time of the peak load. It should be noted that the basic load in this week is about 100 kW higher than the basic load of the annual load duration curve. It should also be noted that the peak load

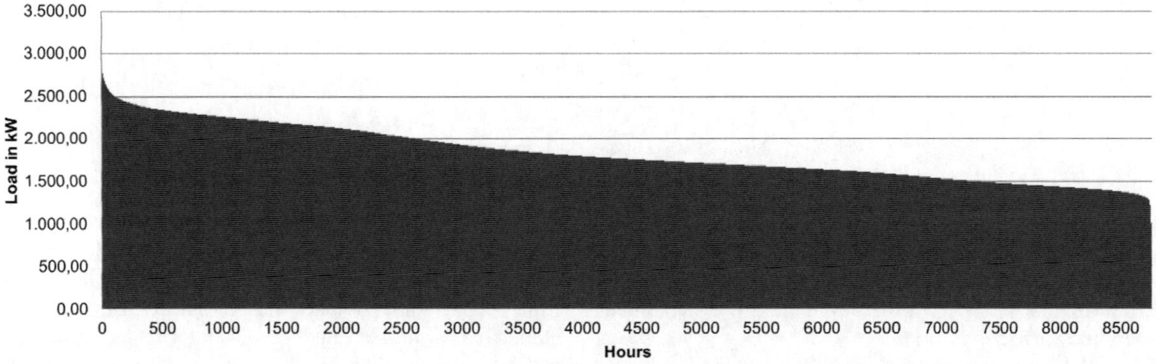

Figure 9. Annual load duration curve

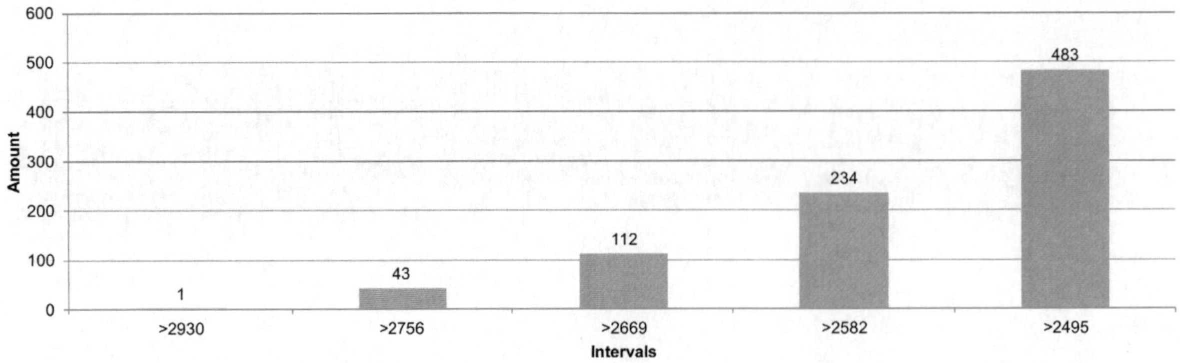

Figure 10. Load Peak Distribution

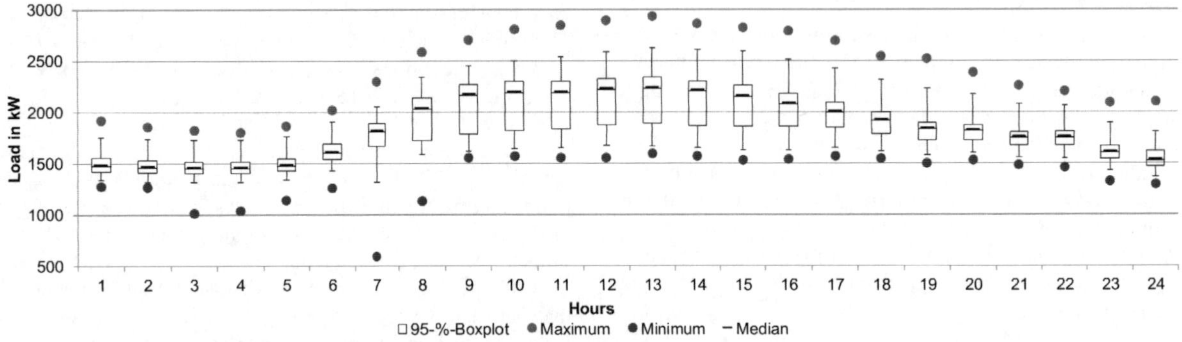

Figure 11. Overall Box-Plot covering the hours of a day

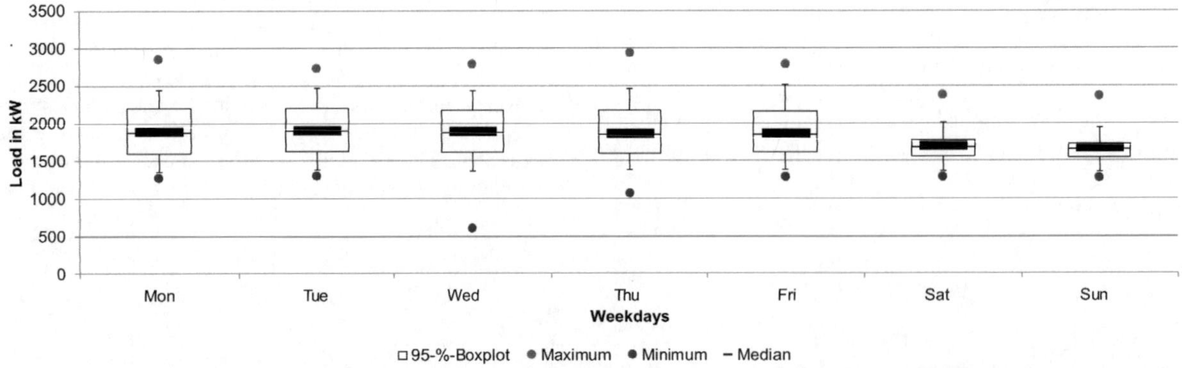

Figure 12. Overall Box Plot covering the weekdays

is not an anomaly, instead the general consumption in this week is very high. The weekends and nights have a reduced load. With regard to the previous assumption that the peak load is due to cooling, it should be noted that July 02, 2015, was one of the hottest days of the month. The maximum temperature was 35.2 ° C.

Figure 10 shows the load peak distribution of the company. The interval lengths are defined by the observation of the top 2.5% of all measured values. If the interval > 2756 kW is considered, it should be noted that less than 50 load peaks are counted in this interval. If the lower bound of the interval is reduced by approximately 100 kW, the number of load peaks triples. The number of load peaks contained in an interval are cumulated in the next interval. Therefore, this visualisation can be used to identify the load management potential. Hence, potential savings can be expected.

Figure 11 shows the box plot covering the hours of a day. It considers all data from the year 2015. Ninety-five percent of all data is located between the vertical upper and lower black lines. Between the maxima (magenta dot) and the upper vertical lines as well as the minima (blue dot) and the lower vertical line 2.5% of all data is located. Based on the medians and the box plots, the nightly reduction of the energy consumption can be identified. The peak load occurs mainly between 8 am and 5 pm.

Figure 12 shows the box plot covering the weekdays. It is noticeable that the median is 200 kW lower on Saturdays and Sundays. The maximum also drops by more than 300 kW. It should be noted that 97.5% of all load points lie between Monday and Friday at a maximum of 2500 kW. An objective of the load management could therefore be to not exceed the threshold of 2500 kW.

The analysis of the measurement presents a strong assumption that the used cooling system is responsible for the measured peak loads. Therefore, the next step would be to break the overall consumtion down to each individual consumer. Since, in reality, it is unlikely to monitor each used consumer, it is usually sufficient to monitor the large consumers and cluster the remaining consumption under "others". In the presented example, the cooling machines can be measured and the share of the overall consumption can be calculated. Figure 13 shows the box plot of the measured cooling machines covering the month. It is noticeable that the median of 1680 kW is almost identical between January and May, and between September and December. During June to August, the median rises to 1900 kW. Peak loads above 2500 kW occur more often during May to August. During summer, the base load and the peak load increases. This proves the thesis that the cooling machines have a mayor impact on the load. After identifying the machine with the largest consumption, load measurements can be implemented.

C. *Possible ways to implementation for load management*

The following section presents different ways to implement load management based on the measurements done in the previous section. Due to the analysis of measurements, there are several opportunities to reduce the peak load in the considered company. As analyzed, the peak load evolves due to cooling machines, which runs with increased power usage when the external temperatures are high.

1) Insourcing: Combined power and heat station

Reducing the consumed energy by producing energy on company's own, this measure is called "Insourcing". Within this measure the usage of a combined heat and power station is recommended. This technology leads to a massive reduction of the required energy from an energy supplier.

In order to use this technology, several parameters have to be considered. In this context, a combined heat and power unit (CHP) was implemented with these parameters:

- $P_{Power} = 365$ kW
- $\dot{Q}_{Fuel,\,HCP} = 955$ kW
- $\dot{Q}_{Heat,\,CHP} = 478$ kW
- $\omega_{HCP} = 0{,}88$
- $\eta_{Power,\,HCP} = 0{,}38$
- $\eta_{Heat,\,HCP} = 0{,}5$
- $\tau_{v,\,HCP}$ = adjustable

The mode of operation of this CHP unit has been designed to be heat-guided. Due to the high demand for heating available all year round, the CHP is operating at full load all year round. It follows that the heat produced can be reduced at any time. Furthermore, the CHP is designed to be used for the utilization of the energy reduction. The type of design is made by entering the electrical power $P_{Power} = 365$ kW into a year duration line. Following this method the result contains 6620 operating hours of the CHP. It is recommended that the CHP should not run in the partial load effiency as often as in the overall load effiency. A service contract was obtained that effectuates that the CHP is only in maintenance when the energy consumption is relatively low, for example, in the morning or at weekend. In the calculated example, the result of the examiniation of a combined heat and power station with 365 kW electrical power was an annual saving of about 55,000 €. The net present value analyzed over 10 years of the investment in the CHP is ca. 2,600,000 €.

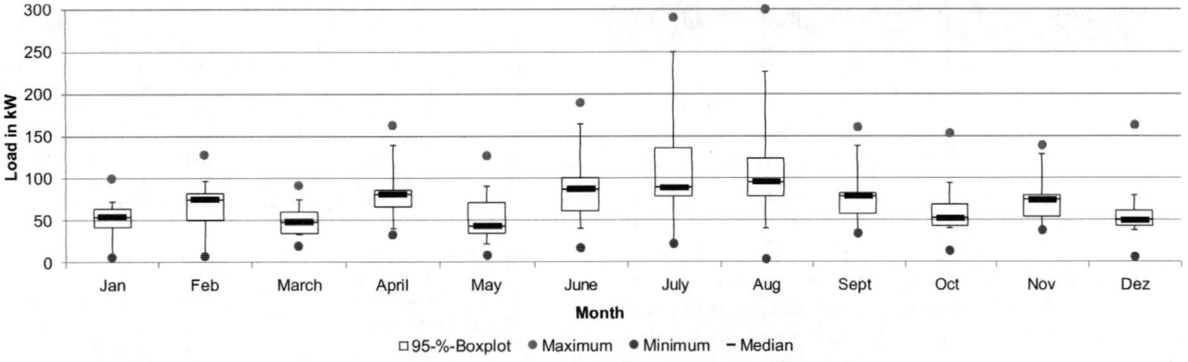

Figure 13. Cooling Machines Box Plot covering the month

2) Insourcing: Emergency power supply

Alternatively, an emergency power supply can used like a CHP. Emergency power supplies are assumed to have a total amount auf 3.5 MW electrical power. In that case, various emergency power supply stations cannot be used parallel since the emergency power supply has to be guaranteed.

In the example calculation, the total annual savings would be more than ca. 60,000 €.

3) Load Shifting: Ice storage

Regarding the definition of load shifting, load intensive processes are identified, which can be shifted in times of lower energy consumption. This approach leads to reduced energy costs. There are two types of cool energy storage technologies: ice storage or cold water storage without icing. Cold water storage technologies have one disadvantage with respect to ice storage technologies. Due to the missing icing process the cold water storage needs much more space to save the same amount of energy. Due to this disadvantage, the ice storage technologie is examined. The relevant parameters of the ice storage are the following:

- $Q_{Storage} = 500$ kWh
- $P_{Peak, Storage} = 150\ kW$
- $n_{SP} = 5$

In order to reduce the peak load by 150 kW, an energy storage amount of $Q_{Total, Storage} = 2427{,}84$ kWh is required.

Figure 14 shows how the usage of the ice storage that reduces the peak load by150 kW. This measure needs five storages to guarantee the load reduction. The calculated potential annual saving in the used example is approximately 15,000 €. Regarding the high cost for investment the net present value is less the net present value of the CHP. In this particular case the net present value of the ice storage would be around 20,000 €.

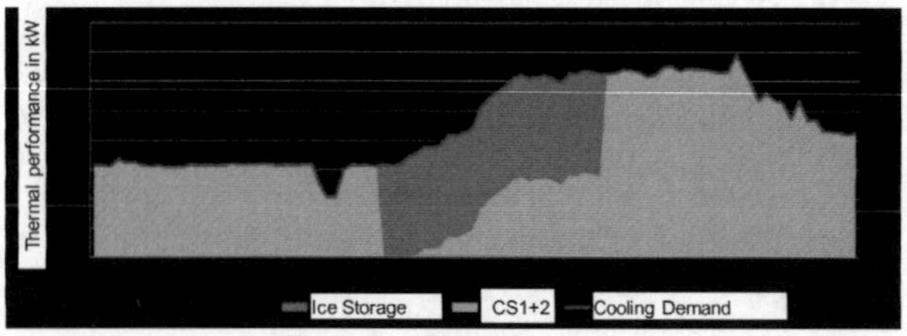

Figure 14. Usage of ice storage

V. CONCLUSION AND OUTLOOK

Load management leads to lower energy costs in companies working in the manufacturing industry. This paper described the requirements that need to be fulfilled to implement load management. With the presented approach, companies are enabled to collect these data and information in a well-structured development. Starting with fundamentals like formulating a company's energy strategy and an energy plan. Furthermore, the company is advised to motivate their employees and to document the whole introduction process.

Besides that, a company must start with a system analysis in order to create a transparent list of all energy consumers. Also, a company must start with measurements in an early stage, to collect necessary data. Energy monitoring systems assist companies in collecting important data and information regarding the energy consumption of machines, etc. Possible circumstances can force companies to reject energy monitoring systems. In this case, the measurement of the energy consumption of prioritized consumers is recommended. This paper presented relevant consumers, which have a high impact on the main peak load in the manufacturing industry. Using these fundamentals and the memorized data and information, energy transparency can be achieved by analyzing collected and memorized data. Therefore, load profiles on all layers, such as buildings, units or consumers must be analyzed following the presented approach.

The application of the approach showed that load measures can lead to lower energy costs. Therefore, the load profiles were analyzed precisely. Due to this analysis, load peaks were identified. Using these results, several load management measures were derived. With a focus on two main measures "insourcing" and "load shifting", two different technologies were introduced to address the measures. On the one hand a combined power and heat station can be used, and on the other hand an ice storage technologies. In the used example calulations, both technologies leads to a annual amount of at least 15,000 €.

Summarizing, load management can be used to reduce energy costs in a company.

ACKNOWLEDGMENT

This article arose during the work of the authors, within the context of the research project FlAixEnergy (project number: 0325819A) funded by the Federal Ministry for Economic Affairs and Energy in Germany. The authors want to thank all donors, supporter and critics.

REFERENCES

[1] J. Hicking, S. Nienke and G. Schuh, "Implementing Load Management in Manufacturing Companies. A Feasible Approach", Seventh International Conference on Smart Grids, Green Communications and IT Energy-aware Technologies. IARIA, Barcelona 21.-25.05.2017, pp. 1–6.

[2] M. Schenk and M. Schumann, "Einleitung - Herausforderungen für die Produktion mit Zukunft," in Produktion und Logistik mit Zukunft: Digital engineering and operation, M. Schenk, Ed., Berlin: Springer Vieweg, 2015, pp. 1–48.

[3] G. Schuh, Produktionsmanagement: Handbuch Produktion und Management 5, 2nd ed. Berlin: Springer Vieweg, 2014.

[4] G. Schuh and V. Stich, Eds., Grundlagen der PPS, 4th ed. Berlin: Springer Vieweg, 2012.

[5] T. Bauernhansl, Energieeffizienz in Deutschland - eine Metastudie: Analyse und Empfehlungen, 2014th ed. Berlin, Heidelberg: Springer Berlin Heidelberg, 2014.

[6] J. Gochermann, Expedition Energiewende, 1st ed. Wiesbaden: Springer Fachmedien Wiesbaden, 2016.

[7] S. Döring, Energieerzeugung nach Novellierung des EEG: Konsequenzen für regenerative und nicht regenerative Energieerzeugungsanlagen. Berlin: Springer Vieweg, 2015.

[8] H. Niederhausen and A. Burkert, Elektrischer Strom: Gestehung, Übertragung, Verteilung, Speicherung und Nutzung elektrischer Energie im Kontext der Energiewende. Wiesbaden: Springer Vieweg, 2014.

[9] BMWi - Bundesministerium für Wirtschaft und Energie, Ein Strommarkt für die Energiewende: Ergebnispapier des Bundesministeriums für Wirtschaft und Energie (Weißbuch). Berlin: Bundesministerium für Wirtschaft und Energie (BMWi), 2015.

[10] M. Geilhausen, J. Bränzel, D. Engelmann, and O. Schulze, Energiemanagement: Für Fachkräfte, Beauftragte und Manager. Wiesbaden: Springer Vieweg, 2015.

[11] BMWi - Bundesministerium für Wirtschaft und Energie, "Energiedaten: Gesamtausgabe: Stand: Januar 2016," Jan. 2016.

[12] Deutsche Bundesregierung, "Energiekonzept für eine umweltschonende, zuverlässige und bezahlbare Energieversorung," Berlin, Sep. 2010.

[13] M. Roscher, C. Maasem, and R. Martynski, "Intelligentes Energiemanagement in der Produktion: Effiziente Energienutzung in der Fertigung durch Energiemonitoren und Lastmanagement," UdZ - Unternehmen der Zukunft, 2014, pp. 20–22, 2014.

[14] H. Seidl, C. Schenuit, and M. Teichmann, "Roadmap Demand Side Management. Industrielles Lastmanagement für ein zukunftsfähiges Energiesystem: Schlussfolgerung aus dem Pilotprojekt DSM Bayern," Berlin, Jun. 2016.

[15] F. Wosnitza and H. G. Hilgers, Energieeffizienz und Energiemanagement: Ein Überblick heutiger Möglichkeiten und Notwendigkeiten. Wiesbaden: Vieweg+Teubner Verlag, 2012.

[16] P. Kurzweil and O. K. Dietlmeier, Elektrochemische Speicher: Superkondensatoren, Batterien, Elektrolyse-Wasserstoff, Rechtliche Grundlagen, 1st ed. Wiesbaden: Springer Vieweg, 2015.

[17] C. Köpp, H.-J. von Mettenheim, and M. H. Breitner, "Lastmanagement in Stromnetzen," Wirtschaftsinf, vol. 55, no. 1, pp. 39–49, 2013.

[18] S. Lehnhoff, Dezentrales vernetztes Energiemanagement: Ein Ansatz auf Basis eines verteilten adaptiven Realzeit-Multiagentensystems. Wiesbaden: Vieweg+Teubner Verlag / GWV Fachverlage GmbH Wiesbaden, 2010.

[19] H. Voss, Modellierung des regionalen Erzeugungsangebots auf dem Elektrizitätsmarkt der Europäischen Union. Berlin: Lit, 2012.

[20] Fraunhofer ISE, Energy Charts. [Online] Available: https://www.energy-charts.de/contact_de.htm. Accessed on: Jun. 16 2016.

[21] B. Diekmann and E. Rosenthal, Energie: Physikalische Grundlagen ihrer Erzeugung, Umwandlung und Nutzung, 3rd ed. Wiesbaden: Springer Spektrum, 2014.

[22] J. Hesselbach, Energie- und klimaeffiziente Produktion: Grundlagen, Leitlinien und Praxisbeispiele, 1st ed. s.l.: Vieweg+Teubner (GWV), 2012.

[23] E. Müller, J. Engelmann, T. Löffler, and J. Strauch, Energieeffiziente Fabriken planen und betreiben, 1st ed. Berlin: Springer Berlin, 2009.

[24] W. Irrek and S. Thomas, "Definition Energieeffizienz," Wuppertal, Jul. 2008.

[25] H. Wannenwetsch, Integrierte Materialwirtschaft, Logistik und Beschaffung, 5th ed. Berlin: Springer Vieweg, 2014.

[26] M. Schenk, S. Wirth, and E. Müller, Fabrikplanung und Fabrikbetrieb: Methoden für die wandlungsfähige, vernetzte und ressourceneffiziente Fabrik, 2nd ed. Berlin, Heidelberg: Springer Berlin Heidelberg, 2014.

[27] S. Hirzel, "Betriebliches Energiemanagement in der industriellen Produktion," Karlsruhe, Sep. 2011.

[28] Energiemanagement - Begriffe, 4602-1, 2016.

[29] J. Kals and K. Würtenberger, "IT-gestütztes Energiemanagement," HMD, vol. 49, no. 3, pp. 73–81, 2012.

[30] Manufacturing Execution Systems (MES) – Kennzahlen für Energiemanagement, 66412-4, 2015.

[31] CRA, "Primer on Demand-Side Management: With an emphasis on price-responsive programs," Oakland, USA, Feb. 2005.

[32] S. C. Bhattacharyya, Energy economics: Concepts, issues, markets and governance. London: Springer, 2011.

[33] Arnusorn Saengprajak, "Efficiency of demand side management measures in small village electrification systems," Dissertation, Universität Kassel, Kassel, 2006.

[34] M. Kruppa, "Lastmanagement im Unternehmen: Grundlagen," 2015.

[35] Z. Hu, D. Maskovitz, and J. Zhao, "Demand-Side Management in China's Restructured Power Industry: How Regulation and Policy Can Deliver Demand-Side Management Benefits to a Growing Economy and a Changing Power System," Washington, D.C., USA, Dec. 2015.

[36] Z. Hu, Integrated resource strategic planning and power demand-side management. Heidelberg, S.l.: Springer; China Electric Power Press, 2013.

[37] D. Y. Goswami and F. Kreith, Energy efficiency and renewable energy handbook. Boca Raton: CRC Press, Taylor & Francis Group, 2015.

[38] M. Kleber, "Leitfaden Lastgangmessung: für das Projekt Teilenergiekennwerte, gefördert durch das BMWi, erstellt durch das Fachgebiet Bauphysik & Technischer Ausbau (fbta)," Karlsruhe, 2010.

GFSM: a Feature Selection Method for Improving Time Series Forecasting

Youssef Hmamouche*, Piotr Przymus†, Alain Casali‡ and Lotfi Lakhal§
LIF - CNRS UMR 7279,
Aix Marseille Université, Marseille, France
Emails: *youssef.hmamouche@lif.univ-mrs.fr, †piotr.przymus@lif.univ-mrs.fr,
‡alain.casali@lif.univ-mrs.fr, § lotfi.lakhal@lif.univ-mrs.fr

***Abstract*—Handling time series forecasting with many predictors is a popular topic in the era of "Big data", where wast amounts of observed variables are stored and used in analytic processes. Classical prediction models face some limitations when applied to large-scale data. Using all the existing predictors increases the computational time and does not necessarily improve the forecast accuracy. The challenge is to extract the most relevant predictors contributing to the forecast of each target time series. We propose a causal-feature selection algorithm specific to multiple time series forecasting based on a clustering approach. Experiments are conducted on US and Australia macroeconomic datasets using different prediction models. We compare our method to some widely used dimension reduction and feature selection methods including principal component analysis PCA, Kernel PCA and factor analysis. The proposed algorithm improves the forecast accuracy compared to the evaluated methods on the tested datasets.**

Keywords*–*Time Series Forecasting; Feature Selection; Multivariate prediction models; Artificial Neural Networks.

I. INTRODUCTION

Time series analysis and data mining incorporates a set of tools, methods, and models for describing the evolution of data over time. Such tools play important role in business analysis and business intelligence systems where they generate new, valuable information by combining trends, forecasts, correlations, causalities *etc.* This additional information can be then used to improve the decision-making process and contribute to more intelligent and efficient decisions.

This article is an extended version of research from [1]. Compared to the previous version, we have discussed possible extensions to the algorithm and significantly expanded the experimental section.

In summary, we try to improve the forecasting of a time series using multivariate models, by selecting only the most relevant varaiables. This leads us to the problem of hidden common factors that may cause multiple variables. To overcome this problem, we propose a feature selection algorithm based on the Granger causality graph. Each time series is represented as a node in the graph and the causality is expressed as edges weights. We follow the classical notion of Granger predictive causality presented in [2], in order to compute the dependencies between each two variables.

One of the first successful univariate time series forecasting models was the Auto-Regressive model [3]. Various versions of this model are still in use today. They are based on the same principle. That is, they take into account historic observations in order to predict the future of variable. Univariate models are limited only to one source of information, and thus, they cannot utilize potentially-exploitable time series. To do better, researchers began to introduce multivariate time series analysis and forecasting models capable of exploiting multiple time series [4]. Many of those concepts are still present in forecasting tools nowadays.

Multivariate analysis increases the complexity of models compared to univariate ones, as multivariate models describe the forecasted time series based on (i) its historical observations and (ii) the historical observations of other series in the dataset. On the plus side, utilizing relevant information from other variables [5] may improve the resulting forecast.

Building a model using all existing variables is usually not an viable option as it may add to much noise to fit an accurate model. For example, in [6], [7], based on two macroeconomic datasets, it was found that using more than $30\% - 60\%$ of the existing predictors does not improve forecast quality and in fact may worsen the results. This rises question how to select relevant variables, that was already investigated in several works [5]–[8].

We can distinguish two popular approaches. One is to enforce the model to discard irrelevant information either by shrinking the coefficients or eliminating them. Shrinkage models, Lasso, Lars or regressors based on neural networks are examples of this approach [6], [7].

The second approach is to use a two step model, where (i) a separate procedure is used to extracts relevant information from multiple variables, and then the selected variables are used to build a multivariate forecasting model. The extraction may be done using feature selection, dimension reduction or by using the notion of causality [1], [5], [8]. In the second step, any multivariate forecasting model can be used (including the ones from previous paragraph).

Our proposed approach design is motivated by industrial needs, where precise forecasts are requested in the presence of huge amount of observed variables. The primary goal was to provide a forecast horizon for a set of variables, which allows to do an educated guess when to buy or sell products. The secondary goal was to detect the frauds in public markets. We mainly work on the prices of raw materials and/or finished products available on public markets.

This paper is organized as follows. First, we discuss the related works (Section II) and prediction models (Section III). Next, we talk about causality measures (Section IV). Then, we discuss our approach in Section V and evaluate its performance in Sections VI and VII. Finally, in Section IX, we summarize our contributions and possible future research.

II. RELATED WORK

Using all the existing variables in a multivariate model has some drawbacks. First for Auto-Regressive based models, if the number of regressors is proportional to the sample size, the ordinary least squares (OLS) forecasts may not be efficient [5]. Secondly, the most accurate forecasts are generally obtained using smaller number of predictors [7], [6]. Thus, in this section we discuss works that deal with the problem of large number of predictors.

Feature selection refers to the act of extracting a subset of the most relevant variables (features) of size k from a set of variables of size $n >> k$. Dimension reduction methods generate a new features with lower dimension from the original features by transforming them. Both of them can be used to optimize the inputs of prediction models. If additionally we are interested with descriptive analysis, feature selection techniques give more information as they select existing variables.

The Principal Component Analysis (PCA) is one of the most common dimension reduction methods used. Based on a set of variables, this method takes advantage of the inter-correlation between them [9]. The idea is to generate the principal linearly uncorrelated variables that describe as much as possible the original variables. The Kernel PCA method is a non-linear version of PCA, that extends it by considering the non-linear relationships between variables using kernel techniques [10]. Factor analysis (FACT) is another technique, similar to PCA in the sense that it generates uncorrelated factors of the original variables, additionally it fits a model of error terms associated with factors [9]. Both PCA and FACT are used to construct the dynamic factor model [11], [12], [5], [13]. It is a prediction model that is designed for high-dimensional time series, or time series where the number of observations exceeds the number of variables. The idea is to find a small number of hidden factors (dynamic factors), that drive all of the observed variables. Thus, each variable can be constructed as a combination of those factors. The observed variables forecasts are constructed based on forecasts of dynamic factors.

Another approach for dealing with many predictors is based on the idea of shrinking the coefficients of irrelevant variables towards (or exactly to) 0. This can be achieved by fitting the regression model with constraints on coefficients. There are numerous well known shrinkage/regularization methods, for instance the Lasso [14] and Ridge [15] methods. While they are associated with the problem of multiple regressions, they can be easily adapted to address the problem of forecasting [16], [17], [6], [18], [7].

Artificial neural networks are also a common choice for solving this problem. In [19], the authors propose an automatic approach for stock market forecasting and trend analysis. A pre-processing step was applied using the PCA in order to transform the data into a set of uncorrelated variables and to reduce the dimension of the input variables. Then, an artificial neural network was used for forecasting the stock outputs, and finally a neuro-fuzzy system is used to analyse the forecasts trends. Similarly, in [8], a two step data mining process was proposed for forecasting daily stock market, using PCA as a first step to reduce the dimension of predictor variables, then, a feed-forward neural network is trained for prediction. In [20], when forecasting time series that represent series of brain images, with a number of variables larger than the number of observations, the authors propose a feature selection method based on PCA, Recursive Feature Elimination and Support Vector Machines. In [21], a two-step forecasting approach was presented to forecast two years of Australian electricity load time series. First, correlation, Mutual Information and instance-based feature selection methods are applied in order to extract the relevant informative lag variables. And second, a multivariate artificial neural network and statistical models are applied to make forecasts.

III. PREDICTION MODELS

In this section, we present a description of prediction models used in this research. Two types of models are discussed, statistical and artificial neural network models.

A. Statistical models

Many prediction models are based on the same principle as the Auto-Regressive model AR(p) [22]. The idea is to expresses an univariate time series as a linear function of its p precedent values:

$$y_t = \alpha_0 + \alpha_1 y_{t-1} + \cdots + \alpha_p y_{t-p} + \epsilon_t,$$

where p is the order of the model, $\alpha_0 \ldots \alpha_p$ are the parameters of the model, and ϵ_t is a white noise error term.

The Moving Average model of order q (MA(q)) has the same expression but for the error terms:

$$y_t = \alpha_0 + \alpha_1 \epsilon_{t-1} + \cdots + \alpha_p \epsilon_{t-q} + \epsilon_t \quad (1)$$

The ARMA(p, q) model [22] expresses errors terms and past values of the time series in the same model. It can be expressed as follows:

$$y_t = \alpha_0 + \sum_{i=1}^{p} \alpha_i y_{t-i} + \sum_{i=1}^{q} \beta_i \epsilon_{t-i} + \epsilon_t.$$

For non-stationary time series, the ARIMA(p, d, q) model [22] is more preferable; it applies the ARMA(p, q) model after a differencing step, in order to obtain stationary time series, where d is the order of differencing (computing d times the differences between consecutive observations).

In [23], the Vector Auto-Regressive (VAR) model was introduced as an extension of the AR model. Consider a k-dimensional time series Y_t, the VAR(p) system expresses each univariate variable of the multivariate time series Y_t as a linear function of the p previous values of itself and the p previous values of the other variables:

$$Y_t \quad = \alpha_0 + \textstyle\sum_{i=1}^{p} A_i Y_{t-i} + \epsilon_t,$$

where ϵ_t is a white noise with a mean of zero, and $A_1, \ldots, A_p$ are $(k \times k)$ matrix parameters of the model.

In [24], the Vector Error Correction (VECM) was introduced. This model transforms the VAR model by taking into account non-stationarity of the time series and by including cointegration equations. To simplify matters, let us consider two multivariate time series (Y_t) integrated of order one, which means all the variables of Y_t are $I(0)$ or$I(1)$, stationary or integrated of order 1. The VECM Model can be written as follows:

$$\Delta Y_t = \Pi Y_{t-1} + \sum_{i=1}^{p-1} \Gamma_i \Delta Y_{t-i} + u_t,$$

where Π is the matrix representing the co-integration equations, which can be generated by VAR model, and Γ_i are the matrix parameters of the VECM model. If $rk(\Pi) = 0$, then there are no cointegration equations, so that the VECM model is reduced to the VAR form applied after differencing time series.

B. Artificial Neural Network Model

ANNS are increasingly popular for forecasting high-dimensional time series. The relation between target and predictors is encoded in a network of neurons characterized generally by a non-linear function. The ANNS are usually able to model time series more dynamically compared to classical models.

The principle of using ANNS in time series forecasting is simple. It consists of transforming the data into a supervised learning problem, where the inputs represent the lagged values of the predictors and the target variables. Then, the network is initialized, commonly with randomly generated parameters. Finally, the network is trained based on its inner objective function (that depends on the network structure, activation function, and other learning parameters). Formally, given a k-dimensional time series $(y_1, \ldots, y_k)$ and a network function f_{nn}, the resulting time series can be expressed as:

$$y_t = f_{nn}(y_{t-1}, \ldots, y_{t-p}, \ldots, y_{k(t-1)}, \ldots, y_{k(t-p)}) + \epsilon_t.$$

During the training step, the parameters of the network are updated through the back-propagation step, using an optimization algorithm, such as Gradient Descent or Stochastic Gradient Descent, which aim to find a local minimum of the error function ϵ_t using some criteria. Popular criteria choices are the mean squared error (mse) or the mean absolute error (mae). Note that other metaheuristics can be used to try to find the global optimum of the error function, such as Genetic Algorithms and Particle Swarm Optimization [25], [26].

In [27], the vector autoregressive neural network (VAR-NN) model is investigated, as an extension of the classical VAR process, based on a multi-layer perceptron. In [28], a comparison between the VAR model and a multi-layered feed-forward neural network has been presented for forecasting macroeconomic variables. It was shown that the neural network has a superior forecasts results than the VAR model in this particular case. In [29], the VAR-NN model shows good performance compared with the VARMA model in the task of predicting non linear functions.

The main drawback of multi-layered perceptron neural network is that the neurons are not able to remember past information. Because each neuron provides an output based directly on the activation function and the input values

$$h_t = f(Wx_t + b).$$

Yet, in time series (and sequences in general), maintaining information inside the network may improve the performance of the model. Recurrent Neural Networks (RNNs) were designed to handle this issue. Their structures allow hidden layers to be self-connected, in a way that output may depend on the current input and its previous state. Mathematically, the function of RNNs neurons can be expressed as follows:

$$h_t = f(Wx_t + Uh_{t-1} + b).$$

Unfortunately, the maintained memory in the network is short, because the current state of network depends only on the previous one. The Long Short Term Memory network introduced in [30] was consequently designed to address this problem. The authors propose a specific structure, by adding extra options transforming traditional neurons into blocks, able to model the mechanics necessary for the network to forget and remember informations. Thus, it can learns how to use long-term information passed through the network in the working memory. The mathematical formulation of a hidden LSTM block can be written as follow:

$$\begin{aligned}
f_t &= \sigma(W_f x_t + U_f h_{t-1} + b_f), \\
i_t &= \sigma(W_i x_t + U_i h_{t-1} + b_i), \\
c_t &= f_t \odot c_{t-1} + i_t \odot tanh(W_c x_t + U_c h_{t-1} + c_0), \\
o_t &= \sigma(W_o x_t + U_o h_{t-1} + b_o), \\
h_t &= o_t \odot tang(c_t),
\end{aligned}$$

where $\odot$ represents the element-wise multiplication x_t is the input vector, (W, U, b) are the parameters of the model, σ and $tanh$ are the sigmoid and tangent activation functions, f_t is the forget gate layer responsible for updating the weight of remembering the previous information, i_t is the input gate layer responsible for updating new information, c_t is the cell state at time t, o_t is the output gate layer, and h_t is to output of the cell.

IV. CAUSALITY MEASURES

Studying the relationships between time series is an important task for multivariate time series analysis, which can be exploited for forecasting. The common measures like Correlation and Mutual Information, are symmetric, so they do not provide enough information about the dependencies between variables, i.e., which variables influence the other. The goal of causality is to detect the impact of one time series on an another one in terms of prediction.

In this section, we discuss two different causality measures, the Granger causality [2], and the Transfer entropy [31]. Let us consider two univariate time series x_t, y_t. The Granger definition of causality acknowledges the fact that x_t causes y_t if it contains information helpful to predict y_t. In other words, x_t causes y_t if a prediction model that uses both x_t and y_t performs better than the one that is based merely on y_t.

We detail here the standard Granger causality test [2], which uses the VAR model with a trend term. The test compares two models. The first one only takes into account the precedent values of y_t, and the second uses both x_t and y_t in order to predict y_t. If there is a significant difference between the two models, then it can be ascertained that the added variable (x_t) causes y_t:

$$\text{Model}_1: \quad y_t = \alpha_0 + \alpha t + \sum_{i=1}^{p} \alpha_i y_{t-i} + \epsilon_t.$$

$$\text{Model}_2: \quad y_t = \alpha_0 + \alpha t + \sum_{i=1}^{p} \alpha_i y_{t-i} + \sum_{i=1}^{p} \beta_i x_{t-i} + \epsilon_t.$$

The next step of the test is to compare the residual sum of squares (RSS) of these models using the Fisher test. The statistic of the test is expressed as follow:

$$F = \frac{(\text{RSS}_1 - \text{RSS}_2)/p)}{(\text{RSS}_2/n - 2p - 1)},$$

where RSS_1 and RSS_2 are the residual sum of squares related to Model_1 and Model_2 respectively, n is the size of the predicted vector. Two hypotheses are tested,

- H_0: $\forall i \in \{1, \ldots, p\}, \beta_i = 0$,
- H_1: $\exists i \in \{1, \ldots, p\}, \beta_i \neq 0$.

Under the null hypothesis H_0 (the hypothesis that x does not cause y), F follows the Fisher distribution with $(p, n-2p-1)$ degrees of freedom. Therefore, the Granger causality test is carried out at a level α in order to examine the null hypothesis. The p-value of the test is the probability to observe the given result under the assumption that H_0 is true. In our case, we consider the causality as one minus p-value in order to express values of causalities in the range $[0, 1]$.

Transfer Entropy is another causality measure based on information theory. Before discussing this measure, it is worth to recall the notion of mutual information between two processes (or two univariate time series) I and J. It measures the mutual dependencies (symmetric) between the two processes. Consider two processes I and J, with probability distribution $p(i)$ and $p(j)$, joint probability $p(i, j)$, and conditional probability $p(i|j)$. The mutual information between the two processes I and J can be expressed using the Kullback entropy as follows:

$$M_{IJ} = \sum_{i \in I, j \in J} p(i,j) log(\frac{p(i|j)}{p(i)p(j)}).$$

The main drawback of this measure is that is symmetric and does not model the transfer of information from one process to another. The transfer entropy was proposed as an extension of mutual information in [31]. And the idea is to add a time shift parameter, that allows modeling the non symmetric transfer of information between processes. Even though Granger causality and Transfer entropy may seem to be based on different concepts, an interesting finding was presented in [32], showing that they are equivalent for variables with normal distributions. The mathematical formulation of transfer entropy from J to the I can be expressed as follows:

$$T_{J \to I} = \sum_{i \in I, j \in J} p(i_{n+1}, i_n^k, j_n^l) log(\frac{p(i_{n+1} \mid i_n^k, j_n^l)}{p(i_{n+1} \mid i_n^k)}.$$

V. OUR PROPOSAL

Our approach focuses on the selection of the top predictor variables by describing their hidden dependencies using bivariate causality. Let us consider $Y = \{y_1, y_2, \ldots, y_n\}$ a multivariate time series and a target variable y. The goal is to select a subset of Y, for which we have the more accurate forecasts of y.

We assume that causality is more important than correlation measures when forecasting time series. Because, in contrast to correlation, causality models the non-symmetric dependencies between variables. In other words, if two variables are correlated, it does not identify which variable has an impact on the other. By considering this hypothesis, one solution is to choose a set of variables having strong causality regarding to the target y. This is equivalent to a univariate feature selection technique that ranks variables based on causality to the target. This approach was already investigated in [33] and [34] using the Granger causality test. The main limitation of those approaches is that they potentially ignore hidden relationship between predictor variables. That is, the same hidden source of information may be exploited despite the fact of using with multiple selected variables.

Let us underline that from a theoretical point of view, there are $\sum_{i=1}^{k} \binom{n}{i}$ possible partitions of size less than or equal to k. Where n is the number of original features, and $k < n$. In the general case, i.e., without fixing the maximum number of predictors k, there are 2^n possible partitions, so 2^n possible models [5]. In addition, the causality is generally not a monotone function. As a consequence, finding the best subset of variables that maximizes the multivariate causality is a NP-hard problem.

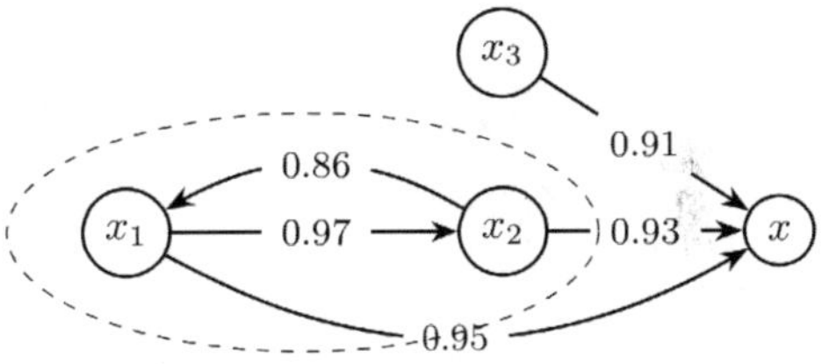

Figure 1. Illustration Of Dependencies Between Time Series Using the Granger Causality Graph.

In Figure 1, we show a small Granger causality graph describing dependencies between 4 variables. Let us try to select two variables as predictors for the target variable x. Selecting variables by ranking them according to causality leads to getting x_1 and x_2 as predictors. However, x_1 and x_2 might provide the same information because x_1 causes x_2.

We propose a new method to deal with this problem based on clustering the causality graph or the adjacency matrix using a clustering technique, such as the Partitioning Around Medoids or the hierarchical clustering.

A. *The proposed algorithm*

The proposed method can be divided into four steps:

- Build the adjacency matrix of causalities between variables.
- Eliminate variables having low causality on the target.
- Cluster the set of the remaining predictors variables, by minimizing the causalities between clusters, and maximizing the causality within clusters.
- Choose one element from each cluster, the one that maximizes the causality on the target variable.

Let us underline that this algorithm is a generalization of ranking methods, in the way that if the number of clusters (input of the method) is equal of the number of variables, then the algorithm will select the first k variables by ranking them according to the causality to the target. In Figure 2, the GFSM (causality-Graph based Feature Selection Method) algorithm summarizes our approach.

Input: Set of predictors time series $Y = \{y_1, y_2, \ldots, y_n\}$, y the target variable, MINCAUS Min-Causality threshold, k the selection size
Output: GFSM-CL the set of the selected variables associated to y

```
for i = 1 to n do
  if causality(y_i → y) ≤ MINCAUS then
    Y = Y \ {y_i}
  end if
  if Y.size() ⩽ k then
    return GFSM-CL = Y
  end if
end for
/* Build the matrix of causalities.              */
Let MC be the adjacency matrix of causalities
for each y_i, y_j in Y such that i ≠ j do
  MC[i, j] = MC[j, i] = 1 − max(causality(y_i →
  y_j), causality(y_j → y_i))
end for
/* The clustering step.                          */
Clusters = clustering(MC, k)
for each Cluster cl in Clusters do
  GFSM-CL = GFSM-CL ∪ arg max_{cl_j ∈ cl} (causality(cl_j →
  y)
end for
return GFSM-CL
```

Figure 2. The GFSM Algorithm.

B. Scalability of the proposed algorithm

Scalability of the algorithm is crucial when handling high-dimensional time series, thus, in this part we discuss it. Granger causality is computed by comparing forecasting accuracy between univariate model and bivariate model (usually followed by significance test). This requires that two forecasting models have to be constructed to compute the Granger causality. An univariate AR model on target variable and a bivariate VAR model with a target variable and one additional predictor.

The algorithm presented uses the Granger causality graph. It requires computation of a set of tuples $G = (P \times P) \setminus \Delta$, where P is the set of predictors and $\Delta = (p_1, p_2) \in P \times P : p1 = p2$. Therefore, we have to compute univariate models for all elements in P and bivariate models for tuples in G. This is trivially scalable as all models can be computed independently. Finally, the results should be grouped by target variable and simple statistical tests of accuracy computed for univariate model on variables $p \in P$, and a bivariate model $(p_1, p_2) \in G$ (simple task in map reduce approach). As a result, we compute the adjacency matrix.

For financial time series it is reasonable to assume that the resulting matrix will have reasonable size and will feet single computation node. In rare cases, when the matrix is very large, scalable clustering algorithms could be used (like k-medoids and other methods investigated in [35] and [36]).

C. Example

Consider $Y = \{y_1, \ldots, y_8\}$ a set of predictors and a target variable y_9. Let us apply the GFSM algorithm in order to select 4 predictor variables from Y that will contribute to forecast y.

1) The matrix of causalities: First, the algorithm computes the Granger causalities between variables in pairs. In this example, we take the matrix of causalities of a dataset containing nine variables:

$$MC = \begin{bmatrix} 1.00 & 0.935 & 0.999 & 0.999 & 0.832 & 0.998 & 0.998 & 0.933 & 0.998 \\ 0.28 & 1.00 & 0.877 & 0.87 & 0.224 & 0.785 & 0.801 & 0.999 & 0.868 \\ 0.033 & 0.656 & 1.00 & 0.106 & 0.479 & 0.944 & 0.775 & 0.082 & 0.905 \\ 0.028 & 0.647 & 0.239 & 1.00 & 0.483 & 0.944 & 0.776 & 0.096 & 0.905 \\ 0.7 & 0.457 & 0.977 & 0.978 & 1.00 & 0.343 & 0.031 & 0.398 & 0.901 \\ 0.808 & 0.417 & 0.818 & 0.817 & 0.906 & 1.00 & 0.997 & 0.431 & 0.722 \\ 0.274 & 0.742 & 0.992 & 0.992 & 0.942 & 0.959 & 1.00 & 0.906 & 0.788 \\ 0.327 & 0.999 & 0.998 & 0.998 & 0.427 & 0.895 & 0.996 & 1.00 & 0.900 \\ 0.304 & 0.071 & 0.581 & 0.584 & 0.205 & 0.448 & 0.999 & 0.754 & 1.00 \end{bmatrix}$$

2) Clustering and selecting the variables: The algorithm partitions the variables based on the symmetrical matrix (as mentioned in the algorithm 2). The idea behind symmetrizing the matrix of causalities is to be able to perform the clustering task. By using the Partitionning Arround Medoids (PAM) [37], let us also underline that this method partitions elements from a symmetric dissimilarity matrix and minimizes dissimilarities within clusters. In our case, the algorithm maximizes causalities within clusters. That is why we use 1 minus the causality matrix as an input of the PAM method.

Then, the algorithm chooses from each cluster the element that has maximal causality on the target. The obtained clustering vector associated to $\{y_1, \ldots, y_8\}$ is $(1, 2, 1, 1, 3, 1, 4, 2)$. And based on the causalities to the target (last column of the adjacency matrix), the selected variables are $\{y_1, y_5, y_7, y_8\}$.

3) Evaluating the clusters: The quality of the causalities founded depends on, first the type of the data, and second, on the evaluation of the clustering task. In our case, we evaluate the quality of the clusters using the following objective function:

$$\text{minimize } G(x) \quad = \sum_i^n \sum_j^n (1 - max(c_{ij}, c_{ji})) \times z_{ij},$$

where

1) $z_{ij} = \begin{cases} 1 & \text{if } y_i, y_j \text{ belong to the same cluster} \\ 0 & \text{otherwise.} \end{cases}$
2) c_{ij} = causality$(y_i \rightarrow y_j)$.

This evaluation can be used in general as measure of causal relationships in multivariate time series. In the example, the value of G is 0.000168.

VI. EXPERIMENTAL EVALUATION

In this section, we describe the experiments design, the datasets used, the forecasting methodology, and the methods and models implemented.

A. Datasets

The experiments are performed on macroeconomic datasets of US and Australia.

- The US macroeconomic dataset [6]: quarterly numeric time series, containing 143 features and 200 observations, spanning the period 1960 – 2008.
- The Australian macroeconomic dataset [7]: quarterly numeric time series spanning the period 1984 – 2015, comprising 117 variables and 119 observations.

These datasets were used in the context of forecasting with many predictors in [6], [7]. Different models were evaluated using those datasets, the naive-benchmark and the AR (4) as baseline models, the dynamic factor model, the VAR model and other shrinkage methods. Both datasets contain three main series, that we focus on in the experiments:

- US dataset: GDP: Real gross domestic product, CPI (Cpi all items (sa) fred), Fedfuns (Interest rate: federal funds (effective)).
- Australia dataset: GDP: Real gross domestic product, CPI (Consumer Price Index), IBR (overnight interbank rate).

B. Methods: feature selection and dimension reduction techniques

We use the Scikit-learn machine learning module [38] for the implementation of the following methods:

- Principal component analysis (PCA) [39].
- Kernel Principal component analysis (Kernel PCA) [10].
- Factor Analysis (FACT) [9].

And we implemented the following two methods:

- A univariate feature selection method using Granger causality (UFSM), similar to the one proposed in [33].
- Our proposal, by generating two versions using two clustering methods in the Algorithm 2. The first one is based on the Parttionning Arround Medoids (PAM) [37] (pGFSM), and the second (hGFSM) is based on the hieearchical clustering [40].

C. Methods: Prediction models

The used prediction models can be classified into three types; baseline model, statistical models, and artificial neural networks (ANNS):

- Baseline model: we use the naive-benchmark (4) model, that predict the next value of a variable based on the mean of the last 4 values,
- Statistical models: we use the AR(4) model and the ARIMA $(4, d, q)$ models (with automatic determination of the parameters d and q, see Section III for details.) to analyse forecasts without the use of predictors. And the Vector Error Correction Model (see Section III for mathematical formulation). We use the implementation from the **forecast R** package [41].
- ANNS models: we use the following strategy to build ANNS models. We transform the data into a supervised learning problem, based on the lag parameter, the target variable, and the selected predictors. Then, we adapt two existing ANNs models to our problem. We use the multilayer perceptron and the Long Short Term Memory networks from the deep learning **python** library; **keras** [42].
  For the model based the MLP structure (VARMLP), we use one hidden layer using a simple rule of thump to determine the number of hidden neurons, $2/3\times(n+1)$, where n is the number of inputs. And for the LSTM based model, we use the same number of units in hidden layer as the number of input variables. In both cases, the models inputs depend on the lag parameter p and the number of predictors k, $n = k\times p$. Then, the networks are trained using back-propagation through time, and the error functions are minimized using the stochastic gradient decent algorithm.

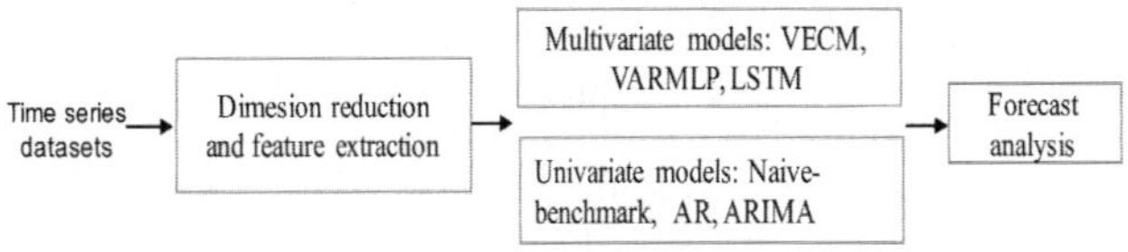

Figure 3. The Used Forecasting Process.

D. Forecasting procedure

We implemented an automatic step-wise forecasting process, as seen in Figure 3. First, It reduces the number of predictors using feature selection and dimension reduction techniques. Second, it applies the forecasting models. And finally, it evaluates the quality of the obtained forecasts. We note that the reduction step is not required for univariate models, because they consider just the target variable to make forecasts. The pre-processing step consists in transforming time series to stationary via differencing, and this step is not required for all models such VECM and ARIMA as they take it into account automatically. For the proposed algorithm, we use the Granger causality test as causality measure. The lag parameter for Granger causality test is automatically determined using the Akaikes Information Criterion (AIC) [43] with a maximum value of 4 equivalent to 4 quarters.

We adopt the same forecasting procedures utilized to forecast US and Australia datasets in [6] and [7]. We consider a lag parameter equivalent to 4 quarters for prediction models. The number of predictions for testing the models is 100 predictions for US dataset and 75 for Australia dataset. Finally, the prediction step is performed using a rolling window procedure (we move one step each time, update models based on last values, and compute the next forecasts), and we focus on the first horizon forecast.

E. Forecast accuracy measures

Two measures of forecast accuracy are used. The classical root mean square error (RMSE), and the mean absolute scaled error (MASE). The MASE is based on the errors of the forecasts and the mean absolute error of the naive method on the in-sample:

$$\text{RMSE} = \sqrt{\frac{\sum_{t=1}^{h}(y_{t+n} - \hat{y}_{t+n})^2}{h}},$$

$$\text{MASE} = \frac{\frac{1}{h}\sum_{t=n+1}^{n+h} \mid y_t - \hat{y}_t \mid}{\frac{1}{n-1}\sum_{t=2}^{n} \mid y_t - y_{t-1} \mid},$$

where h is the number of predictions, $(\hat{y}_{n+1}, \ldots, \hat{y}_{n+h})$ are the forecasts, $(y_{n+1}, \ldots, y_{n+h})$ are the real values.

VII. RESULTS

We show in Tables I and II the forecast accuracy relative to naive-benchmark model using the RMSE and the MASE measures. These experiments are made on an single computer with processor 2,2 GHz Intel Core i7 and 16Gb of RAM. The evaluations are performed by executing the models (in rows) on all the features generated by all the methods (in columns). Due to the computational time limitations, and the large number of the obtained models with the associated subset of predictors, we fix the maximum number of the selected features at 20, and we show only the optimal number k that provides the best performance for each method, with an exception for the method named UFSM, which does no require an input parameter specifying the number of features.

VIII. DISCUSSION

In this section, we discuss the obtained results, and we try to explain some findings. We also compare the global results with papers [6] and [7].

The main observation is that the two instances of the proposed algorithm, i.e., based on the partitioning and the hierarchical clustering techniques, outperform the other methods for most of the target time series. This is especially visible when they are used with artificial neural networks models.

In general, the results reveal that the forecasts of all univariate models used are improved by multivariate models. However, univariate models are competitive for some variables. This is mainly due to the lack of relevant dependencies between some variables. For example, with the GDP variable of Australian datasets, we slightly improved the naive-benchmark model, only by using the pGFSM and hGFSM methods.

When forecasting the CPI variable of Australian dataset, authors of [7] showed that the used multivariate models do not improve the forecast accuracy of the AR(4) and the naive-benchmark univariate models. Nevertheless, we show that when we use the GFSM method with the LSMT model, we improve the accuracy of forecast for this variable. As a consequence, we argue that some of the obtained forecasts in [7] and [6] can be improved using the proposed feature selecting algorithm and neural network models.

In addition, we note that the best results are obtained generally with a number of variables less than 15. This confirms relatively the results in [7], where the best results of multivariate models are obtained using a number of predictor variables less than $20 - 40$.

As a side note, we do not discuss the statistical significance of the forecast accuracy. It is worth to mention that some authors, such as [44], have argued that statistical significance testing of forecast accuracy should be avoided, as test results may be misleading and that practice may actually harm the progress of forecasting field. We also notice that for some target variables, in which, the UFSM method is applied to select the predictor variables, the VECM model could not be fitted, and we do not have predictions for those variables. This is mainly due to the important number of features generated by this method, and this may cause some problems with matrix operations (obtaining singular matrix) when fitting the parameters of the VECM model. To avoid this problem, one should reduce more the number of predictor variables or reduce the lag parameter. Another alternative consists in utilizing artificial neural networks or adopt shrinkage approaches to solve linear models.

Finally, we note that for the PCA and Kernel PCA dimension reduction methods, it is possible to have both automatic number of features k or a specific number given in the input. Currently, our proposal requires from the user the number of features to be selected. It is equal to the number of clusters generated by the clustering method used inside the algorithm. Consequently, this algorithm can be extended to provide an automatic number of features by using some methods of automatic selection of the optimal number of clusters [45], [46].

IX. CONCLUSIONS

In the literature, a little attention has been paid to the role of causality in feature selection for multiple time series forecasting. While the impact of direct dependencies between variables is not negligible in many types of real time series, and the causality may help to detect the most relevant predictor variables. In this paper, we investigated its role and we proposed a feature selection algorithm specific to time series forecasting with the idea of avoiding duplicated dependencies between the predictor variables using a clustering approach. The causality measure adopted for the experiments is the Granger causality, but the proposed algorithm is applicable for other similarity measures, for instance, the transfer entropy.

We have presented a benchmark experiments, by evaluating some two-step approaches, that are based on feature selection and dimension reduction techniques as a first step before applying prediction models. Experiments are conducted on real macroeconomic datasets of US an Australia [6], [7]. And we compared the proposed algorithm to some well known exiting methods, using several prediction models. The results show that the proposed algorithm is very competitive for both datasets in terms of RMSE and MASE as forecast accuracy measures, and works well with the VARMLP and the LSTM artificial neural network models.

In future work, we aim to adopt a more deeper analysis on the graph of casualties than the clustering approach, in order to tackle dependencies between time series. As in the current work, we test our approach on macroeconomic datasets, we also aim to apply it on other type of data, as well as study the applicability of the feature selection methods on the types of the models (i.e., prediction, regression and others).

TABLE I. The Forecast Accuracy Results Using The RMSE Measure, Relative To The Naive-Benchmark Model For AUSTRALIA And US Datasets.

Datasets	Series	Models	RMSE PCA	Kernel PCA	FACT	UFSM	pGFSM	hGFSM
US DATASET	CPI	AR	1.04	1.04	1.04	1.04	1.04	1.04
		ARIMA	1.05	1.05	1.05	1.05	1.05	1.05
		VECM	0.97	0.97	0.95	1.27	0.81	0.76
		VARMLP	**0.54**	0.96	1.00	0.97	0.87	0.86
		LSTM	1.07	1.07	0.56	1.06	0.96	0.90
	GDP	AR	0.92	0.92	0.92	0.92	0.92	0.92
		ARIMA	0.93	0.93	0.93	0.93	0.93	0.93
		VECM	0.97	0.96	0.97		0.88	0.88
		VARMLP	0.88	0.89	0.94	1.25	0.85	0.78
		LSTM	0.90	0.90	0.86	0.87	**0.76**	0.78
	Fedfuns	AR	0.96	0.96	0.96	0.96	0.96	0.96
		ARIMA	0.89	0.89	0.89	0.89	0.89	0.89
		VECM	1.06	1.06	1.21		0.98	0.94
		VARMLP	0.86	0.86	1.12	2.07	0.84	0.80
		LSTM	0.75	**0.71**	0.78	1.16	0.81	0.78
AUSTRALIA DATASET	RGDP	AR	1.06	1.06	1.06	1.06	1.06	1.06
		ARIMA	1.07	1.07	1.07	1.07	1.07	1.07
		VECM	1.24	1.99	1.34	3.28	1.32	1.29
		VARMLP	1.02	1.08	1.15	1.67	1.02	1.02
		LSTM	1.04	1.05	1.01	1.40	1.00	**0.96**
	IBR	AR	0.92	0.92	0.92	0.92	0.92	0.92
		ARIMA	0.92	0.92	0.92	0.92	0.92	0.92
		VECM	1.27	1.85	1.11	2.30	1.01	1.01
		VARMLP	1.23	1.64	1.03	1.64	0.86	0.88
		LSTM	1.14	0.86	1.02	1.71	0.80	**0.75**
	CPI	AR	0.87	0.87	0.87	0.87	0.87	0.87
		ARIMA	1.01	1.01	1.01	1.01	1.01	1.01
		VECM	1.06	1.83	1.03	1.04	1.02	1.02
		VARMLP	0.98	1.03	1.00	1.01	0.78	**0.77**
		LSTM	1.02	1.03	1.00	1.01	0.82	0.88

TABLE II. The Forecast Accuracy Results Using The MASE Measure, Relative To The Naive-Benchmark Model For AUSTRALIA And US Datasets.

Dataset	Series	Models	MASE PCA	Kernel PCA	FACT	UFSM	pGFSM	hGFSM
US DATASETS	CPI	AR	0.87	0.87	0.87	0.87	0.87	0.87
		ARIMA	0.90	0.90	0.90	0.90	0.90	0.90
		VECM	0.87	0.87	0.91	1.52	0.91	0.87
		VARMLP	0.85	**0.83**	0.88	0.96	0.84	0.85
		LSTM	0.94	0.95	0.89	0.97	0.84	0.89
	GDP	AR	0.92	0.92	0.92	0.92	0.92	0.92
		ARIMA	0.90	0.90	0.90	0.90	0.90	0.90
		VECM	0.95	0.95	1.00	0.00	0.91	0.91
		VARMLP	0.90	0.90	0.99	1.26	0.82	0.82
		LSTM	0.92	0.93	0.85	0.89	**0.77**	**0.77**
	Fedfuns	AR	0.95	0.95	0.95	0.95	0.95	0.95
		ARIMA	0.86	0.86	0.86	0.86	0.86	0.86
		VECM	1.17	1.17	1.32		1.04	0.95
		VARMLP	0.93	0.93	1.16	2.06	0.93	0.85
		LSTM	0.80	0.75	0.80	1.21	0.85	**0.82**
AUSTRALIA DATASET	CPI	AR	0.89	0.89	0.89	0.89	0.89	0.89
		ARIMA	1.02	1.02	1.02	1.02	1.02	1.02
		VECM	1.21	1.74	1.11	1.11	1.10	1.10
		VARMLP	1.01	1.05	1.13	1.04	**0.83**	0.88
		LSTM	1.04	1.06	1.03	1.03	0.89	0.95
	IBR	AR	0.89	0.89	0.89	0.89	0.89	0.89
		ARIMA	0.85	0.85	0.85	0.85	0.85	0.85
		VECM	1.33	1.52	1.20	2.18	0.98	0.98
		VARMLP	1.28	1.46	1.20	2.03	0.88	0.91
		LSTM	1.24	1.00	1.11	0.85	0.85	**0.84**
	RGDP	AR	1.05	1.05	1.05	1.05	1.05	1.05
		ARIMA	1.08	1.08	1.08	1.08	1.08	1.08
		VECM	1.37	1.96	1.46	2.98	1.33	1.33
		VARMLP	1.07	1.13	1.15	1.08	1.02	1.07
		LSTM	1.10	1.11	1.06	1.43	**0.99**	1.00

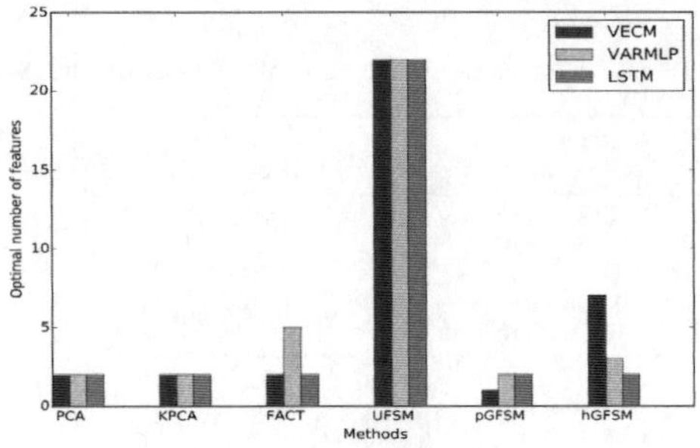

(a) RGDP

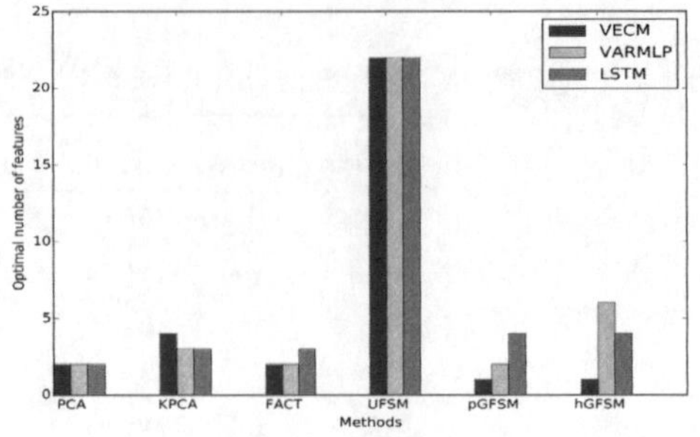

(b) Australia_CPI

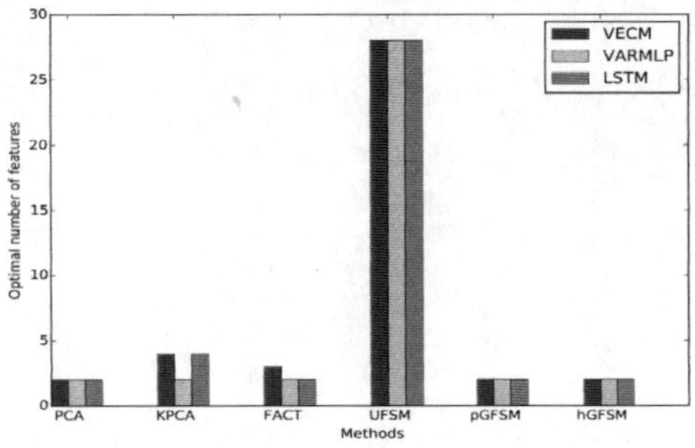

(c) IBR

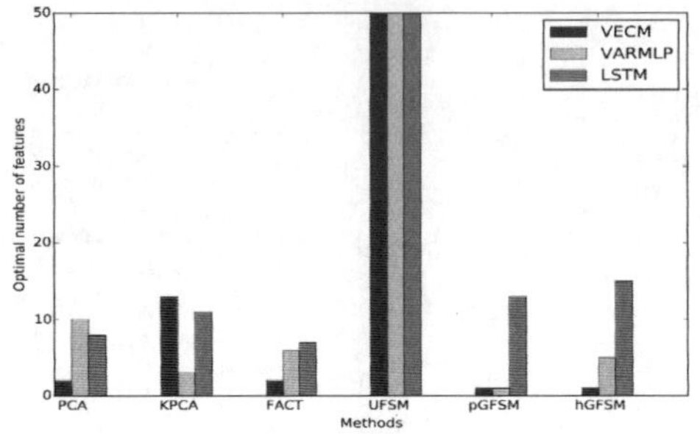

(d) GDP

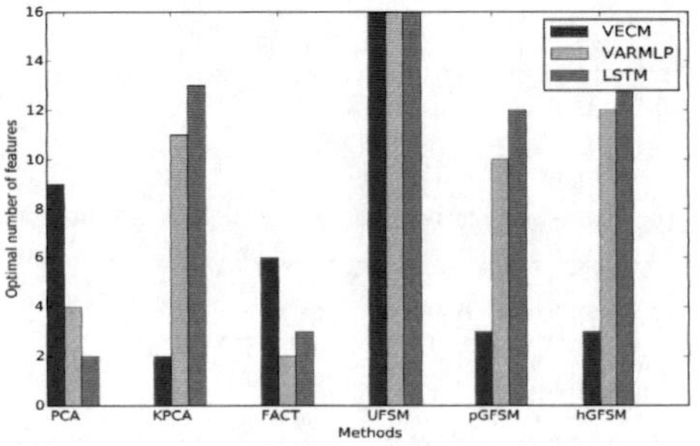

(e) US_CPI

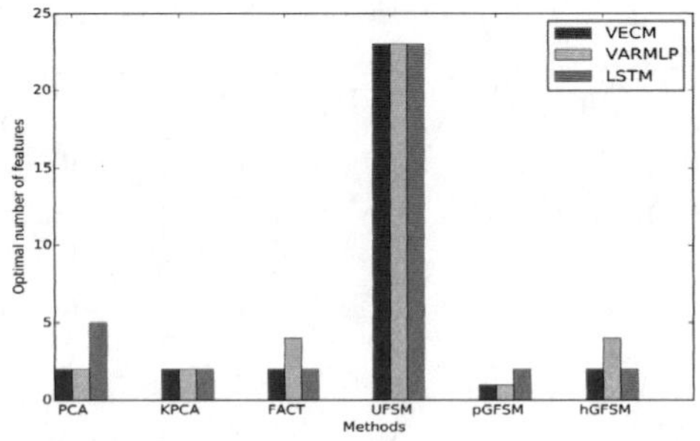

(f) Fedfuns

Figure 4. The Best Number Of Features According To RMSE Of The Methods Used.

REFERENCES

[1] Y. Hmamouche, A. Casali, and L. Lakhal, "A causality-based feature selection approach for multivariate time series forecasting," in DBKDA, 2017, pp. 97–102.

[2] C. W. J. Granger, "Testing for causality," Journal of Economic Dynamics and Control, vol. 2, Jan. 1980, pp. 329–352.

[3] G. Walker, "On Periodicity in Series of Related Terms," Proceedings of the Royal Society of London. Series A, Containing Papers of a Mathematical and Physical Character, vol. 131, no. 818, 1931, pp. 518–532.

[4] P. Whittle, "The Analysis of Multiple Stationary Time Series," Journal of the Royal Statistical Society. Series B (Methodological), vol. 15, no. 1, 1953, pp. 125–139.

[5] J. H. Stock and M. W. Watson, "Chapter 10 Forecasting with Many Predictors," in Handbook of Economic Forecasting, C. W. J. G. G. Elliott and A. Timmermann, Eds. Elsevier, 2006, vol. 1, pp. 515–554.

[6] ——, "Generalized Shrinkage Methods for Forecasting Using Many Predictors," Journal of Business & Economic Statistics, vol. 30, no. 4, Oct. 2012, pp. 481–493.

[7] B. Jiang, G. Athanasopoulos, R. J. Hyndman, A. Panagiotelis, and F. Vahid, "Macroeconomic forecasting for Australia using a large number of predictors," Monash University, Department of Econometrics and Business Statistics, Monash Econometrics and Business Statistics Working Paper 2/17, 2017.

[8] X. Zhong and D. Enke, "Forecasting daily stock market return using dimensionality reduction," Expert Systems with Applications, vol. 67, 2017, pp. 126–139.

[9] I. T. Jolliffe, "Principal Component Analysis and Factor Analysis," in Principal Component Analysis, ser. Springer Series in Statistics. Springer, New York, NY, 1986, pp. 115–128.

[10] B. Schölkopf, A. Smola, and K.-R. Müller, "Nonlinear Component Analysis as a Kernel Eigenvalue Problem," Neural Computation, vol. 10, no. 5, Jul. 1998, pp. 1299–1319.

[11] J. Geweke, "The dynamic factor analysis of economic time series," Latent Variables in Socio-Economic Models, 1977.

[12] J. H. Stock and M. W. Watson, "Forecasting Using Principal Components From a Large Number of Predictors," Journal of the American Statistical Association, vol. 97, no. 460, Dec. 2002, pp. 1167–1179.

[13] J. H. Stock and M. Watson, "Dynamic Factor Models," in Oxford Handbook on Economic Forecasting. Oxford University Press, 2011.

[14] R. Tibshirani, "Regression Shrinkage and Selection Via the Lasso," Journal of the Royal Statistical Society, Series B, vol. 58, 1994, pp. 267–288.

[15] A. E. Hoerl and R. W. Kennard, "Ridge Regression: Biased Estimation for Nonorthogonal Problems," Technometrics, vol. 12, no. 1, 1970, pp. 55–67.

[16] J. H. Wright, "Forecasting US inflation by Bayesian model averaging," Journal of Forecasting, vol. 28, no. 2, Mar. 2009, pp. 131–144.

[17] A. Carriero, G. Kapetanios, and M. Marcellino, "Forecasting large datasets with Bayesian reduced rank multivariate models," Journal of Applied Econometrics, vol. 26, no. 5, Aug. 2011, pp. 735–761.

[18] D. Korobilis, "Hierarchical shrinkage priors for dynamic regressions with many predictors," International Journal of Forecasting, vol. 29, no. 1, Jan. 2013, pp. 43–59.

[19] A. Abraham, B. Nath, and P. K. Mahanti, "Hybrid Intelligent Systems for Stock Market Analysis," in Computational Science - ICCS 2001. Springer, Berlin, Heidelberg, May 2001, pp. 337–345.

[20] H. Yoon and C. Shahabi, "Feature subset selection on multivariate time series with extremely large spatial features," in Data Mining Workshops, 2006. ICDM Workshops 2006. Sixth IEEE International Conference on. IEEE, 2006, pp. 337–342.

[21] I. Koprinska, M. Rana, and V. G. Agelidis, "Correlation and instance based feature selection for electricity load forecasting," Knowledge-Based Systems, vol. 82, Jul. 2015, pp. 29–40.

[22] G. Box, "Box and Jenkins: Time Series Analysis, Forecasting and Control," in A Very British Affair, ser. Palgrave Advanced Texts in Econometrics. Palgrave Macmillan UK, 2013, pp. 161–215.

[23] M. H. Quenouille, "The analysis of multiple time-series," 1957.

[24] S. Johansen, "Estimation and Hypothesis Testing of Cointegration Vectors in Gaussian Vector Autoregressive Models," Econometrica, vol. 59, no. 6, 1991, pp. 1551–1580.

[25] J. N. D. Gupta and R. S. Sexton, "Comparing backpropagation with a genetic algorithm for neural network training," Omega, vol. 27, no. 6, Dec. 1999, pp. 679–684.

[26] K. Khan and A. Sahai, "A Comparison of BA, GA, PSO, BP and LM for Training Feed forward Neural Networks in e-Learning Context," International Journal of Intelligent Systems and Applications, vol. 4, no. 7, pp. 23–29.

[27] D. U. Wutsqa, "The Var-NN Model for Multivariate Time Series Forecasting," MatStat, vol. 8, no. 1, Jan. 2008, pp. 35–43.

[28] A. D. Aydin and S. C. Cavdar, "Comparison of Prediction Performances of Artificial Neural Network (ANN) and Vector Autoregressive (VAR) Models by Using the Macroeconomic Variables of Gold Prices, Borsa Istanbul (BIST) 100 Index and US Dollar-Turkish Lira (USD/TRY) Exchange Rates," Procedia Economics and Finance, vol. 30, Jan. 2015, pp. 3–14.

[29] D. U. Wutsqa, S. G. Subanar, and Z. Sujuti, "Forecasting performance of VAR-NN and VARMA models," in Proceedings of the 2nd IMT-GT Regional Conference on Mathematics, 2006.

[30] S. Hochreiter and J. Schmidhuber, "Long Short-Term Memory," Neural Comput., vol. 9, no. 8, Nov. 1997, pp. 1735–1780.

[31] T. Schreiber, "Measuring Information Transfer," Physical Review Letters, vol. 85, no. 2, Jul. 2000, pp. 461–464.

[32] L. Barnett, A. B. Barrett, and A. K. Seth, "Granger causality and transfer entropy are equivalent for Gaussian variables," Physical Review Letters, vol. 103, no. 23, Dec. 2009.

[33] Y. Sun, J. Li, J. Liu, C. Chow, B. Sun, and R. Wang, "Using causal discovery for feature selection in multivariate numerical time series," Machine Learning, vol. 101, no. 1-3, Jul. 2014, pp. 377–395.

[34] X. Zhang, Y. Hu, K. Xie, S. Wang, E. W. T. Ngai, and M. Liu, "A causal feature selection algorithm for stock prediction modeling," Neurocomputing, vol. 142, Oct. 2014, pp. 48–59.

[35] M. C. K. Babu, P. Nagendra, "IJETT - Survey on Clustering on the Cloud by UsingMap Reduce in Large Data Applications," International Journal of Engineering Trends and Technology.

[36] Y. Wu, Y. Zhu, T. Huang, X. Li, X. Liu, and M. Liu, "Distributed Discord Discovery: Spark Based Anomaly Detection in Time Series," in 2015 IEEE 17th International Conference on High Performance Computing and Communications, 2015 IEEE 7th International Symposium on Cyberspace Safety and Security, and 2015 IEEE 12th International Conference on Embedded Software and Systems, Aug. 2015, pp. 154–159.

[37] A. P. Reynolds, G. Richards, B. de la Iglesia, and V. J. Rayward-Smith, "Clustering Rules: A Comparison of Partitioning and Hierarchical Clustering Algorithms," Journal of Mathematical Modelling and Algorithms, vol. 5, no. 4, Dec. 2006, pp. 475–504.

[38] F. Pedregosa, G. Varoquaux, A. Gramfort, V. Michel, B. Thirion, O. Grisel, M. Blondel, P. Prettenhofer, R. Weiss, V. Dubourg, J. Vanderplas, A. Passos, D. Cournapeau, M. Brucher, M. Perrot, and É. Duchesnay, "Scikit-learn: Machine Learning in Python," Journal of Machine Learning Research, vol. 12, no. Oct, 2011, pp. 2825–2830.

[39] M. E. Tipping and C. Bishop, "Probabilistic Principal Component Analysis," Journal of the Royal Statistical Society, Series B, vol. 21/3, Jan. 1999.

[40] F. Murtagh and P. Legendre, "Ward's Hierarchical Agglomerative Clustering Method: Which Algorithms Implement Ward's Criterion?" Journal of Classification, vol. 31, no. 3, Oct. 2014, pp. 274–295.

[41] R. Hyndman, M. O'Hara-Wild, C. Bergmeir, S. Razbash, and E. Wang, "Forecast: Forecasting Functions for Time Series and Linear Models," Feb. 2017.

[42] F. Chollet and others, "Keras: Deep learning library for theano and tensorflow," URL: https://keras. io/k, 2015.

[43] H. Akaike, "A new look at the statistical model identification," IEEE Transactions on Automatic Control, vol. 19, no. 6, Dec. 1974, pp. 716–723.

[44] J. S. Armstrong, "Significance tests harm progress in forecasting," International Journal of Forecasting, vol. 23, no. 2, Apr. 2007, pp. 321–327.

[45] L. Kaufman and P. J. Rousseeuw, Finding Groups in Data: An Introduction to Cluster Analysis. John Wiley & Sons, Sep. 2009.

[46] R. Tibshirani, G. Walther, and T. Hastie, "Estimating the number of clusters in a data set via the gap statistic," Journal of the Royal Statistical Society: Series B (Statistical Methodology), vol. 63, no. 2, Jan. 2001, pp. 411–423.

Approaches for Securing Smart Meters in Smart Grid Networks

Mustafa Saed
Electrical and Computer Engineering
University of Detroit Mercy
Detroit, USA
saedma@udmercy.edu

Kevin Daimi and Nizar Al Holou
College of Engineering and Science
University of Detroit Mercy
Detroit, USA
{daimikj, alholoun}@udmercy.edu

Abstract— **The Traditional Power utilities are gradually moving towards the Smart Grids. These Grids deploy a very large number of smart meters at the consumers' sites using bi-directional communication networks based on Internet protocols. Smart meters collect consumption data and allow customers other useful functions such as control their consumption electrical power and obtaining current energy usage. With the reliance on the internet protocols, the smart grids become vulnerable to various cyber-attacks. Consumers are worried about their privacy, integrity of their data, availability, and confidentiality when managing their power consumption. In an attempt to contribute to the protection of these smart meters against attacks, threes approaches based on cryptographic protocols are proposed for securing the direct and indirect connection of smart meters to collectors. The security requirements; confidentiality, integrity, and authentication are analyzed with respect to these approaches.**

Keywords- AMI; Direct Connection;Indirect Connecetion; Smart grid; Security

I. INTRODUCTION

Within the smart grid, the Advanced Metering Infrastructure (AMI) and security play a major role [1]-[3]. Smart grids utilize bidirectional communication with consumers to facilitate an information-driven style to indirect energy control and management. To this extent, they deploy large scale smart meters at consumer's sites for bidirectional real time communication using Internet protocols [4]. The smart grid characterizes the new trends of the current power grid nationally and internationally. It emerged in response to environmental changes, improved energy efficiency, and reduced pollution emissions [5]. The smart grid, which is supported by information technology and intelligent control, relies on six components, namely; power generation, transmission, transformation, distribution, consumption and dispatching [6]. As shown in Fig. 1, smart grid refers to the next generation power grid, which upgrades the electricity distribution and management by encompassing a scalable and ubiquitous two-way communication infrastructure to enhance control, efficiency, reliability and safety [7]-[8]. It is, therefore, no surprise that many countries are considering it as the future direction of the power grid [9]-[11].

Smart grids have many components, such as smart meter in their architecture to manage and control the power grid [12]. A smart meter is attached to every house to provide utility companies with more accurate electricity consumption data and customers with convenient way to track their usage information. It interfaces a house's appliances and Home Energy Management Systems (HEMS) on the one hand, and interfaces with data collectors on the other [13].

The Smart meters comprise two main components: an electronic meter that measures energy information accurately and a communication module that transmits and receives data [14]. Based on the importance of AMI and the vital role that it plays within the smart grid [15]-[18], it is very demanding that the AMI be protected from various possible cyber-security attacks [19]. Incorporating the Internet in the smart grid will widely open the door for various security attacks traditionally associated with the Internet.

Undoubtedly, Smart Grid systems will significantly improve efficiency and reliability but at the expense of possibly introducing new vulnerabilities. Hence, smart grid utilization should meet rigorous security requirements [19]. Cyber-security, as a vital challenge of the smart grid transformation must be enforced right at the beginning and not glued when attacks take place [21]. Vulnerabilities are expected in power transmission networks, power grid and zone management [22]-[24]. To eliminate vulnerabilities or at least minimize their impact, strong security measures must be put in place. To reach full customer trust and to ensure excellent permanence of the current power supply, all components of smart grid communication network need to be extremely secure to satisfy the security requirements; confidentiality, integrity, availability, and nonrepudiation [25]-[26].

Consumers do not want others to know how much energy they are consuming or how it is being used (confidentiality). Meter readings and control commands should not be modified while they are being transferred (integrity). The availability of meter reading is critical for utilities and consumers. It is also critical that sending and receiving components and devices cannot deny sending information including readings and commands (nonrepudiation). There are a number of possible attacks on AMI components including denial of service, device tampering, snooping, impersonation, wormhole, black hole and routing attacks. Therefore, AMI demands a reliable and secure communication approach between the smart meters and consumer equipment [26]. The AMI architecture used for this approach will be introduced, and the security of the approaches will be analyzed.

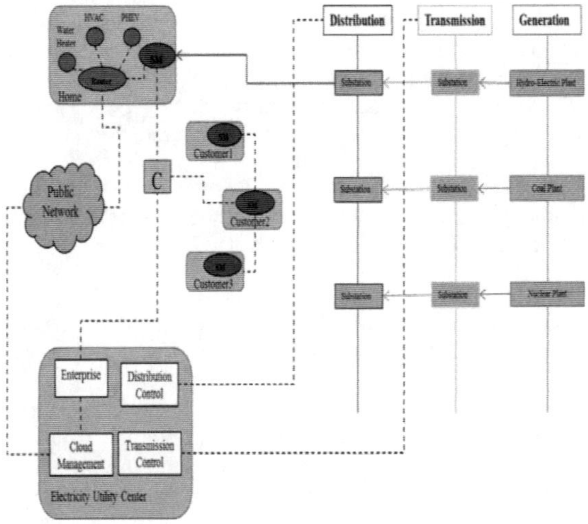

Figure 1. Smart Grid: Power and Information System Architecture.

The reminder of the paper is organized as follows: Related work is introduced in Section II. Section III introduces the AMI architecture & network topology of the smart meter. Section IV deals with the proposed security approaches. The analysis of AMI communication security is presented in Section V. Finally, the paper is concluded in Section VI.

II. Related Work

Vaidya et al. [28] stressed that many of the available schemes for both single-path and multipath routing are not suitable for meshed AMI network. Consequently, they introduced a security mechanism for multipath routing based on Elliptic Curve cryptology, digital signature, and Message Authentication Code (MAC) for such an AMI network. Their approach allows the Certificate Authority to do a lot more work than they should normally do (issuing certificates) including controlling the nodes' creation of public and private key. Nodes (smart meters) perform a number of computations despite their known limited computing power. This also tends to slow the system. Furthermore, a smart meter sends its information to all the neighboring smart meters with no security. This provides a potential attacker the opportunity for attacking more than one goal (smart meter) as they all have the information of the source meter. The neighboring nodes, acting as intermediate nodes, will do more calculations and broadcast the results. This means all other nodes (smart meters) have now the information. This implies, there are many nodes that the attacker can try and many nodes will be affected.

An interesting security protocol for AMI communications in smart grid where the smart meters are interconnected through wireless network was introduced by Yan et al. [29]. Their techniques indicated that the PKI is not desirable and relied on symmetric key cryptology. However, the number of symmetric keys used is large and possibly comparable to the number of keys should PKI has been followed. Furthermore, smart meters have limited capabilities, and therefore, verifying the MAC should have been left to the collector. The authors did not specify what will happen when the two MAC's are not equal. This implies that the integrity of a meter's reading is not handled correctly [30]-[31].

Seo et al. [32] discussed the use of public key infrastructure (PKI) in smart grid and what security requirements need to be implemented in smart grid architecture including the smart meter to secure the smart meter communication in the AMI. The authors did not propose any security technique/protocols to secure the smart grid network but only provided a survey.

Dong et al. [33] proposed a protection scheme for the automation of smart grid system and patch distribution from the control center to data transmission security. Some of the functions were tested on the simulation platform, through intrusion detection system and using field devices such as smart meter. Their proposal considers the security within smart meter but not for the smart meter communication, such as smart meter to smart meter and smart meter to collector [34]. Furthermore, their proposed protection system did not use digital signature to protect against forgery.

Zhao et al. [35] provide the fundamental limit of cyber-physical security in the presence of low sparsity unobservable attacks. It is shown in [36]-[37] that a complete system matrix can be identified using an independent component analysis method. Nevertheless, such attack schemes might not be easy to implement, as all meter data are required to be known and all the meters are required to be controlled. On the other hand, several detection and defense schemes are provided based on the complete knowledge of the system matrix. The off-line method, based on the Kullback-Leibler distance, is proposed to track malicious attacks using historical data [38]. They added their method may not work very well for continuous small-scale attacks. Our work can tackle continuous small-scale attacks through the various techniques that are proposed in the next sections.

Giani et al. [39] utilize the sparse topology information of the smart grid to determine the attack meter sets. However, these works lack the discussion of the system matrix acquisition. In fact, the design of the attack vector relies heavily on precise knowledge of the system matrix. In this case, it would not be easy to obtain such confidential information for an attacker who has limited access to the smart grid. Overall, a feasible unobservable attack scheme based on the incomplete system matrix has not yet been fully investigated. The authors in their proposal were not covering the smart meter communication attack. They only mentioned for the possible vulnerabilities related to attack meter in physical layer.

Li et al. [40] presented an efficient and robust approach to authenticate data aggregation in smart grids. Aggregation refers to the communication between the smart meters and the collector. This is achieved via deploying signature aggregations, implementing batch verification, and signature amortization schemes to reduce communication overhead and number of signing and verification operations, and providing fault tolerance. The authors proposed an efficient authentication scheme for power usage data aggregation in Neighborhood Area Networks (NAN) and smart meter to collector communications. The contributions for this work were represented by deploying digital signatures so that when the collector is out of service, alternative or backup collectors can execute the authentication approach without any additional configuration or setup. Their research also sought to reduce the number of signature and verification operations. However, the research is limited to authentication only. Thus, they are not securing the messages' (reading) between smart meter and collector.

F. Li et al. [41] introduced a distributed incremental data aggregation approach, in which data aggregation is performed at all smart meters involved in routing data from the smart meter to the collector unit. In this research, the authors presented an efficient information aggregation approach, in which an aggregation tree, constructed via breadth-first traversal of the graph and rooted at the collector unit, is deployed to cover all smart meters in the neighborhood. This protocol can let the control unit collect all smart meters' information in the area. Furthermore, to protect users' privacy, all information is encrypted by a homomorphic encryption algorithm. Since no authentication scheme is emphasized, the approach faces the potential risk that malicious smart meter can forge packets, thus causing the smart grid system to fil to detect or diagnose bogus data. Adversaries can maliciously forge their own data to manipulate the aggregation results. Therefore, adversaries and false data reports need to be detected through advanced auditing approaches.

This paper proposes schemes for securing the direct and indirect smart meter-to-collector communications. The schemes are based on PKI. Unlike the work of Vaidya et al., the proposed indirect scheme in our paper allows each node to send the encrypted, authenticated, and signed reading of a smart meter to its successor only (just one node). The successor cannot tell the reading of the predecessor node. If a node is attacked, readings of other nodes will not be affected. Our paper also avoids the need for a certificate authority for both proposed schemes by allowing the collector/substation node to take care of issuing certificates to all smart meters under its authority. Furthermore, nodes do not waste time performing lengthy calculations. In contrast to the approach of Yan et al., PKI provides stronger encryption using public and private keys. It is clear how the keys are created/recreated and exchanged. The messages (readings) are small indicating PKI is the convenient way here. The verification of the hash functions is carried out by the collector, which has more powerful computing capabilities. If the computed hash function is not equal to the received hash function for a smart meter's reading, the collector will reject that reading and inform the substation of a possible attack on that smart meter. Therefore, the integrity of a message (reading) is handled correctly. Furthermore, this proposed idea adds anonymity to the meters by using anonymous IDs, and adds confusion to the order of readings of smart meters using a PRNG. Two different security protocols are proposed to enhance the security of the direct (centralized) communication between smart meters and collector in a smart grid. The proposed work contributed to protecting the two-way direct communication of smart meters with collector through the introduction of two cryptographic protocols. The AMI architecture used for this scheme will be introduced, and the security of the schemes will be analyzed.

III. ADVANCED METERING INFRASTRUCTURE (AMI) ARCHITECTURE & SMART METER NETWORK TOPOLOGY

AMI networks are responsible for connecting a substantial number of devices needed to collect readings from smart meters. As this paper is concerned with securing smart meters to collector communication, only this part of the AMI architecture will be introduced. There are two ways of connecting smart meters to connecters; direct and indirect connections. In direct connection, smart meters directly communicate with collectors to transfer readings and exchange information and commands. For indirect connection, one or more smart meters are directly connected to the collector. The rest are either connected to the nearest smart meters that have direct connection with the collector or through a series of smart meters until the one directly connected to the collector is reached. The collector is responsible for collecting readings from all smart meters within its coverage area (network). Coverage area could include both direct and indirect connection. Figure 2 depicts the direct smart meter-to-collector communication topology. The collector (C) is the central point between the substation and the smart meters (SMs). To clarify the connection, an example of an indirect connection is presented in Figure 3.

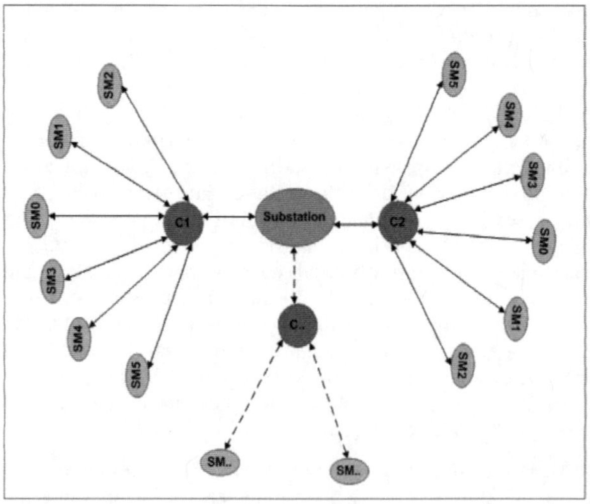

Figure 2. Centralized smart meter-to-collector communication topology.

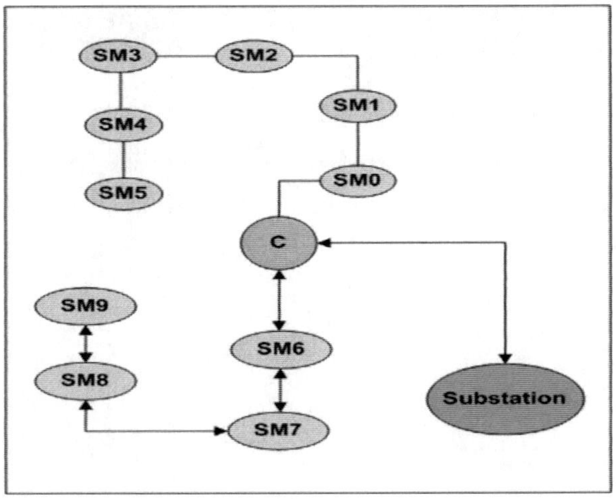

Figure 3. Smart meter-collector indirect connection.

IV. Proposed Security Approaches

Two different security protocols are proposed to enhance the security of the direct communication between smart meters and collectors in a smart grid as describes in section (A) and (B). The symbols and notations used in these protocols are summarized in Table I below.

The approach used for the indirect communication between smart meters and collector will be introduced in section (C).

TABLE I. NOTATIONS & SYMBOLS USED

Symbol	Meaning
SMi	Smart Meter #i, i=1, 2, …n
C	Collector
S	Substation
PUc, PRc, PUi, PRi	Public & Private keys for collector & meter respectively
IDc, IDi, IDS	Identification for collector, smart meter, and substation
Ri	Meter #i 's Reading, i=1, 2, …n
Ki	Symmetric Key shared between collector and meter #i
H(Ri)	Hash value for meter #i 's reading, i=1, 2, …n
Ti	Meter #i 's processor temperature
A-IDi, A-IDc , A-IDs	Anonymous ID for meter, collector, and substation
Ccert, SMi-cert, CRi	Certificate of collector & smart meter i respectively
SM0, SM6	Smart meters directly connected to C
||	Concatenation
E	Encrypt
→	Send to
PRV	Period of validity

A. *Securing direct communication without certificates*

This section relies on public key cryptology. No certificates are needed here. The substation, which is only directly connected to the collector (see Figure 2), will assist in the enrollment and activation part of the protocol. Note that the processor's temperature for each smart meter is used as a random number to further confuse the resulting message.

- Enrollment and activation process:

The Substation in charge authenticates the SMs and the collector. This includes any newly joined smart meter. The substation provides each smart meter with the ID of the collector for authentication purposes, and the public key, PU_c. It also provides the collector, C, with the ID's of the smart meters. The collector sends a message to each smart meter, SM_i, requesting the PU_i of each SM_i. The collector inserts its ID in the message. The request and ID are encrypted with its private key, PR_c. Having verified the collector's ID, each smart meter will send its PU_i and ID_i encrypted with the public key of the collector, PU_c.The collector, C, decrypts the message and verifies the ID_i. If it is valid, it accepts the PU_i. Figure 4 illustrates this process.

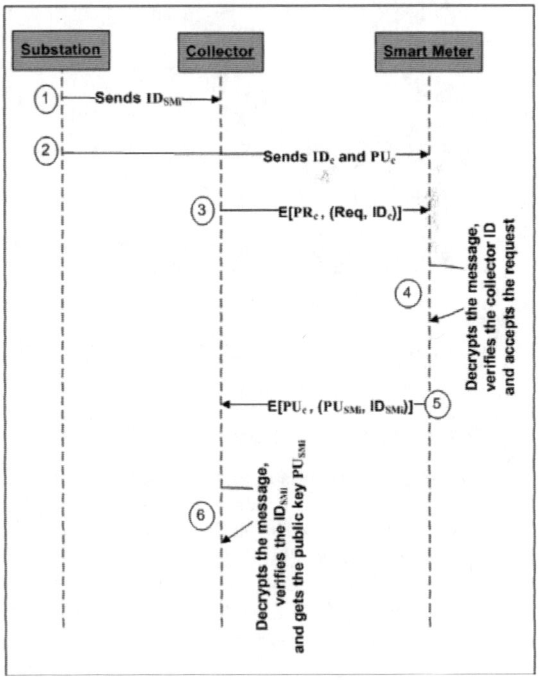

Figure 4. Enrollment and activation-Without Certificate.

- Smart meter to collector security process:

  Each SM_i XORs its reading R_i, with the processor temperature, T_i, to get the message M_i, finds the hash function $H(R_i)$ of the reading R_i, and concatenate M_i, $H(R_i)$, T_i, and ID_i. Note the ID_i is needed to allow the collector to identify the sender smart meter. The resulting message will be encrypted with collector's public key, PU_c, and forwarded to C. Upon receiving the message, the collector, C, uses its private key, PR_c, to decrypt the message. It then XORs M_i with T_i to get the reading R_i and the hash function $H(R_i)$. The collector then calculates the hash value of the extracted R_i and verifies it is equal to $H(R_i)$ to ensure the integrity of the reading.
  This is clarified in Figure 5.

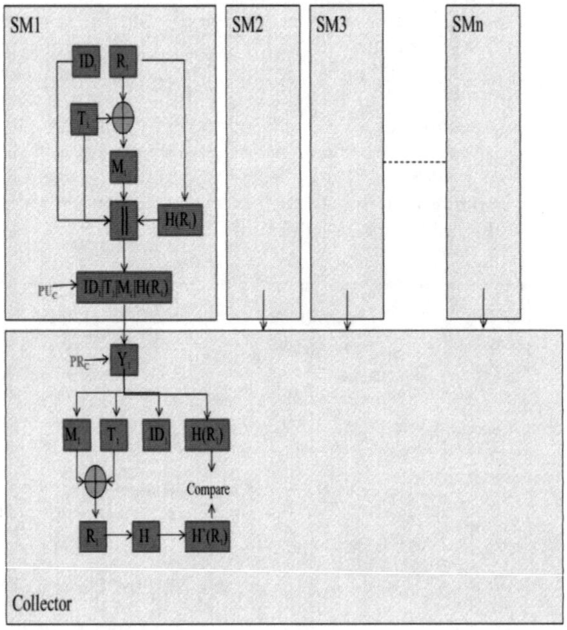

Figure 5. Smart meter-collector security process.

- Key update and exchange process:

  After a predefined number of readings, new public keys for both collector and SMs will be generated and exchanged. The collector uses the old PR_c to encrypt the new PU_c, old PU_i to encrypt the resulting message, and inserts its ID_c before sending it to smart meter #i, SM_i. At the other end, Smart meter i, SM_i, decrypts the received message, verifies ID_c, and gets the new PU_c. The smart meter, SM_i, generates new PU_i and PR_i. It encrypts the new PU_i with the old PR_i, encrypts the resulting message with the new PU_c adds its ID_i, and sends it to the collector, C. C reacts by decrypting the received message, verifying the ID_i, and then obtaining the new PU_i.
  This process is further detailed in Figure 6.

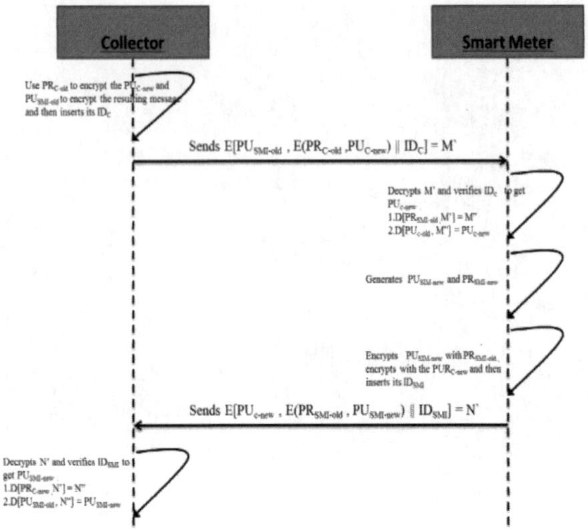

Figure 6. Key update and exchange process.

B. *Securing Direct Communication using Certificates*

This section relies on certificates. These certificates will be issued by the substation to which the collector connects.

- Enrollment and activation process:

  The Substation acts as the Certification Authority (CA). It creates the certificates for all the smart meters and the collector. In these certificates, the real ID of the SMs and collector are replaced with an anonymous ID. These certificates are then sent to the respective party. At the time of setup and installation of the collector and smart meter, the substation's anonymous ID, $A\text{-}ID_s$, and public key PUs, will be provided to the collector and smart meters. This will include any newly added smart meter. The collector and smart meters will create their own anonymous ID_s. Each collector requests its certificate from the Substation. The request includes the public key of the collector PU_c, both ID_c and $A\text{-}ID_c$, and a request message, $C_{Cert\text{-}Req}$, all encrypted with the substation's public key PU_s. This request will be forwarded to S. The Substation creates the collector's certificate, C_{cert}= E [PR_s,PU_c|| $A\text{-}ID_c$|| T_1 || T_2] and then encrypts it with the collector's public key PU_c. The encrypted C_{cert} is then sent to the collector. Note that T_1 is the creation time, and T_2 is the expiration time for the certificate. In a similar way, each smart meter, SM_i, demands its certificate from the Substation. The request includes the public key of the smart meter PU_i, its ID, ID_i, its anonymous ID, $A\text{-}ID_i$, and a request message, $SM_{i\text{-}Cert\text{-}Req}$., all encrypted with the substation's public key PU_s. This request will be sent to the substation. The Substation creates each smart meter's certificate, $SM_{i\text{-}cert}$ = E [PR_s ,PU_i|| $A\text{-}ID_i$|| T_1

|| T_2], and then encrypts it with the smart meter's public key PU_i. The anonymous ID is concatenated to the encrypted $SM_{i\text{-cert}}$ before sending it to the collector. Knowing it is not its ID; the collector will broadcast the message to all the smart meters connected to it. Only the smart meter with A-ID_i can decrypt the message and get its certificate, $SM_{i\text{-cert}}$. To complete the enrollment process, the substation, S, sends a list of ID pairs including the real and anonymous ID's for all smart meters to the collector to enable it to figure out the sending smart meter. This is because the certificate only contains the anonymous ID, and therefore, there is no way the collector can tell who the sender is. The enrollment process is further demonstrated in Figure 7.

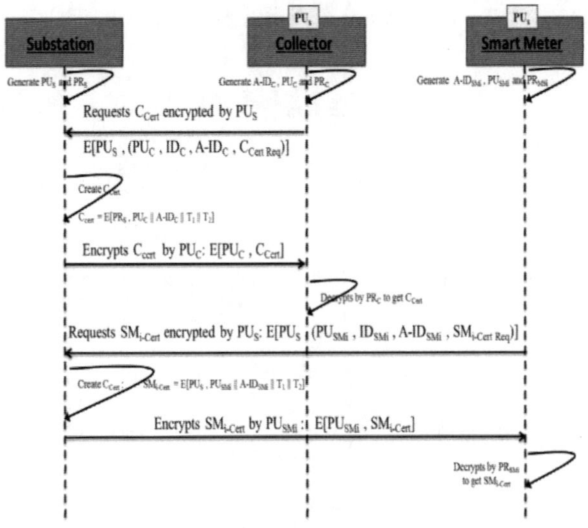

Figure 7. . Enrollment and activation process-With Certificate.

- Smart meter to collector security process:

The collector and each smart meter will exchange their certificates for authentication purposes. Each party decrypts the received certificate to get the public key and ID of the other party. The keys and ID_s are only trusted after verifying T_1 and T_2. Once each party obtains the public key of the other, the smart meter to collector security process of section (A) will be applied.

- Certificate update process:

After a predefined number of readings, new certificates for both collector and SMs will be generated by the substation. The substation will inform the collector and smart meters to create their new public and private keys and to go ahead to request new certificates as above. If either the collector or a smart meter needs to have a new certificate issued as a result of any threat, they can request new certificates from the substation following the process mentioned above.

C. *Securing Indirect Communication*

The approach for the indirect communication between smart meters and collector will be introduced below. In this approach, anonymous ID's (A-ID's) for the smart meters are used. To create anonymous ID's, each smart meter XORs the current ID (real one initially and then anonymous) with the output of a true random number (TRN) generated by a ring oscillator, T_i [42]. Any other true random value can be used instead of or in addition to the one generated by the ring oscillator. In other words, A-ID_i = ID_i XOR T_i for the first A-ID_i, and A-ID_i = Previous A-ID_i XOR T_i for subsequent A-ID_i's. Table I presents the notations and symbols used in these approaches.

- Enrollment-Activation and Certificate Exchange:

In this approach, the collector C should have initially received all the public keys and IDs of the smart meters. On the other hand, the smart meters, SM's, should have the public key of the collector using any secure process. Furthermore, the predecessor and successor nodes for each smart meter are identified during installation and configuration of each smart meter. The node directly connected to the collector has no successor. The nodes at the end of the connection have no predecessors. Note that the scheme will be applied to the upper part of Figure 3 to observe how smart meters SM_0-SM_5 securely send their readings to the collector C. The readings for smart meters SM_6-SM_9 at the lower part of the figure will be collected using the same approach. Each smart meter, SM_i, replaces its real ID_i with an anonymous one, A-ID_i, appends ID_i to it and encrypts both with the public key of collector, PU_c, before sending the resulting message, E(PU_c, A-ID_i || ID_i), to C through the indirect connection (Figure 8).

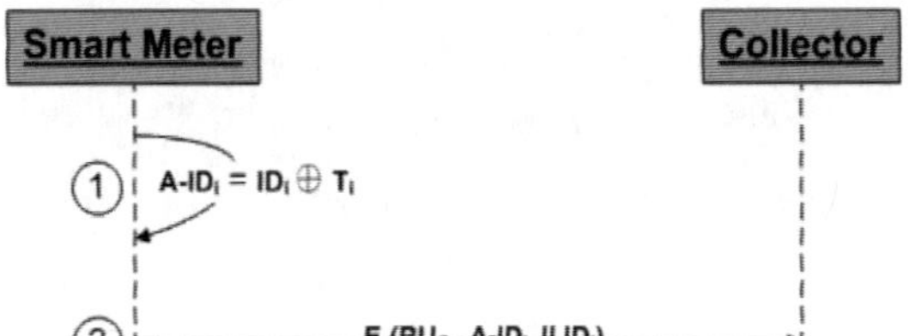

Figure 8. Creating and sending anonymous ID.

The collector, C, creates certificates for each smart meter, SM_i. It appends A-ID_i to the public key of each smart meter, PU_i, and the period of validity

PRV, and then encrypts $PU_i||A\text{-}ID_i||PRV$ with its private key, PR_c to get the certificate for each smart meter ($CR_i = E(PR_c, PU_i||A\text{-}ID_i||PRV)$ since all smart meters have the public key PU_c of the collector. The CR_i is further encrypted with PU_i. Having done that, C then attaches $A\text{-}ID_i$ to the resulting message and forwards $E(PU_i, CR_i) \| A\text{-}ID_i$ to smart meters via SM_0. Certificate creation is depicted in Figure 9 for both the collector and smart meter.

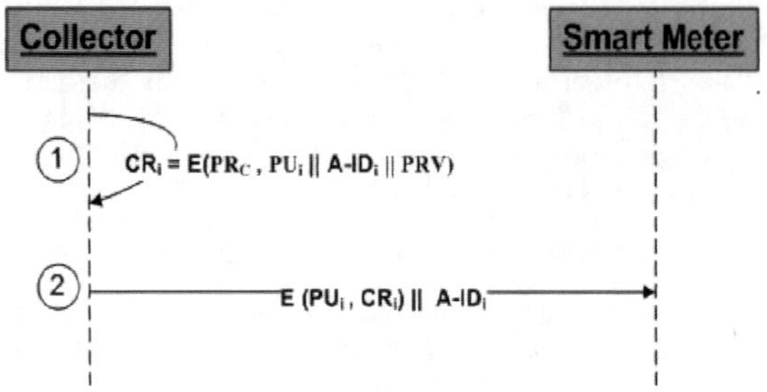

Figure 9. Creating and sending certificates.

Every SM_i checks the $A\text{-}ID_i$. If it is its ID, it decrypts $E(PU_i, CR_i)$ with its private key PR_i to get its certificate. Otherwise, it will forward the message to adjacent smart meters to do the same until all smart meters receive their certificates.

- Secure Reading Collection Process:

Each SM_i XORs its reading, R_i, with the TRN produced by the ring oscillator, T_i, concatenates the resulting message with T_i and the hash function of the reading $H(R_i)$. The resulting message will be encrypted with PR_i to get $X_i = E [PR_i, M_i \| H(R_i) \| T_i]$, where $M_i = R_i$ XOR T_i. To enable the collector to recognize the source meter's reading, $A\text{-}ID_i$ is attached to X_i and both encrypted with PU_c to get $Y_i = E(PU_c, X_i \| A\text{-}ID_i)$. The XOR operation is used to obscure the reading of the meter. T_i is needed to allow the receiver to XOR it with M_i to get R_i. Having done that, R_i will be hashed and compared to $H(R_i)$.

The predecessor and successor nodes exchange certificates to authenticate each other. On successful authentication, the predecessor smart meter encrypts its Y_i with the public key PU_{i-1} of the successor, and forward $E[PU_{i-1}, Y_i]$ to the successor.

The receiving successor decrypts the received message with its private key PR_{i-1}, prepends or appends its own Y_{i-1} and encrypts the two ($Y_i \| Y_{i-1}$, or $Y_{i-1} \| Y_i$, for example) with its successor's public key. This process will continue until all Y_i's have been concatenated at SM_0. Using Figure 3 above, we should have $Y = Y_5 \| Y_4 \| Y_3 \| Y_2 \| Y_1 \| Y_0$ or any other ordering. SM_0 sends Y to C. Any missing Y_i indicates a problem, possibly an attack, within that meter. If this occurs, the collector will reject the received message and report to the substation to investigate the issue. The decision on whether to append or prepend Y_i is based on pseudorandom number generator (PRNG'), which generates pseudorandom bit stream. Y_{i-1} is prepended if the pseudorandom bit is '0' and appended if the bit is '1'. This will obscure the order of Y_i's and make it hard to relate the Y_i's to their smart meters.

To illustrate this, Figure 10 is provided.

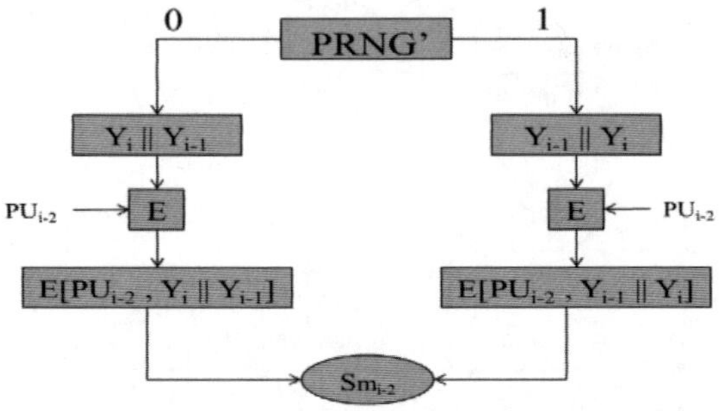

Figure 10. Pseudorandom Number Generator PRNG' operation (Smart mete- to-Smart meter).

The collector, C, uses its PR_c to decrypt Y. Then, based on the $A\text{-}ID_i$, it uses the appropriate PU_i to decrypt each Y_i to obtain $M_i \| H(R_i) \| T_i$ for each smart meter. It XORs M_i with T_i to get the reading R_i. It later finds the hash function of R_i and ensures it is equal to the received hash function $H(R_i)$ to guarantee the integrity of the reading, R_i. Figure 10 illustrates the meter readings collection process.

To simplify Figure 11, $Z = Y_5 \| Y_4 \| Y_3 \| Y_2 \| Y_1$ (order is based on PRNG') is used. Note that smart meter 5, SM_5, has no predecessor, and therefore, no PRNG' unit exists. Only smart meters SM_4-SM_1 have it because they have predecessors (smart meters connected to them, as depicted in Figure 3).

Once the order of Y_i's is decided, the result is encrypted with the public key of the next meter, PU_{i-2}, and forwarded to the next smart meter, SM_{i-2}. The PRNG for SM_0 is not followed by encryption as in Figure 10 because it is forwarding directly to the collector. To illustrate this, Figure 12 is provided.

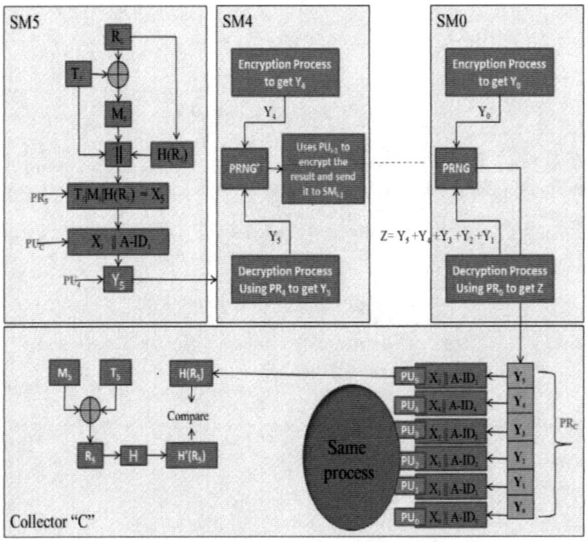

Figure 11. Meter readings collection process.

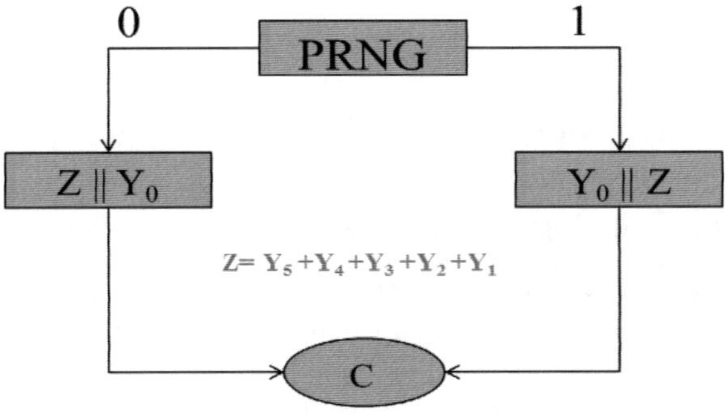

Figure 12. PRNG operation (Smart meter - to - Collector).

- Key Update and Certificate Exchange Process:

After a predefined number of readings or when the validity period PRV of the certificate expires, new keys for both collector and SM's will be generated and exchanged. The collector will use its old PR_c to encrypt the new PU_c and then encrypt the result with the old PUi and attaches A-ID_i prior to sending it to SM_i. The A-ID_i will allow each smart meter to tell if the message is intended for it. The smart meter in question, SM_i, will decrypt this message to get the new public key of the collector. At the other side, each smart meter generates new A-ID_i, PU_i and PR_i, appends the new A-ID_i to the new PU_i, encrypts the resulting message with the old PR_i and then with the new public key of the collector, PU_c. Finally, the old A-ID_i is attached before sending it to the collector. The collector will apply the required series of decryptions to get the new A-ID_i and PU_i of each smart meter. Note that the old A-ID_i is added to allow the collector to recognize each smart meter. Furthermore, new certificates will be generated and forwarded to the smart meters as mentioned above. This is detailed in Figure 13 below.

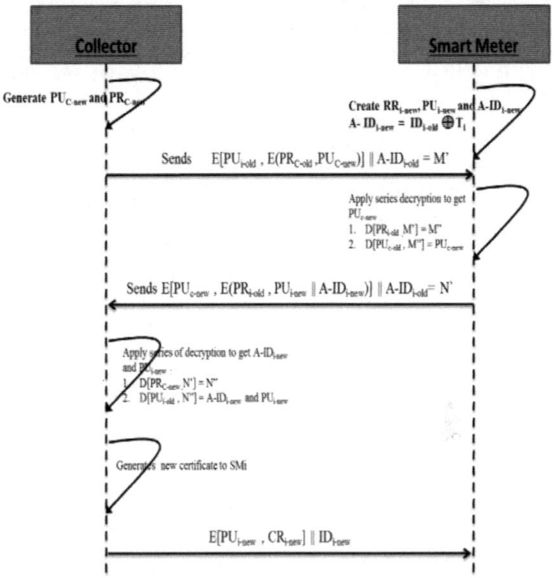

Figure 13. Exchanging new keys, IDs, and certificates.

New keys, certificates, and anonymous IDs are also created and exchanged when an attack is anticipated or has already occurred. An alternative approach is used if the creation and storage of certificates are not desirable due to computing power and memory limitations. For each adjacent smart meter pair, the collector sends the predecessor the public key of the successor encrypted with the public key of the predecessor, and sends the successor the public key of the predecessor encrypted with the public key of the successor. In both cases, the A-IDi is attached to allow smart meters to capture messages belonging to them. Apart from replacing the certificate with the collector providing the public keys for the predecessors and successors, the rest is exactly as in the first approach.

V. Advanced Metering Infrastructure (AMI) Communication Security Analysis

The security of the above schemes is analyzed with respect to confidentiality, integrity, and authentication. Although hash functions can help with intrusion and virus detection, availability cannot be satisfied by cryptology alone (schemes above), and therefore, it will not be part of the analysis. Table II illustrates the security analysis for both proposed schemes.

TABLE II. ADVANCED METERING INFRASTRUCTURE (AMI) COMMUNICATION SECURITY ANALYSIS

Advanced Metering Infrastructure (AMI) Communication Security Analysis		
Security Req.	***Direct Communication***	***Indirect Communication***
Confidentiality	The confidentiality achieved when the message that sent from the SMs to the collector is encrypted using the public key of the collector and the only collector will be able to decrypt and read the received message from the smart meter using the collector private key PR_c. The hash value, $H(R_i)$ of direct approach, is encrypted with the public key of the collector ($Y_i = E\ [PU_c, M_i \parallel H(R_i) \parallel T_i]$). Only the collector with its private key (PR_c) can decrypt the hash value.	The proposed protocol for indirect approach ensure that confidentiality is met through the message that is forwarded to the next smart meter or directly to the collector in the case of SM0 is encrypted with the public key of the collector ($Y_i = E(PU_c, X_i \parallel A\text{-}ID_i)$). Only the party that has the private key (collector), PR_C, can **decrypt** this message.
Integrity	The reading, Ri, in the proposed schemes has its integrity fulfilled through the use of cryptographic hash function, H(Ri). Upon receiving the message, the collector extracts Ri and find its H(Ri). It then compares the computed H(Ri) with the received one. Any mismatch indicates the message has been modified.	The reading, Ri, in the proposed scheme has its integrity fulfilled through the use of cryptographic hash function, H(Ri). Upon receiving a message, the collector extracts Ri and find its H(Ri). It then compares the computed H(Ri) with the received one. Any mismatch indicates the message has been tempered with.
Authentication	The substation, which is only directly connected to the collector (see Figure 2), will assist in the enrollment and activation part of the protocol. The Substation in charge authenticates the SMs and the collector. This includes any newly joined smart meter. The substation provides each smart meter with the ID of the collector for authentication purposes, and the public key, PU_c. It also provides the collector, C, with the ID's of the smart meters. The collector sends a message to each smart meter, SM_i, requesting the PU_i of each SM_i. The collector inserts its ID in the message. The request and ID are encrypted with its private key, PR_c. Having verified the collector's ID, each smart meter will send its PU_i and ID_i encrypted with the public key of the collector, PUc. The collector, C, decrypts the message and verifies the ID_i. If it is valid, it accepts the PU_i. Figure 4 illustrates this process.	The contents of X_i are encrypted with PR_i, and then X_i is encrypted with PUc. Therefore, authentication is also taken care of.

The proposed security protocols introduce an additional enhancement resulting from XORing smart meters' readings with a random value to make it hard for attackers to extract the actual reading. In addition, the replacement of real IDs with anonymous ones will make it hard to relate a reading to a particular smart meter. Finally, the use of pseudorandom number generator (PRNG) introduced further hardship in judging the link between the reading and smart meter. Further, to ensure the message is protected against forgery, digital signature is used.

VI. CONCLUSION

Efforts to establish the Smart Grids are constantly increasing globally. The Smart Grid is a bi-directional communication system enabling customers through their smart meters to administer their energy service and access a number of features including using energy during low cost intervals, reading consumption electricity bills online, and scheduling turning on/off home appliances. These services need to be available when needed, the integrity of meter readings should be preserved, and privacy of these services need to be maintained. Intruders with access to these services can result in a great damage to consumers and the distribution of services by utilities. Comprising one smart meter can result in comprising many others and the collectors. This paper contributed to protecting the two-way direct and indirect communication of smart meters with collectors through the introduction of two cryptographic protocols based on PKI. Securing indirect communication is harder than the direct one because readings have to travel through other smart meters before reaching the collector. The introduced schemes satisfied the security requirements; confidentiality, integrity, and nonrepudiation. Future work will concentrate on verification of theses protocols.

REFERENCES

[1] M. Saed, K. Daimi, and N. Al-Holou, "Securing Indirect Communication for Advanced Metering Infrastructure in Smart Grid," in Proc. EMERGING 2015 the Seventh International Conference on Emerging Networks and Systems Intelligence, pp. 84-90, 2015.

[2] J. H. Khan and J. Y. Khan, "A Heterogeneous WiMAX-WLAN Network for AMI Communications in the Smart grid," in Proc. the IEEE third International Conference on Smart Grid Communication (SmartGridComm), Tainan, Taiwan, 2012, pp. 710-715.

[3] U.S. Department of Energy (DOE), "The Smart Grid: an Introduction," Available: http://energy.gov/oe, [retrieved: November, 2017].

[4] Y. Simmhan, A. G. Kumbhare, B. Cao, and V. Prasanna, "An Analysis of Security and Confidentiality Issues in Smart Grid Software Architectures on Clouds," in Proc. IEEE 4th International Conference on Cloud Computing (CLOUD 2011), Washington, DC, USA, 2011, pp. 582-589.

[5] X. Miao, X. Chen, X. Ma, G. Liu, H. Feng, and X. Song, "Comparing Smart Grid Technology Standards Roadmap of the IEC, NIST, and SGCC," in Proc. 2012 China International Conference on Electricity Distribution (CICED 2012), Shanghai, China, 2012, pp. 5-6.

[6] X. Jin, Y. Zhang, and X. Wang, "Strategy and Coordinated Development of Strong and Smart Grid," in Proc. the 2012 IEEE Conference on Innovative Smart Grid Technologies – Asia (ISGT Asia), Tianjin, China, 2012, pp. 1-4.

[7] U.S. Department of Energy (DOE), Available: www.smartgrid.gov/the_smart_grid, [retrieved: November, 2017].

[8] Y. Yan, Y. Qian, H. Sharif, and D. Tipper, "A Survey on Smart Grid Communication Infrastructures: Motivations, Requirements, and Challenges," IEEE Communications Surveys and Tutorials, vol. 15, no. 1, 2013, pp. 5-20.

[9] A. Ipakchi and F. Albuyeh, "Grid of the Future," IEEE Power and Energy Magazine, vol. 7, no. 2, 2009, pp. 52-62.

[10] R. O'neill, "Smart grid sound transmission investments," IEEE Power and Energy Magazine, vol. 5, no. 5, 2007, pp. 104-102.

[11] H. Tai and E. Hogain, "Behind the Buzz: Eight Smart-Grid Trends Shaping the Industry," IEEE Power and Energy, vol. 7, no. 2, 2009, pp. 96-97.

[12] A. Molina-Markham, P. Shenoy, K. Fu, E. Cecchet, and David Irwin, "Private memoirs of a smart meter," in Proc. of the 2nd ACM workshop on embedded sensing systems for energy-efficiency in building, pp. 61–66, 2010.

[13] E. D Knapp and R. Samani, "Applied Cyber Security and the Smart Grid," implementing Security Controls Into the Modern Power Infrastructure. Newnes, 2013.

[14] Botswana Power Corporation, "A SAP IS-U and Smart Meter," implementation project experience in Botswana, Africa.

[15] I. Joe, J. Y. Jeong, and F. Zhang, "Design and Implementation of AMI System using Binary CDMA for Smart Grid," in Proc. the Third International Conference on Intelligent System Design and Engineering Applications, Hong Kong, 2013, pp. 544-549.

[16] M. Chebbo, "EU Smart Grids Framework: Electricity Networks of Future 2020 and Beyond," IEEE Power Engineering Society General Meeting, Tampa, FL, 2007, pp. 1-8.

[17] D. G. Hart, "Using AMI to Realize the Smart Grid," IEEE Power Engineering Society General Meeting, Pittsburgh, PA, 2008, pp. 1-2.

[18] J. Wang and V. C. M. Leung, "A Survey of Technical Requirements and Consumer Application Standards for IP-based Smart Grid AMI Network," in Proc. the International Conference on Information Networking (ICOIN), Barcelona, 2011, pp. 114-119.

[19] S. Choi, S. Kang, N. Jung, and I. Yang, "The Design of Outage Management System Utilizing Meter Information Based on AMI (Advanced Metering Infrastructure) System," in Proc. the 8th International Conference on Power Electronics, Shilla Jeju, Korea, 2011, pp. 2955-2961.

[20] A. R. Metke and R. L. Ekl, "Smart Grid Security Technology," in Proc. IEEE Conference on Innovative Smart Grid Technologies (ISGT), Gaithersburg, MD, 2010, pp. 1-7.

[21] S. M. Amin, "Smart Grid Security, Confidentiality, and Resilient Architectures: Opportunities and Challenges," IEEE Power and Energy Society General Meeting, San Diego, CA, 2012, pp. 1-2.

[22] G. Chen, Z. Y. Dong, J. H. David, G. H. Zhang, and K. Q. Hua, "Attack Structural Vulnerability of Power Grids: A Hybrid Approach Based on Complex Networks," Physica A: Statistical Mechanics and its Applications, vol. 389, 2010, pp. 595-603.

[23] S. Clements and H. Kirkham, "Cyber-security Considerations for the Smart Grid," IEEE Power and Energy Society General Meeting, Minneapolis, MN, 2010, pp. 1-5.

[24] G. N. Ericsson, "Cyber-security and Power System Communication: Essential Parts of a Smart Grid Infrastructure," IEEE Transactions on Power Delivery, vol. 25, no. 3, 2010, pp. 1501-1507.

[25] M. Wagner, M. Kuba, and A. Oeder, "Smart Grid Cyber Security: A German Perspective," in Proc. International Conference on Smart Grid Technology, Economics and Policies (SG-TEP), Nuremberg, 2012, pp. 1-4.

[26] F. M. Cleveland, "Cyber Security Issues for Advanced Metering Infrastructure (AMI)," IEEE Power and Energy General Meeting-Conversion and Delivery of Electrical Energy in the 21st Century, Pittsburgh, PA, 2008, pp. 1-5.

[27] V. Aravinthan, V. Namboodiri, S. Sunku, and W. Jewell, "Wireless AMI Application and Security for Controlled Home Area Networks," IEEE Power and Energy General Meeting, San Diego, CA, 2011, pp. 1- 8.

[28] B. Vaidya, D. Makrakis, and H. Mouftah, "Secure Multipath Routing for AMI Network in Smart Grid," in Proc. IEEE 31st International Conference on Performance Computing and Communications (IPCCC), Austin, TX, 2012, pp. 408-415.

[29] Y. Yan, Y. Qian, and H. Sharif, "A Secure and Reliable In-network Collaborative Communication Scheme for Advanced Metering Infrastructure in Smart Grid," in Proc. IEEE Wireless Communications and Networking Conference (WCNC), Cancun, Quintana Roo, 2011, pp. 909-914.

[30] G. N. Ericsson, "Cyber security and power system communicationessential parts of a smart grid infrastructure," IEEE Transactions on Power Delivery, Vol. 25, No. 3, pp. 1501-1507, July 2010.

[31] R. Anthony, L. Metke, L. Randy, and Ekl, "Security technology for smart grid networks," IEEE Transactions on Smart Grid, Vol. 1, No. 1, pp. 99-106, June 2010.

[32] J. Seo and C. Lee, "The green defenders," IEEE Power and Energy Magazine, VOL.9, NO.1, pp. 82-90, January/February 2011.

[33] D. Wei, Y. Lu, M. Jafari, P. Skare, and K. Rohde, "An integrated security system of protecting smart grid against cyber -attacks," Innovative Smart Grid Technologies (ISGT), Gaithersburg, MD, USA, 19-21 January 2010.

[34] M. A. Rahman and H. Mohsenian-Rad, "'False data injection attacks with incomplete information against smart power grids," in Proc. IEEE Conf. Global Commun. (GlobeCom), Dec. 2012, pp. 3153-3158.

[35] Y. Zhao, A. Goldsmith, and H. V. Poor, "Fundamental limits of cyber physical security in smart power grids," in Proc. 52nd IEEE Conf. Decision Control, Florence, Italy, Dec. 2013, pp. 200-205.

[36] Y. Huang, Mohammad Esmalifalak, Huy Nguyen, Rong Zheng, and Zhu Han, "Bad data injection in smart grid: Attack and defense mechanisms," IEEE Commun. Mag., vol. 51, no. 1, pp. 27-33, Jan. 2013.

[37] M. Esmalifalak, H. Nguyen, R. Zheng, L. Xie, L. Song, and Z. Han, "A stealthy attack against electricity market using independent component analysis," IEEE Syst. J., to be published.

[38] G. Chaojun, P. Jirutitijaroen, and M. Motani, "Detecting false data injection attacks in AC state estimation," IEEE Trans. Smart Grid, vol. 6, no. 5, pp. 2476-2483, Sep. 2015.

[39] A. Giani, E. Bitar, M. Garcia, M. McQueen, P. Khargonekar, and K. Poolla, "Smart grid data integrity attacks," IEEE Trans. Smart Grid, vol. 4, no. 3, pp. 1244-1253, Sep. 2013.

[40] D. Li, Z. Aung, J. R. Williams, and A. Sanchez, "Efficient Authentication Scheme for Data Aggregation in Smart Grid with Fault Tolerance and Fault Diagnosis," Innovative Smart Grid Technologies (ISGT), 2012 IEEE PES, pp. 1-8.

[41] F. Li, B. Luo and P. Liu, "Secure Information Aggregation for Smart Grids Using Homomorphic Encryption," in Proc. 2010 IEEE Conf. Smart Grid Communication, pp. 327-332.

[42] P. Schaumont, "True Random Number Generation," Circuit Cellar, No. 268, pp. 52-58, Nov. 2012.

International Academy, Research,
and Industry Association (IARIA)
412 Derby Way
Wilmington, DE 19810

CURRAN ASSOCIATES INC.
proceedings.com

ISBN 978-1-5108-5653-0
9 781510 856530

IARIA Annual Congress on Frontiers in Science, Technology, Services, and Applications (IARIA Congress 2023)

Valencia, Spain
13-17 November 2023

IARIA